CENSORING RACIAL RIDICULE

CENSORING RACIAL RIDICULE

Irish, Jewish, and African
American Struggles over
Race and Representation,
1890–1930

M. ALISON KIBLER

The University of North Carolina Press
CHAPEL HILL

© 2015 The University of North Carolina Press
All rights reserved
Designed and set in Arno Pro and Calluna Sans by Rebecca Evans
Manufactured in the United States of America

The paper in this book meets the guidelines for permanence and durability
of the Committee on Production Guidelines for Book Longevity of the
Council on Library Resources. The University of North Carolina Press has
been a member of the Green Press Initiative since 2003.

Cover illustration: Courtesy of The Jacob Rader Marcus Center
of the American Jewish Archives, Cincinnati, Ohio.
AmericanJewishArchives.org

Library of Congress Cataloging-in-Publication Data
Kibler, M. Alison.
Censoring racial ridicule : Irish, Jewish, and African American struggles over
race and representation, 1890–1930 / M. Alison Kibler.
pages cm
Includes bibliographical references and index.
ISBN 978-1-4696-1836-4 (pbk : alk. paper)
ISBN 978-1-4696-1837-1 (ebook)
1. Racism and the arts—United States—History—19th century. 2. Racism and the
arts—United States—History—20th century. 3. Stereotypes (Social psychology)
in motion pictures. 4. Theater and society—United States—History—19th century.
5. Theater and society—United States—History—20th century. 6. Racism in popular
culture—United States—History—19th century. 7. Racism in popular culture—
United States—History—19th century. 8. United States—Ethnic relations—History—
19th century. 9. United States—Ethnic relations—History—20th century. I. Title.
NX180.R3K53 2015   305.800973—dc23
2014035498

FOR DENNIS, JOHN, AND THERESE

Contents

Illustrations

Acknowledgments

Many people and institutions have helped me write this book. It is a pleasure to thank them all here. I appreciate the scholars who read early versions of this work and provided helpful advice along the way: Bluford Adams, Jim Barrett, Una Bromell, Richard Butsch, Malcolm Campbell, Frank Couvares, Janet Davis, Hasia Diner, Jennifer Frost, Ely Janis, Kathleen Johnson, Russell Kazal, Linda Kerber, Alan Kraut, Roger Lane, Timothy Meagher, Fiona Paisley, Lauren Rabinovitz, Terri Snyder, Marc Ross, Leigh Ann Wheeler, and Bill Williams.

I benefited from the scholarly community in the history department and Centre for Women's Studies at the Australian National University. Thanks to Sally Kenney, I was fortunate to spend a semester as a visitor at the Center for Advanced Feminist Studies at the University of Minnesota. At Franklin and Marshall College, my professional home for the past twelve years, I am grateful for the support of my colleagues: Misty Bastian, Dennis Deslippe, Dan Frick, Matt Hoffman, Gregory Kaliss, David Kieran, Maria Mitchell, Mikaela Luttrell-Rowland, David Schuyler, Louise Stevenson, and Carla Willard. They have inspired me with their high standards in their own scholarship and given encouragement at key moments. Alice Drum was the chair of the Women's and Gender Studies Program when I arrived at Franklin and Marshall. Since then she has become an invaluable mentor, book coach, extraordinary editor, and friend. I also thank the students in my "Rights and Representations" seminars for the past decade; your spirited discussions kept the questions about contemporary hate speech connected to my historical research. I learned a great deal from the participants and the leaders—Alan Kraut and Maureen Murphy Nutting—at the National Endowment for the Humanities Summer Institute titled "American Immigration Revisited" in 2009.

Generous financial support gave me the opportunity to write and research full time for two years and also funded several research trips. I appreciate the American Council of Learned Societies Fellowship (2000–2001) and the Rockefeller Fellowship at the Center for Ethnicities, Communities, and Social Policy at Bryn Mawr College (2004–5). I am grateful as well for a Larry J. Hackman Research Residency from the New York State Archives, a one-month residency at the Pennsylvania Historical and Museum Commission, the Lowenstein-Wiener Fellowship from the American Jewish Archives, the Hibernian Research Award from the CUSHWA Center for the Study of American Catholicism at the University of Notre Dame, a Fellowship Grant from the Memorial Foundation for Jewish Culture, a travel grant from the Australian Academy of the Humanities, and a research grant from the Irish American Cultural Institute.

Earlier versions of chapter 2 appeared as "The Stage Irishwoman," *Journal of American Ethnic History* 24, no. 3 (2005): 5–30, and "Pigs, Green Whiskers, and Drunken Widows: Irish Nationalists and the 'Practical Censorship' of McFadden's Row of Flats in 1902 and 1903" *Journal of American Studies* 42, no. 3 (2008): 489–514. Parts of chapter 4 appeared earlier as "Paddy, Shylock, and Sambo: Irish, Jewish, and African American Efforts to Ban Racial Ridicule on Stage and Screen," in *Culture and Belonging in Divided Societies: Contestation and Symbolic Landscapes,* edited by Marc Howard Ross, 259–80 (Philadelphia: University of Pennsylvania Press, 2009). The review process for these publications helped my work tremendously.

Thanks to the knowledgeable archivists at the American Jewish Archives, the Falvey Memorial Library at Villanova University, the John Hay Library at Brown University, the Library of Congress, the New York Public Library, and the State Historical Society of Iowa. Mary Shelley, Meg Massey, and Scott Vine at Franklin and Marshall's Shadek-Fackenthal Library have answered many questions and provided key materials. I am fortunate to be working with the University of North Carolina Press for the second time in my career. I appreciate the careful editing that Petra Dreiser did on behalf of the Press. Thanks to Paul Betz for overseeing the process. And, special thanks also to Jenny Gumbert, a great freelance editor in Lancaster, Pennsylvania.

In Lancaster I am fortunate to be part of the Magpies, a small group of writers and artists who model creativity and courage every day. I appreciate the unwavering support of my family—Dennis, John, and Therese Deslippe. This book has been in the background—and sometimes the foreground—of our family life for too long. Thanks for your patience and good cheer through it all.

CENSORING RACIAL RIDICULE

INTRODUCTION

A male actor impersonates a drunken, clumsy Irish woman. A greedy Jewish pawnbroker lures his female employee into prostitution. An African American man leers at a white woman. For many Irish, Jewish, and African Americans in the early twentieth century, these images on stage and screen were harmful assaults on their reputations, and for some, they were matters of life and death. One hundred years ago, Irish, Jewish, and African American leaders believed that the representation of their race in mass culture helped determine their social status, their safety, and their political ambitions. In turn, they developed varied protest strategies—such as theater riots, boycotts, and backstage lobbying—to combat racial ridicule. Their critique of negative representations thus became a controversial element of nationalist and civil rights campaigns in the late nineteenth century and the early twentieth. Irish, Jewish, and African American activists shared many goals. The leaders in these campaigns were cultural critics who theorized the power of images, sought positive representations, and demanded that American popular culture serve a multiracial democracy. They were also political strategists who often used the attack on images to advance the status of their minority group, to challenge their competitors for leadership of their group, and to establish coalitions with other immigrant or racial communities.

These campaigns reveal how particular Irish, Jewish, and African American spectators interpreted plays, movies, and vaudeville acts. Jewish leaders attacked images of Jewish crime, greed, and immorality. For example, they rejected a series of Montague Glass short stories about Abe Potash and "Mawruss" Perlmutter because Glass was a "Jew depicting his own fellow-Jew as sordid and grasping, with no thought except business and profit and occasionally of cheap pleasure, with no principles other than that everything that one can get away with without being caught is proper and honorable in business."[1] African Americans assailed sensationalistic depictions of lynching in plays and motion pictures, such as in *The Birth of a Nation*, in which Ku Klux Klan members murder an African American man

1

after he pursues a white woman who jumps to her death to end the chase.[2] Black leaders also objected to images of African Americans as incapable of self-government or as a "menace to established society," including the scene in *The Birth of a Nation* in which black Americans drink, carouse, and put their bare feet up on their desks in the state legislature during Reconstruction.[3] Irish activists challenged any mocking depictions of Irish self-government, such as a bomb-throwing radical in the midst of an imagined Irish national government in *McSwiggan's Parliament*, a musical comedy from 1887. African Americans objected to efforts to erect a national monument of "mammy"—as a romanticization of southern brutalities—while Irish Americans criticized misrepresentations of the Irish servant girl, particularly any depiction of her as hulking, drunken, or promiscuous.[4] They disliked simian portraits of the Irish, particularly of Irish women. In 1904, for example, Irish activists protested against a gorilla named Miss Dooley at a zoo in Lincoln Park.[5]

Scholars have studied some of these protests, particularly the African American struggle against *The Birth of a Nation*, but they have not yet examined these three concurrent campaigns together. The immediate overlap of the Irish, Jewish, and African American protests is striking. During the week ending on December 24, 1915, the Pennsylvania State Board of Censors of Motion Pictures, which upheld a variety of criteria for film censorship, including a ban on racial ridicule, cut or modified five scenes from *The Birth of a Nation*. For example, the board cut a scene featuring a close-up of the African American, Gus, salivating as he pursued a white woman. In the same week, the censors also removed scenes that they thought would insult Jews in two motion pictures. They eliminated a scene showing "the stoning and beating of a Russian Jew" from *Reproduction of the Fall of Warsaw*, as well as a subtitle that suggested the hiring of a Jewish woman with a questionable reputation ("I have engaged a Russian girl a—a—er—a—parlor maid") from *The Immigrant*.[6]

These three campaigns against racial ridicule provide much more than a list of the supposed traits that angered Irish, Jewish, and African Americans in the early twentieth century; the protests also show that the perception of insults was relative and competitive. These groups compared their depictions on stage and screen to other groups' images, and they measured the success of their protests against other communities' efforts. The campaigns against racial ridicule—or the Stage Irish, the Stage Jew, and the Stage Negro—recognized that their concerns with visibility and positive representations were heightened in a multiracial setting. An *Irish World* editorial explained its interest in the Stage Irishman in 1899: "To us in America this matter appeals with perhaps greater force than to those in Ireland. We are one among the many races forming the American people, and we have our own honor and that of the land of our fathers to maintain."[7] When Irish American protesters attacked the image of an Irish servant girl—Bridget—in a play at the Harlem YWCA in 1919, they criticized not only her appearance but also her proximity to an African American servant, Dinah. The connection between the different racial characters mattered as much as any particular trait. "Bridget was fitted out with hair that looked like a four-alarm fire and spoke with a brogue," complained an editorial in the Irish nationalist newspaper, the *Gaelic American*. Bridget was presented on the same level as "Dinah . . . another servant [who was] as black as a lump of anthracite." They were "below" the "ladylike" girls in the choir and the other characters in the production who were "normal human beings, with English names." What bothered the Irish American protesters most was that the "negro and the Irish race are the servants, the buffoons, the vulgarians." The *Gaelic American* announced that the "Stage Irishwoman" (Bridget) should be stopped, just as the Stage Irishwoman in early acts— the Russell Brothers and *McFadden's Row of Flats*—had been suppressed by "high explosive eggs" in well-known theater riots in the first decade of the twentieth century.[8] Other accounts of harmful depictions noted the advantageous power of competing groups. For example, when the African American journalist Sylvester Russell criticized the prevalence of "nigger" in popular entertainment, he noted that "the word has appeared mostly from the pens of Irish and Jewish writers."[9] *victims gang up on each other*

As the Irish response to Bridget and Dinah shows, these protests provide windows onto the often contentious relationships between immigrant communities and African Americans. This triad includes two extremes in the history of American minority relations—the strong affinity between Jews and African Americans and the hostility between the Irish and African Americans.[10] The relationship between certain pairings, particularly Jews and African Americans, has received extensive scholarly attention, but the comparison of these three groups remains rare. This work follows the literary historian George Bornstein's recent claim about the importance of tracing the connections and cooperation between these three groups, not just their animosity, in his study of Irish, Jewish, and African American literature.[11] This comparison shows that, contrary to current distinctions between ethnicity (including Irish and Jewish communities) and race (African American), these three groups all constituted "races" in the early twentieth century. The Irish and Jews were "white" according to U.S. law; they were not barred from citizenship and could vote and serve on juries, among other rights and privileges. But whiteness included many separate races around the turn of the twentieth century. According to their own definitions, as well as to the typologies of scientists and politicians, the Celt and the Hebrew constituted distinct races, in contrast to the Anglo-Saxon race.[12]

The overlapping nationalist struggles of these three groups celebrated a correlation of nation and race pride. In the early twentieth century, Irish cultural nationalism fortified the foundation for an Irish race: it cultivated Irish literature and theater, tried to resurrect the Irish language, and offered positive Irish traits—such as being spiritual, rural, and chaste— to counter the English definition of the Irish as wild and childlike.[13] Zionists, a small group of Jewish intellectuals in the early twentieth century, appealed to biological racial bonds as the basis of their nationalist ideology.[14] Black nationalists like Marcus Garvey argued for the superiority of the African race and advocated a variety of strategies to ensure African ascendance, from the success of black-owned businesses to emigration to Africa.[15]

The battles over racial ridicule covered in this book disclose new insights into the history of racial formation. First, Irish, Jewish, and African American responses to racial ridicule show aspects of their "self-perception"—the everyday reactions to racial caricatures often missing in histories of these groups' racial identities.[16] Second, the comparison of these three campaigns discloses different racial patterns, with Jews and Irish Americans struggling with and seeking to jettison identifications of racial otherness, in their own timelines, in the early twentieth century. This history, then, contributes to our understanding of the "slow, gradual and vexed process" of the creation of binary black and white races, as the historian Ariela Gross explains.[17] In particular, this study balances accounts of racial exploitation and intergroup cooperation within American entertainment: immigrant performers and entrepreneurs often perpetuated racist stereotypes in mass culture, but mass culture was also a cause for cooperation among these groups. Jewish, Irish, and African American organizations offered advice to each other, often copied each other, and in some cases joined in other groups' protests.

The motivations and political structures behind the Irish, Jewish, and African American campaigns varied, and the stakes for these three groups differed. Activists interpreted the different risks of offensive caricatures, from the Irish American concern about a loss of race pride to the African American charge that racist images would spark deadly riots. For the Irish, the critique of racial ridicule formed a compelling part of Irish nationalism; for African Americans, it was part of the antilynching battle as well as of efforts to achieve full legal equality; Jews saw it as part of the defense of group rights and civil rights for all. The contrasts here are clear. The Irish in America were not faced with disenfranchisement, segregation, or widespread vigilante violence, but they still saw the campaign against the Irish caricatures—or the Stage Irish—as a way to advance their interests, particularly the goal of Irish independence. Jewish and African Americans, in contrast, linked misrepresentation to the denial of civil rights and vulnerability to violent attack, though the extent of these threats differed. The attack on racial ridicule thus constituted a component of various aspects of these groups' political organizing—cultural revivals, civil rights campaigns, and political nationalism.

Their preferred tactics also varied. While Irish nationalists disrupted theaters to stop particular acts, Jewish and African Americans led the movement for race-based censorship of theater and motion pictures. All groups, however, eventually supported the legal suppression of racial ridicule in the first two decades of the twentieth century, although they were not uniformly enthusiastic about state censorship. Jewish and African Americans wrote and lobbied for the passage of new race-based censorship laws in the first two decades of the twentieth century, but as this book shows, race-based censorship rarely worked in favor of these activists, and it faced increasing challenges from free-speech advocates in the 1920s. In the rising outcry against censorship, the Irish, Jewish, and African American efforts to control racial representation became a symbol of prejudice in censorship, rather than protection against prejudice.

Observers in the early twentieth century often acknowledged the overlap of Irish, Jewish, and African American complaints about their representation on stage and screen. Vaudeville managers, for example, discussed Irish and Jewish sensitivity to these groups' images on stage. One manager, in 1903, kept his eye on the "work of Irish [organizations] against these sorts of turns [Irish caricature]," while others seemed to look out for how "the Irish element" responded to particular acts.[18] Vaudeville managers also worried about pressure from Jewish groups: in 1903, one speculated that "some day the Hebrews are going to make as big a kick as the Irish did against this kind of burlesque of their nationality," and, eight years later, another speculated that a short drama about the expulsion of Jews from Russia might upset Jewish "patronage," even though it was ultimately "in favor of the Jews." He concluded, "It will . . . stir up an agitation for which there is no occasion."[19] Vaudeville managers also noted African Americans who protested by demanding prime seating for acts that particularly appealed to them, such as the black star Bert Williams. When African Americans insisted on box and orchestra seats for a bill that included the African American performers Cooper and Bailey, one manager suggested cutting "coon acts" altogether as a way to avoid the "niggers'" lawsuits and defiance of segregated seating.[20]

A wide variety of performers, journalists, and theater critics thus understood that the protests against the Stage Irish, Stage Jew, and Stage Negro were similar—they belonged together. In 1909, when the vaudeville comedian Joe Welch faced the wrath of angry Jewish spectators because of his crude impersonation of "Hebrew" characters, he wondered about the future of theater comedy and, in doing so, linked these three groups and noted the absence of German protests:

> If we take the Hebrew character from the stage, the stage would lose much. . . . The Irish, or some of the Irish, [are] loudly demanding the effacement of the Irish comedian. As yet we have not heard from the Germans—yet if any race on the face of the globe has been offensively caricatured it is the German race—we may even hear from Booker T. Washington insisting that the negro shall cease to be impersonated. Should things keep up . . . the stage would be without characters and without comedy.[21]

Similarly, an editorial in the Jewish monthly *B'nai B'rith News* in 1910 described the three campaigns together: "Now we have a protest against the 'stage Jew.' Some time ago a crusade was made against the 'stage Irishman.' The colored people have from time to time protested against the 'stage Negro.'"[22] Irish, Jewish, and African American leaders were well aware of the caricatures of the other groups in this trio and often accused the other races of creating them in the first place. Irish nationalists, for example, remarked that the stage should "cease telling the great falsehood that the Jew is a miser."[23] But the Irish also blamed Jews for the caricatures of the Irish: "The gross caricatures of the Irish are part of a propaganda, conducted mainly by Jews, to hold the Irish up to contempt."[24]

Other groups, such as Chinese, Italians, Germans, and Native Americans, occasionally raised their voices with a similar sense of outrage about their depiction. In 1911 Italians protested a movie showing Italian soldiers murdering Arab girls. When New York City officials discharged the rioters, Irish protesters noted that they were not treated with such leniency when they protested against offensive plays and movies.[25] Chauncey Yellow Robe, a Lakota who had attended the Carlisle Indian School, criticized Wild West shows for depicting the Indian as "only a savage being."[26] In addition, he objected to the unrealistic reenactment of the battle of Wounded Knee in the movie *Indian Wars*, which premiered on January 21, 1914. In October of 1913 Yellow Robes wrote that Wild Bill Cody and his costar General Nelson Miles had inaccurately inserted themselves into the battle scene and thus desecrated the hallowed ground "for their own profit and cheap glory." Other reports claimed that Indians were upset that their fighting prowess was mocked in the movie and that the movie unfairly blamed them for the massacre.[27] In 1916 Chinese protesters attacked *The Yellow Menace*, a series of motion pictures that depicted the "utter helplessness of America under present conditions to combat an oriental foe."[28]

Germans also objected to harmful images of themselves, but their efforts were particularly focused on movies related to World War I.[29] A German-American organization, for example, objected to *The Ordeal* in the fall of 1914, because its scenes of cruel acts by German soldiers violated the U.S. position of neutrality in relation to the European conflict and also injured the "feelings of every man who has German blood in his veins."[30] Chicago censors also tried to protect the reputation of German Americans by banning *The Little American* (1917) and *Alsace* (1916)—both appearing during World War I—but censors faced considerable backlash for these decisions. The German—or "Dutch"—caricature on the vaudeville stage may have disappeared because of anti-German sentiment during World War I, not because of German protests, while Irish and Jewish activists pressured performers and managers to alter stereotypes of themselves.[31] The absence of a sustained German antidefamation campaign may be related to internal division within the German immigrant community, to the intense pressure for Germans to subdue their distinctiveness during and after World War I, and to Germans' status as "old stock" immigrants in the face of a new wave of Southern European immigrants. The historian Russell Kazal explains that Germans in the United States experienced divisions of religion and politics, whereas the Irish were unified by Democratic affiliation and Catholicism. Germans in the United States faced far-reaching persecution during World War I, including protests against German-language opera, which led Germans to hide their cultural differences, around the same time that the Irish were rallying around a new Irish free state. When the Irish confidently spoke about "race" pride in the early twentieth century, Germans were increasingly included among the white old stock population of the United States.[32] For these reasons, Germans did not join this triad of movements against racial ridicule.

The Irish, Jewish, and African American groups in this study are not monolithic or unified. Rather, gender and class shaped the representations of Irish, Jews, and African Americans, just as gender and class divided the groups themselves.[33] As the historian Cheryl Greenberg argues, "There is no single black community, no single Jewish community."[34] Although previous scholars have described the Stage Irishman as a generic symbol of the Irish, the representation of the Irish was, in fact, deeply gendered. The Stage Irishwoman—often drunk, lascivious, and manly—was a more controversial caricature than the combative Stage Irishman.[35] In addition, this comparison shows that the early Irish campaign against the Stage Irish was more violent than the other campaigns, but we cannot conclude simply that the Irish were more violent than Jews or African Americans, or that they were "morbidly sensitive" to slights, as the historian Kerby Miller claims.[36] This project suggests that the Irish attack on the Stage Irish did not represent a distinctive trait of the Irish but formed part of a wider pattern of protest by racial minorities in the early twentieth century. The Irish Americans who led theater riots in the first decade of the twentieth century were a particular group of Irish American nationalists fused by working-class masculinity and a radical approach to the fight against British rule.

Each group faced political competition among organizations trying to lead the community: between different strands of Irish nationalism; between radical, conservative, and moderate approaches to African American civil rights; and between quiet, behind-the scenes tactics and a more public approach to Jewish advocacy. Each group also faced internal tensions over class and generation—between elite Jews with Central European roots and recent Jewish immigrants from Eastern Europe; between well-established African Americans and poor migrants from the rural South; and between middle-class Irish Americans and the so-called greenhorn Irish immigrants. Thus, as different factions within each group tried to reform their representation in popular entertainment, they also competed to lead—or represent—their race.

This book provides a new chapter in the history of the so-called culture wars in the United States. For the first two decades of the twentieth century, censorship was a multiracial moral dilemma. By documenting the work of civil rights censors, this study shows that the history of censorship proves more complicated than an "old-fashioned 'heroic' tale of expressive freedom versus moralism."[37] The Irish, Jewish, and African Americans who attacked racial ridicule have much in common with the critical race theorists and feminists who, beginning in the 1980s, advocated for hate speech codes on college campuses and government regulation of pornography and sexual harassment.[38] The terms have changed from racial ridicule to hate speech and "hostile work environment"; and the battleground has shifted from movie theaters and vaudeville houses to universities and the workplace, but the contemporary debates directly link to the struggles of Irish, Jewish, and African American activists in the early twentieth century.[39]

Hate speech has been a century-long conundrum because it exposes two tensions in American democracy—between freedom of expression and equality and between individual and group rights. One of the earliest and most powerful justifications for the First Amendment was that democracy necessitated free expression. James Madison viewed free speech as a key to popular sovereignty. "We the people" demanded a "government by discussion" in which citizens participated in debate unfettered by state interference.[40] Civil libertarians in the late twentieth century argue that the state should not take a side in the "marketplace of ideas"; it should not violate content neutrality in deciding what individuals should think and say. On the other hand, scholars who support hate speech regulations hold that the state needs to be more proactive in creating conditions for liberty and equality, arguing that the lack of government regulation in this marketplace of ideas by no means ensures equal participation. The legal scholar Cass Sunstein, for example, explains that the marketplace of ideas actually depends on a "commitment to political equality," in which no groups are excluded from debate and in which each citizen has roughly the same power as others.[41] Proponents of hate speech regulation today argue that hate speech should be an exception to First Amendment protection, along with incitement to illegal conduct, obscenity, and libel, because hate speech damages social equality. Racial epithets and insults, they argue, are not ideas with social value; they are more like a slap, silencing speakers and causing myriad physical and psychological harms. The feminist legal scholar Catherine MacKinnon argues that pornography is not speech but the act of sex

Waldron

discrimination. The freedom of speech should not be the first freedom; this individual liberty should be balanced against the state's investment in racial and gender equality. MacKinnon, for example, observes that "the First Amendment has grown as if a commitment to speech were no part of a commitment to equality and as if a commitment to equality had no implication for the law of speech."[42]

Some legal scholars, however, reject any opposition between equality and freedom of expression. The former American Civil Liberties Union (ACLU) president Nadine Strossen argues that the First Amendment has empowered groups who are battling discrimination, including civil rights activists, whose sit-ins and marches the "shield" of the First Amendment protects.[43] Government censorship, on the other hand, has proven detrimental to disadvantaged groups. Historically, much of the censorship of sexually explicit materials has attempted to protect women's chastity and has restricted access to information about birth control. Anticensorship feminists thus distrust censorship as a route to equality. As Strossen concludes, "Free speech plays a vital role in defeating doctrines at odds with human rights."[44]

The debates about racial ridicule in the early twentieth century also raised questions about how social difference related to equality. One model of equality is the elimination of "group-based differences"; equality then is based on a universal standard of justice; and "treating citizens equally means treating the exactly the same way."[45] Political activists and theorists have questioned the equation of equality and sameness, arguing that the universal standard is actually the representation of the most powerful groups. In many cases, race-based laws or policies—not simply antidiscrimination statutes that outlaw "taking differences into account"—may be the most effective route to equality.[46] But when disadvantaged groups seek recognition or rights from the state based on difference, they also risk having their status codified as marginal. This minefield of difference and equality plagued the civil rights censors of the early twentieth century. When they asserted the injury of race, they challenged the ideal of civic unity; when they demanded race-based redress from the state, they questioned a color-blind or neutral censorship; and when they demanded power as censors based on their race, they faced dogged charges of partisanship and could speak only for their race.

It is not surprising to find the roots of hate speech controversies in the

Progressive Era, from the late nineteenth century to the end of World War I, when citizens grappled with unprecedented racial diversity after a wave of new immigrants from southern and eastern Europe, when a new powerful medium—motion pictures—spread across the nation, and when a reform coalition backed government intervention for the sake of the public good, even if it compromised individual rights. During the Progressive Era, a wide variety of activists and muckraking journalists exposed social problems related to urbanization, immigration, and industrialization, such as corrupt city government or infectious diseases in tenement housing. Civic activists and politicians then designed solutions, often using social science expertise and usually turning to government plans to alleviate the problems. Progressive reformers emphasized democratic cooperation as a response to unchecked individualism and corporate greed, while they also called on the government to uphold the interests of the community, in balance with individual rights.[47] Individuals needed each other, and they needed state intervention. But just as Irish, Jewish, and African American leaders struggled with representation in censorship, so did Progressives debate how best to express the public will. Some progressive reformers advocated for more direct participation from citizens in legislative decisions. Several states began to allow direct voting on bills passed by legislators.[48] Another Progressive victory was the passage of the Seventeenth Amendment, which instituted the direct election of senators. On the other hand, Progressives also believed that public opinion needed to be managed and developed by elected officials and expert administrators, who would put their assessments of social problems before the public to decide on solutions. New social science graduate programs (in sociology and economics, for example) produced a dedicated group of experts who collected evidence and crafted plans for social improvement. Thus Progressives believed both in a stronger voice for the people as well as in more powerful experts who could implement solutions for the public good.

The three campaigns considered here raise questions about the role of minority groups in the pursuit of the public good during the Progressive Era. Progressive reformers shared a commitment to "the people," as opposed to a "party, faction or interest," but they did not always seek conformity.[49] In the Progressive Era, ethnocentric Americanization programs aimed to assimilate immigrants, and anti-immigration sentiment resulted in severe restrictions on southern and eastern European immigration in 1924. Yet, in the face of this "cultural conformity," some reformers emphasized a pluralistic notion of "immigrant gifts."[50] At Hull House, the premiere settlement house in Chicago, Jane Addams set up programs for immigrants to learn English and civics, as well as engage in recreational activities, to provide respite from the rigors of labor and city living, but she developed respect for immigrant cultures, refusing to see them as an obstacle to American belonging and allegiance. Despite reformers' rhetoric against partisan advocacy, progressivism was a "powerful formula for political action along many social axes," including labor organizations for the working classes and the Urban League and the National Association for the Advancement of Colored People (NAACP) for African Americans.[51] This irony is evident in the protests against racial ridicule considered here, as minority groups sought to represent the public on censorship boards, to shape public taste through education and publicity, and opposed the motion picture business interests. Yet their claims often seemed like a partisan disruption of consensus or special protection.

The campaigns for race-based censorship also found support among many Progressives who downplayed individual free-speech rights. Progressives, in general, were more concerned with the government regulation of capitalism than with a defense of free-speech rights. Most Progressives did not make free expression a priority because they doubted the primacy of individual rights; instead they believed that courts should defer to elected officials' power to promote the "public welfare"—just as they had the power to regulate economic activity for the good of the community.[52] They believed that state censorship—administered by impartial officials—could be necessary for creating a common national culture in the face of divergent immigrant communities. Many Progressives thus backed the censorship of "aliens" and radicals during World War I, arising in part out of Americanization movements. Some of these activists emphasized the authority of "an enlightened bureaucratic elite" who could mold the masses.[53] Other Progressives, however, saw a different relationship between democracy and censorship. Several prominent ones, such as Jane Addams and Louis Brandeis, supported First Amendment rights in the interest of pluralism and democratic participation.[54] Less concerned with the benefits of self-expression to an individual, these reformers advocated open debate as a way to improve democracy. The most controversial film of this period, *The Birth of a Nation*, challenges any clear distinction between the free-speech reformers and the proponents of government regulation.[55] Addams, for example, advocated the suppression of *The Birth of a Nation* despite her free-speech stance. Race-based censorship made strange allies.

First Amendment activism grew in the Progressive Era prior to the well-known campaigns for free speech launched by the political radicals during and after World War I.[56] In particular, new voices and groups emerged to defend "hateful" speech and thought. The Free Speech League, established in 1902 in response to state repression of anarchist speech after an anarchist's 1901 assassination attempt on President McKinley, defended its radical allies and its conservative opponents. For example, the league worked closely with Emma Goldman and Margaret Sanger in their fights for free speech. But under the leadership of attorney Theodore Schroeder, the league defended the speech of political rivals, resisted attaching itself to any particular cause, and supported religious speakers as well as virulent anti-Catholics.[57] The Free Speech League backed the International Workers of the World, a radical union of workers, as well as its rival, the American Federation of Labor.[58]

The defense of hateful speech slowly expanded to question the administrative censorship of movies, which initially seemed uncontroversial because it involved business or entertainment, not "the politically charged issues of the day."[59] But race-based censorship sometimes pierced the apolitical appearance of much motion-picture censorship. D. W. Griffith, for example, launched artistically sophisticated films with claims of historical relevance and realistic portrayals of painful incidents in U.S. history, including racially charged scenes and religious tensions. Attempts to ban his films therefore seemed highly political. Antidefamation campaigns helped place the administrative regulation of American entertainment on the agenda of free-speech activists, persons primarily concerned with political speech. The Irish, Jewish, and African Americans campaigns are a key part of the transition to a "democratic moral authority" in American censorship. In the wake of the moral absolutism of Anthony Comstock in the late nineteenth century and the early twentieth, Protestant leadership gave way to Catholic and Jewish influence in censorship, and a new regime tried to judge images from the perspective of the average person (rather than from that of an impressionable child) and advocated democratic processes for assessing texts.[60]

Griffith, the director of *The Birth of a Nation* and an early proponent of free speech, understood the multiracial context of motion-picture censorship. In his pamphlet *The Rise and Fall of Free Speech* (1916), he emphasized that censorship occurred through pressure from multiple minority pressure groups, not just the African Americans who had objected to *The Birth of a Nation*. He explained how the "wrath of a certain part of our people" interfered with his plans for *Intolerance*, depicting the crucifixion.[61] Throughout the pamphlet Griffith repeats, "Intolerance: The Root of All Censorship," and interjects other examples of narrow-mindedness, such as "Intolerance: Smashed the First Printing Press." He tried to convince censorious groups that their interests were better served by free speech. One of his examples asks Jewish leaders to reconsider their support for censorship, because "Intolerance Caused Kishenef Massacres."[62] The civil rights censors wreaked havoc on his vision of history and his desire to make serious, politically relevant movies: "According to the theory of the censors, the moving picture producers must slavishly avoid the truth, for fear of treading on the toes of races, politicians and individuals. With a censorship board dictating what pictures are produced . . . truth is not to be pictured, but a sugar-coated, virtuously garbed version alone can be presented."[63] His frustrations with censorship, then, were not simply directed at "Mrs. Grundy"—the puritanical female reformer—but at a variety of racial groups, including the Irish, Jewish, and African American censors.

Censoring Racial Ridicule develops chronologically, as it follows first, in chapter 1, the lawless protests (theater riots) and then the emergence of legal state censorship of racial insults. Chapter 1, "The Minstrel Show and the Melee," sets the stage for the rest of the book by tracing the rising social status, internal divisions, and the political mobilizations of the Irish, Jewish, and African American communities. This chapter then examines the relationships between these three groups on stage and in political and social life.

Chapter 2, "Practical Censorship," explores the Irish nationalists who led several prominent theater riots in the first decade of the twentieth century.[64] These riots were theatrical events in their own right. Designed to enthrall an audience, they conveyed ideas about a radical brand of Irish nationalism, about strong Irish manhood, and a distinctive Irish group identity. In fact, however much the protesters wished to dispel negative caricatures of the Irish as drunken brawlers, they also embraced their aggressive assaults on the Stage Irish as a proud part of Irish group identity. Although Irish, Jewish, and African American protesters all used varied

INTOLERANCE

CAUSED KISHENEF MASSACRES

An act of congress to censor the pictorial press is an indirect blow at our boasted freedom of speech.

The constitution endows every citizen with the right to freely speak, write, and publish his sentiments on any subject.

Infringements of the statutes, by indecent or otherwise objectionable pictures, are amenable to the law.

"Hold on, here!"

D. W. Griffith claimed that intolerance was the root of censorship and violence against Jews in his pamphlet, *The Rise and Fall of Free Speech* (1916).

techniques, the Irish nationalists were distinctly violent in their campaign against the Stage Irish. This chapter explains why.

Chapter 3, "Immoral . . . in the Broad Sense," maps the trajectory toward more lawful protests in these campaigns. It focuses on two plays, *The Clansman*, an adaptation of Thomas Dixon's racist fiction, and *The Playboy of the Western World*, John Synge's controversial play from the Irish National Theatre. In the protests against these plays, African American activists pushed for the legal suppression of *The Clansman* because it inflamed racial violence, and Irish nationalists tried to censor *The Playboy* because they saw its depiction of depraved Irish women as indecent. In each case, race was central to the definition of the play's harm to the public. Ultimately, these plays followed different paths: several cities banned *The Clansman*, while *The Playboy* escaped all efforts at legal censorship in major cities, but its producers, under pressure from "gallery censorship," sometimes removed offensive sections.[65] The campaign against *The Clansman* also included alliances between African Americans and Jews, but the Irish battle against *The Playboy of the Western World* was riddled with hostility toward Jews and African Americans. Although these protesters often spoke a common language of racial harms in theatrical productions, they did not make common cause in their search for fair representations.

"Shylock and Sambo Censored" (chapter 4) compares the Jewish and African American paths to supporting race-based censorship of the new medium of motion pictures. Irish nationalists were the leading instigators of theater violence, but Jewish and African American leaders pioneered in the establishment of race-based motion picture censorship in the second decade of the twentieth century. This chapter reveals the common factors contributing to both the African American and Jewish campaigns: segregation, vigilante violence, and exposés of criminality among Jews and African Americans.

Chapter 5, "Are the Hebrews to Have a Censor?" examines how race-based motion picture censorship worked in one city—Chicago, the site of the nation's first motion picture censorship ordinance. In 1907 the Jewish reform leader Adolf Kraus wrote the censorship law, which targeted not only obscenity but also "racial ridicule." Jewish civic leaders then gained considerable control over the representation of Jews in film when the police commissioner recruited them to serve on "citizen juries" in the early years of Chicago motion picture censorship. When the structure shifted to a single civilian censorship board, Jews were well represented, but African Americans struggled to get a token representative on the censorship board. With, first, citizen juries, and then a civilian board, Chicago leaders defended the city's censorship as democratic, compared to police censorship. The power of Jews among citizen censors, however, led to charges of favoritism and prejudice.

The next chapter, "Without Fear or Favor" (chapter 6), investigates how free speech advocates grappled with race-based censorship. First, race-based motion picture censorship created an intense dilemma for reformers who opposed censorship but supported racial equality in their political work. The National Board of Censorship (later National Board of Review), a progressive board that reviewed films in cooperation with producers as an alternative to state censorship, claimed that it did not favor "any one class of audience"; it announced that it was a democratic body that considered only the composite audience. Yet under pressure from the Anti-Defamation League (ADL) and the NAACP, the board began to recommend withholding films that libeled a race. Second, free-speech advocates used examples of race-based censorship, particularly Jewish censorship in Chicago, in their fights against proposed federal motion picture censorship. This chapter shows that the bans on racial ridicule were both a problem for some free-speech progressives and a useful symbol of censorship run amok for reformers fighting motion picture censorship.

The book concludes in 1927 with an analysis of an unusual set of controversies about race and movie censorship. In this key year the ADL battled to transform *King of Kings* (1927) while it was still in production, but felt disappointed in the results; Irish Catholics challenged *The Callahans and the Murphys* and *Irish Hearts* because of the misrepresentation of the Irish *and* of Catholicism, and Irish nationalists failed in their attempt to amend New York City's film censorship law to outlaw racial ridicule. These events show the decline of race-based censorship, the shift from racial to religious identifications among the Irish and Jewish leaders of censorship, and the rise of Catholics in the censorship of morality, more narrowly defined in terms of sexuality.

The roots of the most famous hate speech battle in American history—the proposed Nazi demonstration in Skokie, Illinois, in 1976—reach back to these three campaigns against derogatory productions in the early twentieth century. The rhetoric about the potentially deadly impact of hate speech was not the only similarity between the late-twentieth-century incident and the campaigns against racial ridicule in the early twentieth century; in fact, the legal terrain of the Skokie battle had direct roots in the Irish, Jewish, and African American struggles seventy years before the Nazis set their sights on Skokie. In 1976, a group of American Nazis—the Nationalist Socialist Party of America—announced that it would picket in Skokie, a town in the suburbs of Chicago with a high percentage of Holocaust survivors. Frank Collin, who proclaimed his loyalty to Adolf Hitler's goal of national racial purity, wrote to Skokie town officials for a permit to rally. Jewish leaders, including representatives of the ADL in Chicago, met to discuss the Nazi proposal. The ADL, founded in 1913 in response to virulent anti-Semitism, encouraged the Jewish citizens of Skokie not to oppose or reply in any way to the Nazi request; this "quarantine" approach would withhold the publicity that the Nazis desperately desired. But many of the Holocaust survivors refused to remain silent. They spoke out about the atrocities of Nazi Germany and asserted that the sight of Nazi uniforms in their community would injure them again. They fought to keep their town safe from any Nazi invasion.

The Village of Skokie tried to stop the Nazis by seeking an injunction and by passing several ordinances. One of the ordinances—ordinance 995—made it a crime to display or circulate any text "which promotes and incites hatred against persons by reason of their race, national origin, or religion."[66] The Skokie officials had drafted the ordinance to match a group libel law passed by the Illinois legislature in 1917. In 1950, when the white supremacist Joseph Beauharnais handed out leaflets in Chicago encouraging segregation, accusing African Americans of rape, and warning against any racial "mongrelization," police arrested him for violating this 1917 group libel law. Appeals sent the case all the way to the United States Supreme Court, which upheld the 1917 law in a close 5–4 decision. The majority argued that the legislature was justifiably acting to stem racial violence in Chicago, but the court also undercut the law by noting that it could be "abused" in the future. In a strong dissent, Justice Hugo Black wrote, "The same kind of law that makes Beauharnais a criminal for advocating segregation in Illinois can be utilized to send people to jail in other states for advocating equality and nonsegregation."[67] The only time the Supreme Court addressed the constitutionality of group libel laws, *Beauharnais v. Illinois*, the result was a divided, weak decision. Illinois repealed the group libel law ten years later.[68] Nevertheless, lawyers for the Village of Skokie clung to *Beauharnais* as a judicial opinion in their favor: if the court upheld the 1917 group libel law, perhaps the new ordinance would also pass constitutional muster. It was a slim hope indeed.

Collin challenged all the village's efforts to stop him, including ordinance 995 against hate speech. He found that the First Amendment landscape, which had changed a great deal since *Beauharnais* in 1952, protected inflammatory racist speech. In *New York Times v. Sullivan* (1964) the Supreme Court had also significantly narrowed civil libel when it ruled that citizens could make false statements about public officials as long as they did not act with "reckless disregard for the truth." In this case, the court protected civil rights activists who had taken out an advertisement in the *New York Times* in which they accused Alabama officials of abusing civil rights demonstrators and violating the Constitution.[69] In 1971 the Supreme Court defended the right of Paul Cohen to wear a jacket emblazoned with "Fuck the Draft" while he was in a Los Angeles courthouse. Justice John Marshall Harlan argued that anyone offended by the sentence could simply "avert their eyes" and cautioned against censorship because the back-and-forth of speech was valuable even when it was not pleasant—"the air may at times be filled with verbal cacophony."[70] In *Collin v. Smith*, the United States Court of Appeals (seventh circuit) struck down the Skokie ordinances. The judge found that the ordinance was overly broad: It "could conceivably be applied to criminalize the dissemination of *The Merchant of Venice* or a vigorous discussion of the merits of reverse racial discrimination in Skokie."[71] Collin had the right to demonstrate in Skokie, though at the last minute he decided not to; Nazis enjoyed the protection of the Bill of Rights; and the First Amendment protected hateful speech.

The Holocaust survivors in Skokie were indebted to the Irish, Jewish, and African American activists in the early twentieth century who are the subject of this book. These groups put hate speech—what they called "racial ridicule"—on the political map as part of their nationalist, civil rights, and self-defense campaigns. But it is not just the general concern with hate speech that links them across generations. Jewish and African American leaders drafted laws to ban plays and movies that ridiculed any race; these laws form immediate links to the Skokie campaign seventy years later. Illinois legislators passed a group libel law in 1917 in an effort to stop Griffith's racist *The Birth of a Nation*. These officials borrowed the language of the law from Chicago's 1907 motion picture censorship law, the first in the country, which also banned films that insulted any race or religion. Adolf Kraus, a Jewish civic leader, wrote this law to protect all racial minorities, not Jews alone. In this light, the Skokie hate speech ordinance was, surprisingly, seventy years old.

In May of 1915 a female reformer rose from her seat at a prayer meeting in Brooklyn to denounce motion pictures as the "devil's melting pot."[72] Although she did not refer to race relations, anti-Semitism, or immigrant audiences in her critique, she may well have had multiracial politics in mind because the motion picture world surrounding her was awash in these themes. At this time in 1915, the NAACP confronted *The Birth of a Nation* in city after city. Movie reenactments of Leo Frank's trial had already circulated and newsreels with scenes of his lynching were just a few months in the future. A few weeks before this outcry by reformers, a movie version of Israel Zangwill's play *The Melting Pot* had begun its run. When the play first premiered, in 1908, Jewish groups had protested against its favorable portrayal of intermarriage. While some civic leaders praised the melting pot as a way to incorporate immigrants into the American mainstream, others criticized the loss of immigrant cultures implied by the melting pot. As the Irish, Jewish, and African American protesters would soon discover, within this model it was dangerous to claim power as censors or the need for protection based on racial difference. For racial minorities—white races and African Americans—who sought favorable and accurate representation, American popular entertainment did not constitute a benign melting pot; instead, it was a cauldron of racist caricatures, incitements to vigilante violence, and insults to race pride. The melting pot of American entertainment only encouraged some groups—European immigrants—to melt in the first place, and their upward mobility was often based on the exclusion of African Americans. Despite these inequities, Irish, Jewish, and African Americans used similar rhetoric in their critique of racial ridicule and occasionally found common cause.

Skokie connection
seems odd here, forced

CHAPTER ONE

THE MINSTREL SHOW AND THE MELEE

Irish, Jewish, and African Americans in
Popular Culture and Politics

Two theatrical traditions—the minstrel show and the musical comedy melee—capture the histories of racial caricature as well as the social and political relationships between Irish, Jewish, and African Americans. Theatrical productions and early films repeated racial caricatures of these groups; Irish, Jewish, and African American characters frequently jostled with each other on stage; and Irish and Jewish performers specialized in imitating African American characters. First, minstrelsy stands for the hierarchy of immigrant groups over African Americans and the ways that Irish and Jewish citizens alienated African Americans as they improved their own status in the United States. Significantly, Irish and Jewish performers specialized in blackface performance in their successful careers in minstrel shows and movies. Second, the melee represents the interaction of Irish, Jewish, and African Americans. The melee in popular theater featured different races together in rollicking comic scenes that often erupted into fights on stage. The various racial types were chaotically thrown together through pratfalls, fisticuffs and other stage gags—like dynamite, greased stairs, and flying furniture. The melee often diffused violent tensions between groups, as participants wielded rubber chickens rather than switch blades.[1] Even though these routines often disparaged African Americans most severely and sometimes featured white performers in blackface, they still presented a fluidity of racial characters that were more fully developed than figures in the minstrel show. While the minstrel show asserted racial hierarchy, the musical comedy melee presented a more playful multiculturalism. This chapter explores each theatrical tradition to introduce racial caricatures on stage and to trace the histories of exploitation and mutuality in the relationships between these three groups.

summary

The minstrel show reveals the persistent racist themes of American theater and film as well as the role of immigrant performers in denigrating African Americans. The minstrel show and blackface entertainment thus symbolize a hierarchy among Irish, Jewish, and African American performers in which immigrant groups propelled themselves ahead of black people, beyond a solidifying, biracial color line. The minstrel show grew out of the interactions between Irish and African Americans in places like Five Points, New York, and river towns, where African Americans and Irish lived and worked close to each other.[2] The Irish learned music and dance steps from African Americans, so that new cultural forms, such as tap dancing, emerged. In the minstrel show, a diverse groups of whites, but particularly Irishmen, were able to emphasize their common whiteness to antebellum urban masses in the creation of an abject but fascinating blackness.[3] The minstrel show mocked almost everyone: Irish and German immigrants, Native Americans, and all types of authority figures came under fire in its polyglot humor, but the "central joke" of minstrelsy remained the "smug whiteness" beneath the black makeup.[4] To impersonate African Americans, white performers wore ragged clothes and recited dialogue filled with malapropisms. In the mid-nineteenth century, the minstrel show tended to denigrate slaves as docile and free blacks as incompetent, presenting many images of peaceful plantation life in which "Old Massa to us darkies am good. . . . For he gibs us our clothes and he gibs us our food."[5] Popular among urban northern white men, the minstrel show seems to have assured the working-class audiences of their racial superiority, while also allowing some identification with the rebellious fun of blackness.

The historian Michael Rogin argues that through minstrelsy, "blacked up ethnics entered, even as they helped to create, the American melting pot."[6] The Irish dominated minstrelsy when it became the first distinctively American theater form in the antebellum period. In fact, Dale Cockrell argues that "minstrel shows became, to a certain extent, a product by and for Irish Americans."[7] Performers mocked the Irish on stage; Irish songs with a nationalist theme, such as "The Bonny Green Flat," were popular in the minstrel show, and Irish and African American music and dance styles were often interwoven in songs and sketches.[8] Along with the popularity of Irish themes and the intermixture of Irish and African American cultures, the Irish dominated the blackface impersonation of African Americans. The most famous minstrel show stars were Irish—George Christy, Dan Bryan, Matt Peel, and Ned Harrigan. In addition, Dan Emmett, a member of the

Virginia Minstrels and the author of "Dixie," was born in 1815 to an Irish immigrant family (from County Mayo) who had settled in a Mount Vernon, Ohio, a racially integrated city where he allegedly learned music from free blacks. One performer from Cork—Bernard Flaherty—who specialized in "negro songs and negro dances" in the 1830s and 1840s, was known for his strong accent, "which always clung to him and which suggested his native city rather than the cork he used to burn to color his face."[9]

Jews took center stage when blacking-up reemerged in early-twentieth-century film and peaked on stage around 1910. Jewish women became the premiere "coon shouters" in the first decade of the twentieth century. The so-called coon songs featured Negro dialect, ragtime syncopation, and plantation themes; performers often put on blackface to sing them, but not always. Prior to Jewish women's rise to prominence in the field, May Irwin, an Irish American singer, led the way for female coon shouters in the 1870s. Although she did not perform in blackface, she often acted as the "mammy" to a young African American male performer taking on a "picka-ninny" role in her act. Several decades later, the Jewish stars Sophie Tucker and Anna Held built their careers as coon shouters, Tucker in blackface, Held without.[10] Eddie Cantor got his start singing coon songs written by Irving Berlin, and he went on to play an effeminate African American char-acter, in blackface, with prominent white-rimmed glasses. He also played "Sonny" in a sketch with the West Indian star Bert Williams as "Papsy."[11] Around 1904, Al Jolson began to play a hospital orderly in blackface in a new vaudeville sketch. In 1908, Jolson was a regular in Lew Dockstader's minstrel show, which specialized in reenacting famous white scenarios in blackface. In "Boo Hoo Land" Jolson played "Acie," the assistant to Profes-sor Hightower, played by Dockstader. They set out to explore the North Pole, but end up in a "tribal soup pot."[12] Jolson went on to star in *The Jazz Singer* (1927) and *The Singing Fool* (1928), which involved promi-nent blackface routines. By the time of these movies, blackface was fading on stage.[13]

In the late nineteenth century, musical comedies that specialized in the interactions of immigrant and African American communities became popular. Although they featured performers and producers who had honed their skills in the minstrel show and also involved white performers in black-face, the musical comedy differed from the minstrel show by offering im-migrant characters with more depth within clearer story lines.[14] The foibles surrounding marriages between German, Irish and Jewish immigrants were often themes of these musical comedies. The melee scene formed a regular part of the racial diversity and interaction in tenement neighborhoods in these musical comedies. For example, *The Yellow Kid Who Lives in Hogan's Alley* (1897), a burlesque centered on the jabs between Schultz, a German shoe repairman, and Hogan, an Irish tinker, featured a multiracial melee in which German and Irish characters slip down a set of greased stairs, flipping and rolling over each other.[15] Similarly, in *McFadden's Row of Flats* (1903), an Irish child throws a firecracker into a German bar. The explosion sends the German proprietor and customers topsy-turvy into the street, knocking over Levi, the Jewish tailor, as they rush out.[16]

The main proponents of this theatrical style were Edward Harrigan and Tony Hart, who began to write and perform in full-length musical comedies after their experience in the minstrel show. Their Mulligan Guard plays of the 1870s and 1880s featured Irish, German, Jewish, and African Americans (played by whites in blackface), and, less often, Chinese and English characters in competing military clubs—or guards. One song, from *McSorely's Inflation* (1882), described the diversity of the city:

It's Ireland and Italy, Jerusalem and Germany,
Oh, Chinamen and nagurs, and a paradise for rats,
All jumbled up together in the snow and rainy weather,
They represent the tenants of McNally's row of flats.[17]

Harrigan and Hart reinforced the "common" racial caricatures of the day, but they also emphasized the "democracy" and the "shared plight" of the various racial minorities in these poor city neighborhoods.[18] Harrigan and Hart depicted the entire spectrum of the Lower East Side: here, the Germans are industrious and thrifty, but fat and drunk; the Irish are sometimes clever and joyful, but also combative, oafish, and drunk; Jews (though a smaller part in Harrigan and Hart's productions) are struggling street vendors, focused on squeezing every penny out of their businesses; African Americans pulled out razors in fights and seemed foolish when they tried to convey any kind of sophistication.[19] Harrigan and Hart were not entirely evenhanded in their multiracial representations, however. They tended to put the Irish at the top of their urban hierarchies, giving their Irish characters more depth and also showing their political power, whereas African Americans stayed close to minstrel show stereotypes and appeared menacing toward other characters.[20]

Harrigan and Hart's multiracial productions included at least one "merry melee," and other musical comedies also incorporated this convention. In

The Mulligan Guard Ball, Tommy Mulligan, the son of Dan and Cordelia Mulligan, falls in love with Kitty Lochmuller, the daughter of German immigrants, but Dan Mulligan strongly objects. One setting of the play is a barbershop owned by the African American Simpson Primrose who jokes about the Irish drinking rubbing alcohol. The African American group, the Skidmore Guard, falls through the ceiling onto the Irish group, the Mulligan Guard. Even though the groups squabble and try to separate themselves, they share similar raucous behavior—loud dancing and singing that collapses the floor, which divides them—and the comic frenzy diffuses racial tensions. In the chaos, it was "often impossible to tell who is on top."[21] But the "playfulness" still subjugates African Americans, as white actors in blackface portray the blacks on stage and the Irish Americans take charge in the end and "celebrate" Irish community.[22]

The heterogeneous comedy of the racially diverse melee was also prominent in vaudeville, an explosive theatrical venue that drew together a wide variety of acts, from jugglers to acrobats. The vaudeville aesthetic aimed to produce a quick, intense reaction in the audience; thus its quintessential style was slapstick comedy, with grotesque costumes and crude jokes. At the turn of the twentieth century, a vaudeville program of seven to nine acts regularly included several examples of "racial caricaturists," such as the Dutchman, the Hebrew, the Celt, and the "darkey."[23] White performers could impersonate any racial type, with quick changes of costumes and makeup, including red greasepaint for Irish characters or "sallow" greasepaint for the Hebrew type. Comedians built their careers on their multiracial versatility, mastering many dialects and alternating between Irish, Hebrew, and Dutch caricatures from one act to the next.[24] In vaudeville, then, the confusion of the melee was often embedded in the act of a single comedian or comedy team.

The quick-change comedians built on well-developed racial types in popular theater. The "Hebrew" comedian wore long black clothes and sometimes a fake putty nose. This comic type was either a "fast-talker, very canny merchant" or a "fretful" loser, resigned to the "inexplicable forces of the world."[25] With somber music in the background, Joe Welch, for example, took the stage dressed in ill-fitting clothes, a pointy beard, and his hands hidden in his sleeves. Exasperated and forlorn, he looked at audiences in an awkward period of silence. Then he shrugged, "Maybe you tink I'm heppy?"[26] The popular Jewish stage caricature was often a criminal, sometimes a businessman, often both; he was dirty, "materialistic," "slinking," cheap, and immoral—an insult to the "long suffering, self-controlled, law-abiding" Jewish people.[27] The Stage Jew had "a keen scent for the dollar at any cost."[28] Jewish criminals on stage and screen were willing to break the law for financial gain, and a variety of legitimate Jewish businessmen were depicted as miserly and immoral, if not explicitly criminal.

On the vaudeville stage, "Paddy," the immigrant Irish man, was uproarious and uncouth, in contrast to the plodding German and the stingy Jew.[29] The Stage Irishman had a protruding brow and lips with a pug nose; he was shabbily dressed in green, with bright red or green whiskers on his face and a bottle of whiskey close at hand. The comedian Dan McAvoy appeared "as a huge ape, with a tremendous upperlip, a short stubby nose, and a fringe of bright red whiskers" for his play *His Honor, the Mayor of the Bowery*, in 1905.[30] If his behavior was destructive, lazy, and hapless at times, the immigrant Irish male was sometimes depicted in a positive light as loyal to his working-class neighbors and quick-witted enough to escape a variety of stifling authority figures. For example, Mike Haggerty, the lead character in a series of vaudeville sketches by Will Cressy, is an Irish hod carrier who rejects the pretensions of high society and mocks his daughter's vanity as she tries to gain elite acceptance.[31] The Stage Irish, however, were fundamentally gendered. In contrast to the representation of the upwardly mobile, polite Irish daughter, one popular caricature of the Irish woman was as an overbearing, mannish battle-ax who was also sexually forward and physically uncontrollable. She drank and flirted too much. Cross-dressed actors specialized in this caricature of the Irish woman so often that, even when actresses rendered this hulking Stage Irishwoman, rumors circulated that the performers were in fact men.[32]

Vaudeville performers often presented a confusing jumble of racial types simultaneously by changing rapidly from one type to another or by highlighting the contrast between their racial background and their racial impersonation. Levi and Cohen were two Jewish vaudevillians known as the "Irish Comedians." One vaudeville theater manager described another comedy duo in 1911: "Two Jews singing Irish songs with a little talk . . . is as good an act of the Hebrew brand as has been around in many a day."[33] Joe Weber and Lew Fields also exemplified this comedic borrowing in their act: "Here we are, a colored pair," they explained in thick Yiddish accents. Then they moved into Irish brogue and costume—green breeches, bow ties, and derby hats—for the rest of their routine.[34] The vaudevillian Harry Jolson,

"Hebrew" comedian, Joe Welch. Photo by White Studio ©Billy Rose Theatre Division, The New York Public Library for the Performing Arts

Al Jolson's brother, exemplified the confusion of racial types when he mistakenly used a Yiddish accent in place of an Irish brogue. Although he was well-known for his Jewish characterizations, he was assigned an Irish part for a particular act. But after he marched on stage in an Irish costume, with the accompaniment of "Wearing of the Green," he mistakenly delivered his monologue in "Eastside Yiddish-American gumbo."[35]

While white immigrants had the opportunity to imitate other immigrant groups as well as African Americans, black performers had much less flexibility. African American actors had latitude to impersonate only Native Americans and Chinese immigrants, and sometimes they borrowed from white performers. Overall, however, they succeeded in entertainment when they "never forget they are darkies and never try to do 'white folks' comedy."[36] Young African American actors—the "Congo Bongo Act"—appeared as Native Americans in the first scene of "The Evolution of the Negro"; the act moved through southern plantation life and ended with the performers doing a song and dance routine dressed as waiters in a New York City restaurant.[37] African Americans adopted the darkey dialect and blackface to represent themselves. Managers disliked any African American performer who tried to pass as white, forbade any romantic interaction between white and black characters, and encouraged African American performers to stick to slapstick comedy, rather than serious drama or classical singing. Bert Williams—a West Indian performer who became one of the most successful comedians in the early twentieth century—wore blackface to darken his light skin and spoke in thick dialect to mask his British accent.[38] George Walker, who partnered with Williams in vaudeville and musical comedy, reflected on the strictures on their performances in 1908: "We noticed the colored men had to be comedians and athletic comedians at that. Head stands, flip flaps, and such."[39]

The racism of popular theater and the judgments of African American leaders shaped Ernest Hogan's career. Reuben Crowder, who allegedly changed his name to Ernest Hogan to capitalize on the popularity of Irish comedians, wrote the popular song "All Coons Look Alike to Me" (1899), in which a woman tells her suitor that "all coons look a like to me/I've got another beau, you see/And he's just as good to me as you, nig!/ever tried to be."[40] Although "coon" at this point did not seem to be derogatory, it soon became linked to racist caricatures in popular music and theater. In 1900, after performing a rendition of his famous song on the sidewalk, Hogan faced a mob of whites that looked for famous black performers, shouting

Weber and Fields, vaudeville comedians who specialized in several racial comedy types. Billy Rose Theatre Division, The New York Public Library for the Performing Arts, Astor, Lenox and Tilden Foundations

"Get Hogan and Willams and Walker."[41] He escaped the angry group by running down Broadway and then ducking into the Marlborough Hotel. Instead of protecting African Americans, city police officers joined with the white vigilantes. Sparked by a fight at a police officer's funeral, the riot was a response to the deeper struggles over the city's growing black population, a result of African Americans' northern migration.[42]

Hogan aligned himself with the early NAACP, but he still faced criticism from African Americans who objected to his style of performance.[43] The drama critic Sylvester Russell disliked Hogan's "ignorant" music, which he considered an obstacle to his race's aspiration for middle-class respect-ability.[44] Early histories of Hogan's career linked protests against him with Irish protests against the Stage Irish: "Poor Hogan! As his race rose in the world, they became sensitive to slights as the Irishman who egged *The Playboy of the Western World*, or the rabbis who believe all entrance exami-nations are specially directed against Jews. The verse of 'All Coons Look Alike to Me' was forgotten. The refrain became a fighting phrase all over New York. Whistled by a white man it was construed as a personal insult... Hogan ... died haunted by the awful crime he had unwittingly committed against the race."[45] Hogan was thus an example of all that Irish, Jews, and African Americans had in common—they had all become intolerant of the insults on stage—but also a reminder of the difficult conditions faced by African American performers when compared to immigrant actors. The performances of popular theater celebrated a cosmopolitan ideal and the mutability of identity, but at the same time they affirmed a "dark, racially exclusive side" of American nationalism.[46]

Theater managers and critics used the term "racial comedy" (or dialect comedy) to refer to the Jewish, African American, and Irish imperson-ators. This was not a misnomer. The Celt and the Hebrew were considered distinct white races, not ethnic groups, around the turn of the twentieth century. *The Dictionary of Races or Peoples*, produced by the Dillingham Commission (a House-Senate commission, chaired by the Vermont sena-tor William Paul Dillingham, which investigated immigration reform) in 1911, described a "taxonomy" of European races, including Hebrew, Celt, and Slav.[47] Although they were legally white for the purposes of naturaliza-tion and civil rights, unlike Chinese or Japanese immigrants, Jewish and Irish immigrants were still in between blacks and whites in terms of popular culture and some scientific classification. In the antebellum United States,

African American activists objected to Ernest Hogan's "All Coons Look Alike to Me" (1896). John Hay Library, Brown University

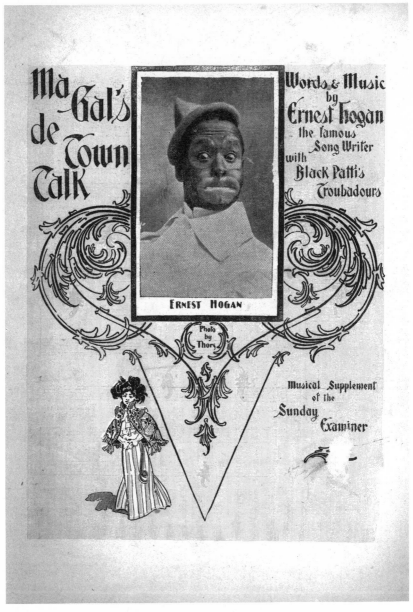

Ernest Hogan in his vaudeville makeup. John Hay Library, Brown University

the Celtic race was "indolent, irrational and childlike," often depicted with a slack simian affinity to African Americans in popular cartoons, with some suggestions of African origins.[48] Racial hostility and the definition of the Irish race played key roles in the 1863 Draft Riots in New York City, in which the Irish attacked African Americans, Native Americans, and white women married to African Americans or Native Americans. The mainstream press blamed the violence on the combative traits of the Irish—a "race of miscreants," according to the *New York Times*.[49] Most nineteenth-century observers saw Jewish success and acculturation as a sign of white superiority, but by the early twentieth century, as Eastern European immigration peaked, Jews emerged as a peculiar race.[50] Around the turn of the century scholars regarded the Jewish race in contradictory ways—praising the race's ambition and capitalist success, but also deriding its greed; they defined Jews as quintessentially modern, but also as old-fashioned in their religious devotion.[51] Commentators claimed that the Jews resembled African Americans because of their swarthy skin tone and inappropriate sexual drive. As the racist populist Tom Watson remarked, the black man's "lust after the white woman is not much fiercer than the lust of the licentious Jew for the gentile."[52] Yet racial identity was not just imposed from the outside; the Jewish and Irish activists in America also celebrated "race pride" as a means of boosting group identity.[53] Some Jews, for example, used a racial self-definition as an argument against conversions for Gentiles marrying Jews, and Irish organizations like the Gaelic League of America, founded in 1898, celebrated Celtic traits, Irish manhood, and Celtic contributions to America as a way to de-Anglicize American and Irish culture.[54]

Irish and Jewish leaders debated racial identity as the racial landscape began to shift from a scheme of multiple racial types, including many European races such as Celt and Hebrew, to a biracial scheme, with Caucasian unity, after World War I.[55] African American migration to urban areas and to the North helped "erode the once-salient 'differences' among the white races."[56] The Irish were increasingly accepted as white, along with Anglo-Saxons and Nordic races, as Southern and Eastern European immigrants became the racially strange immigrants in the racial landscape.[57] Acculturated Jews shifted from considering themselves as a race to identifying themselves as a religious and cultural group. Around 1890, key Jewish leaders put more emphasis on faith as a common bond and on environmental factors. Rabbi Emil Hirsch, for example, shifted from being "adamant" that Jews were a distinctive race in the mid-1890s, to referring to Jews as a nation, then to them as a religious group. The historian Eric Goldstein emphasizes that many Jewish leaders continued to believe in Jewish racial distinctiveness, but they did not want to emphasize it in public discourse, because, with the new prominence of Eastern European Jews, the older generation of Jews had less control over the racial definitions and perceptions of Jews.[58] The attorney Simon Wolf and other members of the American Jewish Committee testified before the U.S. Immigration Commission (the Dillingham Commission) that Jews were a faith group, not a race. Unconvinced, the committee decided to continue the racial classification of Jews.[59]

Just as different racial types put each other down and pushed each other around in comedies on stage, Irish, Jewish, and African American citizens also struggled with their racial otherness and worked to move up, fit in, and fortify group solidarity in the early twentieth century. The social status of Irish, Jewish, and African Americans was improving, in different degrees, through migration, economic advances, and political organizing in the early twentieth century, but they shared a sense of standing outside mainstream American society. Each group also grappled with internal tensions, particularly between an established class and newcomers, and struggled over who or what group would represent it during this period of transition. Irish nationalist factions disagreed about the most effective means of achieving Irish independence and about whether to link Irish statehood to social concerns in the United States. Similarly, self-defense organizations for Jewish Americans and civil rights organizations for African Americans battled their rivals to lead their respective communities.

There was a large migration of Irish to the United States during the famine between 1845 and 1852, when a fungus destroyed five consecutive potato crops, but by 1900 most Irish immigrants already in the United States had left Ireland after the famine.[60] Irish immigrants were concentrated in the northeastern cities of New York, Pennsylvania, Massachusetts, and Rhode Island. They shed their local identities based on roots in rural Irish villages and became "self-consciously Irish."[61] Throughout the nineteenth century, they used violence to protest a variety of grievances, from the draft during the Civil War to the inclusion of Protestant Irish in a New York City parade and labor exploitation in the Pennsylvania coalfields.[62] They displayed a strong collective identity in the Irish American press, at St. Patrick's Day celebrations, and in the Irish nationalist movement, which thrived in the United States. At the same time, they developed a strong sense of victimization, or a "chip on the shoulder"—often because of the perceived discrimination among Protestant employers—that cemented a "high level of group solidarity in politics and the job market."[63] Around 1900, the American-born children of Irish immigrants from the Irish famine of the late 1840s became the dominant force in Irish American life.[64] The status of the Irish in America improved from one wave of immigration to the next, and from one generation to the next, but more slowly than for other immigrant groups. Only 10 percent of Irish immigrants in Boston had white-collar jobs in 1890, but 40 percent of second-generation Irish had moved up to white-collar occupations.[65] They favored government jobs (in sanitation, fire, and police departments) and employment in construction, as opposed to business entrepreneurship.[66] By 1900 the Irish attended college at the same rate as native-born whites, and could point to many prominent examples of political and business success, including Patrick Collins, an Irish revolutionary and wealthy businessman who was elected mayor of Boston in 1901.[67] Yet despite some upward mobility, "the social position of the Irish was distinctly working class, and the immigrant generation was heavily concentrated among the low manual workers."[68]

The Irish in America, then, were divided between those born in Ireland and those born in America, and between those who had achieved middle-class status and those still in the working class. For example, in 1887 the Ancient Order of Hibernians, an Irish Catholic fraternal association, was deeply divided over whether to allow Irish of American birth to join; ten years later it opened membership to both generations.[69] In the 1890s a new lexicon developed to describe this situation: "lace curtain" referred to upwardly mobile Irish, while "shanty Irish" identified the impoverished greenhorns. Irish-born immigrants accused the second generation of lacking race pride and a sense of Irish history. In a debate over "libelous" St. Patrick's Day postcards, an Irish critic attacked Irish women born in America for buying the cards, without concern for "modesty" or Irish "patriotism": "The worst offenders were the ignorant young Irishwomen born in this country who patronized these horrible and indecent cards villifying the land of their fathers and mothers."[70] Class often exacerbated this difference between the American-born and the Irish immigrants. "Assimilation-oriented" Irish in America cringed at the prospect of welcoming poor Irish relatives, whose intemperance might embarrass the new lace curtain Irish.[71] The Catholic Total Abstinence Union (1872), with a middle-class and (often) second-generation Irish leadership, espoused American patriotism, assimilation, and temperance.[72] The Knights of Columbus, founded in 1882 by a "second-

generation Irish curate," distanced itself from the working-class nationalism of the Ancient Order of Hibernians and the Clan na Gael. With their
focus on Catholicism, not Irish race pride, and on America, not Ireland,
the Knights of Columbus attracted white-collar workers.[73]

The Irish also grappled with gender tensions. Irish women tended to
have more independence than other women, immigrant or native born.
They were more likely to head their own families; about 10 to 20 percent
of Irish families had a sole female breadwinner in the nineteenth century.[74]
And a much higher percentage of Irish women migrated and worked in the
paid labor force than women from other immigrant groups. Irish women
were praised as resilient and strong, but women's paid work and independence from men proved controversial. While Irish leaders praised young
women's work, they also criticized the unfortunate circumstances leading
to its need, and they held that married women should never be in the labor
market. Observers also exaggerated and mocked women's independence.
The cartoonist Frederick Opper drew "Biddy" as an imposing ape, shaking
her fist as she stood over her demure employer. The caption says, "The Irish
Declaration of Independence That We Are All Familiar With."[75] In contrast,
Catholic leaders held up Irish women's devotion to family and their chastity,
simultaneously empowering men as protectors of women.

The Jewish community experienced similar fault lines regarding upward
mobility, waves of immigration, and gender in the early twentieth century.
Around the turn of the twentieth century, the Jewish families from Central
Europe—the "German" Jews—who had migrated in the 1830s and 1840s,
encountered large numbers of Eastern European immigrants. Violence,
legal repression, and poverty were pushing Jews out of Russia and Poland.
A series of pogroms began in the early 1880s, and another wave started
in 1903.[76] The German leaders of the Jewish community were concerned
about how the new masses of Yiddish-speaking Orthodox Jews would fare
in the United States. Although their success did not match the German
Jews' accumulation of wealth, Eastern European Jews and their children
still achieved "remarkable . . . occupational and economic mobility."[77] As
the historian John Higham concludes, "They quit the slums in conspicuous
numbers, produced an affluent class of real estate speculators and clothing
manufacturers, and alone among recent immigrants sent a good many of
their children to college."[78]

The different waves of Jewish migrants had contrasting religions, politics, and languages. Jews of Central European (largely German) descent de-

veloped Reform Judaism, which shortened religious services, decreased the use of Hebrew, and, in some cases, added Sunday services. It downplayed Jewish distinctiveness and instead emphasized universal connections with other religions and a secular affirmation of modern American culture.[79] The new wave of Orthodox Eastern European Jews found themselves "repelled" by Reform Judaism.[80] Well-established German Jews also expressed shock at the new immigrants. Middle-class Jews, particularly men anxious about their social status, often pointed to the "Ghetto Girl"—who was crass and garish in her store-bought fashion and excessive make-up—as an example of the vulgarity of the new wave of immigrants.[81] One rabbi described the mutual distrust: Central European Jews thought Eastern European Jews were "ignorant, superstitious, bigoted, hypocritical, cunning, ungrateful, quarrelsome, unclean," while eastern European Jews had this negative assessment of their counterparts: "His ... philanthropy [is] ostentatious and insincere," the rabbi explained, "his manners a cheap imitation of the Gentiles upon whom he fawns."[82] When some social reformers claimed that the Lower East Side was "an African jungle," or that Jews and blacks were equally uncivilized, Central European leaders saw the interrelated risks of their association with African Americans and new Jewish arrivals.[83] Elite Jews in the United States did try to help Eastern European Jews by opposing immigration restriction, funding settlement plans, and encouraging dispersal throughout the United States. But they were embarrassed by the poor, new arrivals and feared that their distinctive appearance and language would heighten anti-Semitism. These elite Jews often remained unaware of their alienating cultural superiority. proof?

African Americans faced Jim Crow segregation, disenfranchisement, and vigilante violence during this period. Their protests against the Chicago World's Fair (or Columbian Exposition), which honored the four hundredth anniversary of Columbus's arrival in the New World and broadly celebrated American progress and empire, provide a snapshot of African American struggles. Blacks objected to their exclusion from any role in planning the fair, as well as to their poor representation in the exhibits. There was no distinct "Negro Department," partly because African American leaders did not agree on the benefits of a separate exhibit, and African American artists and inventors had trouble getting exhibits accepted in other venues. Ida B. Wells, Frederick Douglass, and other black leaders published a pamphlet, *The Reason Why the Colored American Is Not in the World's Columbian Exposition*, to criticize the false sense of American liberty (in the face of the reality of lynch law) and the absence of images of African American progress. The decade of the 1890s marked the peak of lynching in the United States. In 1892 there were 241 reported lynchings; 180 of these occurred in the South.[84] Along with publishing the pamphlet, African Americans also organized the Congress on Africa for a week in August of 1893 to "save American negroes from an obscurity and mortification which the failure to award them place in the Exposition has caused them to feel keenly."[85]

The Supreme Court upheld legal segregation in *Plessy v. Ferguson* (1896), which endorsed separate but equal facilities for blacks and whites. Blacks unsuccessfully lobbied against the passage of state laws codifying segregation and also filed lawsuits against racist practices. In 1883 Ida B. Wells resisted railroad segregation and filed suit against the Chesapeake, Ohio, and Southwestern Railroad for denying her first-class accommodations.[86] Disenfranchisement through poll taxes and literacy tests reversed the gains of Reconstruction for African Americans in the South. Lynching became a terrifying weapon against them between 1890 and World War I in the entire United States, and race riots erupted in northern cities, before and after World War I, including in Springfield, Illinois (1908), and Chicago (1919). Prior to the unusual labor demands of World War I, African Americans were excluded from industrial employment. Even during the war, however, African American men were the "last option" when it came to hiring in industrial factories; they often found themselves overlooked by white unions and used as strikebreakers.[87] African American women had some opportunities outside of domestic service, on the lowest rungs of the industrial ladder, such as in commercial laundries.[88]

Just as earlier generations of Jewish and Irish immigrants moved up the social ladder and confronted new waves of "unrefined" brethren, African Americans also experienced internal divisions when rural African Americans migrated to cities. Pushed by debt, violence, and disenfranchisement in the southern countryside, African Americans were attracted to economic opportunities and the hope of full citizenship. Between 1890 and 1910, approximately 170,000 African Americans left the South in each decade; in the following decade that number skyrocketed to 454,000.[89] Chicago's black population, for example, more than doubled between 1910 and 1920. Life in the North was not free of racism (segregation and rioting marked northern urban history), but African Americans still gained political influence and developed a robust artistic scene—the Harlem Renaissance—in the North.

Despite improved security in the North, blacks still had fewer opportunities than Irish and Jewish citizens. They still received the lowest wages and the lowest-skilled jobs; upward mobility was "virtually impossible."[90]

Like the Jewish confrontation between different waves of immigrants, the northward movement of African Americans also sparked class conflict and inspired elites to launch various forms of uplift. Wealthier African Americans worried that mass migration would undermine their efforts to earn respectable status from whites. They circulated positive images of black domesticity and education to contrast the widespread minstrel stereotypes. But they did not uniformly vanquish minstrel stereotypes; often they simply reserved them for rural blacks. They espoused a class hierarchy in their assimilationist uplift, with them at the top—as opposed to the "so-called primitive, morally deficient lower classes."[91] Black intellectuals sometimes derided recent migrants for their association with urban, low-brow entertainment and regularly criticized cultural styles associated with blacks—the blues and ragtime, for example—while they upheld European ideals of cultural excellence. The Ivy League–educated William Pickens criticized the "Negro of the 'coon song,' and of the slum dive."[92] The National Urban League (NUL), formed from the unification of three service agencies in 1911, focused on training rural black migrants for employment, with a substantial focus on self-help and morality, rather than concentrating on direct legal confrontations with discrimination. Blacks and whites, including a substantial number of Jews, worked together in the NUL.

Despite social and political improvements, all three groups faced slights, coercion, and discrimination because they stood outside the Anglo-Saxon ideal. A movement for strict Americanization, centered on Anglo-Saxon supremacy, emerged at the end of the nineteenth century and peaked during World War I. The emphasis on Americanization had a humanitarian, progressive trajectory, including assistance for immigrants, but it increasingly emphasized loyalty, naturalization, and an uncompromising "100 per cent Americanism."[93] During World War I, various civic groups tried to bolster national unity by stamping out German culture—cutting German language instruction in some states and, in some cases, boycotting German operas.[94] The Espionage Act of 1917 and the expansion of that act, the Sedition Act of 1918, criminalized statements critical of the war effort or of the U.S. government. Officials used the act to silence political radicals, including many immigrants. The intense xenophobia focused most intently on Germans during the war, but it threatened other immigrant groups as well.[95] Anti-

Semitism in the late nineteenth and early twentieth century included the exclusion of Jews from some hotels and resorts, and quotas against Jews in colleges and universities. In 1916, the progressive attorney Louis Brandeis became the first Jewish Supreme Court justice after a long and contentious nomination process in which critics assailed him as a Jewish radical.[96] In the name of national unity and loyalty, social workers, businesspeople, and civic leaders encouraged immigrants to give up Old World customs. Henry Ford, for example, established a compulsory English school for his immigrant workers and his *Dearborn Independent* blamed German Jewish bankers for starting World War I and railed against Russian Jewish immigrants for plotting political revolt in the United States.[97] The "melting pot," he argued, could not include the "aliens who have given us so much trouble, those Bolsheviki messing up our industries and disturbing our civil life."[98] After the war ended, the Justice Department, under the direction of the new Attorney General A. Mitchell Palmer, carried out raids against labor activists and radical organizations, resulting in the deportation of many immigrants, largely eastern Europeans. The second Ku Klux Klan, established in 1915, advocated white supremacy and 100 percent Americanism as its popularity increased in the 1920s.[99] Federal laws restricting immigration, particularly for people from southern and eastern Europe, passed in 1921 and 1924.

All three groups developed organizations to advance what they identified as the primary interest of their communities; these group interests varied among the Irish, Jewish, and African American communities, but the main goals were nationalism, civil rights, and self-defense. Radical Irish nationalists emerged, from a field of intense disagreements over political strategy, as the leaders of the campaign against the Stage Irish, with backing from various mutual-aid societies. Irish nationalist organizations in the early twentieth century animated and fractured Irish American life: the Clan na Gael, which reunified in 1900, supported the violent overthrow of Great Britain, while the United Irish League of America advocated a more moderate approach to achieving Irish independence through the electoral process. Nationalists often argued that respect and autonomy for Ireland led to upward mobility for the Irish in the United States. This "assimilative" trajectory included improved personal habits—obeying the law, the Catholic Church, and the boss.[100] If some nationalist organizing and rhetoric addressed bourgeois desires among the Irish, other aspects refuted it, advocating direct confrontations with Anglo-Saxon respectability. Nationalist leaders also disagreed about connecting nationalism to other social causes. Patrick Ford, the editor of the *Irish World and American Industrial Liberator*, embraced Irish nationalism as well as labor activism and land reform, while John Devoy, the editor of the *Gaelic American*, saw Ford's wide-ranging social critique as diminishing the cause of the Irish revolution, though Devoy also attacked the landlord system in Ireland. Devoy asserted his approach to Irish nationalism: "We are fighting for the Irish people and for the Irish people alone."[101]

Irish nationalist organizations worked with and depended on mutual-aid organizations and Catholic benevolent societies. The Ancient Order of Hibernians, founded in 1836, fought anti-Catholic and anti-Irish bigotry, provided benefits like insurance and educational programs, and by the late nineteenth century endorsed radical Irish nationalism. The Knights of Columbus, established in 1882, also defended the Irish against anti-Catholicism, establishing the Commission of Religious Prejudices to track and challenge the rise of anti-Catholic publications like the *Menace*.[102]

Irish nationalists had some ideas in common with black nationalists and Zionists; and each nationalist campaign in some ways looked outward to connections to other nationalisms. A painful diaspora, struggle for self-determination, and a concern with racist representation marked the three campaigns. As the literary critic George Bornstein concludes, it is remarkable that "both their partisans and their detractors . . . put the three together."[103] Marcus Garvey, the Jamaican-born black nationalist, linked the three movements favorably in 1919: "It is as serious a movement as the movement of the Irish today to have a free Ireland, as the determination of the Jew to recover Palestine."[104] Jewish and African American nationalists regarded Irish nationalism as an inspirational model—it was the "first" nationalism, inspiring other anticolonial movements from India to the British colonies in the Caribbean. Yet as they focused on Irish racial recovery and the establishment of a free Irish state, Irish nationalists sometimes expressed anti-Semitism and racism. Arthur Griffith famously backed an anti-Semitic priest in Limerick and accused Jews of corrupt business practices but Irish nationalism cannot, however, be easily defined as insular and racist; rather, Irish nationalists linked their cause to anticolonialist movements around the globe in the early twentieth century, sometimes expressing admiration for Zionism and the right of Jews to create their own homeland.[105]

Black nationalists formed a key bloc in a new militant coalition that included West Indian migrants and young black artists and writers. They promoted a "militant black diasporic 'New Negro' race consciousness" to challenge the older, more accommodationist model of self-help for African Americans.[106] In 1914 Garvey established the Universal Negro Improvement Association (UNIA) to free Africa from colonial rule and to return all Africans in the United States to Africa. Garvey cultivated race pride as he proclaimed national and cultural distinctiveness of "Africa for Africans."[107]

Garvey often celebrated an affinity between black nationalism and Irish nationalism. Garvey's Liberty Hall in Harlem was named after a Dublin building that housed the Irish Transport and General Workers' Union; it was a focus of British bombing after the 1916 rebellion.[108] After World War I, Garvey announced, "The time has come for the Negro race to offer up its martyrs upon the altar of liberty even as the Irish had given a long list from Robert Emmet to Roger Casement."[109] Connected by anticolonialism, Irish and New Negro leaders sometimes spoke at the same gatherings, and Garvey called a sympathy strike with Irish longshoremen after the first UNIA convention in 1921. Thus, even after World War I, when Irish whiteness became more clear cut and the racial struggle was delineated as black versus white, Garvey still praised Irish nationalism.[110] In other cases, Irish whiteness and racism still disrupted the affinity. As W. E. B. Du Bois wrote, after World War I, "I shall at all times defend the right of Ireland to absolute independence [but] there can be no doubt of the hostility of a large proportion of Irish Americans towards Negroes."[111]

Zionism emerged in the 1890s in the United States, after waves of anti-Semitic violence in Russia and after the Dreyfus Affair in France. The establishment of a Jewish state was one proposed solution to the persecution in Europe. Theodore Herzl's proposal in his 1896 book, *The Jewish State*, to resettle Jews in Argentina or Palestine gained a cross-section of Jewish support, but Zionism remained a "modest" endeavor in the United States until World War I. Reform Jews, at the helm of much of organized Jewish life (including the fight against the Stage Jew) were not, by and large, enthusiastic about Zionism because it clashed with their emphasis on universalism and Americanization.[112] Still, some major Jewish leaders became Zionists in the first decade of the twentieth century—namely Louis Brandeis and Louis Marshall. Zionists like Herzl referred to the Irish nation when he said, "I shall be the Parnell of the Jews."[113] And the Irish linked themselves favorably to Zionism, as Michael Davitt said in 1903: "I have come from a journey through the Jewish Pale, a convinced believer in the remedy of Zionism."[114]

These nationalist campaigns supported new calls for pluralism in the United States, to rebut both the melting pot and the "Anglo-conformity" of "100% Americanism."[115] The Gaelic League challenged the supremacy of Anglo-Saxons in the United States by delineating the Celtic contributions to the country and by pointing to the diversity at the heart of American life.[116] It encouraged "native" dances and songs in amateur entertainments, along with the Irish language. Irish nationalists also took Irish credit for the Star-Spangled Banner.[117] In his 1915 essay in the *Nation*, "Democracy vs. the Melting Pot," Horace Kallen, a Harvard-educated Jewish professor, envisioned multiple European races as different instrumentalists in an orchestra, rather than blending together in a melting pot. Brandeis borrowed from Kallen when he championed a new nationality that "proclaims that each race or people, like each individual, has the right and duty to develop, and only through such differentiated development will high civilization be attained."[118] Kallen, like Brandeis, was a Zionist, partly because he believed that securing a homeland would put Jews on "an equal footing with other ethnic groups."[119] While Irish and Jewish celebrations of distinct racial contributions to a pluralist society only included the white races, Du Bois articulated an early vision of racial pluralism based on black contributions in his 1897 essay titled "The Conservation of the Races."

In contrast to the Irish American protests, the Jewish and African American campaigns against racial ridicule grew out of civil rights and self-defense organizations. Jews in the United States developed an extensive organizational network around the turn of the twentieth century to address the Americanization of eastern European Jews, defend the civil rights of Jewish people, and end the persecution of Jews in Russia and other parts of eastern Europe.[120] The International Order of B'nai B'rith, a Jewish fraternal association founded in 1843, developed a network of chapters across the country. It shared the stage with many other Jewish organizations in the late nineteenth century. The Chicago World's Fair spurred Jewish organizing in many ways. After being denied equal representation at the fair's Parliament of Religions, well-established Jewish women of German backgrounds formed the National Council for Jewish Women (NCJW). The group provided aid to Jewish immigrants, supported religious schools for girls, and backed Progressive legislation—all the while keeping motherhood central.[121] In their effort to Americanize immigrants, the NCJW reformers still cultivated Jewish traditions and espoused a pluralist appreciation of immigration, as opposed to the "conformist" Americanizing organizations, such as the American Legion.[122] The American Jewish Committee (AJC), established in 1906, addressed the anti-Semitic violence in Russia, as well as the civil rights of Jews in the United States. The AJC rejected Zionism as a solution to the European persecution of Jews; this position led more radical Jews, including many Eastern European Jews tired of Central European Jews' leadership, to establish the American Jewish Congress in 1916. Members of the AJC tended to see the American Jewish Congress as too ideological, while the American Jewish Congress expressed dissatisfaction with the AJC's "charity," seeking, instead, "redress."[123]

African Americans also established strong civil rights organizations in the early twentieth century. The scholar and activist Du Bois, who had already lived through a race riot in Atlanta in 1906, was shocked when violent outbreaks spread to the northern capital city of Springfield, Illinois, in 1908. He then joined a group of white and black progressives who, in response to the Springfield riot, established the National Association for the Advancement of Colored People in 1909. The NAACP worked for full legal equality for African Americans through legal challenges to segregation, including segregated seating in theaters, and through publicity denouncing vigilante violence and discrimination. Its insistence on full citizenship set it apart from Garvey's nationalist militancy and Booker T. Washington's conservatism. Washington, for example, praised the leading comedian of the day, the West Indian Bert Williams, for his ability to capture the "natural humor . . . of the Negro" and to achieve great success without any political activism against racism.[124] On the other hand, Du Bois, the editor of the NAACP's monthly *Crisis*, praised the political, antiracist goals of art and circulated his own publicity to correct lies about African American criminality and inferiority.

In their campaigns against racial ridicule, Irish, Jewish, and African American leaders sometimes made similar demands for a pluralist popular culture in which no race was maligned, and sought to defend their particular group by reforming representation. But they also retreated from these inclusive statements to blame each other for their plight. On the one hand, the Irish offered an expansive view of racial ridicule when the *Gaelic American* noted in 1907: "In a country where the theory is to give every one a chance it is an unwise thing to attempt ridicule of race elements. . . . In cosmopolitan America no man has a right to poke fun at his neighbor because of some peculiarity of race or mode of thought."[125] Similarly, the *American Israelite* complained about racial caricature, asserting that the "stage is a cosmopolitan institution. It ought to be above this sort of cheap exploitation."[126] On the other hand, racism was a common theme in the Irish and Jewish campaigns, and in the newspaper coverage of all three campaigns. When a mayor censored *The Clansman* for its insult to African Americans, a critic wondered why African Americans received special protection: "If the Jews have put up so long with 'Shylock,' what excuse can educated white people have for pampering the negroes' overweening conceit by tabooing the 'Clansman' because the ignorant black man imagines himself insulted when shown up in his worst light? Are the negroes better than the Jews?"[127] The noted African American journalist Sylvester Russell, remarked on racism among Jewish theater managers in his letter to the *Indianapolis Freeman*: "Dear Sir: Some of these managers who are drawing the color line are Hebrews. No manager with Hebrew blood in his veins should draw the color line and expect the Americans to cease discriminating against Jews in the exclusive hotel and summer resorts, when they are drawing the race line themselves."[128]

The three groups considered here include two striking pairings in American history—one of affinity, the other of hostility. The Irish have stood out for their animosity toward African Americans, while Jews and African Americans forged an exemplary alliance in the twentieth century. The antagonism between the Irish and African Americans developed despite some common experiences in the nineteenth century. The Irish lived near African Americans in many cities, both groups resented the powerful who had forced them out of their homelands, and both were considered separate races prone to violence.[129] When Frederick Douglass toured Ireland for several years starting in 1845, he noted rural poverty similar to the living conditions of slaves, and he commented on "rapturous [but] melancholy" songs among slaves and Irish peasants: "I have never heard any songs like those anywhere since I left slavery, except when in Ireland. There I heard the same wailing notes, and was much affected by them."[130] In many American cities Irish and African American laborers shared a culture of music, dances, jokes, and dialect.[131]

Despite these commonalities, by the middle of the nineteenth century, the Irish had a "reputation as being among the most intensely racist people in America."[132] This hostility surprised some mid-nineteenth-century observers, who wondered why the Irish, with their recent experience of a "galling, degraded bondage," should reject all efforts to give greater rights to African Americans.[133] Most Irish Americans opposed the abolition of slavery, although there were some powerful exceptions among Irish nationalists, like Daniel O'Connell in the early nineteenth century and, in the 1880s, John Boyle O'Reilly, who defended civil rights for African Americans.[134] Otherwise, the Catholic Church viewed abolitionists as dangerous radicals, and some Irish leaders resented the Protestant, English source of much of the abolitionist campaign.[135] Although many African Americans were sympathetic to the needs of the Irish peasantry, African Americans were second only to the British in the United States in their hostility toward Irish independence.[136]

As the Irish grew more politically powerful and prosperous in the early twentieth century, the possibilities for common cause deteriorated even further; as the historian Arnold Shankman explains, "Blacks could not help but notice that 'Paddy' was rising in the social hierarchy; their own status, on the other hand, seemed to be fixed or on the decline."[137] Established earlier in northern cities than African Americans, in the mid-nineteenth century, the Irish benefited from a burgeoning industrial economy and also carefully protected the benefits of Democratic Party identification, expanding patronage and networks for social service in urban neighborhoods. Irish Democrats largely controlled state and local office by 1900.[138] While the Irish benefited from their allegiance to the Democratic Party and the Catholic Church, African Americans did not have a large enough voting block to make them a political force, and their religious affiliation was not as tightly organized.

Racist hostility toward African Americans and other immigrant groups was intense among the Irish in America. The Irish were prominent participants in mob violence against blacks. For example, they led the 1863 draft riots in New York City, to protest the federal draft law, and attacked African Americans, who represented one of the core causes of the war. Jews also faced Irish hostility. One of the most prominent clashes between Irish and Jews was the 1902 riot at Rabbi Jacob Joseph's funeral. The Orthodox rabbi's funeral lacked adequate police protection as it traveled through the Lower East Side, and the crowd of mourners fought with workers, some of them probably Irish, at the printing company R. H. Hoe and Co. The police who arrived to stop the outbreak injured "hundreds" of Jewish marchers and observers with their clubs. In 1902, more than half of the New York City police force was Irish, and their antagonism to new immigrants, including eastern European Jews, was well established.[139] And in outbreaks of racial violence of the late nineteenth century and the early twentieth, Irish American police officers tended to side with Irish participants.[140] Well aware of Irish prowess as street fighters, other immigrant groups and African Americans went out of their way to avoid Irish enclaves. The Irish were invested in defending their urban space (because they arrived before Jews, Italians, and African Americans in northern cities and because they were prominent in the police force), and they "resented any incursion by newer ethnic groups."[141]

This Irish defensiveness encompassed labor as well. The Irish appeared particularly hostile to African American workers; violence between Irish and black laborers erupted throughout the nineteenth century. In the second half of the nineteenth century, Irish laborers became more hostile to blacks, partly because they were competing with African Americans for menial jobs. The Irish were also sensitive about their association with African Americans because Irish immigrants' hard labor was often described as "slaving like a nigger."[142] But economic competition for jobs does not offer a full explanation for angry white Irish racism.[143] Whiteness did have concrete economic benefits, as race restricted many occupations and "municipal employment."[144] But a broader defense of whiteness also formed part of this violent confrontation with black workers. This defense of Irish whiteness emerged from their allegiance to the Democratic Party, which emphasized a defense of the white working class.[145] It seemed expedient to defend their rights as whites, not as Irishmen, because the latter would have proved unpopular with nativists. According to Timothy Meagher, the "Irish racial hostility [was] a defense of white boundaries."[146]

As opposed to the historic hostility between African Americans and the Irish, scholars have been fascinated by a special alliance between African Americans and Jews.[147] The historian Cheryl Greenberg argues that Jews "embraced racism far less quickly and completely . . . than did most other working-class whites."[148] In 1889 the *New York Age* wrote, "There is a similarity between the Jew and the Negro. One is despised almost as much as the other."[149] Indeed, anti-Semitism, long present in the United States, "calcified" in the late nineteenth century and in the early twentieth. In 1877, Joseph Seligman was barred from the Grand Union Hotel in Saratoga Springs, where he had stayed many times before. In 1907, Bertha Rayner Frank, the sister of Senator Isidor Rayner, left the Marlborough-Blenheim Hotel in Atlantic City when the clerk at the front desk would not book rooms for her nieces because the hotel did not "entertain Hebrews."[150] With the persistence of the Shylock stereotype of Jews as greedy and vulgar, and with the rise of Russian Jews out of the slums, Jews faced new social exclusions. College fraternities were more likely to be closed to Jews, as were many residential areas. Just as eastern European Jews emerged in white-collar jobs, they faced more economic discrimination in hiring.[151] African Americans faced legal segregation in the South and de facto segregation in the North. Northern states prohibited racial exclusion in public facilities, but despite these laws, proprietors of restaurants, theaters, and hotels barred African Americans, or allowed them only in a separate area. The enforcement of the laws was lax, and penalties for conviction small. African Americans regularly challenged theater segregation—when they were barred at the door or were restricted from certain parts of the theater. The *Chicago Defender*, for example, urged its readers to "sue every time [you] are refused in theaters."[152]

It is best to break down "Jews" into separate groups to understand their distinct relationships with African Americans. Many notable central European Jews—such as Julius Rosenwald and Stephen S. Wise—worked closely with African Americans for a variety of reasons: their genuine empathy for the struggles of blacks, their concern that racist violence and disenfranchisement could spread to Jews, and their hope that philanthropic support for civil rights would enhance their own acculturation.[153] But this group was most concerned about its social status, which contributed to their resistance to direct comparisons, and sometimes to their "condescension and paternalism."[154] Wealthy Jewish philanthropists helped African Americans, but at the same time emphasized the need for "black improvement" and also accepted the "principle of segregation."[155] Overall, "the most acculturated Jews in the North remained too insecure in their status to act altruistically toward blacks in a consistent way. Instead, they usually fell into a much more ambivalent pattern."[156]

Eastern European Jews, on the other hand, were more likely to resist whiteness and identify with African Americans. They worked as merchants in black neighborhoods and established some overlapping residential areas with African Americans. Immigrant Jews, in the Yiddish press, drew unqualified parallels between the violence against African Americans and the pogroms of eastern Europe. They called race riots "Negro Pogroms" and accused the police of siding with the attackers.[157]

African Americans often expressed empathy for the suffering of American Jews, and they also admired Jewish accomplishments. Booker T. Washington explained that while Jews were "once in about the same position as the Negro is to-day, he now has recognition because he has entwined himself about America in a business and industrial way."[158] In the following two decades, however, as vigilante violence against African Americans increased, the tone in the Jewish–African American relationship changed. African Americans felt disappointed by the Jewish response to lynchings. Although Jews successfully lobbied the federal government to protest the pogroms in Russia and Romania, the federal government did not take a stand against lynching in the United States.[159] Jewish commentators tended to qualify the comparison of the slaughter of Russian Jews and the murder of African Americans with assertions of African American criminality as the basis of lynching. In addition, some Jews argued that the moral and intellectual advancement of Jews, compared to the "masses of Negroes," undermined the comparison.[160]

The lynching of Leo Frank, a Jewish factory manager in Georgia, revealed differences between African Americans and Jews, but it also became a symbol of their common cause. In 1913, Frank, a Jewish businessman, found himself accused of sexually assaulting and killing an employee at his Atlanta pencil factory. Anti-Semitic claims permeated the trial. Commentators noted a perverse Jewish passion for Christian girls, and, outside the courtroom, protesters shouted, "Hang the Jew."[161] Frank was quickly convicted—and sentenced to death—primarily on the evidence of the African American factory janitor, James Conley. During the following two years, Frank appealed, as newspaper editorials and politicians weighed in on his guilt or innocence.[162] Some observers wondered why the Georgia jury had taken a black man's word over a white man's, believing that Conley was the true culprit. Georgia courts rejected a retrial and the U. S. Supreme Court refused Frank's appeal. After the governor of Georgia, John Slaton, commuted Frank's death sentence to life in prison due to the trial's explicit anti-Semitism, armed guards prevented an angry mob from attacking the governor. The Georgia Populist Tom Watson railed against the commutation, urging Georgia's men to act on the state's "sense of honor and justice."[163] His call for vengeance was answered when twenty-five men took Frank from the prison hospital, where he was recovering from a knife attack, and lynched him in 1915.

Frank's murder stood as a powerful reminder of the Jews' marginal and maligned status in the United States. The trial and appeals process revealed the tensions between African Americans and Jews. African Americans accused Frank's Jewish supporters of inflaming racism to help Frank. Some Jews were willing to exchange Conley for Frank, although Jewish leaders appeared ambivalent in this effort.[164] For example, Jewish newspaper editors reprinted the anti-Conley editorials from the daily press, which characterized him as a "black human animal," but they did not themselves author the most extreme racist attacks on Conley.[165] African Americans, furthermore, were angry that extensive resources and powerful allies backed Frank, whereas the "fifty other lynchings of the year" did not garner this publicity or support.[166] Despite these fissures, Jews and African Americans identified some reasons to cooperate. The *Chicago Defender* asked, "Shall the Jews and Afro-Americans join hands as allies?"[167] Commenting on the mob mentality of the trial, the *American Israelite* explained the dual nature of "race prejudice": "From Anti-Negroism to Anti-Semitism is not so long a step as the thoughtful Georgian would perhaps like us to believe."[168] Several English-language Jewish newspapers, such as the *American Israelite*, supported anti-lynching laws after Frank was killed, and also publicized the lynchings of African Americans.[169] When Louis Marshall joined the NAACP's legal team in 1923, he was particularly interested in an NAACP case that centered on his claim in his appeal of the Frank case to the Supreme Court—that a mob atmosphere had made an impartial trial impossible.[170]

The impulses of insular self-defense and cross-racial identity both emerged from this case. Each group—defensive about its own vulnerability—was willing to switch Jewish and African American scapegoats to strengthen its own position. Yet after Frank's murder Jewish concern with the status of African Americans "intensified" and the case became a symbol of the affinity of African Americans and Jews.[171] Furthermore, in 1913 the B'nai B'rith had created the Anti-Defamation League to battle the kind of anti-Semitism present at Frank's trial. The ADL's founding mission, however, was broader than protecting the civil rights and reputation of Jews; it sought to "secure justice and fair treatment to all citizens alike."[172] As the following chapters show, the Irish, Jewish, and African American campaigns against racial ridicule contained self-defense, hostile competition with other races, and cross-racial ties.

CHAPTER TWO

PRACTICAL CENSORSHIP

Irish American Theater Riots

The wave of protests against racial caricatures began with the splat of a stink bomb on stage. An angry Irish American nationalist was probably the first to let it fly. In 1878 an Irish "mob" in Boston threw "missiles" at Dion Boucicault's *The Shaughraun* because of an uproarious Irish wake, and, in the early 1880s, the Irish disrupted various Harrigan and Hart productions.[1] Theater riots were a controversial centerpiece of the Irish campaign against the offensive caricatures commonly known as the "Stage Irish."[2] In the first decade of the twentieth century, the Irish in America stopped or significantly altered two popular, long-standing productions—*McFadden's Row of Flats* (a musical comedy) and "The Irish Servant Girls" (a vaudeville act by the Russell Brothers). They threw fruit and vegetables on stage, interrupted the performances with speeches and shouts, and also fought in the auditorium. These tactics were common in their campaign against the Stage Irish, in contrast with the law-abiding approaches of the Jewish and African American protests. These Irish riots proved theatrical events in their own right. Designed to enthrall an audience, they affirmed a radical brand of Irish nationalism, strong Irish manhood, and a distinctive Irish group identity. In fact, however much the protesters wished to dispel negative caricatures of the Irish as drunken brawlers, they also reenacted stereotypes of their unruliness. This chapter focuses on two Irish theater riots in vaudeville and popular theater in the United States—one against *McFadden's Row of Flats* and the other against the Russell Brothers—to explain the early contours of the Irish campaign against the Stage Irish. It was a combative approach to representation, particularly sensitive to images of Irish women, and determined largely by offstage developments in Irish nationalism.

CHASE THE BEAST!

"Chase the Beast" was part of the front-page coverage of the battle against the Stage Irishman that appeared in the *Irish World and American Industrial Liberator*, February 2, 1907.

Peter McCahey, a physician who served as secretary of the secret, revolutionary Irish organization called the Clan na Gael, was the common denominator in three important Irish theater riots of the early twentieth century. His path as a theater protester reveals the central contours of the Irish campaign against the Stage Irish. Born in Philadelphia to Irish parents, McCahey joined the Clan and the Ancient Order of Hibernians as a young man. He worked for "complete Irish independence" and led Irish organizations in their fight against American alliances with Britain. As part of his campaign to defeat Britain, McCahey opposed the Stage Irishman. His first participated in a theater disturbance in 1887, when he was arrested after he hissed during *McSwiggan's Parliament*, threw eggs onto stage, fought in the theater, and threatened to burn down any theater that housed the play.[3] Irish nationalists were particularly upset about the depiction of the imagined Irish Parliament—one representative had bright red hair and a "nose that looked like a large carrot," while another member said he planned to put a bomb under the speaker's chair.[4] The actors explained that they did not mean to insult the Irish, just the nationalist "dynamiter, whom every good Irishman has no respect for."[5] The dynamiters, however, were exactly the ones who took offense and decided to stop the show. Many protesters, including McCahey, were arrested, but all were released, the charges dropped, and the play stopped. The Irish relished their success.

McCahey remained active in Philadelphia theater protests. In 1903 he protested against *McFadden's Row of Flats* and, eight years later, led the campaign against John Millington Synge's *The Playboy of the Western World* when it toured in the United States.[6] In between the protests against *McFadden's Row of Flats* and the *Playboy*, Irish nationalists in the United States coordinated with their Dublin brethren when they attacked a team of cross-dressing Irish impersonators—the Russell Brothers—in New York City on the eve of the Irish nationalists' uprising at the controversial debut of Synge's *Playboy of the Western World* in Dublin on January 26, 1907.

As McCahey's career shows, around the turn of the twentieth century, Irish nationalists became more vocal and violent about the representation of Irish men and women as "low, drunken, ignorant and brutal."[7] They objected to images of Irish men as baboons, of animals in the Irish home, and of Irish women as oafish and unfeminine. Historians have thus far focused primarily on the Stage Irishman, which Irish protesters defined as the "English anti-Irish" depiction of the Irish man as "but one degree [removed] from the baboon."[8] While Irish Americans seem to have accepted many representations of the Irish—as jovial, rowdy, and loyal, for example—they rejected the simian Irishman as a British export to the American stage designed to batter Irish dignity and humanity. The president of the Ancient Order of Hibernians (AOH), a large Irish fraternal order with strong ties to radical Irish nationalism around this time, criticized a play in which a caged monkey greeted two passing Irishman with a thick Irish brogue: "How are ye, byes?"[9] More than a decade later, an Irishman stood up in the audience to object to an "Irish . . . buffoon [on stage] throwing dishes at his wife's head and making his home a hell."[10]

The uprisings against the Stage Irish cannot be explained fully by a catalog of offensive traits. Irish protesters sometimes worked to stop a play regardless of the details of the production and, in some cases, political battles or grudges offstage seemed to propel protesters to attack "shopworn acts" that had been purveying drunken, apelike Irish characters for years. The clues about why the Irish chose to attack particular acts and why they often disrupted theaters are located offstage.[11] Indeed, the following comparison of two sets of Irish theater riots reveals that the disturbances were based on new developments, fissures, and gender relations in Irish American nationalism. Most organizations at the forefront of these theater riots advocated the complete de-Anglicization of Irish culture and the liberation of Ireland from Britain by force. Their nationalism by physical force contrasted with the more moderate home rule nationalism, which allowed Irish autonomy in local affairs under the overarching authority of the British Parliament.[12] The Irish nationalists' politicization of culture, along with the competition between moderate and radical nationalists, set the stage for explosive battles over the Stage Irish. By attacking particular details of the play and sometimes rejecting the play regardless of revisions, radical Irish nationalists staged their own aggressive defense of not just their race but their nationalist faction as well. This attack on the Stage Irish, therefore, was more than textual criticism; it was a theatrical event, a show of force and a political platform.

The protests against *McFadden's Row of Flats* and the Russell Brothers also show that the Stage Irishman was gendered, rather than generic. The protesters' critique of the representation of Irish men and women overlapped in some ways: they objected when the Stage Irishwoman, like the Stage Irishman, was portrayed as a gorilla, when she drank too much, and when she was combative and klutzy. Yet in the first decade of the twentieth century, Irish critics in America commented on the distinctive insult of the Stage Irishwoman. They often focused on her sexual excesses, particularly if her promiscuity involved British men, and they attacked the Stage Irishwoman's manliness; she seemed to be too muscular, aggressive, and unattractive. Irish women's sexual morality was symbolically central to Irish men's attempts to free Ireland and establish a secure footing in the United States. As one protester explained, "Irish patriotism and Irish manhood, backed by virtuous Irish womanhood," had already helped build up "this great Republic."[13]

Irish nationalists in Denver first objected to *McFadden's Row of Flats* in late October of 1902. The AOH passed a resolution against the play, and the city's Gaelic League concluded that the play was "wholly devoid of legitimate fun, is indecent, and [is intended] to demean and to ridicule Irish character."[14] Filled with physical gags—slippery stairs and sword fights—and interspersed with vaudeville acts, *McFadden's Row of Flats* followed two saloonkeepers—an Irishman and a German—in their election campaign for alderman. The production drew on two significant theatrical trends of the late nineteenth century: Edward Harrigan and Tony Hart's popular Mulligan Guard plays and the theatrical adaptations of comic strips about immigrant life on the Lower East Side, mainly Richard Outcault's *The Yellow Kid* and Frederick Opper's *Happy Hooligan*. The Mulligan Guard plays and the dramatizations of the comics focused on confrontations between different exaggerated racial types in poor neighborhoods and both featured rowdy mishaps and fights. *McFadden's Row of Flats* resembles Edward Harrigan's *The Mulligan Guard Nominee* (1880), in which Mulligan and his German neighbor, Gustavus Lochmuller, run against each other for alderman. Though Mulligan is a corrupt politician, a heavy drinker, and a raucous fighter, he is also loyal, streetwise, and generous. Historians generally agree that Harrigan's Irish characters were more positive and well-rounded than the other types in his plays. As the literary critic Lauren Onkey explains, the Irish "run" the crowded, racially mixed tenement neighborhoods in these pieces.[15]

McFadden's Row of Flats was one of a dozen theatrical adaptations of the popular Yellow Kid comic strips, which Outcault started to draw in 1895, first for the *New York World* and then for William Randolph Hearst's *New York Journal*. His illustrations focused on Mickey Duggan, the Yellow Kid, a bald Irish boy in a yellow nightshirt. His friends in the neighborhood, including Terrance McSwatt and Liz, put on amateur circuses, parades, and horse shows; they compare their paltry Christmas presents, assault the dogcatcher, and nurse their wounds after a raucous Fourth of July. Mrs. Murphy watches from her window with her bucket of beer handy. The Yellow Kid's observations about the poverty, chaos, and violence surrounding him are recorded in Bowery dialect on his nightshirt. When Outcault moved the comic strip to the *New York Journal* in 1896, E. W. Townsend, an author who specialized in stories about slum children, began to write text to accompany the Yellow Kid illustrations.[16] The Yellow Kid then became a fad, with sheet music, books, and many theater productions devoted to Mickey Duggan and his motley gang.

Although part of the Yellow Kid vogue, *McFadden's Row of Flats* actually shifted the eponymous character to the margins, keeping the chaotic, immigrant urban backdrop. An early review of *McFadden's Row of Flats* noted: "The day of the 'yellow kid' is over. The management seems to have realized this, for the 'kid' is far more in evidence on the billboards of 'McFadden's Row of Flats' than on the stage."[17] The set included a secondhand clothing store, with Abraham Levi as the proprietor, and two saloons—one German, one Irish (The Shamrock). The Irishman Tim McFadden, wearing a red wig with scraggly red or green whiskers, campaigns against a German immigrant, Jacob Baumgartner, in the ethnically diverse neighborhood of Five Points, New York. When McFadden and Baumgartner hold campaign parties at the same ballroom, the two factions begin to fight, trip each other, and roll around the stage.[18] At the end of the play, McFadden and Baumgartner become friends, and McFadden wins the heart of Mrs. Murphy, the drunken widow in the flats.[19]

On March 20, 1903, several Irish men yelled and hissed during the production of *McFadden's Row of Flats* at the Fourteenth Street Theatre in New York City. It got them thrown out of the theater. A week later, at the play's next stop, the New Star Theatre, the protests escalated. Just as the characters onstage broke out into melees, the protesters were involved in similar disturbances offstage. After they threw eggs and vegetables onto stage, five men were arrested, including two laborers and two skilled workers.[20] James Briarty, a foreman of a building crew who escaped arrest, claimed credit for leading the riot.[21] Briarty and others announced their support for the revolutionary Clan na Gael, according to the *New York Sun*: "Wherever plays of this kind appear," the protesters said, "they would be driven out by the Clan-na-Gael and kindred societies."[22] The protesters complained about green whiskers on the Stage Irishman, the appearance of Mrs. Murphy drunk in a wheelbarrow, and pigs in McFadden's flat. Protesters announced their support for the Clan na Gael.[23] Gus Hill, the producer of the play, responded to the New York City protests with a conciliatory gesture: he eliminated the green whiskers from the Irishman's makeup. But Hill was otherwise defiant: He did not remove the drunken Mrs. Murphy or the pig. He also antagonized protesters by adding a song and jokes that mocked the protesters specifically, and Irish nationalism more broadly. Finally, Hill vowed that the show would go on "even if they have to play over a few dead Irishmen."[24] He was angry about what he saw as a cross-country Irish nationalist conspiracy, which began when Irish nationalists in Denver "sent the orders" to stop the play, according to Hill.[25]

Under these tense conditions, *McFadden's Row of Flats* moved on to Philadelphia, where it had played without complaint at least seven times between 1898 and its contentious run there in 1903.[26] Philadelphia theater managers had booked the show year after year since 1898, as a "matter of course," so the Irish attack in 1903 surprised many observers.[27] On March 30, 1903, at the People's Theatre in Philadelphia, Irish "auditors" threw eggs and fought with police and actors during the play.[28] Although Irish nationalists in Philadelphia proclaimed their goal of stopping the play outright, they also attacked several scenes specifically, including a new one that Hill had designed especially for Philadelphia. At the People's Theatre, when Mrs. Murphy arrived on stage drunk drawn by a donkey—the flashpoint in New York City—no one in the audience hissed or threw food.[29] Instead Philadelphia protesters responded to an addition to the play, a comic tune about Irish nationalist agitation. One protester threw the first egg when Arthur Whitelaw sang an original version of "Mr. Dooley" that questioned the judgment of the Irish protesters:

> Now to the Irish, that I see are many in the house.
> There is only a line that I would sing, and this is it—
> There really is no abuse in any part of the play.
> I think you'll agree with me, It's only Irish wit.

Then, "Mr. Dooley" also mocked the political aims of the Irishmen when Whitelaw joked that "if ever this band before the King would play, I'm sure old Ireland ere this would be free."[30] With this addition to the play, the producers may have been trying to inflame, not quell, the protests. Retaliating against Whitelaw's insults to Irish nationalists, the Irish unleashed a barrage of fruit, vegetables, and eggs during his song. The uproar resulted in the arrest of eighteen Irish men. When the play returned to New York City in the second week of April, a theater manager agreed to cut the green whiskers, Mrs. Murphy's donkey ride, and the pig in the parlor.[31] Even though this did not constitute an exhaustive list of the play's offensive traits, the protesters bragged of their success: they had put *McFadden's Row of Flats* under "practical censorship."[32]

Hill was correct to point out that Philadelphia's indignant Irish men were responding as much to nationalists in other cities as they were to the details of his play. New York's Irish activists, for example, had challenged their compatriots in other cities to shut down the play: "The show would not be tolerated here or elsewhere."[33] To live up to Denver's and New York City's calls to action and to counter Hill's defiant stance, Irish nationalists asserted that it did not matter that the "highly objectionable features" had been dropped: "The only way this slum show could secure the approval of self-respecting Irishmen would be by dropping itself out of existence altogether."[34] The defiance of Philadelphia's Irish protesters ran deeper than details on stage.

McFadden's Row of Flats continued to tour throughout the first decade of the twentieth century. Despite the piece's familiarity and the show's rigorous editing, the play still occasionally stirred controversy, as if the memory of some past affront was cause enough to assert belligerent defiance. One Irishman wrote to the *Gaelic American* asking, "How should any society endorse 'McFadden's Flats,' even with its 'objectionable features' eliminated?"[35] The nationalist challenge thus lingered on, regardless of revisions.

With the memory of the *McFadden's Row of Flats* skirmish still fresh in their minds, Irish nationalists turned their attention to the veteran vaudevillians John and James Russell.[36] Known as the "originators of the Irish servant girl act," the Russell Brothers had started the sketch in the late 1870s, but they also performed blackface routines, Dutch (or German) and Yankee caricatures, and impersonations of famous women like Sarah Bernhardt.[37] In "The Irish Servant Girls," the Russell Brothers wore dresses with long, white aprons, and James Russell added a red wig and covered his dress with green ribbons.[38] James called John "Maggie, Maggie" in a gruff voice, and they hit each other with brooms, winked at men in the audience and exposed the underwear beneath their skirts. On January 24, 1907, the Russell Brothers were scheduled to perform their signature sketch at the Victoria Theatre in New York City. A committee of Irish nationalists met with William Hammerstein, the theater's manager, who refused to end the act right away, though he agreed to shorten its run. This was not good enough for the Irish "patriots" who decided to bring their protest directly to the Russell Brothers' "shop-worn" act.[39] When the performers appeared on stage, angry Irish protesters—one hundred of them—stood up, yelled "Take them off," hissed, whistled, and groaned. Thomas P. Tuite, an Irish American war veteran and ardent Irish nationalist, rose from his seat after the catcalls had subsided to address the management and the audience: "Stop it! Stop it! Stop it! or by the eternal we will stop it. For whenever you again bring it on you will be met by clean, manly men who will stop it if they have to stop you."[40] The curtain came down after a few minutes.

The Russell Brothers changed the title of their act to "The Stage Struck Maid," eliminated some of the slapstick comedy, and removed some sexual innuendo for their subsequent booking at the Orpheum Theatre in Brooklyn.[41] Unimpressed with these reforms, Irish activists made their protest more disruptive. During the performance, one man stood up with an egg in his hand, ready to let it fly. "Up boys and at 'em!" he exclaimed, and many Irish compatriots followed his lead. They pelted the performers with eggs and lemons, converting the comedians into a "lemon and egg soufflé," according to one report.[42] Whenever an egg broke on stage, protesters in the audience let out a cheer. Soon the stage looked like a "grocery after the invasion of a bull," and the Russells ran to the wings with yolks and whites dripping down their wigs and costumes.[43] Twenty-two men were arrested for their involvement in the "Orpheum riot," but the charges were later dropped.[44] The Russell Brothers performed for several months outside of the major vaudeville theaters after the protests in New York City and, by 1913, they had left vaudeville altogether.[45]

Why did Irish nationalists choose to attack these particular acts and what do these riots reveal about the protesters? The fights over *McFadden's Row of Flats* and the Russell Brothers were not just a response to British colonialism or Anglo-American elites; the Irish in America were also comparing themselves to other racial groups. These Irish protesters asserted that the Irish were depicted worse than other races. "Even in the vaudeville sketches, where all nations are more or less caricatured," explained an editorial in the *Irish World*, "the German, or the Dutchman as he is called, and the Jew, are accorded some resemblance of humanity. . . . The Irishman alone is an idiot, if not a brute."[46] Revealing another layer of competition, the Irish claimed that other races should also protest but were lagging behind the Irish in their race pride. The Stage Jew was "due for a demonstration," and Germans were too "indulgent" of stage caricatures.[47] In 1907, when the *New York Times* and other papers charged that the Irish were depicted with good humor, just like all other races, the Irish protesters lashed out at the "editorial rot by Anglo-Hebrew newspapers."[48] The "aggressive Irish ethnocentrism" that was so central to these protests against the Stage Irish was directed at American elites as well as other minority groups and against competing nationalist groups.[49]

Offstage, dares and grudges among Irish nationalists helped determine when, exactly, the eggs and rotten vegetables would fly. These uprisings challenge previous historians' contention that upwardly mobile Irish fought against stereotypes of coarse Irish immigrants on stage because these representations challenged their fragile respectability.[50] Some evidence supports the view that Irish activists sought to improve their own reputation by reforming the apelike Stage Irishman. Tuite's eloquent address to the crowd certainly seems to confirm that protesters sought to claim a positive reputation. Similarly, an AOH leader argued in 1906, "The Irish people are not depraved as the stage Irishman might lead many to think."[51] Patrick Ford, a newspaper editor who, by the turn of the twentieth century, had renounced social radicalism, supported the Catholic Church, and had aligned himself with the moderate United Irish League of America, made the attack on the Russell Brothers a front-page story in his newspaper the *Irish World*.[52] He believed that the campaign against the Stage Irish improved Irish respectability in the United States, contributed to the fight against public immorality, and bolstered the moderate Irish nationalist movement along the way.[53] The "pedigree conscious" Irish clearly had plenty of motivation to banish the oafish Irishman from the American stage.[54]

But a close look at the controversy surrounding the Stage Irish suggests that the search for improved social standing was only part of a more complicated story. Tuite's calm address to the theater crowd was, after all, the prelude to a barrage of fruit, vegetables, and eggs. Throughout the campaign against the Stage Irish, protesters often willingly risked the disfavor of American elites by moving beyond resolutions and restrained boycotts to the undignified disruption of theatrical space with fistfights and stink bombs. The editor of the moderate *Irish American* was shocked by the "drastic" form of the attacks on *McFadden's Row of Flats*, and the *New York Times* labeled the Irishmen who rioted over the Russell Brothers in 1907 "impudent ruffians" and "baser fellows."[55] It is not surprising, then, that most of the Irish involved in disrupting *McFadden's Row of Flats* were actu-

The Russell Brothers in "The Irish Servant Girls." Billy Rose Theatre Division, The New York Public Library for the Performing Arts, Astor, Lenox and Tilden Foundations

ally "immigrant, lower-class backers of aggressive Irish ethnocentrism," as one historian described them.[56]

Theater riots were rare in the late nineteenth and early twentieth century, but Irish violence was not. These Irish riots are surprising because they occurred long after theater managers and reformers had cleaned up their democratic, often unruly theater audiences. In the eighteenth century and the early nineteenth, spectators regularly interrupted performances, demanded actors repeat a favorite scene, and reacted violently to any condescending or aristocratic performers. Theater rioting, which peaked in the 1820s and 1830s, formed part of the audience's "prerogatives to act out."[57] In 1834 an anti-abolitionist riot extended to the Bowery Theatre to protest the appearance of an English actor who had insulted the American flag. Class tensions erupted in a riot at the Astor Place Opera House in 1849 in New York City. The Astor Place crowd shouted down the supposedly pretentious English actor William Macready, and a volley of eggs, fruit, and vegetables forced him from the stage. When he returned a few days later, some of Macready's detractors were quickly arrested in the auditorium, but protesters surrounded and attacked the theater. Militia guards eventually fired into the crowd. Twenty-two were killed and 150 were injured.[58] In the second half of the nineteenth century, theater managers began to silence their audience's traditional combativeness, reduced prostitution at theaters, and encouraged middle-class women and children to attend—toward the goal of adding moral restraint and respectability to the atmosphere. Instructions in playbills advised spectators to avoid whistling, stomping, talking loudly, or distracting others. Audiences were now supposed to respect the "artistic authority" of the dramatic actor; as spectators became more passive, more reverential of the actor, they lost command of their stage.[59]

The Irish were well known for their violence in sectarian clashes and labor disturbances after the Civil War. In 1912, one writer aptly described "the Gaelic sympathy with rebellion in almost any form."[60] He was drawing on a long history. In 1870 Irish immigrants attacked a Protestant-Orange parade in New York City. The Molly Maguires, a clandestine group of miners in the anthracite coalfields of Pennsylvania, used violence to improve their position in the workforce throughout the 1870s. In 1893, Irish longshoremen battled black and Italian strikebreakers in Brooklyn.[61] Irish gangs were known as particularly aggressive street fighters, poor Irish canal workers showed high levels of interpersonal violence, and Irish brawling was a frequent feature of July Fourth and St. Patrick's Day celebrations.[62]

In the early twentieth century, Jewish and Polish boxers, as well as Italian gangsters, often took Irish names to take advantage of the "pugnacious Irish reputation and perhaps also to minimize ethnic discrimination."[63] Displays of physical strength, bravery, and racial pride were keys to Irish masculinity.

It is therefore not surprising that violence often played a role in the Irish nationalist campaign against the Stage Irish. Irish leaders regularly declared that resolutions were fine but insufficient; courageous men needed to do more.[64] On December 30, 1902, three months prior to the uproar over *McFadden's Row of Flats*, a "small riot" broke out in Springfield, Massachusetts, during Eddie "Monkey" Weston's performance of *A Hot Old Time* when Weston appeared with "fiery red hair, eyes that blinked like monkeys . . . and loose baggy trousers."[65] After many men had yelled at the stage, several patrons were removed from the theater and one man, accused of hitting the theater manager, was arrested. In San Francisco, in 1907, Irish protesters—the St. Patrick's Day Celebration Committee—lobbied the theater manager to stop *The Belle of Avenue A* because of the depiction of immodest, drunken Irish women. When these protests failed, they disrupted the show in the theater. After the uproar, some commentators blamed "rowdies who behaved riotously and assaulted policemen."[66] A few years later, Benedict Fitzpatrick, of Irish ancestry, climbed up a stepladder and smashed an electric sign advertising "Casey," a "pug-nosed, squint-eyed, bald-headed man." Police arrested him when he reached the ground.[67]

If there was not actual violence, the possibility of violence often lingered in the background of Irish protests. Said one protester tired of negotiations with managers: "No more going with hat in hand [to theater managers] and humbly begging them to cut out this 'objectionable feature' or that one." He reasoned that the managers would break contracts with offensive acts "when we have 'put the fear of god in their hearts' and not before then."[68] Another Irishman claimed that if the resolution failed, "rotten eggs" would do the job.[69] In Butte, Montana, the AOH and leaders from the Robert Emmet Literacy Society met with Mayor John MacGinness and convinced him to prevent the production of Dreamland Burlesquers because the posters advertising the show included a "negro leading a baboon by a chain . . . the features of the animal were those . . . of the time-worn caricature [of the Irish]."[70] The mayor decided to prohibit the show and arrest the performers based on a state law that forbade the creation or maintenance of a "nuisance." A large crowd gathered in front of the Grand Opera House ready for action ("with missiles to salute the visiting Thespians"), but they dispersed when the manager announced that the play was cancelled. With this victory behind him, James H. Lynch, an AOH leader and the head of the committee that lobbied the mayor, praised the "sober and manlike manner" of the crowd.[71]

An examination of the nationalist groups involved in this violence helps explain the tactics and timing of these uprisings. When the leader of the home rule movement, Charles Parnell, was embroiled in a divorce scandal in 1890 and then died in 1891, Irish nationalists in Ireland and the United States lost momentum. Though political agitation continued, with such achievements as the Wyndham Land Act of 1903, which provided incentives to Irish landlords to sell land to tenants, the goal of home rule, which seemed to be in the "dim future," no longer captured the passionate commitment of the Irish.[72] The question of Ireland's "distinct national civilization"—what set the Irish apart from the English—became the major issue of the turn of the century.[73] The reunification of the Clan na Gael in 1900 and its broader campaign, alongside the Gaelic League and the Ancient Order of Hibernians, to de-Anglicize Irish and American culture set the stage for the campaign against the Stage Irish.

Founded in 1867, the Clan na Gael attracted men who were frustrated with political negotiation and who enjoyed the "aura of adventure that surrounded the group's shadowy undertakings," including bombings and assassinations.[74] In this way, the Clan na Gael picked up where the violent Fenian Brotherhood had left off in the 1870s. The Clan also found new allies to promote a superior, distinct Irish culture at the turn of the twentieth century, including the Gaelic League, founded by Douglas Hyde, the son of an Anglican minister, in 1893.[75] The Gaelic League was active in the United States, where its critique of Anglicization undermined the "Anglo-Saxon idea of American nationality."[76] The league refused to take a side in the debate between physical-force nationalism and the more moderate home rule proposals, but its program of ending British influence fit particularly well with the Clan na Gael's support for violent, anticolonial revolt, as well as its celebration of the Celts as a superior "fighting race."[77] The AOH, the largest of the Irish benevolent fraternal societies with almost two hundred thousand members in 1908 (including its ladies' auxiliary), also supported the Gaelic League, advocated Gaelic sports, and pushed for more Irish history in schools, along with attacking the Stage Irish, in the midst of its "most militantly Irish phase" in the early twentieth century.[78]

The Clan na Gael stood at the forefront of the *McFadden's Row of Flats* protest in Philadelphia in 1903, while the Clan na Gael and the Gaelic League took the lead against the Russell Brothers in 1907. Meetings about the *McFadden's Row of Flats* protests occurred on Clan turf, the Irish American Club House, at 726 Spruce Street in Philadelphia, and the leading spokesmen were Clan organizers.[79] Peter McCahey, a physician who helped run the Clan na Gael, took a prominent role the protests.[80] Six of the nine members in the organizing committee were affiliated with the Clan na Gael, including McCahey; Patrick O'Neill, a Clan supporter with fund-raising experience for the Irish Land League; and Henry Carney, a Clan member since at least 1892 and a leader of the protests against *The Playboy of the Western World*.[81] Information about the Irish men arrested for their role in the disruption of *McFadden's Row of Flats* matches the background of the Clan's working-class, Irish-born base. Seventeen of the eighteen men arrested were reportedly born in Ireland.[82] In addition, the apprehended men were concentrated in semiskilled and unskilled occupations.[83] Although the Clan leadership often included doctors and judges, rank-and-file members tended to work mainly in lower-end jobs—"workers at the very bottom of the economic hierarchy."[84]

Around 1900 the Irish of Philadelphia maintained a dense network of Irish nationalist organizations, with the same fissures that marked nationalist politics in Ireland and the United States—a competition between moderate or home rule nationalists, largely middle- and upper-class Irish, and radical nationalists, with a base of working-class, immigrant Irish men.[85] Prominent Philadelphia Clansmen donated funds for Irish causes, financed Clan members' business ventures, such as opening saloons (which often became hubs of Clan activity), and attempted to disrupt British power and influence by any means necessary, including dynamite.[86] Radical nationalist organizations like the Clan na Gael expressed fiery resistance to home rule nationalism as a "betrayal of everything national."[87] Major Henri LeCaron, a British spy who had infiltrated the Clan na Gael, identified Philadelphia in the late nineteenth century as the most powerful stronghold of revolutionary Irish activity.[88] He was particularly concerned about Philadelphia's Luke Dillon who worked on a variety of radical ventures, including the bombing of a Canadian canal near Buffalo, New York, in 1900. Philadelphia was also home to prominent moderate nationalists. In 1908, for example, the Philadelphia attorney Michael Ryan became president of the United

Irish League of America, an organization that worked for increased peasant land ownership and helped establish a popular foundation for John Redmond's "rejuvenated home rule movement."[89]

In the uprising against the Russell Brothers a few years later, the Clan na Gael and the Gaelic League took center stage. James C. Lynch, the past president of New York's Gaelic League, explained that ninety-one members of the Gaelic League had launched the initial outburst against the Russells, and then prodded other organizations to follow.[90] Patrick J. Donnelly, a lawyer who came to watch the arraignment of the Russell Brothers' rioters, explained, "It is only recently that Irishmen have come to realize what their ancestors really were. Through the light cast upon the history of Ireland, through the efforts of the Gaelic League, representatives of the race living in this country have learned that their forefathers were not at all the remarkable characters they have been depicted on the stage."[91] Newspaper reports claimed that the Ancient Order of Hibernians and the Clan na Gael were also central to the protests.[92]

Physical force nationalism relied on its working-class base. The violence of these nationalists' protests against the Stage Irish affirmed this working-class orientation because the aggressive tactics were an affront to many upwardly mobile Irish in America.[93] In Worcester, Massachusetts, almost 90 percent of one AOH division were manual laborers, and just over 70 percent of new members between 1897 and 1902 had been born in Ireland.[94] The AOH in Butte had an overwhelmingly immigrant, blue-collar base, though this organization also drew the older, stable members of Butte's working-class community.[95] Throwing eggs at the Stage Irishwoman, or threatening to throw eggs, thus appears to be one component of what the historian Timothy Meagher calls the "Irish immigrant male culture, the rowdy masculinity of the 'bhoys.'"[96] And these acts fit well with the Clan na Gael's distinctive "cult of male revolutionary 'brotherhood.'"[97] The Clan and the closely affiliated AOH were also involved in raucous holiday celebrations, in which Irish men played sports, drank heavily, and fought to "let off steam and settle old scores."[98] In these contexts, rowdiness was an acceptable assertion of Irish pride. Rather than searching for mainstream respectability, these Irish theater rioters flaunted racial difference and solidarity as well as "belligerent masculinity."[99]

The mainstream press and more conservative Irish nationalists condemned the violent tactics. One letter to the *New York Times* objected to the behavior of the "rabble": "I resent the attitude assumed by these ignorant ruffians as 'champions of my race.'"[100] Although John Finerty, the first president of the moderate United Irish League of America (UILA), criticized the Stage Irish, he only advocated a boycott, stopping short of the Clan na Gael's violent approach to the Irish caricature on stage.[101] To defend themselves, the Irish protesters refused to apologize for their violence and attacked "mild protest" as ineffectual, although they sometimes sought to deflect full responsibility and emphasized the peaceful appeals that they tried before direct action in the theater.[102] The failures of quiet lobbying, in their view, justified their disruptive methods.[103] To defend their rioting, Irish Americans tried to broaden the definition of respectability to include race pride. The *Irish World* remarked, "They are gentlemen. They are good citizens."[104] Another editorial in the *Irish World* explained:

> Respectability, as the world has it, position, calling, property, and all that, has no weight with us; character is the true test of respectability; but we may mention incidentally that there was solid and uncumbered property a-plenty to pledge as security for these "rowdies;" . . . [the protesters] will be found in every case to represent intelligence, character, good homes, and clean lives—men with whom the theatrical scum have so little in common that they cannot understand. What is more, they represent all that is intelligent, decent and patriotic in the race, and the race . . . will stand by them.[105]

This account undermines the equation of respectability with wealth, emphasizing instead racial solidarity.[106]

The "radical-conservative divergence" within Irish American organizational life is important in explaining more than different opinions about disruptive tactics; it also helps us understand the timing of these uprisings.[107] The Clan na Gael, part of the radical faction, reunited in 1900, after a hostile split dating from the 1880s.[108] Strengthened by its reunification, the Clan na Gael launched its rough, steadfast campaign against the Stage Irish to set it apart from its rivals in headlines in the nationalist press and to compete with the moderate nationalists to represent the Irish in America. The United Irish League and its American branch, the UILA, run by John Redmond's moderate Irish Parliamentary Party, celebrated a series of achievements, including the introduction of land reform measures and its first national convention, during the controversial run of *McFadden's Row of Flats*. Denver Hibernians and Gaelic League members—Clan allies—fired the first shot in the *McFadden's Row of Flats* war in the midst of a UILA campaign. The UILA was building membership with a celebration in Chicago in August 1902 and its inaugural national convention in Boston on October 20, 1902, just a little more than a week after the Denver outcry over *McFadden's Row of Flats*. The Clan na Gael and its radical allies tried to undermine the UILA's constitutional nationalism at every turn. The Clan, for example, amended its own constitution with a statement that it was "'treason' to belong to the Irish League or to aid or support it in any way."[109]

The Clan na Gael rejected what it saw as Redmond's conciliatory approach to parliamentary affairs in the early twentieth century. Redmond, for example, supported George Wyndham's land reform package, which emerged from a conference of landlords and tenants in December 1902. This legislation set out the terms for tenants to purchase land; it provided government aid to tenants and incentives to landowners, such as the appropriation of 12 million pounds of bonus payments to landowners.[110] This divisive bill was introduced on March 25, 1903, approved by the United Irish League in April, and passed by parliament in August. The upcoming land bill, according to Redmond, would be "an important step toward home rule."[111] Similarly, Finerty praised the "mere introduction of the measure [as] a monumental victory for the masses of Ireland . . . due to the splendid leadership of John E. Redmond."[112] The *Gaelic American*, edited by the national Clan na Gael leader John Devoy, called the Wyndham Act a "fraud land bill," charging that it favored affluent farmers.[113]

Opposition to the Wyndham Act often ran parallel to an attack on *McFadden's Row of Flats*. The Wyndham Act was introduced in parliament in the midst of the protests against *McFadden's Row of Flats* in New York City, right before the second skirmish in this city on March 27, 1903. Edward T. McCrystal, the president of the Gaelic League of New York, disregarded the reforms of the Wyndham Act and turned the focus back to national Irish culture. He asserted that this "concession" to the Irish would not derail the fight for a "separate entity": Irish peasants, he predicted, would not "halt on the high road to victory, for the bribe of a mess of pottage."[114] Then, two days after the Wyndham Act was introduced in 1903, McCrystal took a seat at *McFadden's Row of Flats* at the New Star Theatre. He objected to the image of the Irish on stage and, though he was not arrested, spoke out in support of the Irish men who were detained for resisting arrest and rioting in the theater: "We now unite in the belief that the native of Ireland, or the son or grandson of an Irishman, should not submit to have his countrymen held up to constant ridicule. . . . As an American . . . I believe that we should unite in objecting unless we are to regard ourselves solely as Anglo-Saxons, and for my part I do not claim to be one."[115] His critique of *McFadden's Row of Flats* resembles his critique of the Wyndham Act. In the face of home rule nationalists' negotiation of political details and celebration of incremental reforms, competing nationalists may have tried to bolster their side with aggressive opposition to the Stage Irish.

Just as offstage conflicts shaped the challenges to *McFadden's Row of Flats*, the trigger for the attack on the Russell Brothers also occurred outside of "The Irish Servant Girls"; in fact, the motivation was likely a controversial play that debuted outside of the United States. The protests against "The Irish Servant Girls" coincided with the opening of J. M. Synge's *The Playboy of the Western World* in Dublin, which rioters targeted in the same week in 1907. On January 26, two days after the first attack on the Russell Brothers in New York City, Synge's play had its tumultuous debut in Dublin at the Abbey Theatre. This week is even more remarkable because it also featured a protest in Tuam, County Galway, on January 27, 1907, when a group of Gaelic Leaguers and other protesters objected to two upcoming plays, *A Coastguard's Daughter* and *The Wild Irish Boy*; these plays were not shown. One protester explained that the plays "did not hesitate to revile our Irish women."[116] *Playboy* features the "peasant women of Mayo contending in their lusts" for Christy Mahon, a man who has, they believe, murdered his father.[117] At the play's Saturday evening opening, many members of the audience hissed angrily during the second act, some in Gaelic, when actors referred to female peasants in their "shifts" or underclothes.[118] By Monday night conditions had deteriorated so much that W. B. Yeats, one of the Abbey Theatre's founders, called in police to arrest disruptive spectators. At that evening's performance, one angry patron referred to the fight against the Russell Brothers when he reportedly yelled, "What would not be tolerated in America will not be allowed here."[119] The protesters insisted that the play should be withdrawn, but Yeats and other leaders of the theater stood fast, and with continued police surveillance, the protests decreased by Thursday night. As the *Irish World* aptly noted, "The stage-Irishman conflict is becoming . . . worldwide."[120]

New York City protesters in January 1907 may have been responding to simmering discontent in Dublin. Although the riots against the Russell Brothers preceded the outburst against *Playboy*, the controversy over Synge gained in intensity several years earlier, and his nationalist critics widely anticipated the debut of *Playboy*. This explosive week in theater history is thus probably anchored in Synge's career, not in the Russell Brothers' tours.[121] The coincidence of these transatlantic riots supports the theory that protesters planned both uprisings carefully. Lady Augusta Gregory, director of the Abbey Theatre, claimed that the protests in the United States were organized from Dublin, and protesters in the Abbey Theatre shouted out a reference to the Russell Brothers.[122] Clearly, Irish nationalists coordinated these events.

Irish nationalists perceived similar insults to Irish women in these two productions, on both sides of the Atlantic. The controversy over *The Playboy of the Western World* was largely a debate about the nature of the Irish peasant woman, while the protests against the Russell Brothers focused on the Irish peasant girl working as a domestic servant in a new urban environment. Many assessments of Synge's play pointed specifically to the images of immoral peasant women as the play's downfall. The sexual assertiveness of Pegeen and Widow Quin, the references to "shifts" in the second act, the young women's presence in a shebeen (or whiskey shop) and Pegeen's unchaperoned night with Christy disturbed many patrons. These objections coalesced into a critique of the disreputable peasant woman. As one protester asked, "Is it necessary for me to say that in no part of Ireland are the women so wanting in modesty as to make advances to a total stranger, much less to a criminal?"[123] And another critic concluded that the play was a "protracted libel upon Irish peasant men, and worse still, upon Irish peasant girlhood."[124]

The debates over *Playboy*, *McFadden's Row of Flats*, and the Russell Brothers share an overwhelming focus on protecting the image of Irish women. All three productions featured flirtatious and aggressive Irish women, and often drunken Irish women or Irish women in saloons. The Stage Irishwoman was a contentious issue because she raised questions about Irish women's sexual morality, a topic tightly correlated with national pride; about the status of employed Irish women; and about the lack of proper—or civilized—gender roles among the Irish. *McFadden's Row of Flats* and the Russell Brothers featured promiscuous and hard-drinking Irish women. Irish protesters, in fact, found the Stage Irishwoman more infuriating than the Stage Irishman. As the *National Hibernian* stated, "If the 'Stage Irishman' represented the very lowest and vilest traits of the Irish character, his spouse did worse."[125] The *Gaelic American* reported, "They do object to the drunken creatures who are put on the stage as Irish characters.

It is far worse to so portray an Irish woman."[126] The extreme insult of the Stage Irishwoman served an important function for Irish nationalists in America; the Stage Irishwoman seemed to galvanize Irish men to defend the race. One of the defenders of the rioters against *McFadden's Row of Flats* explained that the Stage Irishwoman could halt his race's drift into Anglo-American apathy: "The instant that you turn the batteries of abuse against Irish women, you arouse the fighting blood of the meekest among the sons of Erin."[127] Furthermore, in 1905 the *Irish World* almost welcomed the Stage Irishwoman: "There seems to be an inclination now to insult and caricature Irish women, and it may be well, because this may serve to arouse people more thoroughly to the contumely and calumny which is boldly heaped upon them."[128]

Throughout the campaign against the Stage Irish, Irish protesters focused on several depictions of drunken Irish women: along with the Russell Brothers and Mrs. Murphy, the Irish also attacked Kitty Fogarty in "The Factory Girl," Mrs. McCluskey, in the *Belle of Avenue A*, and "Judy O'Trot." Mrs. Murphy from *McFadden's Row of Flats* had been a long-standing character in Outcault's comic strips and in Townsend's accompanying text. Draped in a checked shawl with her white hair pinned up, Mrs. Murphy watches the chaotic activities of the children in her alley, with her whiskey jug or bucket of beer nearby.[129] She often asks the kids in the alley to rush "t'Kel's for a pint of beer"; she drinks beer instead of tea, and a sign in the flats advertising Mrs. Murphy's Thanksgiving reads "Roast Turkey—Yes, Everything will be roasted and everybody will be roasted—Come."[130] Kitty Fogarty, according to the *National Hibernian*, was a "shrieking, drunken woman, with wildly disheveled red hair, a blackened eye and generally besotten aspect."[131] In *The Belle of Avenue A*, Mrs. McCluskey drinks too much and leaves the stage with two English men. She asks in confusion, "If it just the same to you men, whose wife am I?"[132] The Irish also attacked "Judy O'Trot," an Irish peasant woman who looked "more like a half-drunken savage than a woman. She used vulgar and demeaning language, and seemed to delight in being able to imbibe freely of whiskey."[133]

Female drinking on stage was contentious because it led to sloppiness and promiscuity. Protesters objected to the loose sexuality of the Russell Brothers' servant girls and of Mrs. Murphy. These characters were eager for romance, but undesirable in their manliness. One review of the *McFadden's Row of Flats* in Philadelphia explained that "the portrayal of Mrs. Murphy, Queen of the Flats . . . is but little behind what the posters would lead one to expect."[134] Mrs. Murphy appears in all three acts of *McFadden's Row of Flats*. She arrives on stage in a drunken stupor in Act 1; she dresses up as the Queen of England—a "rale lady"—and fights with her daughter in Act 2, and she kisses Tim McFadden in Act 3. She's argumentative, flirtatious, and unattractive—the antithesis of a real lady. Though drinking provides the backdrop for much of the play, it is Mrs. Murphy who first appears on stage intoxicated. According to the script, the police officer who pushes her on stage in a wheelbarrow explains, "I found her down in the alley and this was the only way I could get her home."[135] He tips the wheelbarrow over and she slides out. Mrs. Murphy then asks him to "go and get five cents worth of oats."[136] Mrs. Murphy put off people with her bad breath and her ugly face. McFadden exclaims, "Let's run away," then clarifies, "From each other."[137] Mrs. Murphy says, "My face is my fortune," and McFadden retorts in an aside to the audience, "Faith then she's broke."[138] Although these jokes come at Mrs. Murphy's expense, McFadden still tries to kiss her in Act 1 and embraces her in Act 3. He asks, "Will you change your name to McFadden?" And she answers enthusiastically, "In a minute."[139]

Although Irish tradition had accommodated the female drinker by the late nineteenth century, Irish community leaders were embarrassed when Protestant reformers noted the drunkenness among Irish women, because it was a manly public display, a sign of poverty and lawlessness, as well as a fall from the virtue associated with women in Ireland. Irish men drank more than Irish women within a male-dominated pub culture, but Irish women drank far more than women from other immigrant groups. Between 1884 and 1890 in New York City, 1.16 Irish women in a thousand died from alcoholism, while German women died at a rate of 0.12 per thousand.[140] "In America, where village controls seem to have been weakened, female drinking took a quantum leap forward," concludes the historian Hasia Diner.[141] The Irish in America upheld liquor dealing as an honorable occupation for widows, and Irish women were central to the "kitchen grog shops" that were the locus of drinking prior to the rise of saloons in the twentieth century.[142] But bourgeois reformers declared the unlicensed kitchen pub immoral and illegal. Catholic priests and Irish journalists attributed the problem of Irish women's alcoholism to poverty, domestic discord, and the decadence of American urban life.

The Russell Brothers insulted Irish women's sexual morality and also questioned Irish men's heterosexuality. The brothers' "symbolic suggestions of unspeakable depravity" outraged protesters.[143] One of the comedians fell on his back and exposed his underwear, while the other flirted with men in the audience. The Russell Brothers' act was a "libel on the purest race of womanhood that God ever created."[144] The Russells' choice of feminine attire did not just make them manly Irish women; it also made them sexually suspect Irish men because the genre of transvestite performance was increasingly attached to homosexuality in the early twentieth century. Accounts of their act noted that they "pirouetted" on to the stage and described their cowardice when they ran offstage during the barrage of fruit and vegetables—"their knees knocked and their teeth chattered."[145] By 1913, Julian Eltinge, the most popular female impersonator of the time, had to defend himself against charges of effeminacy. The reputation of the average female impersonator was a "creeping male defective who warbles soprano and decks himself in the frocks and frills of womankind."[146] When Irish nationalists sent the Russell Brothers slinking off the stage, they triumphed over an image of Irish male effeminacy and sexual deviance.

This particular victory bolstered the protesters' respectability and decency. The "rowdies" became clean men of good character, while the performers, on the other hand, transformed into "low-lived ruffians."[147] By focusing on sexuality, the protesters could celebrate their masculine strength because they were good fighters who protected virtuous Irish girls from slander. During the trial of those arrested at the Orpheum Theatre, the judge explained that "no man, especially an Irishman, would sit still and witness a performance that was ridiculing his mother or sister."[148] In this case their rowdiness was not ironic; it fit well into the martial manhood cultivated by the Gaelic League (and the Gaelic revival in general), the Clan na Gael, and the AOH in the campaign against the Stage Irish.

As a symbol of traditional national culture and racial superiority, Irish women's sexual behavior was under careful scrutiny, so the Stage Irishwoman was held to high moral standards. According to the protesters, the Stage Irishwoman maligned the exemplary "modesty" of the "womanhood of the race."[149] Indeed, Irish nationalists and Irish Catholic leaders in the United States regularly asserted that Irish women were more virtuous than women of other nationalities. These claims were based on post-famine traditions of sexual control in Ireland, where rates of premarital sex and illegitimacy were low compared to those in other countries.[150] According to the historian Patricia Kelleher, Irish women's remarkable chastity was a "source of self-esteem and a credit to women's reputations."[151] Even anti-Catholic and anti-Irish critics "grudgingly admitted that Irish women 'preserve the abstinence from sexual vice which distinguishes them so honorably at home.'"[152]

A final contentious image in the *McFadden's Row of Flats* was the pig in the Irish home. One editorial explained one of the fallacies in *McFadden's Row of Flats*: "Now, pigs are not members of the household of Irish families, and the impropriety of 'McFadden's Row of Flats' must be realized by any person who sees the play."[153] This complaint was not unique to *McFadden's Row of Flats*. Two weeks before the outburst over this play, the *National Hibernian* complained that the Stage Irishman with a "florid face, porcine features and a touch of acquired brogue, [seems] to succeed in drawing crowded houses."[154] The Irish had long been depicted as pigs—with snouts and fat cheeks—and as living too closely with pigs.[155] As the historian Peter Way explains, the Irish were seen as having the "muscles and minds of apes and the manners of pigs."[156] A 1901 cartoon in a monthly humor magazine, *Judge*, shows an inspector looking into the hut of the Irish American Muldoon family. He asks, "How many have you in your family, Mrs Muldoon?" and she answers, "Tin, sur; counting ther ould mon an ther pigs."[157] The Irish, through association with pigs, seemed to be dirty and indiscriminate, willing to live in filth, like their garbage-eating swine. The identification of the Irish with pigs was also a class stereotype, for the pig in the household was a sign of peasant life. It required little capital or land to raise pigs, while prosperous landowners kept sheep and cattle.[158]

The pig in the Irish home had gendered dimensions. Irish nationalist protesters often objected to images of Irish women interacting with pigs. Critics of *McFadden's Row of Flats*, for example, assailed a poster showing an "Irishwoman sleeping with a pig in the room."[159] Around the same time, in a long complaint, members of the United Irish American Societies in New York City attacked St. Patrick's Day cards with a young Irish woman posed in front of a "sleek pig": "Other lands raise pigs in far greater numbers than Ireland, and are far more intimately associated with them as domestic assets, yet there is no disposition to typify a particular country, say Denmark or Holland, as pig dependent. This is reserved for Ireland with its covert suggestions, and Irishmen resent the implied imputations."[160] The presence of the pig raised questions about the Irish woman's domestic skills and her feminine reputation generally. Indeed, the beastly Irish woman implied many overlapping insults.

The attacks against the Russell Brothers focused in particular on rescuing the reputation of one group of Irish working women in the United

States—domestic servants. The Gaelic League, Clan na Gael, and their allies in the early twentieth century often objected to depictions of the clumsy, backward maid. For example, in 1904 Irish activists objected to a male actor's impersonation of a domestic servant, Maggie, because when a "doctor advised her to rub some medicinal oil on her chest, she rubbed it on the ice-chest."[161] The Gaelic League also criticized the AOH in Pittsfield, Massachusetts, for showing *The Finish of Bridget McKeen*, an Edison film produced in 1901, which shows Bridget struggling to set a fire. After several bumbling attempts, she pours kerosene into the stove. The resulting explosion vaults her into the air in a large puff of smoke. The final shot focuses on her gravestone: "Here lies the remains of Bridget McKeen,/Who started a fire with kerosene."[162] This film is part of a fairly long list of "numbskull stories" about Irish domestics, including other early films like *How Bridget Served the Salad Undressed* (Biograph, 1900).[163]

Irish women, who often migrated as single women, dominated household service in the United States throughout the nineteenth century. Hasia Diner describes domestic service as "an almost universal experience for women of Irish origin in the United States," noting that in 1900 60.5 percent of all women born in Ireland who worked in the United States were employed as domestic servants.[164] By 1920 Irish women provided the majority of servants in Boston, Philadelphia, and New York, before African American women moved into these jobs.[165] Employers and observers widely criticized the Irish maid as incompetent and dirty. Usually without upbringings that prepared them for middle-class housework, Irish immigrant women often did not know how to prepare many dishes, how to clean "glass or silverplate" or "dust carpets."[166] Religious conflict also created friction between Irish Catholic servants and their Protestant employers. Catholics were accused of being spies for the pope and of baptizing Protestant babies while employers were away. In addition, critics charged the Irish servant girl with too much independence, too much rebelliousness—she was willing to leave one job for a more lucrative one, often talked back to her mistress, and displayed her "Hibernian temper."[167] Cartoons also mocked her as a direct participant in the Irish revolution. In this way, arguments about the problem of the Irish domestic servant raised questions about whether the Irish, in Ireland, were capable of self-government, and whether the Irish in America could be assimilated into democracy.[168]

Bridget McKeen and the Russell Brothers' cross-dressed maids fit a stock image of the Irish domestic servant—the older Irish woman who was large,

THE CHICAGO
PUBLIC SCHOOL INSULT.

A Caricature Drawing Exhibited at a
Public School Entertainment in
Chicago, and Put Forward as a
Representative Irish Woman.

Irish-Americans are taxed to pay for
such insults. This brutal caricature
was drawn by a graduate of the high
school.
Is it well to teach contempt for womanhood in the public schools at a time
when our city is horror stricken by weekly murders of women?
    —The New World, Chicago.

Irish nationalists objected to this "brutal" caricature of an Irish woman. *Irish World and American Industrial Liberator*, February 3, 1906.

masculine, and loud. She was also unattractive, incompetent, and insurrectionary. In her description of Frederick Opper's cartoons, the historian Maureen Murphy describes one extreme, "Biddy Tyrannus, an enormous, menacing figure who threatens her employers."[169] The maid's masculinity, as the historian Andrew Urban notes, differentiated her in two ways: she signified Irish lack of civilization because of their uncouth gender roles; the men were loafers, while the women were strong and in charge. In addition, the Irish maid's big feet and muscular arms also set her apart from the "refined . . . women who . . . were responsible for her supervision."[170] American popular culture often portrayed hardworking, beleaguered Irish women who "could quaff the flowing bowl, use her fists, feet or tongue better than her husband."[171] A 1903 editorial in the *Irish World* aptly summed up the misrepresentation of the Irish: "The Irishman is a drunken 'loafer,' who will not work, spends half or all of his wife's earnings, and beats her into the bargain."[172]

The frequent transvestite portrayals of Irish maids—and of other Irish women—on stage intensified the gender reversal in the portrayal of the Irish. Cross-dressing was prominent on the popular stage around the turn of the twentieth century. Gilbert Saroni made a career on stage and in early film by portraying ugly "old maids," while Julian Eltinge, known for his extravagant gowns, offered makeup and fashion advice to female fans. The Irish maid, in particular, was often portrayed by a man on stage. Daly and Devere, like the Russell Brothers, depicted Irish maids who were both sexually loose and manly. Their transvestite Irish maid, Bridget, spoke with a heavy brogue, boxed with men, and bungled her employer's requests.[173] In Bernard Gilmore and John Leonard's early Yellow Kid contribution,

Hogan's Alley (1896), Mrs. Michael Hogan was played by a male actor and Liz, a minor character in Dumont's *Yellow Kid of Hogan's Alley*, was a cross-dressed character.[174] Surveying the manly Irish women on stage, the *Gaelic American* objected to the notion that "masculine voice, and masculine coarseness . . . were essential to a successful and true representation of an Irish woman on stage."[175]

The attacks on the cross-dressed maids of the Russell Brothers struck the heart of the gendered insult to the Irish. Protesters tried to reclaim the morality of Irish women, rescue Irish masculinity, and thus reassert appropriate gender roles in Irish social relations. The campaign against cross-dressers also allowed protesters to defend the image of Irish women without actually attacking female performers on stage. Prior to the Russell Brothers incident, protesters had been criticized for an "unmanly" attack on actresses. A letter to the editor of the *New York Times* called the protesters cowardly and low class. As proof of their weakness, the author pointed to the men's attack on a female performer on stage, whom he described as a "defenseless woman honestly endeavoring to earn her living." "No worthy son of Erin," he concluded, "will lend his moral support to cowardly dastards who egged defenseless women."[176] In this light, the cross-dressed Russell Brothers provided the ideal target for patriotic, manly protesters.

The context of gender reversal in these popular caricatures of the Irish helps explain the aggressive response from male nationalists. Irish nationalists on both sides of the Atlantic exhibited hypermasculinity as one avenue of colonial resistance. This was a response to the theories of colonialists like Matthew Arnold who described the Celtic race's excitability and sentimentality and proposed an advantageous mix of masculine and feminine in the melding of Celtic, Germanic, and Nordic types. Built on notions of Irish "ineffectuality," Arnold's complementary vision supported the need for English rule over the Irish. In retaliation, the Gaelic Athletic Association, founded in 1884, offered Irish men the opportunity to redeem their masculinity through rigorous sport and military training.[177] Similarly, Irish leaders claimed that the Irish would rise in their "battalioned might" against insults on the stage.[178] The war records of some of the campaign's leaders, such as McCrystal and Tuite, reinforced the revolutionary ideology and male dominance of many of the supporting organizations. In these protests against the Stage Irish, men took on soldiers' traditional roles as the exclusive protectors of women.[179]

The protests against the Russell Brothers' servant girls reveals both esteem for Irish working women and paternalistic concern for their vulnerability in the context of American commercialism and politics, and an attempt to keep Irish women subordinate. In opposition to the denigration of the Irish female servant as immoral, critics of the Russell Brothers defended Irish domestic servants as a "reputable class of Irish women."[180] Many Irish American commentators described them as self-sacrificing women who endured hardships for the economic well-being of their families. The Irish maid was also a symbol of Catholic suffering in a hostile world. And some reinterpreted her imposing size in caricature as the admirable strength necessary for hard work.[181] Yet in discussions of the Stage Irishwoman, single Irish women also appear endangered by the American labor market, political movements, and sensational mass culture.[182] A 1905 article commented on a working girl's "daily temptations," and a doctor's letter in the *Irish World* in 1907 explained that many Irish girls lost their virtue during their trips to New York: "There is not a mother in Ireland who would trust her daughter there without adequate protection."[183] In addition to protection from the moral corruptions of work in the city, young Irish women needed to be shielded from political movements attempting to improve women's status. Ten days before the uprising against the Russell Brothers, an article in the *Irish World* worried that Irish women in America would become ensnared in the movement of "modern woman" and blamed "exaggerated Feminism [in] England and America" on the increasing "number of bachelors."[184] Male authority was undermined not only by the popular images of Irish men's ineffectuality but also by women's movements that challenged patriarchy. The protection of Irish women, through the attempts to correct her image on stage, was one stab at this unstable gender hierarchy.

The Russell Brothers' critics seem to have been more comfortable exalting motherhood than defending the Irish working woman.[185] The Irish mother stood above the domestic servant on the nationalist scale of appropriate feminine sacrifice and morality. According to one journalist, "any true man with a good Irish mother would resent" "The Irish Servant Girls."[186] It was not only the protesters but also the beleaguered performers who relied on this powerful icon. John Russell defended himself and his brother by disclosing their Irish heritage, and Percy Williams, the manager or the Orpheum Theatre, the site of the riot, also took to the stage to tell the audience that his mother was Irish—"the best woman God ever let live."[187] It did not make for a very clever defense. In earlier protests nationalists had argued that if the creator of an offensive caricature was Irish, the insult was even greater. The *Irish World* press fired back at the Russell Brothers: "Were your Irish mothers drunken, vulgar and indecent?"[188]

The protesters' nationalist discourse in praise of Irish mothers matches the Gaelic League's construction of the ideal woman as a transcendent mother, a "self-effacing cipher," and a spiritual inspiration—all female role models that shared a "static negation of sexuality."[189] The pure Irish woman stood as a defense of the superiority of Irish culture over English and American society and as the conservator of Irish culture through her influence in the home.[190] Hyde, for example, claimed a connection between proficiency in Gaelic and a "genuine moral superiority."[191] For the Gaelic League, motherhood was the fullest expression of a woman's national pride. Hyde had long argued that mothers were the key to stemming language loss. In particular, Mary Butler's Gaelic League pamphlet, *Irishwomen and the Home Language*, declares that "woman reigns as an autocrat in the kingdom of her home. . . . The spark struck on the hearthstone will fire the soul of the nation."[192]

On April 4, 1903, the *Irish World* published a song to celebrate the triumph over *McFadden's Row of Flats*, particularly over Mrs. Murphy and the donkey:

> McFadden dear an' did you hear the latest song afloat,
> Of how your "Flats" was ancient-egged an' how your ass was
>   smote? . . .
> You thought you would great laurels win when at the "Star"
>   you'd shine,
> But when the hen-fruit came your way a fear crept up your spine.
> "I'm done," you cried; "no, never more my donkey will be seen,
> Nor will my lady ride him out a-wearin' of the green."[193]

The practical censorship of an act did not just concern cross-dressed maids, green whiskers, drunken women, and pigs, though protesters offered a spirited critique of these details. The theater riots were manly dares, defiant displays, and recruiting tools not only in the battles between Irish nationalists and Anglo-Saxon authority but also in the fiery debates between Irish nationalists themselves. The theater rioters of 1903 and 1907 were not as interested in mainstream respectability as they were in demonstrating Irish race pride—led and defended by male protectors. In these ways, the clumsy Stage Irishwoman and the Irish men who threw garbage at her had key supporting roles in the transatlantic drama of Irish nationalism and migration. She gave the rioters respectability because her sexual depravity justified their violence and helped them demonstrate their masculine honor.

After the first decade of the twentieth century, Irish theater riots against the Stage Irish faded as Irish nationalists turned their attention to war—World War I, the Easter Rebellion, and the Anglo-Irish War. Reasoning that Great Britain was overburdened with involvement in World War I, Irish nationalists decided to launch an uprising on the Easter weekend of 1916, even though they recognized their slim chances of success.[194] The Clan na Gael backed the Irish Republican Brotherhood and brokered deals for arms and supplies from Germany in preparation for the rebellion. British troops quickly suppressed it, but when they decided to execute the leaders of the uprising, public opinion on both sides of the Atlantic turned against them. Following the executions, Irish American nationalism favoring physical force flourished.[195] A new nationalist group, the Friends of Irish Freedom (FOIF), joined the Clan na Gael in attacking anything it considered British propaganda and in mocking John Redmond's moderate stance. Born at an Irish Race Convention in 1915, the FOIF shared the Clan's radical nationalist perspective, but it was a more open organization. Many Clan leaders also held power in the FOIF. Under the leadership of the Clan member and New York Supreme Court Justice Daniel Cohalan (who was Devoy's close friend), the FOIF had eighty-seven branches by 1916 and 225,000 members by 1920.[196]

In their cultural criticism during World War I, Irish nationalists demanded favorable images of the Easter Rising, defended their patriotism, and tried to undermine Great Britain during the war. In 1917 the FOIF, the Clan na Gael, and the Gaelic League objected to the film *Whom the Gods Destroy*, which followed three friends' involvement in the Irish rebellion. Irish nationalists believed it slandered the heroes of the revolution: "We hope to induce the proper authorities to prevent such slanders. If they won't, then [it] will be time for us to take the matter into our hands and adopt other methods."[197] These protests spread from Boston to New York and New Jersey.[198] Irish nationalists met with theater managers and public officials to have the movie removed. When Vitagraph explained that the picture was not offensive because the actors were Irish, the protesters quickly rejected this excuse—it had not even worked to protect the Russell Brothers.[199] A few months later, Irish nationalists in the United States approved of a play, *Ireland's Easter*, written by two Irish priests, in May of 1917.[200] The *Gaelic American* also criticized *Irish and Proud of It* as a blatant propaganda tool of the British. The play was offensive not only because of the portrayal of a drunken, rough-housing Irishman—Patsy Brennan—but also because it showed Irish soldiers fighting for Belgium, not for Irish independence. When the play introduced the Irish leader John Redmond, the audience hissed "traitor." Redmond's conciliatory approach to British authority had fallen out of favor.[201] Irish nationalists also became embroiled in debates about patriotic songs: they objected to "My Country 'Tis of Thee" because it had the same melody as "God Save the Queen," and they deemed all English songs, including "It's a Long Way to Tipperary," un-American.[202] In these ways, Irish nationalists defended their patriotism, questioned their opponents' loyalty to the United States, and defined un-Americanism as any support for England.[203]

Although the context of World War I changed Irish nationalists' approach to the Stage Irish in fundamental ways, some glimmers of the riotous tradition remained. Irish nationalist groups objected to the film *Kathleeen Mavourneen*, which featured Theda Bara as an Irish peasant woman who must accept a loveless marriage because of her poverty. Accounts of the protests did not offer many details about offensive parts of the movie, but in San Francisco protesters did complain about "pigs in an Irish parlor"— a hallmark of *McFadden's Row of Flats*—and the Irish peasant woman in the backward Irish countryside had been a noxious image throughout the campaign against the Stage Irish. In this case, the violence of the protest also matched earlier controversies. The FOIF first lobbied theater managers, but then accelerated to a conflict in a San Francisco theater. Young men in the gallery rushed into the projection room, seized the film, and smashed the equipment.[204] When the FOIF recounted its attack on the character, Bridget O'Flaherty (a lowbrow and roughneck Irish servant girl) at the Harlem YMCA in 1919, it linked the conflict to the Irish battle against *McFadden's Row of Flats* and the Russell Brothers. The FOIF acknowledged that the fight against the Stage Irishwoman was never ending: it required "eternal vigilance."[205]

CHAPTER THREE

IMMORAL . . . IN THE BROAD SENSE

Censoring Racial Ridicule in Legitimate Theater

Irish nationalist protesters willingly risked arrest in their drive to stop offensive productions in vaudeville and musical comedy. But these leaders,
along with African American and Jewish activists, also increasingly tried to
get the performers arrested. They often succeeded. This chapter examines
how protesters began to use lawful means to censor two plays that they
thought constituted harmful racial insults. African Americans attacked *The
Clansman* in 1905 and 1906, while Irish nationalists in the United States
started their assault on *The Playboy of the Western World* in 1911. Elements
of the earlier disruptions remained—a lone egg tossed at *The Clansman*,
for example, and more extensive disturbances of *The Playboy of the Western
World*. But a clear trajectory toward more lawful protests emerges in these
campaigns. In the protests against *The Clansman* and *The Playboy of the
Western World*, activists turned to the law to suppress racial ridicule; each
campaign culminated in a court battle in Philadelphia. African American
activists pushed for the legal suppression of *The Clansman* because it inflamed racial violence; Irish nationalists tried to censor *The Playboy* because
they deemed its representation of depraved Irish women indecent. In each
case, race proved central to the definition of the play's harm to the public.
Police in Providence, Rhode Island, apparently connected the two plays,
explaining to worried supporters of *The Playboy of the Western World* that
"they had had the same trouble about a negro play said to misrepresent
people of colour."[1] Despite these perceived similarities, the plays followed
different paths: several cities banned *The Clansman*, while *The Playboy*
escaped all efforts at legal censorship, though its producers, under pressure from "gallery censorship," sometimes removed offensive sections.[2]
The campaign against *The Clansman* also included alliances between African Americans and Jews, while the Irish battle against *The Playboy of the

Western World was riddled with Irish hostility toward Jews and African Americans.

Thomas Dixon, a minister, lawyer, and writer, drew on two of his previous novels to create *The Clansman*. In *The Leopard's Spots*, published in 1901, African Americans take violent revenge on whites, lust after white women, and cheat their way to power in the state legislature. Only the vigilante punishments of the Ku Klux Klan bring order and white supremacy back to the South. Three years later, Dixon published a second book about the injustices supposedly suffered by whites during Reconstruction—*The Clansman: A Historical Romance of the Ku Klux Klan*. Still espousing the dangers of African Americans and the necessity of removing them from the United States, this novel became even more successful than *The Leopard's Spots*. Following the blueprint of *Uncle Tom's Cabin*, popular both as a novel and then as numerous theatrical adaptations, Dixon wrote a play based on his previous Reconstruction novels.[3] Just five years later, Irish nationalists attacked *The Playboy of the Western World* when it toured in the United States in 1911. The Irish nationalist critique of the play was well known, following the riots in Dublin in 1907. Irish and African American protesters had some similar complaints: the plays did not present their people as capable of self-governance, emphasizing instead their lawlessness and sexual wantonness. The Irish were livid that their women were portrayed as lustful, while African Americans worried that the image of sexually voracious black men could lead to violent reprisals.

Scholars have already shown that obscenity prosecutions were inconsistent and unpredictable in the history of American theater. The regulation of racial ridicule proved even more uncertain.[4] The comparison of these two plays shows that one of the factors determining eventual suppression was offstage violence. In particular, the context of lynching and race riots was fundamental to state censorship of racial ridicule. Although progressive civil rights activists stood at the forefront of efforts to censor *The Clansman*, the bans built on and redirected the long histories of regulating African American entertainment and suppressing productions that challenged white supremacy. Officials censored *The Clansman* after the Atlanta race riot of 1906, referring both to it and to the largest protest against the play, a meeting of about one thousand African Americans outside the Walnut Theater in Philadelphia, as evidence of the likelihood of further violence. African Americans planned restrained protests, perhaps to keep the focus on whites as the perpetrators of social unrest, and advocated state suppression of the play to prevent violent outbreaks. Irish protesters, on the other hand, sustained their penchant for direct confrontations within the theater. At the same time, they also launched a new tactic: they tried to take the moral high ground as anti-obscenity censors. Indeed, observers often compared *The Playboy* and *The Clansman* to the prominent obscenity crises in the theater of the early twentieth century: *Mrs. Warren's Profession* and *Sapho* were controversial because of the sexual nonconformity of the lead female characters. Yet the plays considered here take us beyond the reaches of obscenity to the racial dimensions of theater's potential social harm, or immorality in "its broad sense."[5]

These two plays show how race shaped the understandings of the "bad tendency of speech" in censorship controversies of the early twentieth century. The protection of public welfare from this alleged bad tendency was the most common approach to theatrical censorship, and to the First Amendment in general, during the first two decades of the twentieth century. While judges gave state officials broad authority to define the tendency of speech, public officials agreed that degrading public morals and causing unrest made up the central aspects of "bad tendency" during this period. The First Amendment did not protect speech that caused violence or harmed community morals. Obscenity, first and foremost, caused moral harm. William Blackstone defined obscenity in English common law as "writings, pictures or the like, of any immoral or illegal tendency."[6]

Most theatrical censorship in the late nineteenth and early twentieth century regulated obscenity, which the historian Helen Horowitz summarizes as "sexually exciting words offered openly to a broad public for sale."[7] Anthony Comstock, a Civil War veteran and social reformer active in the Young Men's Christian Association (YMCA), bolstered federal obscenity law in 1873 to include bans on information about abortion and contraception circulating through the national mail service. He then became an agent for the United States Postal Service to help enforce the law, and also the head of the New York Society for the Suppression of Vice (NYSSV), an anti-vice committee that had split from the YMCA. The Supreme Court's treatment of obscenity relied on the bad tendency test when it claimed that the Comstock Act's ban on mailing obscene publications protected the people from a "demoralizing influence."[8]

The leaders of these campaigns against *The Clansman* and *The Playboy of the Western World* moved beyond traditional obscenity claims in two ways: they tried to broaden the notion of immorality to include racial injustice and they also argued that the plays in question were "spark[s] in a powder house."[9] The second strategy, the charge of inciting violence, fit well within the censorship framework of the early twentieth century. American courts often moved beyond obscenity in their identification of types of speech that threatened to undermine morality. Criminal news and police reports, for example, were censored because they caused "public demoralization."[10] More important, the tendency to provoke violence among listeners was a crime. Police regularly punished radical speakers for inciting the "lawlessness of hostile audiences."[11] The National Civic Federation, a conservative reform organization that included many lawyers as members, explained that "civil authorities are not required to sit idly by while incendiary speeches incite mobs to destroy order, peace and property."[12] Authorities often interpreted this quite broadly, even stopping some radical activists before they had the chance to speak. Others crafted a more narrow definition: they held that the First Amendment did not protect speech that provoked an "immediate" disturbance.[13] In the campaigns against *The Clansman* and *The Playboy*, African American and Irish critics claimed that the plays and their authors caused social unrest, but other observers focused on protesters as the dangerous element.

In the debates surrounding *The Clansman* and *The Playboy*, politicians and journalists referred to two other controversial plays—*Sapho* and *Mrs. Warren's Profession*. Censors found *Sapho* and *Mrs. Warren's Profession* problematic in the early twentieth century "because the productions immediately attracted enthusiastic audiences by their supposedly risqué treatment of fallen women."[14] In New York City, protesters held that *The Clansman* was "analogous" to *Mrs. Warren's Profession* and *Sapho*, and was "every bit as immoral and dangerous as either of these."[15] "Parricide," a critic of *The Playboy* remarked, "is not more a fit conception about which to build a modern play than was prostitution in Mr. Bernard Shaw's 'Mrs. Warren's Profession.'"[16] The Colored Citizens Protection League appealed to the mayor of New York City, the Democrat George McClellan, to stop the play, but journalists in the black press acknowledged that it would be hard to prove that the unsavory play was "incendiary and immoral"—the prerequisites for censorship.[17] Irish and African American activists pressed these comparisons with *Sapho* and *Mrs. Warren's Profession* to expose the inconsistency of official censors and to encourage censors to include racial ridicule in their cultural critique.

The attacks on *Sapho* and *Mrs. Warren's Profession* formed part of a new assault on legitimate theater. Lowbrow theater, namely burlesque, had been a prime target of the NYSSV. Whereas past attempts at stage censorship had castigated "theatrical enterprises in general [or] improper costuming and dance," aspiring censors in 1900 began to attack the sexual themes in realist plays.[18] A top concern of censors was the depiction of sexuality—including the sexually suspect woman, prostitution, and homosexuality. According to the theater historian Katie Johnson, fifty new plays about prostitution appeared in New York between 1898 and 1922.[19] "Brothel dramas" became the "prevailing" genre on the legitimate stage in the 1910s, despite the interventions of Comstock and city censors.[20] The inconsistency of censorship shows that sexuality was not a simple target in legitimate theater, because just as daring displays of sexuality stirred up censorship controversies they also provided a powerful defense of the art of Broadway—"a sign of [the theater's] highmindedness and seriousness."[21]

The first twentieth-century scandal in the legitimate theater centered on *Sapho*. Clyde Fitch's adaptation of Alphonse Daudet's novel of the same name debuted on February 5, 1900, at Wallack's Theatre. The star and producer, Olga Nethersole, won fame by getting out of bed barefoot in *Camille*, and giving her male costar a full kiss in *Carmen*. Nethersole did more than play transgressive women; she was an unmarried, successful businesswoman, one of the few female producers in theater. Her position as the producer of *Sapho* and her passionate acting style added fuel to the flames.[22] Nethersole portrayed Fanny Le Grande, a well-known courtesan, who has an illegitimate son and who embarks on an affair with a young student. In the most shocking scene, the student, Jean Gaussin, carries Fanny upstairs to spend the night with her.[23] After attempting suicide, Fanny is reunited with her child's father. Although she does not love him, Fanny agrees to marry him and build a life as a wife and mother. Fanny defied the binary categories of good and bad women of the day. She was no naive victim; she was passionate and maternal.

Social reformers were outraged by the "Sapho plague."[24] On February 20, 1900, Nethersole and her male costar, Hamilton Revelle, were "arrested for corrupting public decency."[25] The arrests generated a "mania" about the play.[26] The sale of the novel on which the play was based increased, and new companies began to tour with burlesques of the play. Nethersole continued to perform Fanny before enthusiastic crowds when she was released on bond. Following a dramatic trial, in which Nethersole appeared in outlandish costumes and recited dialogue from the play, the star was acquitted after the judge instructed the jury not to consider the sensibilities of a young girl in the audience, but the "sensibilities of people at large." Two days later Nethersole reappeared as Fanny. The audience cheered her so enthusiastically that she had to bow twenty times before the fans quieted.[27]

Four years later, Comstock battled another sexually transgressive woman on stage—Mrs. Warren, a wealthy, intelligent brothel owner who escaped factory work through prostitution. She is the main character in *Mrs. Warren's Profession*, a play by George Bernard Shaw, an Irish author whom Comstock labeled the "Irish smut dealer."[28] Shaw maneuvered his play through the British censors only by cutting significant scenes and changing references to prostitution. Still it was not staged for a public English performance until 1925. Shaw defended his play, arguing that it was an indictment of the economic oppression that made prostitution a reasonable option for women.[29]

The American run of *Mrs. Warren's Profession* had an auspicious start in New Haven, at the Hyperion Theatre on October 27 1905. The town's mayor, John Studley, closed the show after opening night. Under Studley's orders, the chief of police revoked the Hyperion's license until Nethersole's company left the city. After the preview in New Haven, *Mrs. Warren's Profession* opened in New York City to large crowds and a reinforced police presence on October 31, 1905. When the police commissioner William McAdoo came to opening night to assess the play, he declared it "an offense to the morals of the public," shut it down, and arrested the cast, manager, and theater owner.[30] In July of 1906 the Court of Special Sessions acquitted them of violating the obscenity laws, explaining that "the unlovely, the repellent, the disgusting in the play are merely accessories to the main purpose of the drama, which is an attack on certain social conditions relating to the employment of women."[31]

The victories for the performers and producers of *Sapho* and *Mrs. Warren's Profession* reveal cracks in the anti-obscenity crusade of the day. Each acquittal challenged the traditional definition of obscenity, which had been established by a British case, *Regina v. Hicklin*, in 1868, and accepted by American courts in 1879. In the vindication of *Sapho*, the judge rejected the idea that the text should be judged from the point of view of the most vulnerable viewer; in *Mrs. Warren's Profession*, the court ruled that a play could not be obscene based on just one section of the text. Although these prosecutions failed, the risk of more still affected Broadway content. Censorship threats forced producers to make changes to two white slavery dramas—*The Fight* and *The Lure*. John Sumner, then head of the NYSSV, also led a charge against *Aphrodite* in 1919, but city officials did not follow through.

The attacks on legitimate theater were only partially successful for several reasons. First, the Hicklin Rule for obscenity posited a vulnerable viewer who needed to be protected from immoral productions; censors tried to emphasize the potential harm to youthful viewers. As one critic wrote of *Sapho*: "To see it may ruin the life and happiness of a boy or a girl forever."[32] But this was not often a winning argument, because the Broadway audience "believed itself eminently capable of self-governance."[33] Second, nineteenth-century approaches to obscenity were beginning to break down in favor of the more democratic regulation of American culture. Comstock and his NYSSV, with its puritanical outlook, became the frequent target of ridicule. At the same time, some Catholic and Jewish leaders became more involved in anti-obscenity activity. According to the historian Andrea Friedman, an "interfaith movement" emerged as the status of prudish Protestant anti-vice crusaders declined. Friedman describes how a "democratic moral authority" emerged in the wake of Comstockery to regulate culture: the new regime judged images from the perspective of the average person (rather than from that of an impressionable child) and advocated democratic processes for assessing texts.[34] Through the 1920s, self-regulatory schemes gained ground, and in the 1930s, state regulation, with jury trials, took center stage.

The shifts to more democratic censorship schemes occurred amid these racial groups' grassroots protests over racial ridicule. One critic observed that "theatrical affairs in which the subject of race or religion figures, have frequently experienced the weight of unofficial censorship."[35] The activists compared their efforts to stop offensive productions with obscenity cases as well as other complaints about racial insults. In Patterson, New Jersey, the African Americans who lobbied the mayor to stop *The Clansman* noted that he had earlier banned a play that caricatured the Irish.[36] In 1907 a Chicago critic connected the protests against the Russell Brothers to debates about *The Clansman*, just after *The Clansman* controversy had died down.[37]

African American protesters, however, focused most extensively on how censorship officials treated *The Clansman* and *Uncle Tom's Cabin*, which activists and officials considered racially inflammatory. Theatrical versions of Harriet Beecher Stowe's antislavery novel had proven popular throughout the late nineteenth century and the early twentieth. Though some versions of the "Tom show" included minstrel show characterizations and happy endings that idealized the plantation South, one production, by George Aiken and George Howard, stayed true to the "abolitionist pathos" of Stowe's book.[38] The play ended with the death of Uncle Tom and did not romanticize plantation life. One minister in Washington, D.C., complained about *The Clansman*: "I am of the firm belief that the Civil War was brought on by the appearance of Mrs. Harriet Beecher Stowe's play, 'Uncle Tom's Cabin,' and while I do not think the Dixon play will carry nearly so much influence, yet it is not right that it should be allowed to continue."[39] Dixon also encouraged the comparison. Stowe's antislavery narrative motivated his career. He committed himself to challenging *Uncle Tom's Cabin* and to eclipsing its successes as a novel and a play. After watching one of the hundreds of *Uncle Tom's Cabin* companies put on the play in 1901, he wrote *The Leopard's Spots: A Romance in of the White Man's Burden*, which sold more than one hundred thousand copies just a few months after its publication, and helped establish Doubleday, Page as a successful publisher by ultimately selling more than a million copies. Dixon saw his fiction as a sequel to and "refutation" of *Uncle Tom's Cabin*, in which he emphasized the suffering of whites after the Civil War.[40]

The links between *Uncle Tom's Cabin* and *The Clansman* ran deeper than Thomas Dixon's literary motivations. Protests against *The Clansman* began around the same time that the Daughters of the Confederacy successfully lobbied the Kentucky legislature to ban theatrical productions of *Uncle Tom's Cabin*. In 1906 the legislature outlawed the production of racially inflammatory plays, or theatrical performances that "tend to create racial feelings and prejudice."[41] Southern lawmakers targeted the abolitionist version of the play by passing laws against plays that incited racial prejudice, intended to mean black prejudice and violence against whites.[42] In the South the play proved controversial because, as some critics argued, it "slurred the fair name of Southerners" and was likely to "inflame race prejudice among the large class of Negro citizens."[43] These concerns about African American reactions to *Uncle Tom's Cabin* fit with other efforts to control African American audiences. In Lexington, Kentucky, for example, other reformers and religious leaders, including the black Methodist AME church, attempted to control nightlife associated with working-class African Americans. These "ignorant and dissolute" blacks were a distinct source of disorder because of assumptions about sexual excess and aggression.[44] The language of the Kentucky ban on *Uncle Tom's Cabin* remained vague

S. Joe Brown, who pressed the
Des Moines city council to pass
a law to bar *The Clansman*.
State Historical Society of
Iowa—Iowa City

enough that progressive critics of *The Clansman* could use it for their own
ends. But, as the rest of this chapter will show, the efforts to censor racist and antiracist productions often shared alarm over "unruly" African
Americans.

Clansman protesters did not just use the so-called *Uncle Tom's Cabin* law
to their own ends; in at least one case, they successfully lobbied legislators
to pass new laws banning plays that incited a racial hatred. Whereas officials
and protesters often claimed that the play should be banned as immoral or
as encouraging violence, the city of Des Moines tried to censor it because
of its racial defamation. After the play appeared once in 1906, apparently
inciting racial "disturbances," S. Joe Brown, an African American attorney
in Des Moines, introduced a bill in 1907 to ban exhibitions and performances that inflamed racial feeling.[45] Brown's ordinance stated: "No person
shall . . . exhibit, sell, or offer for sale any . . . book, picture magazine or other
thing for exhibit or perform or assist in the performance of an indecent,
immoral, lewd or inflammatory play . . . calculated to encourage or incite
rioting, breaches of the peace or lawlessness of any kind or to create a feeling of hatred or antipathy against any particular race, nationality or class
of individuals."[46] The law, however, was not published in time to stop *The
Clansman* in March of 1907. Brown claimed that the play was "destructive

of good morals and good order, productive of race hatred and mob violence and has been prohibited in a number of the leading cities o the country."[47]

From the date of its opening, on September 22, 1905, in Norfolk, Virginia, the play faced criticism for being an inaccurate representation of African Americans and for inciting violence. In the first year of its tour, neither of these claims stopped the play. Critics of the play challenged Dixon's claims of historical accuracy. One letter to the *Atlanta Constitution* called the play a "perverted mixture of truth and falsehood."[48] Another writer called it an "overdrawn picture of conditions that existed nearly 40 years ago."[49] Dixon fought back by offering $1,000 to anyone who found any historical inaccuracy in the play.[50] Southern supporters of Dixon also vouched for the truth of the play: "It is true that South Carolina, as other Southern states, was bankrupted by the negro legislature; that the ignorant blacks were encouraged by Thaddeus Stevens and other radicals of the North to usurp the white men."[51]

One of the strongest early critics of the play was Joseph Silverman, the chief rabbi at New York's prominent reform synagogue Temple Emanu-El from 1888 to 1922. In early January of 1907 Dixon began to refer to Silverman's "bitter attack" on the play.[52] Silverman's stance against *The Clansman* is not surprising because in several of his civic and religious positions he debated race and religion on stage. As president of the Central Conference of American Rabbis, he worked against anti-Semitism in public schools, including drives to ban texts like *The Merchant of Venice*. As a member of the Committee for Religious Congress at the Chicago World's Fair, he was particularly concerned about the representation of Judaism at the World's Parliament of Religions.[53] As a delegate to the Actors' Church Alliance (ACA), Silverman may have been attempting to improve the image of Jews in the eyes of Protestant reformers, many of whom were particularly critical of Jewish control of the theater around the turn of the twentieth century. By placing himself on the side of theatrical reform, Silverman may have hoped to counter this characterization of Jewish "Shylocks" in the theatrical world. Furthermore, at ACA events, he decried religion in theatrical productions because he believed that religious plays were ultimately seeking converts to Protestantism and Catholicism, not Judaism. In other words, he saw the attempts at Christian indoctrination on stage that he protested against in public schools.[54] He was not just concerned about the status of Jews. Silverman also challenged discrimination against African Americans. He spoke out against the racial and religious prejudice of the Ku Klux Klan: "We Jews can fully sympathize with any people that is similarly dealt with."[55]

Silverman also began to criticize anti-Semitic portrayals on stage and on screen—a trend that he continued through the first two decades of the twentieth century. First, he expressed his concerns about anti-Semitism in Oberammergau's Passion Play because of its depiction of Jews as Christ-killers. Two years after criticizing racism in *The Clansman*, Silverman spoke up at the 1908 Executive Committee Meeting of the B'nai B'rith to seek the formation of an agency to defend "the Jewish name." This proposal resulted in the establishment of the Anti-Defamation League.[56] In 1910 he railed against the Stage Jew as a "stench in our nostrils, a disgrace to the country, an insult to the Jew, and a discredit to the stage."[57] In his critique he also noted the success of the Irish Americans in their fight against the Stage Irishman. Between assailing *The Clansman* and following the Irish campaign against crude Irish caricatures, Silverman was fully immersed in the multiple confrontations against racial ridicule in the early twentieth century.

The debates about the historical accuracy of *The Clansman* overlapped with charges that it incited violence; the latter charge proved a more powerful claim in the drive to censorship. Critics charged that the images of lustful, violent, incompetent blacks inflamed racial tensions to the point of violence. Yet observers still debated whether the play or protesters caused disorder or whether black or white spectators were likely to react violently. The answer to these questions changed as the play traveled around the country and determined whether the censors' response affirmed or challenged the play's racism. Even when city officials censored *The Clansman* in response to African American protesters, they often reinforced the danger of the protesters, not of the play.

Critics noted the "enthusiastic" reception of the play in the South, but they also described the play's incitement of racial violence.[58] An editorial in the African American newspaper the *New York Age* observed that the play was "dragging its slimy serpentine length through the South and rekindling fires of prejudice."[59] The protests often helped fill the theaters for the play's successful run. After audience members hissed in Columbia, South Carolina, several African Americans tried to speak to Dixon, but he refused. The protesters stated the play "would do great harm in inciting a strike between the races."[60] A southern critic compared the play to a lynching: "It is no tribute to the merit or the usefulness of the play that people rush to see it. In Texas last year, trains were run, crowded with eager citizens, to see a negro burned to death."[61]

The notions of black anger toward whites and an easily inflamed African American audience were central to the battle over *The Clansman*. Dixon and his supporters emphasized the "savage mood" and "wild threats" of African Americans.[62] They were adamant that their unruliness should not determine the fate of *The Clansman*. In Decatur, Alabama, city officials responded to complaints about the incendiary nature of the play by announcing that African Americans would be banned from the show if it appeared in the city.[63] Other accounts of the potential for violence left open the possibility of white or black instigation. The South Carolina Woman's Christian Temperance Union seemed worried about the lower class of both races when it issued a statement condemning the play because it incited the "lawless element to deeds of violence."[64] An editorial in the *Atlanta Constitution* held that the play led to the "formation of lawless bands of both races seeking revenge for fancied wrongs."[65]

African American critics argued that the play inspired white violence against blacks. One 1906 editorial linked the play directly to lynchings: "The impression that seems to prevail and to which Tom Dixon so effectively appeals to the galleries, that the antipathy to the Negro rises from his crimes against womanhood, is simply not true."[66] Other critics noted that the play "[created] in the minds of the whites a feeling of hostility" and also recounted the chain of assaults and near misses in relation to the play: "When *The Clansman* showed in Savannah a riot was narrowly averted and a young Afro-American doctor perched high in what is locally styled the 'buzzard roost' came near being seriously hurt in an attempt to jump out of the window. In Macon, Ga., the white audience not only hissed the Afro-Americans in the gallery, but apparently wanted to lynch some of them.... In Atlanta, at the first performance, an Afro-American who applauded one part of the play had his head hit with a club for his temerity."[67] Ten months later *The Clansman* was linked to a much bigger incident that fundamentally transformed the climate for censorship—the Atlanta race riot of 1906.

Although the play was controversial for racial antagonism, it was not banned until the aftermath of the riots that shook Atlanta in September 1906. During the summer of that year, tensions had increased over lynchings in Atlanta and Chattanooga. White leaders complained of a "rape menace," candidates for election stressed the race issue, and sensational press reports

Act II of *The Clansman*, in which the African American governor, Silas Lynch, confronts the white Cameron family in the parlor of their home. TCS 29, Harvard Theatre Collection, Houghton Library, Harvard University

lent sympathy to white men's efforts to "protect our women."[68] On September 22, in the midst of a "general sexual hysteria," ten thousand armed white men gathered on the outskirts of the African American neighborhood and attacked black-owned saloons, pool halls, and restaurants.[69] When police officers swept through the neighborhood, African Americans fired on them, killing one. Police then arrested hundreds of black residents and killed four citizens during their search. Calm did not return to the city until September 27. Twenty-five African American men died and several hundred were wounded. The historian Pete Daniel concludes that irresponsible newspaper editors, politicians, and police "shared the blame with the white mob."[70]

The Clansman may have played a role in fomenting the violence in At-

Act III of *The Clansman*, in which the Ku Klux Klan apprehends and prepares to lynch Gus. TCS 29, Harvard Theatre Collection, Houghton Library, Harvard University

lanta. At its first appearance in the city, in early November 1905, *The Clansman*'s audience became unruly and police had to silence the racial hostility. During the play African Americans cheered at unexpected places and offered enthusiastic support for black characters. When whites cheered "lynch him" when the black villain was captured on screen, black spectators in the segregated gallery began to taunt the whites below. The management turned on the lights to quiet the audience, and then called the police, who arrested several people.[71] *The Clansman* supported the racist commentary of black crime and social danger. In particular, the sensationalist press featured black men menacing white women just before the riots in September 1906. The afternoon of its start, the *Atlanta Evening News* and the *Atlanta Journal* both featured articles about black men assaulting white women.[72]

The advocates of censorship enjoyed favorable conditions in the fall of 1906, with the Atlanta riot behind them and municipal elections in three northern cities ahead of them in the fall. Immediately after the riot, censorship calls referred to the violence in Atlanta. The mayor of Macon, Georgia, stopped the play "in view of the race riots in Atlanta." Birmingham and Montgomery, in Alabama, also banned it.[73] Northern cities followed suit: Philadelphia, Harrisburg and Lancaster, Pennsylvania, and Wilmington, Delaware. Censoring *The Clansman* seems to have been part of the negotiations between African Americans and the Republican Party. Republican officeholders delivered some patronage to African Americans and helped a few blacks get elected to the state legislature after 1910, but African Americans remained disillusioned with the Republicans and sought, largely unsuccessfully, to find other avenues to political power.[74] Mayor John Weaver, a Republican, stopped the play in Philadelphia, a few weeks before elections in November 1906, and Republican police commissioners, with the approval of the Republican Mayor, Horace Wilson, did the same, a few days later, in Wilmington, also during election season. In Wilmington, Republicans accused Democrats of bringing *The Clansman* to the city to "make political capital."[75] Dixon charged that African Americans complained to "make politicians come to their knees on the eve of an election."[76] Another letter to the editor in Lancaster accused Republican politicians of "truckling to colored voters," explaining that "this country is coming to a pretty pass when municipal authorities of boss-ruled cities can set themselves up as stage censors, and suppress a play that a large number of decent educated white people wish to see."[77]

After the Atlanta riot, protests against the play expanded, and its defenders often discussed the mob violence of protesters. The play had appeared in Philadelphia without significant protest before the Atlanta riot, but about one month after it, African American antilynching activists and ministers led a protest against *The Clansman* in Philadelphia.[78] One of the leaders of the campaign, Nathan Mossell, had been active with clergy in antilynching activism in Philadelphia of the 1890s.[79] Philadelphia's African American population doubled between 1890 and 1910. Many of the roughly sixty-three thousand African Americans in Philadelphia at the end of the nineteenth century had migrated from the South and brought with them memories of southern mob violence. Though Philadelphia was the site of multiple ethnic tensions, the city's black population was the major target of violence.[80]

Philadelphia African Americans were shocked by the lynching of George

White in Wilmington, Delaware, in 1903. An African American farmhand accused of raping a white high school student, White was burned at the stake. The event was widely publicized throughout Philadelphia, which was closely linked to Wilmington through business and trade. A minister in the African Methodist Episcopal church, Montrose Thornton, led the black opposition to vigilante violence. He remained in Wilmington through 1907, long enough to witness the arrival of *The Clansman* in his hometown and in nearby Philadelphia. By 1912 he moved to the Charles Street AME Church in Boston and began to work closely with the civil rights leader William Monroe Trotter. Trotter and Thornton galvanized the African American community in Boston to oppose the showing of *The Birth of a Nation*, the film version of *The Clansman*, in the city in 1915. The local and national fight against vigilante violence undergirded the drive to suppress *The Clansman* and *The Birth of a Nation*.[81]

African American preachers in Philadelphia sent out "a call to action" on October 20, 1906: "Lynchings have been encouraged by the play. . . . We, the citizens, have determined that it shall not play at the Walnut Street Theatre during the coming week."[82] Three days later a crowd of African Americans gathered outside that theater when *The Clansman* was scheduled. One report estimated that two thousand blacks came to protest, with another one thousand whites to observe the event.[83] At the start of the play, one black man threw an egg at the stage from the gallery. Someone shouted, "We want no Atlanta here" (referring to the recent race riots), and then African Americans ran from the gallery to join the crowd on the street.[84] Police arrested the egg-thrower, Henry Jenkins, and, according to one report, clubbed him on the head and led him, with a bleeding scalp, outside. The Philadelphia *North American* noted that "hundreds of Negroes swarmed" around Jenkins and threatened the police.[85] When the director of public safety tried to break up the group, the crowd surged around him, but ministers calmed the protesters and they eventually dispersed quietly: "That there was largely no bloodshed is largely due to the action of a number of negro ministers and leaders, who moved among the crowd of angry men and urged them to be quiet."[86] Press reports referred to "mob law" and a "frenzy," but the black press denied these descriptions; as one article put it, "There is no truth in the statement that there was a riot for there was none."[87] This was a double bind for African American protesters: they did not want to be mislabeled as an unlawful mob, yet the sensational descriptions of violence at the Walnut Street Theatre helped their case for censorship.

Following the Walnut Street protests and appeals from African Americans, Mayor Weaver banned *The Clansman* because he believed the "tendency of the play is to produce racial hatred."[88] He noted that the play caused prejudice among whites, but he characterized African Americans as uncontrollable in the face of *The Clansman*. He elaborated: *The Clansman* "has aroused our colored citizens to a state of frenzy and if permitted to go on I believe would produce a very bitter feeling on the part of our white citizens to our colored brethren"[89] He also affirmed the protesters' claim that *The Clansman* ridiculed African Americans: "The play holds up a whole race to ignominy and ridicule," he concluded, "instead of bringing all classes together."[90]

When Dixon sought an injunction to halt the mayor's order in court, he encountered a spirited defender of the black protesters—Judge Mayer Sulzberger, a Jewish civic leader whose family had migrated from Baden in what became Germany in the mid-nineteenth century. As a dedicated Republican, Sulzberger was linked to the politicians who had banned the play in Pennsylvania. The courtroom was "jammed to suffocation" with a large group of African American spectators, including the ministers who had planned the protest. This hearing was a showcase for the key arguments for and against the play.[91] Dixon upheld the historical accuracy of *The Clansman* and criticized protesters for creating disorder. When Dixon read parts of the play out loud, with considerable dramatic flair, and then defended its truth ("I have documentary evidence for the truthfulness of every scene"), Sulzberger "impatiently" interrupted: "What do we care for that. History may be as false as a lie itself. Don't weary us with such matters. You can write a history of Pennsylvania from the records of the penitentiary, but that would not make it correct."[92] Many spectators cheered Sulzberger. A short time later Dixon stated that he had read more than five thousand volumes about Reconstruction. Sulzberger mocked him: "You mean to say that you have read 5,000 volumes on this subject?"[93] Then he chuckled.

Dixon and Sulzberger debated whether the protesters or the play were the source of danger. Dixon said to the judge, "It is a grave commentary on civilization that a mob of colored rioters can constitute themselves as censors of the drama and . . . close a historic theatre." But Sulzberger kept the focus on the play's incitement of violence and misrepresentation of African Americans. Sulzberger asked Dixon about the conclusion of the play, in which the Ku Klux Klan arrests the play's villain. "Oh! Then the government of the State is displaced and usurped by a body of citizens

Mayer Sulzberger, the judge who sparred with Thomas Dixon over *The Clansman*. Temple University Libraries, SCRC, Philadelphia, PA

who run things to suit themselves."[94] When Dixon complained about the egg-throwing in the theater, Sulzberger again disagreed, "So you make yourselves the judge and police the audience, I see. . . . The audiences may applaud, but may not show their disapproval."[95] Sulzberger and the director of public safety, Robert McKenty, agreed with Mayor Weaver that the African American preachers who organized the demonstration should have had "better sense."[96] But the city officials kept the primary focus on the play as the cause of violence. Later, the city solicitor challenged Dixon: "The whole tenor of the play then is derogatory to the colored man?" The audience burst into applause. Sulzberger quieted the courtroom. Weaver then took the stand to defend his decision, stating that he did not intend to endanger even "one citizen" for the benefit of "box office receipts." The crowd murmured its approval.[97] Sulzberger, in his final decision, explained that the "true object of the play . . . was to prove that the negro was so degraded as to be unable ever to improve his condition." He affirmed that the mayor had the power to stop a play that he thought would disrupt the public peace.[98]

Sulzberger may have been sympathetic to the leading African American advocates of Philadelphia because he was involved with organizations that were turning their attention to the harm of the Stage Jew. Several months before he heard *The Clansman* case, Sulzberger had started his six-year term as president of the new American Jewish Committee (AJC). The AJC drafted civil rights legislation to stop discrimination against Jews at American resorts. In 1907, for example, Louis Marshall, another AJC leader, began the process of amending an 1895 New York civil rights law to prohibit hotels from printing advertisements stating that the establishment would "refuse accommodations on the basis of a patron's race, color or creed."[99] In addition, Sulzberger denounced racism when he decided a case in favor of an African American man who had been refused service at a Pennsylvania inn. He wrote, "It appears . . . that men who have skin of various degrees of whiteness or yellowness or muddiness believe that they are the final sum of the Creator's wisdom, and that anybody whose complexion substantially differs from theirs is an inferior creature." Sulzberger found that the law, while not "powerful enough to overcome social prejudice," was able to "manage public matters." He found for the African American plaintiff, but awarded only nominal damages.[100]

The Clansman continued to tour through 1908, with some difficulties. In Harrisonburg, Virginia, in 1907, a theater electrician cut the lights (and the phone lines) in the first act of the play. A Des Moines city ordinance, passed after The Clansman played in the city in 1907, targeted productions that created racial animosity.[101] The first two seasons of The Clansman expanded race-based censorship unpredictably and unevenly, sometimes using the laws intended to ban Uncle Tom's Cabin, and also established a powerful justification for the suppression of the film adaptation of The Clansman—The Birth of a Nation—about a decade later. But before The Birth of a Nation unleashed another round of censorship debates, the Irish entered the fray to assert the racial harms of the Stage Irish in The Playboy of the Western World. Their path, for various reasons, was much different than the path of the African American campaign against The Clansman.

The Playboy of the Western World, the most famous play of the Irish national theater revival, started its American tour at the Plymouth Theatre in Boston in September 1911. It was already well known to Irish nationalists because it had a long, violent history. Gossip about the play's slurs on Irish woman-hood swirled around the play's debut in Dublin in 1907. Irish nationalists interrupted the middle of the third act, when Christy, the playboy, says, "It's Pegeen I'm seeking only, and wat'd I care if you brought me a drift of chosen females, standing in their shifts itself." The audience uproar drowned out the rest of the play. They challenged Synge's assertions of realism—in his introduction to the play he said that all the language had been "heard among the country people of Ireland, or spoken in my own nursery before I could read the papers."[102] Similar to complaints about *The Clansman*, Irish protesters objected to Lady Gregory's claims that *The Playboy* was "a true picture of Irish peasant life."[103] In other words, "It all comes down to truth or falsehood of the picture presented."[104]

The history of *The Playboy* riots contrasts sharply with the African American reaction to *The Clansman*. Irish nationalists proudly pledged disorder in the theater, though they did not always follow through. When they launched missiles of vegetables and stink bombs, they did not apologize. In general, however, they did take a more restrained course of speeches and boos in the auditorium than during earlier theater protests, and, from the start of *The Playboy* tour, they tried to get the law on their side. Irish nationalists did not succeed as official censors, in contrast to the African American victories over *The Clansman*. While the critics of *The Clansman* emphasized incitement to violence, those attempting to censor *The Playboy* focused on indecency and anti-Irish characterizations, with some marginal references to incitement to violence.

A noted Irish author, Seamus MacManus, summarized the series of un-Irish aspects of the play: "This play pictures these modest Irish maidens as tumbling over one another to win a blackguard, whose fascination is that he murdered his father. And, apart from the gross immodesty and repulsive vulgarity which the Irish colleen stands for in this play, I know of no other viler libel that could be put upon her than, as in the play, to show her throwing herself at the head of a scoundrel . . . throwing herself at him because he was now her ideal hero."[105] The Irish American press railed against the play as immoral and disrespectful to the Irish, particularly to Irish women.[106] "All the women jostling each other to pay court to him [the playboy]" upset Irish activists; they "force their attentions on the men, and the place selected for the contests for the possession of a man is the shebeen house."[107] When the Clan na Gael focused on the misrepresentation of Irish peasant women's sexuality in the play, it connected charges of indecency with claims of racial and national insult.

Controversy surrounding *The Playboy* died down in the following several years in Ireland, but the play was again embattled during its first American tour, beginning in 1911. Warnings in the Irish American press helped Irish communities prepare for the Boston opening. Irish American leaders compared the upcoming *Playboy* tour with the earlier Dublin riots over

Synge's play and with the attacks on *McFadden's Row of Flats* and the Russell Brothers: "We pledge ourselves as one man . . . to drive the vile thing from the stage, as we drove 'McFadden's Row of Flats' and the abomination produced by the Russell Brothers."[108] The memory of these rowdy uprisings was important, because even when the Irish protesters were orderly, the possibility of a rambunctious disruption remained a real threat. Thus, even when the confrontation did not move beyond boos and hisses, the tension between legal suppression of *The Playboy* and disruptive protests shaped the tour.

At the Boston opening of *The Playboy of the Western World*, the protest remained relatively restrained, limited to editorializing in the Irish nationalist press and hissing and booing in the theater. Spectators did not throw things or interrupt with speeches. Police officers removed the angry Irish spectators.[109] Harvard students, specifically recruited by Lady Gregory, countered the boos of Irish Americans with applause. The *Boston Globe* reported that "every hiss seemed to be . . . promptly met by applause."[110] Irish nationalist leaders explained that the protest would have been more robust if Abbey Theatre managers had not already radically "made over" the play. Only editing, they claimed, averted a riot.[111]

Protesters still hoped that the mayor would use his power to stop the play as a violation of the city's obscenity regulations. William Leahy, the Harvard-educated, Irish secretary to Mayor John Fitzgerald, as well as a city censor, represented the mayor at the play. He and the mayor surprised their Irish constituency by holding that the play was not obscene. Leahy reported that the play had "been softened from the original" by actors, and that, although the play was "rather coarse in parts," it was not obscene: "If obscenity is to be found on the stage in Boston, it must be sought elsewhere, and not at the Plymouth Theater."[112] He directly addressed the protesters' claim that the play gave a false image of the Irish, claiming "the sum of it all is not Ireland."[113] Irish nationalists conceded that Leahy was competent to judge obscenity, and that there was nothing obscene in the play. But they still asserted the connection between obscenity and racial insult. Leahy, they argued, was not competent to judge whether the play was an accurate representation of Irish life: "He knows absolutely nothing about Irish peasant life."[114] Furthermore, they claimed that the whole "tendency [of the play] is immoral," even if there was no scene or line that was "positively immoral or obscene."[115]

In Providence and New Haven, the play's next stops, the early pattern continued: protests remained reserved and efforts at official censorship failed. Protesters claimed the play had been edited to avert protests; Lady Gregory denied the charge. Congressman George F. O'Shaunessy, a Galway-born lawyer and legislator active in New York City politics prior to moving to Rhode Island, led a committee of Irish activists, many from the Ancient Order of Hibernians.[116] The committee met with the manager of the Providence Opera House, who then spoke with Lady Gregory. Gregory announced that no concessions were made to the Irish committee, and she touted the police commissioner's approval. But the Irish protesters said she lied; they claimed a "great moral victory" because of the eliminations from the play. The *Gaelic American* reported the most controversial parts were not in the play at the Providence Opera House, including references to "shifts" and the suckling of the black ram by the Widow Quinn. Lady Gregory quickly rebuffed this claim: "We gave the play to-night exactly as it has been given in London, Oxford, Cambridge . . . and the other night in Boston."[117] Defensive about their subdued protests in the theater, Irish nationalists claimed that they would have taken more decisive action in the theater if they had not been "lulled" by the promise of a clean presentation. But the extensive police presence, more than any broken promise, may have proven a more decisive factor.

Irish nationalists tried to use the threat of direct action for leverage in their backstage negotiations with producers and the police. The *Gaelic American* reported that a "wasp" editorial criticized O'Shaunessy for the "intimation of disorder in a theatre."[118] O'Shaunessy then explained, in a defensive letter, that he had "waited upon the Police Commissioners to suggest to them the advisability of suppressing the production unless the objectionable features were deleted. At no time, either directly or indirectly, did I suggest the possibility of any disorder arising in consequence of the play being allowed to be produced without expurgation, although the inference that I did so is almost unescapable from your published statements on the subject."[119]

During *The Playboy*'s New York engagement the disturbances increased; critics called the response a "Donnybrook Fair."[120] Early in the play, protesters stood up and called out, "Put 'em off," then hissed. Thomas P. Tuite, a Civil War veteran and nationalist who had been active in previous uprisings against the Stage Irishman, stood up in the auditorium and said, "decorously," "I protest against this play as an outrage on human nature, as an American citizen and an Irishman."[121] The *New York Times* reported that

Irish spectators then unleashed "a shower of vegetables that rattled against the scenery and made the actors duck their heads and fly behind the stage setting for shelter."[122] Witnesses reported some fights in the theater and noted that many spectators had been drenched in a foul-smelling, milky potion. A spectator in the gallery tossed a potato onto the stage, hitting an actress, Miss Magee, who "glared" defiantly back at the crowd.[123] Reports of the number of arrests vary widely—from ten to two hundred. Many who were not arrested found themselves simply tossed out of the theater during the first act. Once officials had quieted the venue, the performers started over from the beginning. Hisses and a few potatoes continued to punctuate the play. Seven of the people arrested were fined and police released three without fines.

The violence was controversial, both among the Irish community and among non-Irish observers. An editorial in the *Christian Science Monitor* explained that the "tactical folly of the methods" would be obvious to "less emotional and more rational objectors." These methods cast the Irish activists as hot-tempered and disorderly—just the images some Irish were trying to remedy—and also attracted more attention to the play, making "friends for the company, Lady Gregory and Mr. Yeats."[124] Another journalist observed that the protesters' behavior simply proved "the Gaelic sympathy with rebellion in almost any form," which was one of the offensive themes of Synge's play.[125] The Irish leaders responded by denying that the protest took place, and by claiming that it was spontaneous, not prearranged. Yet even their disclaimers contained an element of pride: "There was what the papers call a 'riot' in descriptions full of exaggeration, but they all admit that was the most remarkable and determined demonstration ever made against a play in a New York theatre."[126] They also placed blame on Jewish police officers who became "brutal" in the theater, and also Jewish theater managers and Jewish newspapers, who ran New York City "to suit themselves," according to an Irish editorial.[127] They continued to disparage Jews, calling Lady Gregory a "Shylock."[128] In general, the Irish tried to redirect attacks on their own propriety by emphasizing Jewish immorality.

The Irish protesters also defended themselves by making comparisons to another group of protesters—a group of Yale football players who had trashed the Hyperion in New Haven when a singer's risqué act was cut short. On a Saturday evening after a Yale football game, the curtain had come down surprisingly early on Gaby Deslys's *Vera Violetta* at the Hyperion. The city's police censor had contacted the theater manager after the

The Latest Emanation of "The Mind of Ireland."

THE "PLAYBOY" AND HIS PROTECTORS.

A cartoon mocking *The Playboy of the Western World*, William Butler Yeats, and Lady Augusta Gregory. *Gaelic American*, December 2, 1911

previous evening's performance and the play was shortened, partly in anticipation of a rowdy football crowd. When the show stopped abruptly, with no explanation, Yale students ripped up the chairs, broke the stage footlights, and destroyed other decorations in the theater. Then they rushed the stage, tried to bring up the curtain, and fought with the stagehands, who responded by turning fire hoses on the audience. Performers and protesters rushed out of the theater, as more students arrived from a nearby dormitory to throw rocks at the theater. News reports estimated that eight hundred men were involved in the riot—"the wildest football night riot in history."[129] Six spectators were arrested. Five of them—all Yale students—were released on bail. A Yale dean, Frederick Jones, backed the students: he criticized the police for arresting the students because he believed they had not participated in the riot, and he accused them of treating the students too roughly. Police dropped the charges against a lawyer who had also been arrested and then apologized for his arrest.[130]

Irish American nationalists maligned the Yale rioters for several reasons. For one, the opportunity to critique Yale students was particularly satisfying to Irish nationalists because Ivy League college students had backed *The Playboy of the Western World*. Lady Gregory, often bragged that college students truly appreciated the literary genius of the play, which she said was included on some Ivy League reading lists. Gregory recalled that Harvard and Yale "demanded" engagements of The Playboy, and in Boston, Harvard students had cheered it on in response to the hisses and shouts of Irish Americans.[131] Irish American nationalists, then, relished this chance to cast the literary, Protestant elites of Yale as an unruly mob of sexual deviants. In this light, the Irish American protesters were respectable though unfairly maligned gentlemen. Second, the contrast with the Yale riot proved important in the Irish attempt to defend the Playboy rioters. Their protesters fought against immorality, not for more illicit sexuality, as the Yale students did. They did not receive an apology from the theater manager, though the Yale undergraduates did. An editorial in the radical Gaelic American summarized the comparison: "Let it not be forgotten that the protest of the Yale students who wrecked the Hyperion Theatre was on behalf of 'hot stuff' while the dignified protest of the men and women at Maxine Elliott's Theatre was against obscenity and vile presentations on the stage. But the Yale students belonged to a 'respectable element' and that covered their sins."[132]

Irish protesters in New York City failed in their efforts to have city authorities censor the play for "endangering public morals." But their pressure forced some modifications. Actors assured the chief magistrate, William McAdoo, that they had edited out troublesome lines about "shifts."[133] McAdoo decided that the play did not warrant suppression, although he acknowledged problems. He explained that the play did offend one segment of the audience, those who believed it was a "brutal piece of alleged realism intended to depict, to their disadvantage, social and moral conditions in a part of Ireland."[134] He said he understood Irish resentment, but stopped short of condemning the play for maligning the Irish. In addition, he observed that the play included "coarse suggestiveness," yet he did not think it was as explicit or "salacious" as in other recent plays. He did not recommend censoring the play because a "play may offend against good taste, truth, racial pride, national tradition and religious conviction, and yet not be of such an immoral character as to call for suppression."[135] When The Playboy appeared in Chicago later in January, Mayor Harrison declined to use his discretionary power to stop it. An Irish American alderman, Mike McInerney, pushed the city council to pass an order to the mayor to halt the play. Harrison, after deliberating with his staff and reading the play, decided not to ban it because he considered it neither immoral nor indecent. But

Harrison took an even stronger free-speech position than earlier officials. He acknowledged a certain danger of the play leading to violence, but he concluded that "it does not follow that because the delivery of a speech or the acting of a play is liable to lead to a breach of the peace it is such an abuse of the right of free speech as to justify the authorities in preventing it."[136] The play ultimately enjoyed a "tranquil premiere" to a sparse audience on February 6, 1912.[137]

When *The Playboy* moved on to Philadelphia, the Irish protesters did not throw anything on stage or fight, according to newspaper accounts. Yet this did not stop the press from calling their response to *The Playboy* a riot. On January 15, at the play's debut at the Adelphi Theatre, Irish spectators hissed and shouted when Pegeen Mike's father departed, leaving her with the "the playboy" overnight. Various nationalists stood up to speak against the play; they interrupted actors and tried to shame spectators into leaving. Joseph McGarrity, a leader of the Clan na Gael, stood up first, announcing, "Shame on you Irish players, and shame on a play which is a disgrace to Ireland." As police escorted him out, he shouted, "Shame on any decent woman who will see this play or act a part in it."[138] Joseph McLaughlin, the vice president of the Ancient Order of Hibernians and the owner of a bar in Philadelphia, took the floor to denounce the play. Some spectators who recognized him shouted, "Put the saloonkeeper out." The police did just that. Twenty-nine Irishmen were ejected; two were arrested.[139] At the second production, fourteen men were arrested after they disrupted the play with hisses, coughs, and cries of "shame." Press reports acknowledged that the Philadelphia protesters, unlike their New York brethren, did not throw "substantial missiles" at the opening night, although they did resort to tossing eggs and cakes following the production.[140] Forewarned by the conflicts in New York City, police were well prepared for the disruption in Philadelphia. It is difficult to say whether the intense police protection or Irish design created the vigorous yet restrained protest.

The Irish nationalists asked, "What meaning has the word morality in Lady Gregory's mind?"[141] Joseph McGarrity's and Joseph McLaughlin's speeches in the theater, as opposed to the vegetable missiles in New York City and other sites, helped position the protesters as moral censors. They tried to claim the same moral and artistic plane occupied by Lady Gregory and other promoters of *The Playboy*. One article in the *Gaelic American* stated that the "only dramatic things are done by the audience when 'the Playboy' is presented ... they are spontaneous ebullitions of feeling, show-

Joseph McGarrity, Irish nationalist who opposed *The Playboy of the Western World*. Joseph McGarrity Photographs and Realia Collection. Digital Library @Villanova University. This work is licensed under a Creative Commons Attribution-ShareAlike 3.0 Unported License.

ing that Irish people in America have still red blood in their veins and think and act like real human beings, these manifestations constitute true 'Art.'"[142] McLaughlin added, "I hold that a man who attends a performance has as much right to show disgust as approval."[143] In this light, those who interrupted the play were the artists; they had the right to freedom of expression.

Irish Americans now pressed their objections to the play in terms of decency and public order, with marginal references to the play's misrepresentation of the Irish. A committee of Irish nationalists, representing the Ancient Order of Hibernians, Clan na Gael, and other societies, visited the mayor. Mayor Rudolph Blankenburg, a recently elected reformer, answered, "If an Irish Mayor of Boston does not object to the play, here seems to be no justification for action by myself."[144] The Irish nationalists noted Philadelphia's refusal to recognize the racial prejudice in the play, particularly in comparison with the apparent sympathy of the Pittsburg press to this argument. "Anything that aggravates racial or religious prejudices is to be deplored."[145]

The protesters tried a new tactic in their pursuit of official censorship

Joseph McGarrity with friends and family at Atlantic City. Joseph McGarrity Photographs and Realia Collection. Digital Library @Villanova University. This work is licensed under a Creative Commons Attribution-ShareAlike 3.0 Unported License.

on January 17. Based on affidavits drawn up McGarrity, the Irish players were arrested for violation of the McNichol Act of 1911, which prohibited "lascivious, obscene, indecent, sacrilegious or immoral" plays. McGarrity held that the play was immoral, blasphemous, and a misrepresentation of the Irish.[146] It was a bold move for a liquor dealer to claim the upper hand in morality. One journalist remarked on the irony of a saloon-keeper taking actors to court for the "protection of Ireland's good name."[147] In the afternoon, on January 19, 1912, Magistrate Carey held a hearing of the Irish players. The city's director of public safety, testified that he and his wife found nothing shocking about the play: "There was nothing to offend the most devout and reverent of women."[148] McGarrity then explained that he thought the play was "immoral and blasphemous" and that he had a right to express that opinion in the theater.[149] Judge Carr, however, asked why he did not simply leave the theater. John Quinn, one of the attorneys for the actors, turned the charge of immorality back on McGarrity. The play itself was not immoral, so a person who thought it was "must have a depraved mind. I am ashamed that men should come here and insult womanhood with their views. The American people are too good a judge of the Irish race to agree with them."[150] The defenders of the play also pointed to the absence of any public disturbance in Boston, New Haven, and Providence. The judge quickly dismissed the charges without explanation.

The success of the African American struggle against *The Clansman* had conservative roots and overtones. It was based as much on fears of unruly African Americans as it was on the goal of stopping racial ridicule; it was also built on the laws used to suppress critiques of white supremacy. Above all, the censorship of *The Clansman* underscored African American vulnerability. The immediate context of race riots and lynchings made the case against *The Clansman* urgent. If the violence outside the theater propelled more censorship of *The Clansman*, the Irish protesters' disorder in *The Playboy*'s auditoriums did not inspire bans. The unapologetic rowdiness of the Irish nationalists, in contrast with the orderly meetings of the black protesters, showed that the Irish enjoyed a level of physical safety that allowed them to battle to control the American stage on their own terms. They had more success with direct confrontations than they did when saloon owners accused *The Playboy* of indecency in court. Gallery censorship, though somewhat sanitized, remained the calling card of Irish nationalists.

These plays not only raised questions about the harms of racial ridicule; they also introduced questions about the appropriate methods and boundaries of censorship. Dixon put himself on the side of free speech and blamed city officials for buckling under the "mob of colored rioters [who] constitute themselves as censors."[151] A critic of the Chicago city council's order to suppress *The Playboy* worried that a majority of aldermen had not even read or seen the play. He concluded, "If we are going to kill freedom of speech let us be systematic about it."[152] A decade after *The Playboy* controversy in the United States, stronger calls for free speech emerged along with a search for more democratic means of censorship. In 1922, New York City's chief magistrate accepted a plan for a "Play Jury," twelve jurors drawn from a large pool of citizens from a variety of professions (not theater or social reform, to ensure impartiality).[153] Yet complaints about racial misrepresentation could still yield bans if they hid behind obscenity. In the 1920s a nascent free-speech organizational network battled the flimsy use of obscenity as a cover for politically and socially significant speech.

Charges of racial ridicule and obscenity converged again in 1923, when *The God of Vengeance*, by the Jewish writer Sholem Asch, was barred under

New York City's obscenity statute. The play depicted a rabbi who ran a brothel but tried in vain to protect his daughter from a life of immorality. A lesbian prostitute ultimately seduces her. *The God of Vengeance* had played in Yiddish theaters since 1907. The theater historian Nina Warnke shows that the Yiddish press debated the censorship of the play when it first opened, but in 1923 when the play appeared in English on Broadway, the debate erupted in the mainstream press. The shift to Broadway made elite Jews of German descent anxious about how Eastern European Jews represented them to Gentile audiences. City authorities investigated the play after Rabbi Silverman, then retired from Temple Emanu-El, complained about the play's unfavorable depiction of Jewish religious leaders. Officials bypassed the Play Jury and convened a grand jury instead. The charges of defamation incited the legal action against the play, but the grand jury debated whether or not the play's prostitutes and lesbians made the work obscene. The local statute outlawed plays "which would tend to the corruption of the morals of youth or others."[154] The cast and Harry Weinberger, the play's producer, were found guilty of violating the local anti-obscenity statute in May of 1923. The appellate court affirmed the lower court decision without comment in June 1924.[155] This was the first play to be convicted under the anti-obscenity statute in thirty years, but the conviction was overturned.

The conviction ignited a legal drama that pitted First Amendment advocates—the Free Speech League and the more conservative American Civil Liberties Union (ACLU)—against one another as their leaders debated whether or not *The God of Vengeance* constituted a politically significant free-speech case. Did *The God of Vengeance* contain controversial, unpopular ideas, or was it simply an immoral play? The ACLU was not interested in protecting immoral entertainment, but it was concerned about "freedom of opinion." Weinberger had helped defend Emma Goldman and other radical speakers in their court battles, and he was upset that obscenity served as a legal cover for the real complaints against the play. As he explained, there was the "Jewish side" and the question of whether the play was "'obscene, indecent, immoral or impure, which tends to the corruption of the morals of youth and others,' which is what the law requires the play to be before it is a violation of law."[156]

Rabbi Silverman was not alone in his attack on the play's anti-Semitism. Several Jews complained directly to Weinberger about how the play humiliated Jews. One Jewish patron wrote, "When Jews have so much to contend with in our social problems from race or religious prejudice . . . why add more fire to it with a vicious phase of a part of Jewish life?"[157] Weinberger tried to convince some Jewish leaders to support the play. He urged Samuel Schulman, a well-known rabbi, "to see whether or not this play written by one of the greatest living Jewish writers of modern times, acted almost entirely by a Jewish cast and a Jewish manager and a Jewish owner of the theatre, could by any stretch of the imagination be considered anti-Semitic. That it is not immoral is beyond question." He pressed Schulman to consider whether the play was any more anti-Semitic than *The Scarlet Letter* was "anti-Christian?"[158] Schulman refused to get involved and rejected the comparison with *The Scarlet Letter*. "Jews are being attacked from all sides. And a Jewish author and Jewish players should consider whether they should present anything which might contribute to increase antipathy against the Jews."[159]

Weinberger's efforts to expand support for the play show the fissures in the early free-speech organizations in the United States. Throughout the appeals process Weinberger worked with his colleagues in the Free Speech League (FSL) to convince Roger Baldwin and the ACLU to defend his play, but Baldwin had "very strong doubts" about the case.[160] The two main groups at the time, the FSL (founded in 1902) and the ACLU (established in 1920), differed in their approach to the First Amendment rights of performers and producers in commercial entertainment. Nearly two decades prior to the establishment, the FSL defended individual expression broadly, without exceptions for obscene or racist speech. It defended free speech as part of its "libertarian radicalism," but it did not focus on "needy radicals"; instead, it defended "nonpolitical" speakers, religious speakers, and dramatists, as well as radicals.[161] The FSL also defended the principle of free speech regardless of the viewpoint or content of the speech: it never refused to assist a beleaguered speaker on "ideological grounds."[162]

Theodore Schroeder, a leader of the FSL and a prolific writer and theorist about free speech, agreed to help Weinberger. Weinberger's case fit well with Schroeder's position of defending all speech, regardless of the particular viewpoint, and treating obscenity cases in the theater as politically significant. Schroeder concluded that the Constitution "made no exception for any particular class of intellectual 'evils,' but protected them all alike."[163] Schroeder, in particular, opposed the suppression of *The Clansman* in Philadelphia; he saw this as a case of shutting down the "discussion of the negro problem in the North." He advocated that officials "suppress disorder which might possibly result from discussion than to suppress freedom of speech itself."[164] Weinberger and Schroeder lobbied the ACLU, but the ACLU rejected the FSL's expansive approach to censorship, ignoring obscenity and censorship in the arts in its early years to focus primarily on political speech, which it deemed important for the search for truth in a democratic society.[165]

In their case to Roger Baldwin at the ACLU, Schroeder and Weinberger did not emphasize that attacks on obscenity in the arts should become a prominent free-speech issue, though Schroeder wrote extensively about this elsewhere. Rather, to convince Baldwin of the play's importance, Schroeder and Weinberger emphasized the defamation claims raised against the play, even though these were not the legal basis of suppressing the play. These objections about the depiction of Jews, they argued, were an attempt to stifle an unpopular opinion, not a crusade against immorality. Weinberger and Schroeder compared *The God of Vengeance* to *What Price Glory*, a pacifist play that featured two drunken, vulgar marines who were hardly the "selfless patriots who populated previous American war dramas."[166] Military officials had complained to the mayor of New York City that the play maligned the Marine Corps, and others complained to the Department of Justice, arguing that the play violated a section of the National Defense Act barring individuals outside the military from wearing army, navy, or marine uniforms. The producer cut some of the lines, but otherwise the complaints did not deter the play's successful run.[167]

Weinberger and Schroeder pursued the comparison of *What Price Glory* with *The God of Vengeance* because Baldwin had already accepted the former play as a free-speech issue. Weinberger explained to Baldwin that censors attacked *What Price Glory* because it maligned the military: "I suppose if the play was written the other way round, the Army and Navy officials would be in favor of it."[168] Then Weinberger elaborated on another similarity: both plays were attacked as immoral, but were actually censored for the viewpoints they presented:

> Just as in the "What Price Glory" play, the real argument against the play is that it is a pacifist play and in case of indictment they should be indicted on the basis that the play is either immoral because of its swear words ... or if the US indicted on the ground that it interferes

with the recruiting, while in the case of the "God of Vengeance" the real objection of certain Jews is that it showed the Jews in a bad light.[169]

In general, Weinberger complained about liberals veering "off when the cry of 'immorality' or 'obscenity' is raised, not fully realizing that liberties are destroyed under a thousand pretexts of all kinds, from 'blocking traffic,' 'disorderly conduct' 'inciting to riot,' 'obscenity.'"[170]

Baldwin believed that *What Price Glory* was a "free speech matter" but he did not accept the analogy with *The God of Vengeance*.[171] He explained that the latter case is "not primarily one of freedom of opinion—it is one of censorship on the ground of morality. . . . 'What Price Glory' much more clearly involves the issue of freedom of opinion. . . . We do not believe that the right of the public to censor plays on the ground of morality can be questioned."[172] Weinberger countered: "I do not get what distinction you draw, if any, between the 'God of Vengeance' which represents a picture which some Jews object to, and 'What Price Glory' which picture some military and naval men object to."[173] Two days later he elaborated on the essential similarity of these controversial plays:

> Every worthwhile play is consciously a piece of propaganda, to put across some kind of message of social consequence. Whether that message is spoken in the ordinary way of a sermon or lecture, or is accompanied by a theatrical stage setting and stage clothing, surely must be immaterial to its classification as raising a free speech issue when censored. Think of this in relation to present discussion over the censorship of a pacifist play ("What Price Glory") and I am sure you must see what I mean. In the "God of Vengeance" case the proposition is: can a phase of life be shown even if it is about Rabbis.[174]

Weinberger and Schroeder thus pressed these questions: Was the theatrical depiction of a minority group, particularly the representation of that group as sexually immoral, politically significant? Did the misrepresentation of a minority on stage or screen invite a rational debate, leading to the discovery of truth? At this point, the ACLU answered no.

While these civil rights groups differed in their approach to obscenity and theatrical productions, they were in agreement in their opposition to race-based censorship. Schroeder believed that minority political views were often wrongly censored as "obscenity."[175] In contrast, Zechariah

Chafee, who often worked with the ACLU, claimed that obscene words were not an "essential part of any exposition of ideas [and] have a very slight social value as a step toward truth."[176] Furthermore, obscene or profane utterances, he explained, did not invite "counter -argument."[177] Chafee's views seem closer to Schroeder's, however, in his concern about the censorship of views about race relations. Chafee, for example, briefly mentioned the injustice of censoring unpopular views about race relations, including films and plays: "There are always men who want the law . . . to nip opinions in the bud before they become dangerous because they may eventually be dangerous," wrote Chafee. As an example, Chafee listed not only speeches in the South calling for the abolition of slavery but also plays like *Mrs. Warren's Profession*. He also objected to a section of a federal sedition bill that banned appeals to racial prejudice in the mail. Such an exclusion, in Chafee's view, would "suppress all but the most carefully guarded presentations of the wrongs of the negro."[178] In his footnote to this section, he criticized West Virginia's restrictions on race irritation in the movies.[179] Similarly, Schroeder, in *Free Speech for Radicals* (1916), expressed concern about the Philadelphia's "suppression of a play obnoxious to the negro population."[180] In this light, the protests against *The Clansman* and *The Playboy of the Western World* did more than expand the network of race-based censorship; they also caught the attention of early free-speech activists who began to see the political significance of censoring entertainment. As the following chapters show, race-based movie censorship built on the traditions established by African American and Irish theater protests. Minority groups demanded representation as censors, but learned that race-based censorship laws did not consistently favor them.

CHAPTER FOUR

SHYLOCK AND SAMBO CENSORED

Jewish and African American Campaigns for
Race-Based Motion Picture Censorship

The censorship struggles over racial representation in legitimate theater quickly moved to the regulation of the new medium of motion pictures. In 1907, the African American attorney S. Joe Brown succeeded in getting Des Moines to pass an ordinance against any "inflammatory play . . . calculated . . . to create an antipathy for any particular race, nationality or class of individuals," but it failed to stop its intended target, *The Clansman*. Black activists turned to this law, however, when they tried to stop *The Birth of a Nation*, the film version of *The Clansman*.[1] Just eight months after Des Moines acted against *The Clansman*, Adolf Kraus, a Jewish lawyer, philanthropist, and civic leader in Chicago, drafted the nation's first motion picture censorship law. This new law did not simply ban "immoral or obscene" films; it also allowed police to obstruct any movie that "portrays depravity, criminality or lack of virtue of a class of citizens of any race, color, creed of religion and exposes them to contempt, derision or obloquy."[2] In his actions, Kraus was likely responding to *The Clansman*, but also to the American Jewish Committee's effort to ban hotel advertising that defamed any race or announced a racially discriminatory policy, and to George Kibbe Turner's sensationalistic account of Jewish criminals in his *McClure's Magazine* article of April that year.[3] Thus, with some overlapping motivations an African American pioneer in Des Moines and a Jewish leader in Chicago passed censorship laws designed to protect not only their respective group but other minorities as well. This chapter focuses on how African Americans and Jews arrived at this same point of race-based motion picture censorship.

For Jews and African Americans, the pain of social exclusion, the shame of accusations of criminality, and the fear of violence motivated their efforts

to reform racial representations in popular culture, converging, in particular, on the censorship of the new medium of motion pictures. Yet these
similarities and the common endpoint should not obscure the differences
in the gravity of the threats facing each group. While African Americans
battled the scourge of lynching in the United States, Jews also knew the fear
of vigilante violence: they were shocked by the lynching of Leo Frank and
the violence against Jews in Europe. But they were, undoubtedly, safer than
blacks in the United States. The image of Jewish criminality was predomi-
nantly one of dishonest business practices, but the image of the African
American rapist was often at the root of vigilante violence against blacks.
Jews faced several high-profile exclusions from summer resorts and started
a campaign to stop these, while African Americans faced pervasive segregation in public accommodations. During this period, the African American
focus on ending discrimination in public amusements took priority over
reforming images on stage and screen. Representations insulted Jews, but
they endangered African Americans.[4]

Jewish organizations became involved in antidefamation activity around
1907, six years before the establishment of the B'nai B'rith's Anti-Defamation
League (ADL) in 1913. When the ADL became the leading self-defense
agency after 1913, it took over the work of a variety of groups, including the
Central Conference of American Rabbis (CCAR) and the National Council of Jewish Women (NCJW).[5] The campaign against the Stage Jew had
emerged from two "needs": a competition over who or what organization
would lead (or represent) the Jews and a rise in the affronts to Jews in the
early twentieth century. In this section I situate the ADL's ascendance in
competition with other Jewish voices, and compare the broad campaign
against the Stage Jew with African American efforts to challenge inaccurate,
harmful images.

Jewish leaders began to focus on the representation of Jews in advertising
in response to discrimination against Jews in hotels and resorts. In the most
famous case, Judge Henry Hilton rejected the wealthy businessman Joseph
Seligman from the Grand Hotel in Saratoga Springs in 1877. After this incident, Jewish exclusionary policies spread to less affluent establishments and
increased over time. In the Catskill Mountains, for example, in the 1890s,
surveys noted advertisements stating "No Hebrews Taken." This kind of
"race prejudice" was most pronounced in areas with many Jewish vacation-
ers. But the restrictions were not limited to resorts: Jews were largely barred

from private schools and college fraternities, and they were segregated in the housing market through the use of restricted covenants in urban areas.[6] In May of 1907, a clerk at the Marlborough-Blenheim Hotel in Atlantic City denied a room to Bertha Rayner Frank: "We don't entertain Hebrews," the clerk told Frank, the sister of Maryland senator Isidor Rayner. Her story then became front-page news in the *New York Times*, which reported that many Jews had sought rooms in Atlantic City but that the hotel management had told them: "The patronage of Hebrews is not solicited."[7]

One of the oldest American Jewish organizations, the American Jewish Committee (AJC), responded to the Frank incident with a legislative agenda. Well-established Jews had founded the AJC in 1906 against a backdrop of Russian pogroms: a devastating wave in October 1905 in western Russia had left more than two thousand people dead, injured, or homeless.[8] The organization's founders had been born in the United States or educated there, but culturally they hailed from Central Europe—usually from the region that became Germany in 1871—with careers in law or business, and many had extensive philanthropic experience. The AJC's goals were "not stated as efforts to solve anti-Semitism but merely to protect the civil and religious rights of Jews and care for the victims of disaster."[9] Convinced that anti-Semitism was primarily a European problem, the AJC directed much of its early work toward Europe, including relief for European Jews. The AJC fought against passport restrictions on American Jews who wanted to travel in Russia; it also protested the U.S. Immigration Act of 1907, which increased the head tax on arriving immigrants, and objected to a 1909 bill classifying Jews as a race in the 1910 census.[10] The AJC avoided public demonstrations and attention that would disrupt the "image of integration," preferring the "private approach of the shtadlan or *Hofjude*—the rich and influential Jew who interceded with Gentiles on behalf of his brethren in a spirit of benevolent paternalism."[11]

In 1907, in the context of local snubs and European violence, the AJC began working to amend civil rights legislation in New York State and to outlaw anti-Semitic resort discrimination and the advertisement of those exclusions. With this effort, Jews joined African Americans who had worked to expand and enforce civil rights legislation in the state since the early 1890s, but Jews diverged from blacks by focusing on defamatory advertising rather than unequal access. State civil rights laws had become paramount after 1883, when the Supreme Court had ruled the federal Civil Rights Act of 1875 unconstitutional. In 1895, African American legislators secured the passage of a new civil rights law in New York, which increased the types of venues covered by and the penalties for violating it. After 1895, New York guaranteed all people equal access to "inns, restaurants, hotels, eating houses, bathhouses, barber shops, theatres, music halls, public conveyances on land and water, and all other places of public accommodation or amusement."[12] When African Americans tested the law soon after its passage, they found considerable compliance, except in bathhouses, but a few years later, surveys of restaurants and theaters showed that the law had not been effective. Hotel and restaurant proprietors used different strategies for discouraging African American patronage, including discourteous service or poor seating.[13]

Jews expressed little public interest in the 1895 legislation, but after the Bertha Rayner Frank case in 1907, the AJC turned its attentions to hotel discrimination and New York's civil rights law. Louis Marshall, a lawyer and one of the founders of the AJC, was one of Frank's friends. He believed that the scandal of her exclusion could prompt the passage of a law to remedy the wider problem. He encouraged the New York state senator Martin Saxe to introduce a bill to broaden the state's 1895 antidiscrimination law. Saxe, whose district included the west side of Manhattan, had the support of African Americans and Jewish voters.[14] Marshall wanted to extend the list of sites where people were protected from discrimination, because the original list did not include resorts. The most significant departure from previous revisions was Marshall's proposed ban on offensive advertisement, such as "No Jews and Dogs Permitted."[15] Marshall convinced his friend, Adolph Ochs, the editor of the *New York Times*, to publish an editorial supporting the bill, and also wrote to the New York governor Charles Evans Hughes to try to persuade him of the harms of anti-Semitic advertisements. Despite this lobbying, the Saxe Bill died in the Judiciary Committee because of the opposition of the conservative New York State Senate.

Six years later the bill reached the assembly floor, in the hands of a New York City Democrat, A. J. Levy. Now known as the Levy Bill, the legislation included a more expansive definition of hotels as public accommodations and banned the advertising of discriminatory admission practices, but it did not otherwise extend the 1895 act's prohibitions. The Jewish authors used inclusive language in the bill, protecting "persons of every race, faith, creed or color."[16] It passed the Assembly and Senate in 1913 and went into effect on September 1, 1913, when Democrats, particularly those representing New York City, gained more power in state politics. In 1913 the state legislature was more Democratic than it had been in 1907, and the number of Jewish voters in New York had dramatically increased since 1907, as approximately forty thousand Jewish immigrants settled in the state in that six-year period.[17]

Jews had drafted a law that protected minorities broadly, thus showing an affinity with African Americans, but in other ways Jews distanced themselves from African Americans in the discussion and in the implementation of the civil rights law. In the debate over the law, many Jews reported little support for equal access, but significant enthusiasm for the ban on insulting advertisements. The focus on advertising set them apart from African Americans who struggled against widespread exclusion from and segregation in public accommodations but who were less concerned with advertising because the segregation of African Americans was so well known that it did not need to be advertised. Marshall admitted that "the admission or exclusion of guests . . . is a matter in which I have but little interest."[18] The publicity committee of District 6 of the B'nai B'rith, the precursor to the Anti-Defamation League, also complained only of the insulting advertisements, not of the discriminatory policies behind them: "Whether a certain social circle bars Jews or whether certain hotels regard Jewish patronage as undesirable is of little consequence to us. When, however, these facts are used in such a manner that they will poison the mind of the public and the same is so advertised that the public are led to believe that the Jew is unfit and undesirable, then it is our duty to resent the insult, to protect the goodly name."[19] The 1913 law, therefore, did not align Jewish and African American interests. Although African Americans followed the bill's progress, many saw it as catering only to Jews. The black press thus paid little attention to the law, probably because African Americans did not see the law as significantly affecting them.[20]

Throughout the debates concerning the law, Jews expressed anxiety about any links between African Americans and themselves. Some argued that such a law was necessary because "the Jew cannot take position with the negro [sic] as an undesirable in places offering accommodations to the general public."[21] On the other hand, Rabbi Max Heller wrote in the Cincinnati-based American Israelite that little would be gained by the legislation and that it also entailed the risk of associating Jews with African Americans in the public mind: "The whole force of prejudice against the negro [sic] would be arrayed against Jewish advocates of civil rights legislation."[22]

For fifteen years after the passage of the New York civil rights law, the

AJC and the ADL pressed for other states to institute similar laws, but they often adapted the wording to focus on religion and nationality, undermining the more inclusive terminology of race. In Pennsylvania, for example, the ADL and the AJC advocated for a similar law beginning in 1915, and, in 1917, the Pennsylvania state legislature passed a law preventing the "publication and distribution of discriminating matter against any religious sect, creed, class, denomination or nationality."[23] By 1926, seven states had passed laws against discriminatory advertising and access: Illinois, Colorado, Connecticut, New Hampshire, Pennsylvania, Maine, and New York.[24] The laws supported by the ADL and AJC usually addressed both advertising and access, but insulting advertising seemed to be more important to these Jewish groups and, in some cases, constituted the law's sole focus. New Hampshire, for example, banned discriminatory advertising, not the practice of discrimination; it prohibited "advertising intended or calculated to discriminate against any religious sect, class or nationality, or against any member thereof, as such, in the matter of board, lodging or accommodation, privilege or convenience offered to the general public at places of public accommodation."[25] In the ADL's first annual report, published in 1915, the organization's president, Sigmund Livingston, explained, "The chief evil is not the discrimination but in the method by which that discrimination is made known."[26]

An anti-Semitic advertisement in *Outlook* tested the new law in New York. In May of 1913, this advertisement simply stated, "No Jews allowed." Marshall wrote to the editor, Lawrence Abbott, asking him to cancel the ad without any legal enforcement. Abbott claimed the advertisement's publication had been inadvertent, and that if he had known about it ahead of time, he would not have published it, regardless of the law. Marshall felt that Abbott's agreement to remove the text affirmed the law's power. But the advertisement ran again with new phrasing—"Gentiles only." Marshall believed that the law was comprehensive enough to stop that wording as well, but he was wrong. Hoteliers began to use new terms for exclusion— "restricted clientele" and "churches nearby," for example—which all readers understood to indicate discriminatory practices.[27]

One key motivation for Jewish anti-defamation work was segregation from summer resorts; another was the sensationalistic assertion of Jewish criminality in 1907 and 1908. Beginning in April 1907, with the publication of George Kibbe Turner's exposé titled "The City of Chicago," Jewish criminality in relation to prostitution became a controversial topic. Turner claimed that the procurers of prostitutes in Chicago were largely "Russian Jews."[28] In September of 1908, Theodore Bingham, the New York City police commissioner, issued a controversial report on immigrants and crime in the city. In the *North American Review* article he estimated that Jews were responsible for half of all the crimes in New York City.[29] He claimed that Jewish crime mainly involved property and that is was only natural that persons not physically fit for hard labor became criminals: "[Russian Hebrews] are burglars, firebugs, pickpockets and highway robbers—when they have the courage."[30] He put particular emphasis on the dangers of white slavery. In November 1909, Turner wrote another article on immigrants and prostitution, this time focusing on New York City, "Daughters of the Poor," which again appeared in *McClure's*. This piece revealed innocent immigrant girls lured into white slavery; many of the accounts involved Jewish men and prostitutes.

The Jewish response to these charges of criminality reveals the breadth of concern with representation of Jews in the press and in popular entertainment as well as the tensions within the Jewish community, mainly between older and newer immigrants. The AJC and the elite Jews of New York City, such as Louis Marshall and Jacob Schiff, both affluent Jewish philanthropists from German-speaking families, did not initially offer a strong rebuttal, but they ultimately competed with the Eastern European Jews to right Bingham's wrong. Their lack of interest in public sparring over this matter was tied to Marshall's belief that the charges were "partly true" and to "uptown" Jews' distrust of the angry "immigrant leaders." Some Jewish leaders also discreetly acknowledged Jewish participation in organized crime.[31] Indeed, Jewish social workers and civic leaders had been working against Jewish crime in the years leading up to the release of Bingham's report. Historians have noted that Jewish involvement with crimes of physical violence was low, but that their participation in white-collar crime was significant.[32]

While the AJC remained reserved, Jews from the Lower East Side became loud and angry—at Bingham and at the complacency of other Jews. Some scholars suggest that the "self-righteous" and "heated" Jewish reactions to Bingham, Turner, and others suggest Jewish culpability.[33] The *Tageblatt* asked, "When someone refused to allow a [Jewish] aristocrat into a Gentile hotel, the Jewish four hundred did not rest until the guilty party had been dismissed; and now—they are quiet! Is it because the ones insulted are Russian Jews?"[34] Four Yiddish dailies called Commissioner Bingham an anti-Semite and his essay a lie.[35] They criticized Marshall and

Schiff for their "inexcusable passivity," yet the East Side Jews understood their dependence on these "men of influence."[36] It was not just the lackadaisical, chaotic response that bothered the East Side Jewish community; it was also the apparent disdain for the Jewish immigrant population.

On September 13, 1908, Marshall began to negotiate a deal: Bingham would publically retract his charge of Jewish criminality, and East Side Jews would no longer demand Bingham's resignation and instead accept the case as closed. Marshall would also announce that the controversy was over. The pressure of a new coalition of East Side Jewish groups and the AJC forced Bingham to retract his charges. But this did not bring closure on the issue. There was ongoing conflict between the characterization of the immigrant quarter as an ideal slum—with a healthy community spirit—and this "painful disclosure of decadence and communal helplessness."[37] The Jewish ghetto needed a strong voice to defend the Jewish name. Angry that their numbers did not translate into power and that the spokesman for Judaism did not seem to represent them, East Side Jews set out to establish a democratic committee that represented the full spectrum of Jewish life, including Zionists, socialists, the Yiddish press, downtowners, and uptowners. A diverse group of Eastern European Jews met in New York several times in the fall of 1908, without the AJC's participation or support; its goal was to organize Jewish life in New York City, protect Jewish rights, and work to improve community health.[38] This new coalition—the Kehillah—joined with the AJC on the condition that the AJC "shall have exclusive jurisdiction over all questions of national or international character affecting the Jews in general."[39] The Kehillah's executive was made up of members of the AJC's Executive Committee; in this way, the Kehillah became a local arm of the AJC. Its role in Jewish defense work was to investigate the role of Jews in white slavery and to establish crime-prevention programs, such as the Bureau of Social Morals, established in 1912, to help clear the Jewish name. The Kehillah started a committee for the Good Name of Immigrant Peoples, which in 1915 "secured the suppression of many objectionable advertisements, moving picture films, and theatrical performances."[40]

But the Kehillah did not ultimately "command wide public attention as a communal spokesperson."[41] Uptown Jews were not sure that self-defense was the best and only response: "The lesson [the Jewish quarter] drew from Bingham's charges was the need for a powerful and aggressive voice to defend the Jewish name; it expected Kehillah to be that voice. But for uptown Jews, who tacitly admitted the existence of criminality, the antidote was the development of a more healthy community."[42] Uptown Jews thus held on to the power to speak for and defend the Jewish community, despite some struggles, and they affirmed the focus on reputation and image—a decision that animated the battle against the Stage Jew.

Journalistic exposés of prostitution and organized crime were not the only source for exaggerated images of Jewish criminality. Jewish criminals, particularly in the realm of white slavery, were popular characters in plays and films of the early twentieth century. Jewish leaders noted that the Stage Jew was a "cheap John" with "no ambition except to make money."[43] The ADL elaborated: "Whenever a producer wishes to depict a betrayer of public trust, a hard-boiled usurious money-lender, a crooked gambler, a grafter, a depraved fire-bug, a white slaver or other villains of one kind or another, the actor is directed to represent himself as a Jew."[44] Jewish criminals on stage and screen were willing to break the law for financial gain, and a variety of legitimate Jewish businessmen were depicted as miserly and immoral, if not explicitly criminal. Anti-Semitic arguments around the turn of the twentieth century blamed Jews—greedy, stingy, and licentious—for the decay of a variety of social institutions in the modern age. Their commercialism, according to populists, was the engine behind dehumanizing industrialism; their unyielding attention to profit, according to anti-obscenity activists, compromised art and morality in the press and the theater.[45] The historian Stephen Carr describes the claims of an "international Jewish conspiracy" in this way: "While Jewish capitalists squeezed the middle and lower classes, the anarchist Jew threw bombs, the journalist Jew printed lies and half-truths, and the entertainment Jew polluted high culture."[46]

The CCAR, the NCJW, and the International Order of B'nai B'rith actively campaigned against the misrepresentation of Jews, particularly the image of the Jewish criminal. An organization of reform rabbis established in 1889, the CCAR began working to alter the image of the immoral, greedy Jew in the first decade of the twentieth century.[47] The CCAR's campaign against the Stage Jew emerged from its Committee on Church and State, which at first focused on keeping sectarianism out of public life and pushing the Bible out of public schools. This initial agenda broadened to include the misrepresentation of Jews in school texts and mass entertainment.[48] Within this context, the committee campaigned against the inclusion of *The Merchant of Venice* in public schools, because Shakespeare's Shylock was an "unscrupulous, usurious, vindictive, bloodthirsty fiend."[49] He loves his ducats more than his daughter, starves his servant, and believes that money is the source of happiness. Despite this critique, the play was a controversial text for the CCAR. Many Jewish leaders recognized that some actors and writers had tried to make Shylock a "hero"; the *American Israelite* also reported on one actor's explanation that "Shylock's condition may be described in three words—madness through persecution. And his frenzy was confined to that one thing—his treatment by the Christians."[50] Others worried that the play's standing as a classic and its universal recognition made it too difficult to challenge. But critics also argued that the play's ongoing popularity had done more harm to Jews than the crucifixion myth.[51] Some rabbis at the CCAR believed that the attempt to keep *The Merchant of Venice* out of public schools would make more progress against anti-Semitism than asking "theatrical managers to eliminate some types of the stage-Jew."[52] Despite some disagreement, the committee had many successes in battling the play. In 1916 the New Haven Board of Education prohibited *The Merchant of Venice* in its schools.[53] Two years later the Board of Education in Portsmouth, Virginia, also voted to remove Shakespeare's piece.[54]

In 1909 the attack on the Stage Jew also became part of the agenda of the Committee on Church and State. At this point the committee adopted Rabbi Joseph Silverman's motion "dealing with the caricature of the Jew on the stage and in current publications."[55] At its next conference, in 1910, the committee recognized that the "scope of its work has been widely enlarged and includes efforts to thwart attempts at belittling the standing of the Jew as well as to protect him against any infringement up on his constitutional rights."[56] The committee began to correspond with New York theater managers and contact local newspaper editors when "Jew" was applied to "malefactors."[57] William Friedman, the chairman of the Committee on Church and State, wrote to the National Theater Managers' Association, to Marcus Klaw and A. L. Erlanger (booking agents), J. J. Shubert, Martin Beck, and other powerbrokers in American theater. Although the *New York Times* assessed the lobbying of theater managers as a successful cooperation, Friedman admitted the difficulty of the effort: "It required much correspondence and was very difficult to induce others to live up to their agreement."[58] For example, the *American Israelite* noted that, despite agreeable correspondence, one vaudeville circuit still booked the "Clown Hebrew impersonator . . . Julian Rose's Levinsky's Wedding."[59]

The focus on persuading managers to stop the Stage Jew fits with the CCAR committee's overall emphasis on "tact" and its preference for private protest. In its program for stopping Bible reading in public schools, for example, it advised meeting with the Board of Education first and moving to more public measures "only if they appear obdurate."[60] The may have chosen the quiet strategy of backstage lobbying because it did not want to attract any more public attention to scandals in culture industries associated with Jews. Furthermore, it may have hoped that its coreligionists would be sympathetic to the campaign. Indeed, when J. J. Shubert replied to Friedman, he suggested his support was based partly on his Jewish heritage: "I quite agree with you that all such are in worse than bad taste, and even if such performances had no effect whatsoever on a large number of theater goers, we ourselves would be distinctly opposed to ridiculing our own race."[61]

But this suggestion of religious and racial solidarity often backfired, particularly when Jewish protesters identified the Stage Jew as a reflection of the greed of Jewish theater managers, editors, or performers. When the Katch Company used Jewish caricatures to advertise in the *Cloak and Suit Review* in 1910, the *American Israelite* charged that it "would hardly caricature their own coreligionists unless there was a money profit in doing it."[62] Julian Morgenstern, rabbi and professor at Hebrew Union College, agreed: "It is mighty bad when a man in order to make a few paltry dollars or as he invariably puts it, 'in order to make a living for his family,' will libel his own people."[63] This critique of Jewish entrepreneurs' support for the Stage Jew made the Jewish businessman seem even more materialistic because he put money over community solidarity.

Though some of their rhetoric reinforced the image of Jews as "vulgar" and "haggling," Jewish leaders also challenged the accusations of Jewish cultural corruption in a variety of ways.[64] First, they often rejected the idea of American theater's decadence. Objecting to an actor's claim that "most of the theatrical managers were low-browed Jews," one article in the *American Israelite* explained that "the American stage today is cleaner and decenter than that of any other country in the world."[65] Second, Jewish protesters sometimes acknowledged the complexity of cultural control. The *American Israelite* attacked Sigmund Lubin, a movie producer, for overseeing films that defamed Jews, though it recognized that Lubin did not "directly supervise the production of these pictures."[66] In another case, a Jewish manager explained to his critics that "the exploitation of such a character in this piece is not my fault and was beyond my control."[67]

At the same time that the Committee on Church and State began its attack on the Stage Jew, the International Order of B'nai B'rith, founded by Central European Jews in 1843 as a fraternal order, also took up this charge. At the start of the twentieth century, the B'nai B'rith was a solidly middle-class organization facing increasing competition from new Jewish organizations over the leadership of a growing and diversifying Jewish community. The B'nai B'rith struggled with immigrants and the new American Jewish Committee over how to best respond to the Russian pogroms. The B'nai B'rith revised its mission as the defense of Jewish rights, in contrast to its nineteenth-century emphasis on charity and social services.

In 1908, Sigmund Livingston, born in Germany in 1872 and raised in Indiana, established a new standing committee, the publicity committee of District Grand Lodge 6 of B'nai B'rith. The committee's charge was to "see to it that the cause of the Jews shall be everywhere properly championed, and the name of the Jew shall everywhere be upheld as synonymous with a high sense of moral obligation."[68] Livingston believed the behavior of Eastern European immigrants had caused the rise in anti-Semitism in the United States. He worried that the misdeeds of new immigrants increased anti-Semitism against all Jews. He identified the core problem as "the Jew that disregards business ethics, or violates the rules of morals, or perverts his civil power, or transgresses the laws of this land."[69] The solution, according to Livingston, was moral "housekeeping" among Jews and a strenuous defense of the Jewish public image.[70] By 1912 the committee had developed a national scope—publishing articles against anti-Semitism and also protesting against insulting incidents around the country.

Around the same time, the National Council of Jewish Women developed a program of cultural uplift and antidefamation work. Beginning in 1893, affluent Jewish women of central European descent and members of reform congregations had established the NCJW at the Parliament of Religions at the Columbian World's Fair. This new organization emulated other women's reform groups in many ways but also carved out a distinctly Jewish path. The NCJW worked to improve education and health care and to reform prostitution and commercial leisure based on women's heightened moral sensibilities and their maternal responsibilities. They also tried to counter Christian missionary work, focused on the education of Jewish women, and established themselves as models of Jewish American womanhood in their efforts to uplift eastern European Jews.[71] The NCJW cultivated the "instinctive shrinking from the vulgar" among Jewish women.[72] This kind of rhetoric resembled the work of the Woman's Christian Temperance Union, which had launched a Department for the Suppression of Impure Literature (later the Department for the Promotion of Purity in Literature and Art) in 1883. The NCJW's attention to the misrepresentation of Jews was dwarfed by its concern with crime and sexual immorality. Cordelia Kahn, who launched the first Purity of the Press Committee in Philadelphia, noted in the first national report that the Portland section of the NCJW "sent a protest to the papers against the use of the word 'Jew' or 'Jewish' when publishing wrongdoing on the part of our faith, inasmuch as religious affiliation was not stated in regard to other persons."[73] A few years later, in the Program of Work for 1911–1914, the attempt to attain a clear press meant a press "free from . . . prejudice, distortion, from baneful news of crime and scandal."[74]

The trial and lynching of Leo Frank spurred the founding of the Anti-Defamation League of the B'nai B'rith, which consolidated and intensified the battle against anti-Semitism. Jewish groups did not agree about how to handle Frank's predicament, but the case ultimately gave antidefamation high priority, concentrated in the hands of the new organization. Frank's friends had appealed to the American Jewish Committee for help. Louis Marshall did not want to do anything to help Frank "from the standpoint of Jews" and favored quiet pressure on Southern newspapers;[75] the AJC did not want to appear to defend Jewish criminals.[76] But Marshall devoted much of his time to helping Frank's lawyer and ultimately led the campaign to commute Frank's sentence.[77]

B'nai B'rith, on the other hand, transformed the publicity committee of District 6 into the Anti-Defamation League in response to Frank's trial. In September of 1913, Adolph Kraus, the president of B'nai B'rith from 1905 to 1925, called together fifteen prominent members of the order in Chicago to form the ADL's executive committee. The founding statement refers to the Frank case: Anti-Semitism, Kraus argued, "has gone as far as to attempt to influence courts of law where a Jew happened to be a party to the litigation."[78] Even more important for this study is the founding statement's reach beyond the protection of Jews. The ADL proclaimed that its "ultimate purpose [was to] secure justice and fair treatment to all citizens alike and to put an end forever to unjust and unfair discrimination against and ridicule of any sect or body of citizens."[79] In this way, the ADL tried to reach beyond Jews to other races, religious groups, and nationalities in its civil rights work.

The ADL was a consolidation and reinforcement of multiple antidefamation voices within Jewish organizations. In 1914 the Committee on Church and State stated that it had returned to its original charge and left "the work of protesting against the caricaturing of the Jew . . . and the defamation of the Jewish name to the Anti-Defamation League."[80] By 1920 NCJW leaders acknowledged that the organization's campaigns to reform popular culture had receded, while the ADL was busy focusing on the "offenses against [the Jewish people] on the vaudeville stage, in the movie houses, in daily . . . or monthly journals."[81] The ADL also eclipsed its immigrant Jewish competitors of the Kehillah in New York City. In April 1914, a year after the ADL's founding, the Kehillah's Committee for the Good Name of Immigrant Peoples, which had been active since at least 1909, met to discuss the "imputation" of Jews in film, particularly related to arson. A few film companies, including Edison, sent a representative to the meetings, but they told the assembled citizens that they should simply contact that National Board of Censorship.[82] Maurice Simmons, the chair of the committee, reported that the board announced its efforts to end the vilification of the Jewish race in November of 1915. He concluded, "The libeling of the Jew in 'films' had assumed alarming proportions and was the subject of complaint from every section of the country."[83]

Because of their contrasting approaches to the Frank case, the ADL and the AJC seem to have taken divergent approaches to antidefamation: while the AJC preferred a quiet approach and focused on overseas problems, the ADL was more public in its advocacy for American Jews. The AJC convinced the ADL to cancel plans for public agitation, including mass meetings, against the guilty verdict.[84] As Marshall wrote in 1916, "It [the AJC] seeks to inform itself of all cases where Jews are subjected to wrongs and discrimination, but its functions are not to act as public defender. The American Jewish Committee has no public office to perform."[85] These contrasts, however, obscure a central agreement: both groups supported the amelioration of anti-Semitism through legal avenues. Although some scholars assert that the ADL advocated censorship reluctantly, it is clear that the ADL and AJC were both "vigorous supporters of 'censorship' in their campaign to eliminate anti-Semitism from popular culture."[86]

Although it used other tactics as well, the ADL included state censorship in its arsenal from the beginning: "The immediate object of the League is to stop, by appeals to reason and conscience, and if necessary by appeals to the law, the defamation of the Jewish people."[87] When the ADL first looked systematically at anti-Semitism in motion pictures, it believed that the large number of Jews involved in making motion pictures would work in its favor. But the ADL would soon face disappointment when some of these Jewish manufacturers merely told the ADL that it was "supersensitive" and ignored the organization altogether.[88] The ADL then surveyed existing censorship boards about their policies toward movies "which grossly and maliciously caricature any people." It advocated for a national board of censorship, under government control, and also pushed for more state and local censorship boards: "Until there is created a National Board of Censorship under Government authority, if such is practicable, state or local censorship would be of much help to the League."[89] The ADL soon developed a model motion picture censorship ordinance that outlawed movies maligning any sect, race, or religion. Thus, by consolidating multiple voices and responding to several injuries—from segregation to lynching to stereotypes of criminality—the ADL became the leading advocate of race-based motion picture censorship.

Taking a different route, African American activists arrived at the same point of support for race-based motion picture censorship. The NAACP took a leading role in reforming the image of African Americans in the early twentieth century. On February 12, 1909, a biracial group of sixty, including at least four Jews, sent out a "Call" for people to join a new organization devoted to improving the status of the Negro.[90] Most immediately, the group was responding to a race riot in Springfield, particularly shocking because of the symbolic impact of Lincoln's birthplace. William Walling, a southerner who worked in Illinois as a labor activist and whose wife was Jewish, concluded that the violence against African Americans was worse than Russia's persecution of the Jews. Walling's wife, Anna Strunsky, had a basis for comparison because she had served a prison sentence in Russia for her radical political activities. While the impetus for the new organization was to stop the spread of violence, the "Call," considered by some NAACP leaders to be its manifesto, also emphasized the civil rights and full integration of African Americans.[91] The NAACP's first annual report outlined its goals of ending discrimination in education, citizenship rights such as voting, and all areas of the law. The leadership encouraged members to monitor and write letters to the press regarding "any and all matters where the rights of colored people were at issue."[92]

At the National Negro Conference in 1909, leaders focused on the refutation of black people's supposed mental and physical inferiority.[93] At the end of the conference, the activists agreed to establish a permanent organization, with its headquarters in New York City. In 1910, the executive committee of the NAACP created the position of director of publicity and research for W. E. B. Du Bois, in which he enjoyed considerable independence to publish the association's monthly magazine, the *Crisis*. By 1915, two of the organization's seven work areas involved media criticism: ending public slander and publishing the truth about "the colored American and his difficulties." In particular, the organization in its early years focused on correcting lies in the press to stem vigilante violence and discrimination. Leaders of the NAACP believed that the press had inflamed racial feeling leading up to the Atlanta and Springfield riots. Walling, for example, held the local press partly responsible for the Springfield riot because it had blamed African Americans for crime, and he also noted the state's lack of remorse when an Illinois newspaper blamed the violence of 1908 on the "general inferiority" of black people.[94] "The public must be kept informed," NAACP chairman Oswald Garrison Villard explained; "the facts must be gathered and assembled. This requires effort. Facts are not gotten out of one's imagination. . . . Public opinion is the main force upon which the Association relies for a victory of justice."[95] In fact, Du Bois sometimes went so far as to claim publicity as the organization's main work, and favorable public opinion the primary goal. "All our work," he announced in 1914, "might be characterized as publicity work."[96]

African American journalists and civil rights leaders also tried to change the terminology used to identify them in the press. The argued against racial insults like "darkey" and "nigger" and, in a larger campaign, insisted that "Negro" be capitalized. An editorial in the *Crisis* noted that the words "darkey" and "nigger" were as insulting to African Americans as "sheeny" to Jewish people and "mick" to the Irish.[97] The NAACP agreed with Lester Walton, the managing editor and theater critic at the *New York Age*, who argued that "Negro" should be capitalized "just the same as . . . 'Jew' and 'Irish.'" Walton wrote to the Associated Press (AP) in 1913 to advocate for the capitalization of the term. "In the daily press you frequently read an article which is written something like this," explained Walton: "'Every race was represented at the conference. . . . The Indian, Japanese, Italian, Chinese and negro were much in evidence.' What a rank injustice to the Negro to use a lower case 'n' in this instance!"[98] Although some publications, such as *Outlook*, and *Century*, and several daily newspapers began to capitalize "Negro," Walton felt discouraged because the majority of newspapers did not adopt his recommendation: "Whether this marked reluctancy to use the capital "N" is due to sentimental reasons or based on a desire to steadfastly adhere to rhetorical standards made hundreds of years ago I have been unable to ascertain."[99]

Jews had a more influential lobby and enjoyed more success in their campaign against the misuse of "Jew" in the press. In 1913, around the same time that Walton appealed to the Associated Press, Adolph Ochs and members of the executive committee of the newly established ADL also wrote to the AP to offer advice on the proper use of the words "Jew" and "Jewish." Ochs explained that a person's Jewishness should not be noted in the press, whether the author was discrediting or praising the person—as in "JEWISH criminal" or "JEWISH physician"—because the subject's Jewishness did not have any connection to the "conduct entailed." He also noted that "Jew" should not be used as a verb, as in, to "Jew down."[100] Just two years later, Livingston described considerable success: "The campaign of education which we had carried out was showing its results and in comparatively few instances did the improper use of the words occur."[101]

The NAACP and the ADL shared a commitment to eradicating lies and negative caricatures as the source of prejudice and discrimination, but the scope of their campaigns diverged. Jewish antidefamation efforts focused on popular entertainment, while African Americans largely addressed lies in the news media.[102] The founding statement of the ADL put the Stage Jew front and center: "For a number of years a tendency has manifested itself in American life toward caricaturing and defaming Jews on the stage, in motion pictures."[103] African Americans, on the other hand, attacked racist lies in the press that led to violence and injustice, as well as incorrect or disreputable terminology; their critique of popular entertainment remained muted. In May of 1913, the Crisis reported that one of its main areas of work, "Publicity and Information" should "stop the conscious and unconscious enmity of the daily and weekly press and seek to abate scurrilous headlines and contemptuous and belittling reports; it should send letters, answer attacks, visit the editors; furnish the papers with news of events."[104] In 1912, for example, the Crisis condemned examples from southern newspapers calling for the lynching of the African American boxing champion Jack Johnson. The press had "quite lost its head on the matter."[105] Du Bois affirmed these challenges to the press as "censorship of the press," which he deemed a necessary corollary to the organization's own favorable depiction of African Americans in its monthly magazine.[106]

Prior to the campaign against *The Birth of a Nation*, the NAACP only occasionally criticized images of African Americans in entertainment; instead, it focused on battling segregation and correcting lies about the causes of lynching. Nevertheless, in 1912, the *Crisis* explained that the images on stage and screen perpetuated the secondary status of African Americans:

> True it is that this country has had its appetite for facts on the Negro problem spoiled by sweets. In earlier days the Negro minstrel who "jumped Jim Crow" was the typical black man served up to the national taste. It was the balmy day when slaves were "happy" and "preferred" slavery to all other possible states. Then came the sobering of abolition days and war, when for one horrified moment the world gazed on the hell of slavery and knew it for what it was. In the last fifteen years there has come another campaign of Joy and Laughter to degrade black folk . . . We have had audiences entertained with "nigger" stories, tales of pianos in cabins, and of the general shiftlessness of the freedman, and concerted effort to make it appear that the wrongs of color prejudice are but incidental and trivial. . . . This is the lie which *The Crisis* is here to refute.[107]

Along with this critique of the portrayal of African Americans, the *Crisis* condemned the use of the word "Nigger" onstage.[108] In addition, the magazine noted African American musical innovation as a positive influence on American music. Du Bois wrote, "The Negro may be looked down upon by the white man, but it is a significant thing that the white man is now getting his musical inspiration from the Negro."[109]

If the early NAACP voice on images of African Americans on stage and screen remained muted, other African Americans spoke out forcefully. Drama and entertainment critics in the black press discussed unfavorable portrayals of their race and the need for more shows produced and performed by African Americans. In 1904 the African American theater critic Sylvester Russell attacked sheet music publishers and performers for using "nigger" in songs: "The ignorant 'stink-weed' variety performer who thinks he pleases in forcing this word upon the public is very much mistaken."[110] Four years later Lester Walton hoped that "colored shows will wield far more influence in making acceptable stage types depicting Negro life than any other influence" and, two years before *The Birth of a Nation*, he questioned whether the motion picture industry was "properly presenting to the world at large the American Negro."[111]

The *Crisis* regularly discussed the artistic accomplishments of African Americans and the political purposes of art, but the NAACP's examination of popular entertainment focused extensively on equal access to public amusements, instead of on images of African Americans.[112] The organization challenged segregation in employment, education, and housing, but also in theaters. The association's leaders advocated for the enforcement of existing civil rights laws in northern states and encouraged African Americans to bring suits when they were discriminated against in entertainment venues. The New York Vigilance Committee, a branch of the NAACP led by Joel Spingarn, began "pushing cases of discrimination in places of public amusement."[113] This committee set up groups of black and white customers to seek admission to theaters in New York City, and then filed suit against those that violated New York State civil rights law.[114] In May of 1912, for example, a New York court held that African Americans could not be barred from sections of the auditorium and the Vigilance Committee also forced a movie theater to change its segregation policy.[115] Jane Addams praised this effort as part of campaign to "secure the enforcement of the civil rights laws on the books." In 1913 the Vigilance Committee, with its emphasis on "creative direct action," merged with the NAACP's National Legal Committee.[116] The NAACP's success in integrating public amusements spread beyond New York to cases in Illinois, California, Ohio, and Pennsylvania.[117]

Under Du Bois's leadership, publicity became central to the NAACP's antilynching campaign. The NAACP offered lawyers for accused African Americans, but its main weapon was the exposé.[118] The organization launched investigations, then publicized its findings as widely as possible; in this way, the antilynching campaign in large part constituted a "publicity campaign."[119] In its first annual report, the NAACP recounted that it had given "publicity to and assisted in the hard fight for life made by Steve Greene," who had shot his white employer in self-defense.[120] If good publicity could prevent lynching, then bad publicity, including popular theatrical productions and motion pictures, could cause lynching. As shown, many African American leaders criticized *The Clansman* for inciting violence against black people. In addition, African American theater critics linked the new motion picture industry to lynching. In 1909, Walton criticized a movie theater's publicity: "John Smith of Paris, Texas, Burned at the Stake. Hear His Moans and Groans. Price One Cent." He wondered, "Where do the elements of education come in so far as the picture in question is concerned?"[121]

In 1915 African Americans and Jews converged in their efforts to use the law to censor racial ridicule in motion pictures. But their paths of censorship were quite different. Jewish motion picture initiatives preceded African American attempts to censor racist films. In addition, although Jews and African Americans launched similar efforts to ban motion pictures that promoted violence, the African American campaign, much more than the Jewish one, maintained a focus on antiviolence. The Jewish campaign against anti-Semitic films, beyond movies about the Leo Frank lynching, spanned a broader range of images. Finally, when African Americans turned to censorship to fight *The Birth of a Nation*, they faced a legal landscape different than did their Jewish brethren; they confronted a tradition of censoring images of black power, such as black boxing champions and productions that criticized white supremacy. For example, Kentucky passed an early "Uncle Tom's Cabin" law in 1906 at the urging of the United Daughters of the Confederacy; the law banned theatrical performances that "tend to create racial feelings and prejudice."[122] In the early twentieth century, Memphis periodically censored movies because of race; the city censors suppressed a 1914 film version of *Uncle Tom's Cabin* because it might cause racial unrest.[123]

Government censorship of images of black power reached state and federal levels in the bans on films of boxing matches. In 1909 Iowa outlawed all prize-fighting films, to stop showing an African American, Jack Johnson, beat a white fighter, Tommy Burns, for the heavyweight title. Between 1909 and 1912, other state censors worked quickly to ban the film of the fight, as well as subsequent films of Johnson's victories over white challengers. Boxing had long been controversial, with bans in some states by the end of the nineteenth century, but the concern with Johnson's affront to white supremacy led to film censorship at the local and national level. Johnson publicly flouted Jim Crow conventions—in his romances with white women, his lavish lifestyle, and his "braggadocio appearance."[124] In 1910 Johnson knocked out Jim Jeffries, his white challenger who stated that the purpose of his fight was to prove "that a white man is better than a negro."[125] Reformers claimed that racial violence would likely erupt from the film. Southern Democrats in the United States House and Senate made the Johnson fight films a federal issue 1912, on the eve of another Johnson bout, when they introduced a bill to ban "the importation and interstate transportation of films or other pictorial representations of prize fights."[126] The bill passed the House and Senate in July of 1912, after a new film of Johnson's victory over Jim Flynn had started to circulate. Although the law did not target fights in which whites fought blacks, lawmakers specifically referred to Johnson and race relations in their debate over the film. The Tennessee congressman Thetus W. Sims said the bill would stop "moving-picture films of prize fights, especially the one between a negro and a white man."[127]

Considering this background, it seems unsurprising that African American leaders hesitated to advocate censorship. Some observers noted the contradiction between their progressive impulses: "They hate injustice to the negro and they hate a bureaucratic control of thought."[128] Joel Spingarn was reluctant to embrace censorship of *The Birth of a Nation* because any suppression of the film, he reasoned, could also be used to censor *Uncle Tom's Cabin*.[129] Other NAACP leaders were also defensive about the campaign for censorship, wondering in particular if their efforts would simply attract more attention to the film. One *Crisis* editorial explained: "Of course, it is difficult under such circumstances to select a feasible method or campaign to counteract the undoubtedly vicious influences of this widely viewed picture. If Negroes and all their friends were free to answer in the same channels, by the same methods in which the attack is made, the path would be easy; but poverty, fashion and color prejudice preclude this. We have therefore sought vigorously through censorship to stop this slander of a whole race."[130] Censorship, in this case, was justified only because African Americans did not have equal access to media to influence public opinion in their favor.

Like black Americans, Jews knew that the power of censorship could be directed against them. The historian Andrea Friedman shows that Reform rabbis became active in the anti-obscenity movement "as much in response to anti-obscenity campaigns as to the existence of obscenity." They hoped their participation could undermine Christian beliefs about lax morals among Jews, and they tried to counter the argument of many anti-obscenity activists that Jewish producers caused cultural decay. Reform rabbis also found that much work against obscenity conflicted with "Reform Judaism's self-definition as a modern religious movement, in an era when individual autonomy and relaxed sexual mores were two of the primary denoters of modernity."[131]

Jewish and African American doubts about censorship seem to have been outweighed by the perceived danger of the new medium of motion pictures. The ADL in 1915 explained: "No other instrument in modern civilization is so wide-spread in its influence and makes so profound an impression upon the child-mind." As opposed to damaging literature, movies "now vividly presented [anti-Semitism] before the eyes of the unmatured, ignorant or the uncultured."[132] Similarly, James Weldon Johnson argued that *The Birth of a Nation* was more dangerous than the play or the original book: "Every minute detail is vividly portrayed before the eyes of the spectators. A big, degraded looking Negro is shown chasing a little golden-haired white girl for the purpose of outraging her, she, to escape him, goes to her death by hurling herself over a cliff. Can you imagine the effect of such a scene upon the millions who seldom read a book, who seldom witness a drama but who constantly go to the 'movies'?"[133] He concluded that the Irish had stopped the play *McFadden's Row of Flats* for insulting their race, so African Americans should do the same.[134] For Johnson, the concern was not just with the beguiling new technology of motion pictures but with the accessibility of motion pictures to illiterate, uneducated, and poor patrons.

The ADL took the lead in establishing censorship of racial ridicule. The ADL legislative agenda paired its movie censorship ordinance with its civil rights law banning discriminatory advertising: both laws worked to protect the reputation of Jews and other minority groups.[135] The ADL, however, remained uncertain about how wide to cast its net in protecting minorities from ridicule in film. In its questionnaire to states and municipalities about movie censorship, the ADL asked specifically about whom they protected from insult: "Does the censoring body attempt to censor pictures which grossly or maliciously caricature any people, or which are designed to insult those of a particular religion?"[136] In some cases the ADL distanced Jews from racial categories: in 1915 it announced that Jews were a religious group, with "no reasonable basis for comparison [with] the negro, the Chinaman, the Irishman or the Italian." The report clarified that the organization was seeking a rule to prevent any film that attacked any "religious body."[137] On the other hand, the ADL reported that "in energetically endorsing and helping the enactment of these ordinances, the League feels that it is doing a work that will rebound not only to its credit, but will benefit all classes of people."[138] A draft of its censorship law in 1914 followed an inclusive approach by including a ban on movies that ridiculed any "sect, race or religion."[139]

The ADL's indecision about the wording of the ordinance relates to debates over how Jews wanted to define themselves and to their relationships with African Americans. At the same time that the ADL was experimenting with different terminology for the censorship ordinance, leading Jewish activists were debating whether or not Jews should be considered a "race." The early twentieth century saw new problems with Jewish racial designation, partly related to the arrival of Eastern European immigrants, which made it more difficult for the Americanized leaders to control group definition and racial difference.[140] The core of Jewish leaders—"laymen [not rabbis] prominent in law, business, academia and philanthropy"—exhibited increasing defensiveness about racial group definition.[141] Louis Marshall was anxious about any statements affirming racial identity because he discouraged any distance between Jews and the American mainstream, while Jacob Schiff referred to himself as a "faith-Jew" rather than a "race-Jew."[142]

The ADL decision to protect racial and religious groups in its model movie ordinance shaped state censorship in Pennsylvania and Maryland. Pennsylvania's censorship legislation passed in 1911, but the board was not established until 1913. The Maryland State Board of Censors was established in 1916.[143] Beginning in 1913, the ADL successfully lobbied Pennsylvania and other states to ban racial and religious ridicule.[144] In 1915, the Pennsylvania State Board of Censors Rules and Standards stated, "Plays which hold up to ridicule any sect (religious or otherwise) will not be approved."[145] Maryland excluded "inflammatory scenes and titles calculated to stir up racial hatred."[146] The Maryland board noted that the "Anti-Jewish Defamation League" lobbied it heavily.

The year 1915 proved a landmark in the history of race-based motion picture censorship. First, the Supreme Court upheld government censorship of motion pictures in its *Mutual Film Corp. v. Industrial Commission of Ohio* decision. The Court concluded that movies were an amusement business, not part of the press or politics.[147] Second, in 1915, Jews protested against motion pictures that depicted the lynching of Leo Frank, while African Americans attacked *The Nigger* and *The Birth of a Nation*. These groups often used the laws spearheaded by the ADL. An examination of this year shows that Jews and African Americans shared concerns about depictions of lynching on screen, but their efforts to regulate racial representation in movies still differed. Jewish censorship demands focused on Jewish foibles on screen more broadly—from images of an overweight Jewish woman to portrayals of immoral Jewish businessmen—while African Americans attacked, more narrowly, images of violence against blacks. Jews sought protection from embarrassment and disrepute; African Americans sought safety.

The Frank case became the subject of numerous newsreels and films, which were targets of censorship controversies. During Frank's appeal and after his lynching, Frank's defenders and detractors worked to control his representation on film. They acknowledged that films about the case might sway the outcome of the appeal and that images of the lynching could inspire further violence. While Frank's appeal was in process, several films of the trial appeared favoring his innocence. A fifteen-minute documentary, *Leo M. Frank and Governor Slaton*, was on the bill in New York City in theaters owned by Jewish entrepreneur Marcus Loew. The Jewish connections allegedly angered those seeking to avenge the death of Mary Phagan, Frank's alleged victim, and may have fueled the mob murder of Frank.[148] The film historian Michael Bernstein notes that Frank's lynchers also helped revive the Ku Klux Klan, and would have cheered on Griffith's *The Birth of a Nation*, because Griffith's drama and Frank's murder shared the core narrative of avenging a rape.[149]

Censors banned motion pictures of the Frank case for a variety of reasons: preserving the public peace, avoiding interference in an ongoing trial, and protecting a class of people (in this case, Jews).[150] At the urging of the "Jewish people of Sacramento," the city's Commission of Education (also the city censor) agreed to ban all films representing the Frank case a few months after his murder.[151] The National Board of Censorship and the New York City license commissioner banned *The Frank Case*, a five-reel reenactment by George Roland, in 1914 because it advocated Frank's innocence while the case was in appeal.[152] The newsreel showed crowds at the lynching, but not the actual violence of the lynching.[153] The Chicago censorship board also rejected *The Frank Case* "because it portrays a story of a criminal case now pending . . . and has a tendency to disturb the public peace."[154] But in 1915 the Chicago censor added another reason in his reappraisal of the film, referring to a clause in the ordinance prohibiting the issuance of permits for pictures tending "to create contempt or hatred for any class of law abiding citizens."[155]

The ADL and the AJC both worked to suppress movies of the Frank trial and lynching. Jewish activists criticized depictions of the lynching or of Frank's hanging body, which some newsreels included.[156] For example, a rabbi from Harrisburg, Pennsylvania, was proud of his success at "moral suasion" when he encouraged the Pennsylvania Motion Picture Censorship Board to cut sections of a film that depicted the lynching.[157] In Philadelphia, police officials seem to have been responding to Jewish concerns when they urged theater managers not to show any films related to Leo Frank.[158]

Newsreels of Frank's lynching were in circulation at the same time as *The Birth of a Nation*.[159] The African American press noted the coincidence and censors' different responses. Reacting to a *Mutual Weekly* newsreel that included images of Frank's hanging body, the *Indianapolis Freeman* explained: "Exhibitions of moving pictures of the body of Leo Frank as it swung from the limb of a tree near Marietta, Ga. after the mob had done its work were stopped by the police. This is as it should have been. Any exhibitions that are inflammatory, causing friction between races should be stopped." The editorial carefully compared movies of the Frank lynching with *The Birth of a Nation*, acknowledging that both films insulted a race, but that many Jews were still backing the tour of *The Birth of a Nation*, despite Jewish claims of being "friendly to the Negroes." The similarities between Frank films and *The Birth of a Nation* only went so far, as this editorial stated that there was no doubt which film would injure the greatest number of people.[160] In 1915 two films related to the lynching of African Americans appeared—*The Nigger* and *The Birth of a Nation*; both became the center of censorship controversies.[161] *The Nigger* follows a southern governor's dilemma when a political opponent threatens to reveal that he has an African American grandmother. Rather than make a deal with his opponent, he resigns and decides to work for African Americans in the state. The movie includes an earlier incident in his life when, as a sheriff, he failed to prevent a lynching. The film alludes to the burning of the man. The NAACP was divided in its response to the film. Mary Childs Nerney, NAACP national secretary, worried that attacking *The Nigger* would detract from the campaign against *The Birth of a Nation*. Du Bois did not find the movie objectionable, and Nerney wrote to the Cleveland branch of the NAACP that the film was "on the whole sympathetic to the colored man."[162] But for many, the concerns about the lynching overrode the broader arc of the movie.

Also within the antilynching framework the NAACP launched a campaign against *The Birth of a Nation*, in January 1915, with the help of other organizations, such as the Urban League. Throughout the movie's national run (and then in subsequent releases in the twentieth century), the NAACP tried to stop the film through government censorship, pressure on advertisers, printed editorials, sermons, boycotts, and confrontations at movie theaters. Race-based censorship regulations proved central to the NAACP campaign. The NAACP succeeded in suppressing the film in some cities by

Rabbi Stephen Wise, a strong critic of *The Birth of a Nation*, *The God of Vengeance*, and *The King of Kings*. Courtesy of The Jacob Rader Marcus Center of the American Jewish Archives, Cincinnati, Ohio. AmericanJewishArchives.org

pressuring existing movie censorship boards and other public officials and by working to get new race-based legislation passed. Like the Frank case, *The Birth of a Nation* was the basis of alliances and tensions between Jews and African Americans. Prominent Jews in the NAACP, such as Spingarn, worked to stop the movie and several rabbis delivered sermons against it.[163] The NAACP thanked the *Jewish Criterion* for its "splendid" editorial opposing the film in 1915.[164] Rabbi Stephen Wise, one of the founding members of the NAACP and a member of the National Board of Censorship, also opposed the film. When the board approved the film, Wise spoke out against the decision, described the movie as an "indefensible libel upon a race," and lobbied the New York mayor directly to stop it, referring to the Irish attack on *The Playboy of the Western World*.[165] Yet some African Americans accused Jews of being responsible for *The Birth of a Nation*. An editorial in the *Indianapolis Freeman* stated that the movie's owners were Jews. "There is much money wrapped up in those *Birth a Nation* pictures," the author explained. He noted Jewish overtures to African Americans in terms of civil rights, but then found the contradiction: "Yet in the face of this we find launched amid us the most insinuating Yet in the face of this we find launched amid us the most insinuating vehicle of hate known to our race."[166]

The NAACP's initial and overriding complaint was that the movie endangered African Americans because of its negative and historically inaccurate images of black people: the film encouraged lynching. Although the film did not include an actual lynching scene (probably because it would have certainly been cut by censors), it encouraged lynching by emphasizing the "illegitimacy" of state officials, affirming the myth of black male criminality, and creating spectacular crowd scenes. Critics at the time observed that the fervent response to the movie replicated the "mob mentality" of a lynching.[167] They noted that both *The Clansman* and *The Birth of a Nation* produced "the spectacle of black lynching and society's tolerance of it" by cultivating race hatred and repeating lies about African American men's lust for white women as the cause of lynching.[168] The *Crisis* reported on Rolfe Cobleigh's speech, in which he said that the movie's favorable portrayal of the Ku Klux Klan—that "lawlessness was justified"—was a "dangerous . . . false doctrine."[169] The NAACP paired attacks on the film with accounts of actual lynchings. The June 1915 edition of the *Crisis* assailed *The Birth of a Nation* as an "exaltation of race war," then reported on lynchings in Georgia.[170]

But the threat of violence was more complex than the prospect of further lynchings. Some proponents of censorship argued that the movie's incendiary quality would cause riots. Leaders of the NAACP usually focused on the film's potential to cause and endorse lynching, but they also began to refer to the possibility of social unrest related to protests against the film. In Atlantic City, for example, city officials stopped the play for fear of hostility among citizens in the "black belt," particularly given threats overheard among African Americans in the saloons."[171] On September 8, 1915, Nerney advised a local branch to "say . . . [the play] 'The Clansman,' when it was produced in Philadelphia some years ago, caused most serious riots and was taken off."[172] Indeed, in Philadelphia, with the memory of the disruptions surrounding *The Clansman* in mind, city officials stopped the movie when they learned that many African Americans had purchased tickets to the play.[173] This approach proved problematic due to its suggestion that African Americans were dangerous, rather than the movie itself. One activist encouraged Nerney to emphasize "the idea of trouble among the negroes, as your strongest hope for suppression, but without any hint that you have been holding them back."[174] Leaders in the NAACP worked carefully to emphasize that African American protesters were trying to halt violence, not create it.[175]

In 1917, when *The Birth of a Nation* was banned in Cleveland (after approval by the State Board of Censors, a reversal of its previous rejection), a judge discussed the danger of suggesting that the film would cause a disturbance of the peace. In his detailed decision, he expressed his dislike of the film and of the medium in general (for catering to "base passions"), but he overruled censorship anyway. If activists granted that the film would disturb the peace, they also admitted to African American unruliness—an "uncalled for slander upon these citizens," according to Judge Foran. He advised African Americans to stop giving the film free publicity.[176]

Several state censorship boards cut insulting images of African Americans and Jews from motion pictures. About a month before it decided on *The Birth of a Nation*, the Pennsylvania board stopped a film about the Frank trial and lynching, after complaints from a Harrisburg rabbi. Ellis Oberholtzer, a prominent member of Pennsylvania's censorship board, also responded favorably to Joseph Krauskopf, a Reform rabbi from Philadelphia, who criticized *Mrs. Van Alden's Jewels* for its insult to Jews.[177] He agreed to cut several scenes.[178] In the same year, the Pennsylvania censors ordered revisions in *The Nigger* and in *The Birth of a Nation*: the Fox Film Company had to change the title of *The Nigger* to *The New Governor* and to eliminate the use of "nigger . . . in all cases." In particular, the board instructed the company to cut scenes of shooting and brick-throwing and to change "Go in to your nigger sweetheart" to "Go in to your black sweetheart."[179] The board ordered eight modifications in *The Birth of a Nation*, including reductions in the scene in which Gus chases Flora and the elimination of the view of a "negro putting bare feet on a desk" in the legislature. The board also removed the scene in which an African American woman "fondles" Austin Stoneman's arm.[180] Stoneman was a thinly disguised Thaddeus Stevens, a Pennsylvania abolitionist. Censors in Pennsylvania acted to protect his reputation, not just African Americans. Oberholtzer, for example, wrote to a theater manager in Philadelphia: "I am glad you are making some eliminations in *The Birth of a Nation*, so that the memory of old Thad Stevens will not be quite so much outraged in his own State. He was the greatest figure which we contributed to the Nation during the Civil War period. I think that the makers of this wonderful picture have made altogether too free with his reputation, along the lines which I object to."[181]

While Jewish activists pioneered bans on racial ridicule in state motion picture censorship boards prior to *The Birth of a Nation*, the NAACP worked to expand the censorship of racial ridicule after the controversial film appeared. Jewish-backed laws tended to be more inclusive than

NAACP-authored ones, using language to protect races, religions, and nationalities, not race alone. The ADL model act referred to "any sect, religion or race." The legislative responses to *The Birth of a Nation*, however, often isolated race. The city commissioners in Phoenix, Arizona, in a special session passed a new ordinance to target *The Nigger*; it banned "any act, exhibition, attraction, amusement or language therein which shall in anywise tend to excite race hatred or prejudice."[182] At least five cities passed new laws or amended old ones to stop *The Birth of a Nation*. John Hopkins, the only African American city council member in Wilmington, introduced one ordinance in June 1915: "No person, firm or corporation shall exhibit within the limits of the City of Wilmington, any moving picture that is likely to provoke ill-feeling between the white and black races."[183] A few months later Tacoma amended its statute to cover not just obscene or immoral performances but also ones that tended "to incite race riot or race hatred."[184] Denver, St. Paul, and Wichita also passed laws to censor *The Birth of a Nation*. Only St. Paul's law covered motion pictures that tended to "create race or religious prejudice."[185] The laws did not always have the intended result. Despites its new law, Tacoma, for example, did not suppress *The Birth of a Nation*. The Denver city council voted to censor the film, but a court injunction allowed it to be shown.[186] St. Paul stopped *The Birth of a Nation* but not because of the ordinance.

Courts often rejected the argument that *The Birth of a Nation* would "incite racial prejudice because of the uncomplimentary stereotyping of blacks."[187] The first censorship struggle over the film, at its premiere in Los Angeles, resulted in a judge overruling the city council's cancellation of the movie and granting an injunction to Griffith. In his ruling the judge explained to the African American protesters: "My advice to you is to wholly disregard this matter. . . . The mere reproduction of the pictures cannot change your standing in the community."[188] *The Birth of a Nation* went on to have a successful run in Los Angeles. Griffith would succeed in getting injunctions to stop censorship of the movie throughout the country. With some dejection NAACP leaders noted that Griffith had secured injunctions in several cities in which the NAACP had initially succeeded in suppressing the film—in Chicago, Providence, and Pittsburgh, for example.[189] When the Pittsburgh mayor banned *The Birth of a Nation* in 1915 even though the State Board of Censors had approved he film, the Allegheny County Court of Common Pleas enjoined the mayor because his action was not based on the two justifications for censorship—"apt to cause a breach of peace" or "subversive of public morality."[190] An Illinois judge also dismissed race-based censorship, proclaiming, "No race or nationality has greater right under the law than any other has."[191] In several cases, city officials refused to ban the movie because the defamation of African Americans fell outside the city's censorship laws, which covered only immorality and obscenity. Baltimore police declined to take action because they could only suppress the film if it was "vulgar or indecent."[192] In Boston, Mayor Curley said that he found the movie to be an "outrage upon colored citizens" but that he could not stop it.[193] He cut two scenes, probably because he believed they were immoral or obscene, in keeping with the censorship statute.[194] But a Boston judge overruled him and cut only one scene—Gus's pursuit of Flora—because of immorality; he did not consider race in his censorship.[195] Spokespersons for the NAACP responded by arguing that immorality should be "construed in a broad sense as anything hostile to the welfare of the general public."[196]

In the campaign against *The Birth of a Nation*, opponents of the film used laws banning racially inflammatory movies, but when these laws did not exist in particular locations, they also tried to ban the film using more common terms of censorship laws—immorality and incitement to violence. Throughout the campaign against the movie, the NAACP referred to its racial defamation and its threat to public decency.[197] At a hearing in Boston, African American critics lambasted both the film's racial hatred and its sexual excesses.[198] And in New York City, the NAACP referred to the film as "an offense against public decency . . . and an unjust appeal to race prejudice."[199]

The NAACP and the ADL used their censorship campaigns for broader organizational goals, not just the suppression of particular representations. The NAACP's attack on *The Birth of a Nation* helped the young organization establish a national reputation and gave its local chapters experience in political organizing.[200] In Atlantic City, NAACP leaders remarked that a protest would help "place the name of the Association before a great many persons" and predicted that a demonstration in Trenton would "increase our membership." The historian Thomas Cripps holds that gaining publicity and new members shaped the organization's immediate attacks on movies, plays, and the press.[201] The NAACP's battle against *The Birth of a Nation* supported its expanding antilynching campaign. It lobbied for the passage of a federal antilynching bill and, in 1919, published a study of lynching that demonstrated that less than 20 percent of the approximately

2,500 African Americans murdered even faced accusations of rape.[202] The historian Robert Zangrando argues that the organization carefully used its response to vigilante violence to "mobilize the black community, achieve recognition, add new members, both black and white, and solicit funds in the fight against lynching."[203] At around the same time, the ADL pushed the B'nai B'rith away from philanthropy toward defense work as a way to gain a leadership position within a Jewish community torn by "institutional competition, geographic rivalry, and a distrust of immigrant Jews." By 1920, the ADL had helped to "anchor B'nai B'rith on the map of the American-Jewish community."[204]

The Jewish and African American paths to race-based censorship of motion pictures had much in common, such as a rebuttal of images of criminality and the struggle against lynching. But strong contrasts also mark their journeys. When Jews attacked hotel segregation, they focused primarily on the shameful advertisement of Jewish exclusion, whereas African Americans fought for the enforcement of civil rights laws, including their right to choose their seats freely in theaters. Although Jews, through their work with the NAACP, helped guide the organization's effort to stop *The Birth of a Nation*, Jewish and African American organizations did not form a coalition to lobby for and implement race-based censorship. Nonetheless, these two groups did meet on the same ground, using the inclusive wording of race (sometimes along with religion and other categories) in the standards of censorship boards throughout the country and agreeing about the need to protect minority groups from certain movie representations. Yet the two groups defined the harm of motion pictures in contrasting ways. While Jewish censors posited that defamatory images injured their reputations, African American censors often argued that racist representations inspired whites to assault them. Successful censors, however, often pointed to African American unruliness as the true danger. The twists and turns of the censors' efforts to protect Jews and African Americans thus surprised these well-intentioned, progressive advocates of censorship. The impact of this type of protective censorship on Jews and, to a lesser extent, on African Americans in one city—Chicago—is the topic of the next chapter.

CHAPTER FIVE

ARE THE HEBREWS TO HAVE A CENSOR?

Jewish Censors in Chicago

Chicago's 1907 motion picture censorship law, the inauguration of motion picture censorship in the United States, did not simply ban "immoral or obscene" films.[1] The law gave Chicago police the power to ban any film that was "obscene, or portrays depravity, criminality or lack of virtue of a class of citizens of any race, color, creed or religion and exposes them to contempt, derision or obloquy, or tends to produce a breach of the peace or riots, or purports to represent any hanging, lynching or burning of a human being."[2] Adolf Kraus, a Jewish attorney, civic leader, and the law's author, discussed the persecution of minorities when he reflected back on the purpose of the law at a hearing in 1920: "There might be some attempts against the minority–to wipe them out, that it is not safe. Now should pictures be tolerated, say for instance the prosecution of negroes and burning them at the stake."[3] The founding vision of Chicago's race-based censorship was indeed inclusive, spanning immigrant groups and African Americans, the white races as well as African Americans. But in practice, Chicago censorship did not protect all races equally. In fact, Jews gained more power than other minority groups in the censorship process, but only as experts on anti-Semitism. Jewish censors thus held unusual power, and remained marginal at the same time. Critics of Chicago censorship charged that the system of minority groups regulating their own image was unfair and impractical. As one movie industry representative asked, "Are the Hebrews to have a censor? Are the Catholics to have a censor? . . . And then we must not forget the women. They will want a censor and if the woman censor is a suffragist, the anti-suffragist will want a censor."[4]

By 1909 Chicago had the highest density of nickelodeons—with 407 theaters, or one per 5,350 people—of any city in the world. New York City had one nickelodeon per 11, 250 people. As the historian Julie Ann

Lindstrom explains, Chicago was definitely not the "second city" of nick-elodeons.[5] Nickelodeons, located in poor neighborhoods, were widely accessible to immigrants and working-class patrons, women and children. "Nickel madness," as the historian Kathleen McCarthy states, proved an "extremely democratic phenomenon."[6] A diverse coalition of Chicago progressives turned its attention to movie reform in the first decade of the twentieth century: the Juvenile Protective Association, the Chicago Woman's Club, the City Club of Chicago, and Hull House. Scholars have described this coalition primarily as a struggle to protect children, with battles along class and gender lines as well.[7] The *Chicago Tribune* reported that the "mushrooming" nickel theaters were demoralizing children because they were essentially "girl shows," with women's bodies on display; because they featured lurid trials on screen; and because they instructed spectators about how to commit crimes. The Juvenile Protective Association, which helped establish a juvenile court system, assessed the condition of five-cent theaters in 1907. It exposed poor ventilation in the theaters and reported violations of child labor laws.[8] The City Club of Chicago, a civic organization founded in 1903, debated, but did not agree on, a proposal to bar unaccompanied minors from movie theaters.[9] Some reformers worried that motion pictures sowed the seeds of "class hatred" in their depictions of strikes and labor violence.[10] With that critique in mind, Chicago's movie censors tried to draw up immigrants and the working class into a unified, moral culture by transforming motion pictures into an artistic "counter attraction" to compete with other cheap amusements.[11] Jane Addams of Hull House (the premier settlement house in the United States) hoped that the cheap thrills of movies would be improved to higher standards of art and literature, envisioning the democratic potential for film as an invigorating fantasy life to the urban poor.[12]

The coalition of reformers pushed for government supervision of motion pictures because it wanted to overcome social disruptions, protect women and children, and prevent crime.[13] But Kraus also moved further to endorse censorship for the protection of racial and religious minorities. This multicultural commitment built on the reformers' social thought already outlined by historians—the desire to protect the vulnerable, the support for social cohesion, and even a commitment to social justice. While women seemed to need protection from risqué films, racial minorities needed protection from racial ridicule; while nickelodeons alarmed some reformers because of their working-class appeal, movies with racial caricatures seemed to encourage dangerous racial divisions. But race-based censorship was a particularly problematic expansion of these censorship debates. Many observers viewed race-based censorship as an unwieldy growth of censorship (Did every racial minority deserve representation as a censor?) and as the epitome of special interests' corruption of rational censorship. The case of Jewish censorship in Chicago exposes the perils of race-based censorship.

Chicago's censorship law passed judicial review in *Block v. City of Chicago* (1909). The Illinois Supreme Court chief justice, James Cartwright, argued that movie audiences, because of their "age, education and situation in life" were entitled to "protection against the evil influence of obscene and immoral representations."[14] Cartwright did not discuss the race-based provisions of the law, perhaps because censors did not act on them until 1914. The law initially put all censorship authority in the hands of the police, but during the following decade, civilian censors gained more power. In 1913, Major Metellus Lucullus Cicero Funkhouser became the second deputy superintendent of police, a new position created to oversee all censorship activities. Funkhouser experimented with using ad hoc "citizen juries" to review films and, in 1914, a new civilian censorship board, with eleven members, replaced the police censors, although all censorship was still under the authority of the second deputy, Funkhouser. Movie producers and free-speech advocates challenged police as unfit censors, so Funkhouser began to include more citizens in the decision-making process to make censorship appear less authoritarian. Jewish interests in banning anti-Semitic caricature shaped the formation of citizen juries, the appointments to the civilian censorship board, and the enforcement of the board's race-based standards.[15] These Jewish citizen censors held unprecedented authority to control their own image in Chicago.

Jewish censors gained power in Chicago in 1914—a transitional year in the history of motion picture production.[16] Around this time, Protestant cultural control of motion pictures—in the hands of the so-called Edison Trust and the National Board of Censorship—collapsed. In 1908 Edison joined with other filmmakers to create a patent trust—the Motion Picture Patents Company—which charged nonmembers fees for using patented cameras, projectors, and raw film stock. The eight members of this trust bankrolled the National Board of Censorship. By 1912, however, many new producers were making movies outside of the Patents Company; they had taken over half of the market. Motion picture entrepreneur Carl Laemmle initially worked within the system of the "Trust," as he named the Patents Company, but then decided to fight it in 1909.[17] Laemmle and many of the other new independent producers were Jewish, most from Eastern Europe, with a few from Central Europe. Sigmund Lubin, on the other hand, was one of only two Jews in the trust. They came to movie production through the ownership of nickelodeons in their immigrant neighborhoods, unlike the Protestants who spent their early careers as inventors or entertainers.[18] Edison's group tried to push the independents out through litigation and "economic pressure."[19] But by 1914 the trust had disintegrated and, in 1915, the Supreme Court provided the final blow when it ruled that Edison's group violated fair trade. The battle between the independents and Edison's monopoly had been more than a business competition: according to Neal Gabler, it was also "generational, cultural, philosophical, even, in some ways, religious."[20] These independents consolidated into various companies to establish the eight companies of Hollywood: all the founders or heads of the "Big Eight" were Jewish.[21]

The shifts in the motion picture business coincided with changes in the image of Jews on film. Historians generally agree that Jewish characters received more favorable representation from 1900 to 1920, once Jews gained more power in Hollywood. In cinema's "primitive" years the Jew on screen was usually a "scheming merchant" or a conman, greedy and deceitful, or an outright criminal. In *Levinsky's Holiday* (1913), for example, a clothing merchant takes his son to the circus where the father agrees to become the target in "Hit the Nigger," rather than pay his entrance fee like other customers. Levinsky realizes that his son is making a profit from his role in the game by selling the rotten eggs that spectators throw at the father, which makes him praise his son. Scholars suggest that early producers, mostly Gentiles, did not consider the "very real injury" that such "distorted caricatures did to contemporary Jews."[22] But by the end of World War I, the Jew in motion pictures had become an icon of Americanization; films often ended with Jewish-Gentile intermarriage and showed hardworking Jews leaving the ghetto. Several scholars suggest that the prominence of Jewish producers created this more sympathetic portrait of Jews on screen. The film historian Thomas Cripps, for example, holds that the sentimental, Americanized image matched the "assimilationist experience of the Jewish studio bosses."[23] This chapter shows that Jewish producers make up only one part of a more complicated story. At the same time that the power in motion picture production shifted to Jews, Jewish censors gained the authority to regulate the image of Jews on film as censors in Chicago. Chicago's censorship regime thus pitted Jewish producers against Jewish censors.

Several factors explain the rise of Jewish censorship in Chicago: the rich organizational life of Jews of Central European descent in this city, the Anti-Defamation League's influence in its home city, and the links between prominent Jewish reformers, many in the legal profession, and the Democratic city administrations. In 1907, Chicago and Philadelphia had 100,000 Jewish residents, second only to New York City. By 1927, Chicago had surpassed Philadelphia, with 325,000 Jewish citizens, compared to New York City's 1.7 million.[24] The first Jewish residents of Chicago were immigrants from the southwest of what became Germany in the mid-nineteenth century. They hailed from Bavaria, Prussia, Bohemia, and Austria. The United States warmly received this group, according to the historian Edward Mazur, while the later wave of Jewish immigrants from Eastern Europe met with a hostile reception.[25] Many became financially successful, rising to top of the clothing industry, in manufacturing and retail.[26] The highest-paid rabbi in the world at that time was Emil Hirsch, of Chicago's Reform Sinai Congregation, with a salary of $12,000 in 1887. Julius Rosenwald, the president and chairman of Sears and Roebuck and a premiere philanthropist, was a member of the Hirsch's congregation. In 1885, Hirsch's temple shifted to a Sunday Sabbath; Hirsch explained this as a result of Jewish success in a Christian world: "With very rare exception, all Jewish business houses are open. . . . Which would be wise, to lose all our religion or simply to change our Sabbath day?"[27] While the success stories of Central European Jewish merchants are often dramatic, these affluent businessmen were far outnumbered by the skilled craftsmen and laborers. And their wealth did not match the fortunes and power of the "gentile American oligarchy that controlled heavy industry and directed the flow of investment" around the turn of the twentieth century.[28]

This group of Chicago Jews was not only active in Jewish philanthropy and community development, with national headquarters in Chicago; it also led urban reform beyond the boundaries of organized Jewish life. Members were also allied with the Democratic administration of Mayor Carter Harrison II. Jewish organizations in Chicago led the Jewish anti-defamation work: the Anti-Defamation League (ADL) emerged out of B'nai B'rith's District 6, which included Chicago, and was the home district of its national president, Adolf Kraus. Chicago was also the home of the

National Council of Jewish Women (NCJW). In 1905, the B'nai B'rith, under Kraus's leadership, moved its headquarters to Chicago and remained there for twenty years.

Leaders of B'nai B'rith and the NCJW had united to fight against the Stage Jew before the founding of the ADL. In April 1913, prominent Chicago Jews formed the Anti–Stage Jew Vigilance Committee; the founding members are a who's who of organized Chicago Jewry. The NCJW was well represented, with Babette Mandel, Jennie Purvin, and Hannah Solomon serving on the original committee.[29] Kraus, of the B'nai B'rith, and Tobias Schanfarber, an officer in the Central Conference of American Rabbis, were also founders. The committee was composed overwhelmingly of Reform Jews, who had roots in Central Europe. The organizations represented had already displayed an interest in the representation of Jews in mass culture, through campaigns for "purity" in the press and efforts to stop *The Merchant of Venice*, among other causes. The mayor of Chicago, Harrison, also ranked among the members of this pre-ADL committee, and he seemed sympathetic to Jewish concerns when he staffed his city censors.[30]

In this milieu Kraus possessed the skills and interest to pioneer antidefamation work. Born in Bohemia in 1850, he came to New York City at the age of fifteen and moved to Chicago at twenty-one to embark on a distinguished career in public service, law, and publishing. During his six years on the Chicago Board of Education, he served two terms as its president and also worked on the committee for textbooks. In 1891 he began to work with Carter Harrison I in his publishing venture, the *Chicago Times*, and helped make it profitable when he took over editorial control.[31] In 1893, Harrison appointed him as his "corporation counsel," a position Kraus retained until Harrison's assassination. He became president of the Civil Service Commission in 1897. During his term as president of the B'nai B'rith, from 1905 to 1925, he pushed the international organization toward antidefamation work in the United States.[32]

Kraus was active in Chicago's campaign against prostitution, in which he tried to both protect the reputation of Jews and to end crimes against vulnerable women. He responded forcefully to George Kibbe Turner's April 1907 exposé of Chicago prostitution in Chicago in *McClure's Magazine*. Turner alleged Russian Jews were predominant in this area, but after a separate investigation, Kraus argued that only 20 percent of the traffickers were Jewish.[33] With Julius Rosenwald's backing, Kraus and B'nai B'rith hired Clifford Roe, a former assistant state attorney who had worked on

Adolf Kraus, author of the 1907 motion picture censorship ordinance in Chicago. Courtesy of the B'nai B'rith International Archives at the American Jewish Archives, Cincinnati, Ohio. AmericanJewishArchives.org

Adolf Kraus, 1905-1925

white slavery cases, to "work independently" against prostitution.[34] Kraus insisted that no Gentile be arrested until "every Jew engaged in the business" was in jail.[35] In 1911, after the publication of the Chicago Vice Commission's report on prostitution, Kraus joined the Committee of Fifteen to "aid the public authorities in the enforcement of all laws against pandering and to take measures calculated to suppress the 'white slave' traffic."[36] Kraus worked with his friend Julius Rosenwald on this committee, but most members were Protestant.[37]

Kraus may thus have been responding to several factors—local, national, and international—when he drafted his inclusive motion picture censorship law. Turner's exposé on white slavery, which prompted Kraus's reform activity with the Committee of Fifteen and may have also informed his efforts to protect the image of Jews, appeared in April 1907, six months before the city council passed Kraus's law. Kraus was probably aware of organized Jewry's efforts to stop insulting advertisements of anti-Jewish admission policies at resorts and of attacks on *The Merchant of Venice* and on vaudeville comedians. In addition, the context for considering the vulnerability of minorities included pogroms in Europe. In April 1903, forty-seven Jews were killed in the Kishineff pogrom; then, two years later in Odessa, more than eight hundred lost their lives in the violence. Finally, Kraus also likely knew about laws passed in other cities, such as Des Moines, to censor Thomas Dixon's *The Clansman* and prevent racial violence. The editor of the *Des Moines Register*, Harvey Ingham, was, like Kraus, a Jewish leader who backed African American causes.[38] After the Atlanta riots in September of 1906, for which *The Clansman* may have provided one spark,

Dixon boldly predicted that riots would follow in New York and Chicago. The Chicago newspapers covered other incidents in which *The Clansman* seemed to inspire lynchings. Then, in 1906, the *Chicago Tribune* endorsed the suppression of the play: "An author who insults a race of citizens and then complains about lawless interference with white men's rights is hardly the man to be trusted to assist in the elevation of the American stage."[39]

Kraus and other Jewish leaders were active within this nexus of advocacy for Jews specifically and social reform more generally. Other prominent Jews in Chicago worked in both worlds, while many also shared Kraus's alliance with the Democratic Party and his success in the legal field. Like Kraus, Julian Mack and Hugo Pam combined their legal backgrounds, Democratic allegiances, leadership in Jewish organizations, and activism in non-Jewish reform groups with their support for Jewish censorship. Mack, whose grandmother had emigrated from Bavaria, was a Chicago attorney who did some of his early work at the Chicago World's Fair, determining whether or not "Little Egypt" violated decency standards.[40] Mack, like his friend Julian Rosenwald, worked closely with Mayor Carter Harrison II, who rewarded him with an appointment as Chicago's civil service commissioner. He soon moved on to become a judge on the Circuit Court of Cook County, then on the Juvenile Court in 1904. Mack's trajectory resembles Kraus's: both received appointments from Democratic mayors, and both served as presidents of the Civil Service Commission. Mack spoke out in favor of an age limit for five-cent theaters in May 1907.[41] The reformers working with juvenile justice were extensively involved in motion picture reform.

Several Jewish "club women" also pioneered Jewish censorship in Chicago. Like Pam, Kraus, and Mack, these women transcended racial and religious lines in their reform work. Mrs. Ignace J. Reis, part of the 1913 Chicago group that worked against the Stage Jew, served on women's censorship juries, for *Smashing the Vice Trust*, for example, and on a Jewish women's jury for *Rebecca's Wedding Day*. Along with being active in the NCJW, Reis was also a leader of the Travelers' Aid Society, which aimed to protect women, girls, and children from "evil" when traveling alone.[42] Other Jewish women, including Hannah Solomon and Mrs. Herman Landauer, were active as Jewish censors based on their work in women's clubs generally, not just Jewish organizations.[43] Solomon, who served on the Chicago Motion Picture Commission in 1920, and Landauer were leaders in the NCJW as well as in the Chicago Woman's Club.[44]

Major Metellus L. C. Funkhouser, vigilant Chicago censor. Chicago History Museum

In 1913, five years after Kraus's law went into effect, Major Funkhouser became Chicago's new "censor of public morals."[45] He quickly gained a reputation as a strict censor—a "prudish old maid," as one critic put it.[46] He allegedly rejected three times as many films as his predecessor and more than the National Board of Censorship. "Funkhouserism," one anticensorship activist explained, is "a menace to the rights that made this country free."[47] This kind of criticism prompted him to experiment with more flexible censorship processes. A few months after his appointment Funkhouser began to seek out groups of citizens to review plays and movies, including businessmen and club women, but the new advisors would not "sit as a board of censorship."[48] The citizen juries proffered a key opening for the new ADL. As Funkhouser searched Chicago for citizen-censors, Jewish advocates readily stepped forward and enforced the race-based censorship rules they had helped create. The relationship between Funkhouser and the ADL was so close that the ADL not only lobbied the board but Chicago censors contacted the ADL about films they thought Jewish leaders might find offensive.[49] The ADL explained the favorable process in Chicago: "To wait for the picture to be shown and then register a protest was, of course, quite useless, as but very few theaters book a film for more than one day's run. . . . This opportunity was accorded us through the courtesy of Mayor Carter H. Harrison of Chicago and Major MLC Funkhouser, Second Deputy Superintendent of Police, who permitted the Managing Board [of the ADL] to inspect all films which had Jewish characters in the cast."[50] Funkhouser believed that particular groups—a racial minority, a profession, women—should rule on films that featured them. For example, a special committee of children's advocates reviewed and rejected *How Villains Are Made*.[51] He also invited a group of army officers to review *The Trap* because it featured a drunken military man. In the case of *The Trap* (and many other films), Funkhouser turned to a jury after he had already approved the film, so his reliance on the specialized citizen juries was often a backup plan when citizens criticized his decisions. Funkhouser defended his committee or "jury" system as democratic: "It is true that I allow a committee to censor the pictures. They act as a jury. They witness a picture and cast their opinions in a ballot box. Then I revoke the permit or allow the picture to be shown, according to their verdict."[52] This approach made censorship seem more open and also dampened criticism from likely lobbying groups.

On February 17, 1914, Chicago's censorship moved into the hands of a ten-person civilian board under Funkhouser's supervision.[53] This shift raised the status of the citizen censors, who had previously served on ad hoc juries at Funkhouser's discretion, and decreased the power of police screeners who had ruled on films. The civilian censorship board featured a new system of representation. The board itself was "representative" of the diversity of Chicago, with one Jewish member, one Catholic member, one Polish censor, and—eventually—an African American representative. Four of the original five appointees were women, including Miss Eva Loeb (nominated by Judges Pam and Mack, Rabbi Emil Hirsch and forty-six Jewish women's clubs), Mrs. Christine Field (endorsed by the Chicago Commons Woman's Club) and Mrs. G. F. Karr (backed by Catholic priests).[54] Particular social service organizations, such as Hull House and the Juvenile Protective Association, also sent representatives to the board.

The censorship board and the citizen juries constituted contrasting approaches to representing racial and religious minorities in the assessment of movies. With the board, the mayor sought a diverse group to inspect all films, while the citizen juries gathered to comment only on films related to their particular social group. The civilian censorship board may have been an attempt to tame both police power and the demands of pressure groups like the ADL. The two systems, however, overlapped, as Funkhouser turned to citizen juries if protesters objected to the board's decision about a film.

Funkhouser thus used citizen juries for additional inspections to settle debates about provocative movies[55]

Although other professional and women's groups were often assembled to decide on a particular motion picture, Jewish juries were the most common in 1914. The ADL's first success was the suppression of *Rebecca's Wedding Day* in late January 1914. Funkhouser recalled that the picture initially "got by us. . . . Even the Jewish people on the board did not catch it."[56] Then Kraus and others "had all the hide off of [him]," according to Funkhouser, and he assembled a committee of Jewish women to view the film.[57] After they decided it was "odious"—and a potential "cause of prejudice against the Jewish people"—Funkhouser revoked the permit. The *Chicago Tribune* announced that this action was the "first move in the campaign started by the recently formed Anti-Defamation League."[58] Funkhouser explained that "whenever a picture relates to the Jewish race I will have it first viewed by a committee."[59] Critics attacked the censors' decision about *Rebecca's Wedding Day*. "This was a comedy no one but a few individuals could take exception to. . . . what chance have we to produce a comedy with an Irishman, Englishman, Swede, German, or any other civilized nationality?"[60] In one of many lawsuits, the Mutual Film Corporation questioned the rejection of *Rebecca's Wedding Day* "because Rebecca weighs 300 pounds and falls through the bottom of a cab on the way to church. Had Rebecca been Irish or German there would have been no objection, but Mr. Funkhouser says the picture ridicules the Jewish race. Jewish citizens of high intelligence who have seen the picture see nothing but the real humor in the picture and enjoy it as they enjoy Potash and Perlmutter stories."[61] But the ADL prevailed, and its success was not just local; it announced that *Rebecca's Wedding Day* was "suppressed in practically every part of the country."[62]

Film manufacturers, outraged at the banning of *Rebecca's Wedding Day*, asked of the censors: "Whom do these women represent?"[63] This was a complicated question. They clearly represented the Jewish community, but many of the Jewish women also transcended race and religion. Mrs. Herman Landauer, for example, frequently represented the Chicago Woman's Club.[64] But she was also on the Jewish jury that endorsed *The Merchant of Venice*, after making one cut.[65] Later, she was on a women's jury that banned a movie on white slavery, *Smashing the Vice Trust*, in March 1914.[66]

These Jewish women censors participated in the rise of female censors, whose authority rested in their ability to speak for children and other women. Funkhouser described his reliance on female censors in this way: "Very often it was not an unusual thing for us to send out for the ladies connected with the welfare of the city to come in and see the picture. We thought they were better people to pass upon them than we, as to the influence it would have upon the children or their disposition."[67] In the twentieth century female reformers justified their participation in censorship campaigns through maternalism—their supposedly innate desire and ability to protect children—not through their own pure sexual standards, as many had in the nineteenth century.[68] With this maternal mission, female reformers earned spots on censorship boards across the country. The New York and Pennsylvania state censorship boards reserved one spot on their three-person panels for a woman.[69] Middle-class women ultimately made up most of censors on the National Board of Censorship. The historian Lee Grieveson notes that, by 1912, 57 of 75 censors were women, and in 1915 the number of women had risen to 100 of 115. In 1917 the Kansas Motion Picture Censorship Board had become the first state board to be "composed entirely of women."[70] Female censors seemed to be the "great policing force of the business" or, as one observer dismissively noted, "the new indoor sport [censorship] has attained great popularity among the ladies."[71] Free-speech proponents also singled out Funkhouser for catering to a "small coterie of women" and endorsing a "prudish hysteria."[72]

One month after Jewish women rejected *Rebecca's Wedding Day*, another Jewish jury assembled to re-evaluate *The Merchant of Venice*, which had received a permit earlier. This jury was a group of men and women, perhaps because the main character was not a woman and the film was serious "art." The committee included Adolf Kraus, Judge Hugo Pam, former judge Philip Stein, and Mrs. Herman Landauer, who had previously reviewed *Rebecca's Wedding Day*. Pam and Kraus had been active in the 1913 attack on the Stage Jew, just prior to the formation of the ADL. Stein had been active in defending Jewish interests against Christian standards and led the drive to have the Chicago World's Fair stay open on Sunday.[73] A permit for *The Merchant of Venice* had been issued earlier, but some Chicago Jews lobbied Funkhouser to revoke it. Funkhouser decided to convene the citizen jury: "I intend to be fully satisfied that the character of Shylock is portrayed in such a way that it will not be conducive to the baiting of a race the city should protect from unwarranted prejudice as much as any class of its citizens."[74] After the screening in city hall, Rabbi Abram Hirschberger spoke out "strenuously" against the film being shown to children, particularly in regard to the scene "showing Shylock groveling on the ground and clutching his beloved money."[75] Yet the group approved the film and made only one alteration: the phrase "the Jew" in one subtitle was changed to "Shylock." Funkhouser conveniently placed himself outside the debate: "It is not a personal matter with me."[76]

Through the Jewish juries or the regular civilian board, censors regularly edited or banned altogether movies that featured Jewish characters and themes. The ADL celebrated its success: "In practically every instance our recommendation was accepted."[77] Along with *Rebecca's Wedding Day* and *The Merchant of Venice*, which attracted widespread attention, the ADL and Jewish censors quietly shaped many other censorship decisions. In January 1914 the Chicago officials refused a permit to *A Stage Door Flirtation*, with "two Yiddish sports," along with *The Missing Diamond*.[78] One month later, the Chicago censors suppressed *One of the Finest* and *How Mosha Came Back*.[79] When they did not ban movies, censors sometimes cut some scenes to improve the representation of Jews. They edited *Deborah* by slicing two subtitles: "Perhaps money will induce the Jewess to release him" and "The Jewess willingly accepts the money." On September 14, 1914, the Chicago censors cut out several subtitles from *The Daredevil Detective*: "Rosenzweig will pay a big price for them [the jewels]" and "at Rosenzweig's." On this same day, the board ordered cutouts of *Oliver Twist*. Although the reports mention nothing about the representation of Jews, it is likely that Jewish activists complained about the character Fagin, as they did later, in 1921.[80]

Often the ban on racial or religious disparagement intersected with the disapproval of the depiction of unlawful acts. A central rationale for the rejection of films was the depiction of Jewish criminals; six movies were denied in 1914 for this reason. A report of the board's censorship activities in 1918 ranked the number of feet deleted for eight offending subjects. The depiction of "unlawful" acts ranked first on the list, accounting for nearly 50 percent of all material cut (or 31,000 feet of deleted film). "Race" was the cause of deletions on six occasions, accounting for only 254 feet of cut film. Race ranked seventh out of eight subjects, with creed as the least popular.[81] The attention to depictions of crime sometimes covered anti-Semitism as well. Chicago censors eliminated the first reel of *Rose of the Alley*, which featured Fagin, a Jewish peddler who recruits a girl to a life of crime: "Fagin . . . has her in his clutches, and compels her to pick pockets, showing her, throughout the first part of the first reel, how it should be done."[82] In addition, the Chicago permit for *The Mystery of the Amsterdam*

Diamonds was cancelled in June 1914.[83] The ADL objected to this movie because the main criminal was Jewish. The board also officially rejected *The Master Cracksman* because it made a "hero out of a criminal."[84] Chicago censors noted two assaults on police officers, a robbery, and other objectionable scenes, but the ADL objected to the "fence" being made up as a Jew—Moses—and to a scene in which Moses "is shown fondly kissing his money."[85]

On February 15, 1914, Carl Laemmle's Universal Motion Picture Manufacturing Company launched a series of advertisements attacking Funkhouser. Born in Württemberg (which became part of Germany in 1871), Laemmle had strong ties to Chicago. His announcements denounced Funkhouser's restrictive standards ("You peremptorily tell us to stop showing pictures which are shown and approved in every other city") and mocked his individual power ("You are confident you know more about moving pictures than the half million Chicagoans who pay to see them every day").[86] Laemmle accused Funkhouser of failing to understand that scenes of crime and drinking often taught powerful moral lessons against vice.[87] But after Funkhouser had allowed Jewish leaders to reexamine *The Merchant of Venice*, the ads specifically attacked Jewish power in the censorship process. First, Laemmle described the Jewish censorship work as divisive and undemocratic; he alleged that Funkhouser protected "one class of people more than another": "Why should you consider them any more than the Irish, the Germans, the Dutch, the Scandinavians, or any other American citizens?"[88] Second, Laemmle suggested a political motivation behind Funkhouser's deference to Chicago Jews: How would these Jews in "high positions" "thank" Funkhouser for the privilege of censoring?[89] Laemmle's ads focused on how Funkhouser manipulated the review process by referring to citizen juries. He accused Funkhouser of wanting to reject *The Merchant of Venice* (in the advertisement from February 18 he said Funkhouser was "in serious doubt" about the film), but ultimately letting Jews hold the responsibility for a controversial decision: "Didn't you want some one else to be the goat?"[90] Movie producers thus described Funkhouser's use of citizen juries, particularly Jewish juries, as a dangerous political game. The juries insulated him from criticism, yet also won him political support from the groups of jurors. In these ways, Laemmle accused "Candidate" Funkhouser of using censorship to aid his political ambitions.[91] In response, the ADL wrote to Laemmle directly, claiming that "these advertisements are pernicious, offensive and indiscreet in their attack upon Jews and Jewish organizations.... [The advertisements] tend to instil [sic] prejudice in the minds of some against the Jewish people."[92] The attack on Funkhouser's Jewish juries centered on the impracticality and the injustice of having one minority group control images on screen. Jews, in general, were not censors for the whole community; thus their decisions on behalf of Jews registered as deviations from democratic decisions. The more power Jewish censors accrued to regulate images of themselves, the more suspicion they aroused as biased censors.

Critics charged that Funkhouser's citizen juries were unfair and partisan—a far cry from Funkhouser's pronouncements about the juries as models of democracy.[93] Some critics complained of exclusion from the juries: African Americans, for example, wanted to sit on a jury, but Funkhouser never asked them. Others argued that Funkhouser's system relied on those who complained most often: a citizen jury was a "packed jury."[94] In response, he characterized his committees as juries of "good men and women [who] cast their opinions in a ballot box" and rendered a "verdict."[95]

Despite escalating criticism from movie producers, the censors' bans on negative Jewish characters continued through the spring and summer. Chicago censors denied permits to *The Partners* (March 1914) and *The Peddlers* (May 1914), both of which they deemed to ridicule Jews. The rejected *In the Czar's Name* for depicting the "mistreatment of Jews" and *His Trade* for showing Jewish vandals.[96]

By the fall of 1914, after their advertising campaign had failed, movie producers seemed to become more cooperative. The activity of the Chicago censors put so much pressure on the filmmakers that they sometimes voluntarily withdrew their movies at the ADL's urging. Leon Lewis, the secretary of the ADL, explained in the November 1914 *Motion Picture Bulletin* that Laemmle had canceled the Chicago tour of *The Fatal Wedding*, which the ADL compared to *Rebecca's Wedding Day*.[97] "It is quite apparent that within two or three months after we had commenced our campaign, motion picture manufacturers were giving considerable attention to the communications which we sent to them."[98] Laemmle met with the ADL after the Chicago censors had notified the ADL about *The Fatal Wedding*. At that meeting Laemmle apologized for the film, explaining that it had been issued "through an oversight."[99] He then promised that "no films which tend to bring the Jew into ridicule or contempt should be manufactured in the future."[100] Vitagraph, in November of 1914, invited the ADL to send representatives to inspect two of its films dealing with Jewish life before their release.[101] When advocacy groups could speak through a censorship board, manufacturers listened. The ADL hoped to extend its antidefamation ordinance for this reason: "Wherever it is found that negotiations with the film exchanges, municipal authorities, or the theatrical managers, are unproductive of results, the model ordinance, which has been drafted, [should] be introduced in the local council and support for the same sought from all civic societies."[102]

The Chicago board was not as vigilant about the representation of other groups, though it did not ignore them altogether. The case of *How Mosha Came Back* illustrates the censors' disparate treatment of minority groups. The regular civilian board rejected the movie on February 27, 1914; members of the ADL attended the screening and "were present when [the film] was condemned."[103] In the movie, Mosha, a "98 pound weakling," becomes a prize fighter in his dream and knocks out the world champion—an Irish fighter. The ADL opposed the film because Mosha was presented "in caricature." But critics of Chicago censorship argued that the suppression of *How Mosha Came Back* for demeaning Jews ignored the Irish: "This was done although an Irishman got the worst of the spat, in which he got mixed up with a Jew."[104] In 1914, Chicago's censors sometimes suppressed films for insulting a variety of racial minorities, foreign groups, and Catholics. It rejected *Nipped* "because of tendency to disturb public peace and creating prejudice against Japs [sic] and Mexicans."[105] It denied permits to at least two films because they were anti-Catholic. *Renunciation* allegedly insulted the Catholic community because it showed a monk carrying around with him "the photograph of the sweetheart of his youth and [who] at the end tears it up and throws it at the image of the Virgin Mary."[106] *Pieces of Silver* met with rejection because of its tendency to "create religious prejudice."[107] Chicago censors also cut several films that depicted lynchings that same year: *A Desperate Chance*, *The Partners*, and *Condemned*. The last of those was suppressed because it portrayed a riot and mob rule.

African Americans certainly perceived Jewish authority in censorship that they did not have. The leading African American newspaper, the *Chicago Defender* noted in March 1914 that Jews had successfully rejected two movies because they "burlesqued" Jews. "First a determined effort for representation on the board of censors, and then a close scrutiny of the reels submitted will soon enable the *Chicago Defender* to display a headline like this: "Colored Women's Clubs Keep Race from Ridicule."[108] A few months later, the paper attacked two movies: the first showed an illiterate black man stealing a chicken and the second, *Mother of Men*, focused on a slave stealing a white baby. Asking "where is [the] censor board?" the *Chicago Defender* claimed that the "degrading pictures of the race" should not have passed the censor in the first place.[109] The newspaper also criticized *Levinsky's Holiday* for passing the censors without any editing of "Hit the Nigger," a carnival game the protagonist plays in the film. African Americans, the publication asserted, seemed to be the last group left to lampoon: "It used to be 'Hit the Jew' or 'Down with the Irish' but alert members of those races watch with hawk-like eyes any attempt to belittle their people."[110]

African American struggles for representation among Chicago censors and for reform of the images of black people occurred during a period of rising political power for African Americans in the city. In the late nineteenth and early twentieth century, Chicago attracted many educated and politically active black migrants. One of these new arrivals, Robert S. Abbott (who decided to stay in Chicago after he performed at the Columbian Exposition), founded the *Chicago Defender* in 1905.[111] The population of Chicago's so-called Black Belt had reached about 30,000 by 1910, but this increase was dwarfed by the great migration following World War I. By 1935, the African American population had reached 250,000. A group of white and black Progressives, including Jane Addams, formed a committee to support the NAACP in 1909; the Jewish philanthropist Julius Rosenwald was also an early and regular contributor to NAACP causes in Chicago. In 1913, this committee became the NAACP's first affiliate. The growing black community increasingly tried to achieve better representation in city and state legislative bodies. With the backing of the local NAACP branch, two African Americans—Robert Jackson and Sheadrick Turner—were elected to the state senate in 1914. By 1915 Chicago's African Americans made up the majority in the second ward and elected Oscar De Priest as the first African American alderman—a goal they had pursued for many years. The *Chicago Defender* wrote of these efforts, "We must have a colored alderman, not because others are not friendly, but because we should be represented just the same as the Irish, Jews and Italians."[112] The success of these black politicians was tied not only to civil rights organizing but also to African American links with Mayor William Thompson's Republican machine, which came to power in 1915. Drawing on his New England abolitionist heritage, Thompson supported racial equality, and Chicago African Americans upheld him as the "second Lincoln."[113]

African Americans in Chicago worked to enhance their power in city and state politics, including the city's censorship board. The *Chicago Defender* wrote repeatedly about the need for an African American on the censor board, as it was a political body, like the school board or city council that served tax payers.[114] It noted that Jewish organizations had backed Eva Loeb for the board, and that Catholics had recommended Mrs. G. F. Carr, acknowledging the "obvious" need for them to "protect their races from ridicule." But African Americans, "more maligned" than other races, lacked representation. By mid-March, the *Chicago Defender* noted that the censorship board was busy and understaffed, but had still not reached out to an African American citizen.[115] Finally, on March 21, 1914, Mayor Harrison appointed Reverend A. J. Carey to the board. Born into a Georgia slave family, Carey attended Atlanta University and moved to Chicago in 1896 to become pastor of Quinn Chapel AME church. He also became active in Chicago politics and civic causes.[116]

Gaining representation on the board seems to have helped African Americans in some ways. After Carey joined, the censors cut *Hen Fruit* in October 1914 because of its portrayal of "tramps and negro stealing chickens."[117] The *Chicago Defender* also bragged that Carey had censored several "race pictures" from a white firm in New York that East Coast censors had let pass.[118] In March 1915, Alonzo Bowling, a sociologist and educator, was appointed to the board to replace Carey. He was discharged in April but reappointed in May, after his "troubles" [had been] "readjusted." Carey supported him.[119] The presence of a single African American on the board did not have an impact on the biggest censorship controversy in the city—the debate over *The Birth of a Nation.*

Compared to the many movies with Jewish characters censored in Chicago, *The Birth of a Nation* had a much easier path to exhibition. It first passed review in an irregular way, when the wife of Chicago's mayor previewed the film with the mayor's secretary, Charles Fitzmorris, though not the censorship board.[120] After this "private exhibition," the police superintendent issued a permit, without any cuts. In light of the intense discussion of the film around the country and the forced edits and bans in other cities, observers expressed surprise that Chicago's censorship board, considered one of the nation's strictest, was not "permitted to use [its] cutting implements in this instance."[121] African Americans protested this unusual path to exhibition, pointing to the film's celebration of "the mob hanging a nigger" and other scenes of "race hate."[122] They were also angry that that "no colored people had been present at the city hall showing [with Mrs. Carter Harrison]."[123]

Two weeks later, after significant protest and the end of Harrison's term, the new mayor, William Hale Thompson, decided to revoke *The Birth of a Nation*'s permit for several reasons. First, he said that the recreation of Lincoln's assassination could cause crime in the city: "Anything of that kind simply breeds crime," he announced.[124] Second, Mayor Thompson acknowledged that he was responding to lobbying from African Americans, explaining that "the negro is entitled to protection from class hatred."[125] Although it seemed unequivocal, Thompson's decision was actually weak, because he also admitted to not having seen the movie; instead he based his decision on the opinions of the black protesters and on the views of "[s]ome of my friends who have seen it."[126] In addition, the abrupt shift in the censorship decision from one administration to another made it seem particularly political. Movie producers were gratified, then, to see a swell of public challenges to censorship after Thompson's decision: The *Moving Picture World* remarked, "Especially has the incident [Thompson's ban] been prolific of good in that it has enlisted powerful public opinion on behalf of moving pictures."[127] Under pressure from censorship foes, Thompson offered one possible solution—gather African American leaders to get their approval of the film. He suggested to the producers of Griffith's film that they assemble "thirty or forty colored ministers and let them pass on the picture."[128] This did not happen.

The supporters of *The Birth of a Nation* instead sought an injunction to stop Thompson's ban for several reasons. They alleged that his revocation of the permit was illegal because it occurred outside of a three-day period of review and was not based on any violations of the permit. They also claimed the ban constituted an unjust interference with the contracts and profits of the movie producers, who had invested $30,000 in Chicago as result of the permit. Judge William Fenimore Cooper, of the Illinois Cook County Superior Court, rejected the mayor's decision, elaborating that *The Birth of a Nation* had "good and bad" black and white men, and other films, on a regular basis, contained "the debased type of the white race of different nationalities."[129] The situation thus made it unwise and impossible to censor racial insults. He concluded: "Any race or nationality so offended can best give the lie to the bad characters so presented by continuing to conduct themselves as law abiding citizens who do not expect greater rights from the law than it allows all other men or nationalities."[130]

The run of Griffith's film in Chicago spelled a defeat for African Americans on several levels. Unlike white women, Jews, and particular professional groups, African Americans had not been consulted as a jury to determine the fate of a film that depicted them. When they did manage to influence the mayor's decision, a judge overruled the ban and specifically rejected racial ridicule as a basis of censorship. Chicago officials thus rebuked African Americans as censors and undermined race-based censorship.

Although African Americans lost in their local struggle over *The Birth of a Nation*, their escalation of the battle to the state level demonstrated their growing political power. After the Chicago showing of the film, the African American legislator Robert Jackson took the language of the Chicago city ordinance and introduced it into the House of the General Assembly in 1915, where it became state law in 1917. Jackson's efforts show how African Americans and Jews used the same tools—in this case, a law written by Adolf Kraus—but were not allied in the laws' implementation.

Jackson was elected to the Illinois House of Representatives after success in civil service and private business as well as civil rights activism. He became the highest-ranking African American in Chicago's postal system and also a wealthy businessman through a printing business and his involvement with Negro League baseball. He focused on improving the image of African Americans in film and elsewhere, such as securing state funding for a celebration of the fiftieth anniversary of black emancipation.[131] He worked to end segregation and lynching and to block antimiscegenation laws, including one directed at heavyweight champion Jack Johnson.[132] His hostility to *The Birth of a Nation* combined a concern with images and practice, as he concluded that the film favorably portrayed lynching and thus "forc[ed] a prejudice" against African Americans as a class.[133]

Jackson's censorship bill faced Jewish opposition, but it also had significant Jewish support in the state legislature. Chicago's local censors opposed it because they saw it as an affront to "home rule." Indeed, Jewish censors would likely see their authority in censorship diminished because so much of their input depended on local Chicago networks. In this way, Jackson's bill pitted local Jewish interests against African American statewide censorship. But Jackson also relied on the Jewish senator Samuel Ettelson, who pushed the bill through the Senate. The senator had been active in the pre-ADL committee to combat the Stage Jew in Chicago.[134] Jackson and others articulated a multiracial vision of censorship as "the protection of the rights of all races who are held up to scorn and contempt and pictured as criminals," but some supporters of the bill drew a more narrow group of racial victims as they maligned Jewish movie producers as "embittering hundreds of thousands of our citizens" with their greed.[135] Finally, as the bill was amended and revised in the state legislature, race dropped out as a category of censorship. The ADL then opposed the final wording of the bill because it "would not permit the ruling out of films which incite race prejudice."[136]

The bill failed in 1915, but Jackson introduced race-based censorship again in 1917. His chances had improved in 1917, after the Supreme Court's 1915 decision upholding state censorship of motion pictures, *Mutual v. Ohio*. In addition, the context of World War I gave Jackson additional urgency when he argued that the race-based censorship law protected a race of people who had shown great "devotion to the flag of the nation."[137] The bill prevailed. But enforcement was lax, partly because of inadequate funding and partly because of the state supreme court's earlier decision in favor of *The Birth of a Nation*. Thus, neither the Chicago law nor the identical state law stopped the blockbuster. The law's inclusive language could have helped build a coalition of Jews and African Americans, but the implementation of the law actually encouraged fragmentation and alienation, as Jews in Chicago were invited to censor as Jews about Jewish films While they had much less clout, African Americans, like Jews, found they could not represent Chicago; they were race-censors.

Funkhouser's censorship came under increasing fire after the controversy surrounding *The Birth of a Nation*. Not allied with urban reform and uninterested in motion pictures, the new mayor, "Big Bill" Thompson, proved less supportive of Funkhouser's role. He openly criticized Funkhouser for various transgressions, and the Chicago City Council introduced several plans to curb Funkhouser's power.[138] In 1916, the chief of police began to overrule Funkhouser's decisions and announced a new system in which the chief of the civilian censorship board, W. F. Willis, would report directly to the chief of police. The city attorney explained that this shift followed the law, but "it seemed to be taken for granted . . . that Maj. Funkhouser's decisions were final and unreversible. If the chief so desires he can appoint a representative to censor the pictures and can act on the recommendations of his representative rather than on those of Maj. Funkhouser."[139] Funkhouser continued his work, however, and fought back against the new chief of the board, charging that he was a lax censor and friendly to movie producers.[140] The *Chicago Tribune* announced that Funkhouser was no longer the "final arbiter" of films, but some of his censorship decisions still remained unopposed.[141] In 1917 the city council introduced another plan to undermine Funkhouser's power. It would require the entire censorship board to affirm Funkhouser's decision to block any film.[142]

Funkhouser hurt his standing when he banned films that insulted the German American community. He had followed the lead of Mayor Thompson, who denounced foreign entanglements as he courted the Irish and German vote in preparation for a run for the Senate.[143] But in 1915 and 1916, Funkhouser seemed unpatriotic when he stopped two movies for being anti-German: *The Ordeal* and *Alsace*. The Chicago censors concluded that *Alsace* was "strongly anti-German and would tend to create contempt and hatred for a law-abiding class of American citizens, namely those of German birth."[144] Funkhouser's suppression of *The Ordeal* was in step with the commissioner of licenses in New York City, who threatened to revoke the license of any theater that showed the film. *The Ordeal* featured a young man dreaming of going to war, the Franco-Prussian War of 1870, in which cruel German soldiers murder his family. When he awakes from his dream, however, his family is safe. Funkhouser and the New York City license commissioner agreed that the movie was likely to raise "racial strife" because of its misrepresentation of the German army.[145] The New York Supreme Court, however, issued an injunction to stop the ban on the movie in New York City. The opinion exposes the debates at the heart of minority groups, representation, and censorship:

> The court must assume that the term American includes all classes of citizens, native and naturalized, irrespective of where they originally came from, whether it be Germany or any other country. The court cannot give judicial sanction to the grouping of American citizens of different classes, and shape or color its decrees in accordance therewith; so that, what has lately become known as "hyphenated" citizenship has no place or standing.[146]

Funkhouser's Chicago critics noted that this opinion seemed to mock the censor.[147]

In 1917 and 1918, new censorship controversies arose around Funkhouser's decision to ban films that reflected poorly on Germans. He banned *The Little American*, starring Mary Pickford, because it showed German troops preparing to execute French prisoners and threatening to rape a young American woman. One review praised the film as pro-American, but Funkhouser saw it as an insult to German Americans in Chicago. As he had many times before, he responded to criticisms by assembling a citizen jury to decide for itself. But this time his jury got out of hand: he invited one hundred people to review the film, with a vote for each viewer. They passed the film.[148] William Brady, a representative of motion picture's interests, testified before the city council's Committee on the Judiciary against Funkhouser's powers and in favor of film's "patriotic purposes."[149] Funkhouser replied to the committee that censorship did not concern his personal power but the ordinance itself: "No film which casts any reflection on any race or religion is allowed," he said. Censorship was not a "one man institution."[150] In 1918 Funkhouser ordered cuts to D. W. Griffith's *Hearts of the World*, which supported the U.S. war effort. One of the film's promoters contacted the U.S. district attorney to investigate Funkhouser's treasonous censorship. Griffith's defenders questioned Funkhouser's patriotism and derided his "German sympathies."[151]

Chicago's judiciary committee stripped Funkhouser of his power in May 1918.[152] He still had some supporters: women's clubs and the ADL backed his retention at the judiciary committee hearings.[153] But the mayor suspended Funkhouser for improprieties and insubordination, charging that he had misused the vice investigation fund in "shadowing" prominent citizens.[154] Funkhouser appealed the dismissal and won. Then Thompson fought back by eliminating the position of second deputy superintendent of police. Funkhouser's days as the morals czar of Chicago were over. Thompson succeeded in getting rid of one of his political opponents and pushing back the Progressives.[155]

The censorship of racial insults did not end with Funkhouser and the new Thompson administration, but the scrutiny of images of Jews declined. This shift may be due to improvements in the representation of Jews on screen and the shifting city administration in Chicago. Thompson was a Republican, whereas the previous Democratic administrations had been more connected to Jewish supporters. Censorship seemed to favor African Americans more often in the Thompson administration. *The Bar Sinister* was banned in September 1918 because it "tended to create hatred and contempt for the African race." An African American jury, including antilynching activist Ida B. Wells, was also assembled in 1919 to review *The Homesteader* for its depiction of N. L. McCraken, a Chicago clergyman and the father-in-law of the filmmaker, Oscar Micheaux. It approved the film, however.[156] In 1921 at least one film, *The Scar of Shame*, was prohibited because of the poor representation of black people. Censors targeted only two films for the misrepresentation of Jews—*Heart of Gold* in 1919, and *Nothing to Think About* in 1921, but they banned several films for insulting Catholics in the 1920s: *Bride for a Knight* (1923), *Bishop of Hollywood* (1924) and *Let No Man Put Asunder* (1925).[157] Censors protected the Irish once, in 1921, by banning *Strangers Beware* for its tendency to create "hatred for the Irish."[158]

Chicago's founding censors wrote a law that benefited many minority groups, not only Jews. The city's experiment in representing racial minorities within censorship seemed remarkably inclusive and democratic—with citizen juries and a diverse civilian board. Jewish and African American legislators cooperated in the passage of the 1917 state motion picture censorship law, which brought the city's ban on racial insults to the state level. But Jews, particularly Jewish women, gained more power in censorship than other racial groups. Uneven access, as well as ongoing doubts about the wisdom of protecting of *any* racial minority through censorship, led to complaints about the unfair politics of Chicago censorship. As one critic noted, "Restriction is often the result of the organized zeal of minute minorities rather than the expression of a consensus of a community's opinion."[159] In general, racial minorities were sidelined because, as they gained power over the representation of their particular group, they could not stand in for the whole community. They represented division, not consensus. As the next chapter shows in more detail, this conundrum became a symbol of the weakness—the prejudice—of censorship in a democracy.

CHAPTER SIX

WITHOUT FEAR OR FAVOR

Free-Speech Advocates Confront
Race-Based Censorship

Civil rights censors argued that government censors should ban films that caused racial prejudice, while free-speech advocates like the filmmaker D. W. Griffith worried that censorship itself was "bitter prejudice."[1] What, then, did these opposing sides mean by "prejudice"? They agreed that it indicated narrow-minded or irrational belief. But civil rights censors saw prejudice in motion pictures as a barrier to racial and religious equality. The ADL, for example, referred to motion pictures as "dangerous instruments of prejudice."[2] The opponents of government interference, however, worked to stop prejudice in censorship, by which they meant political partisanship or narrow advocacy for one group, rather than the whole nation. As one free-speech supporter said, censorship was often based on "local prejudice," or opinion, not fact.[3] Thomas Edison echoed some Progressives when he touted the uplifting qualities of movies: it "will wipe out narrow-minded prejudices which are founded on ignorance, it will create a feeling of sympathy and a desire to help the down-trodden people of the earth."[4] Prejudice proved a particularly loaded term in this period of Progressive reform in which activists and intellectuals sought to heal increasingly volatile national divisions and put great faith in bureaucratic supposed experts to devise solutions to social problems. There was widespread agreement that progress depended on the elimination of prejudice. But the most effective tool for eradicating prejudice—expert, racially sensitive censorship or unfettered motion pictures—was the subject of intense debate.

This chapter examines the confrontation between free-speech advocates and the civil rights censors who supported race-based interventions as the campaign for free speech expanded and the scope of race-based censorship contracted. Griffith, a pioneer in politically provocative and historical movies, regularly confronted the National Board of Censorship, inciting turmoil in the board over its standards; he became a forceful free-speech advocate, helping stave off federal motion picture censorship.[5] Lawyers for Griffith pioneered free-speech claims for businesses in their case against Ohio's film censorship law before the Supreme Court in 1915.[6] The American Civil Liberties Union, founded during World War I, battled wartime restrictions on political dissent, but it also began to object to the censorship of racist and religious hatred, such as the Ku Klux Klan's publications or Henry Ford's anti-Semitism in the *Dearborn Independent*. Griffith's racially and religiously inflammatory films usually made explicit political or educational claims, so free-speech activists, who tended to focus on protecting politically subversive speech, became more critical of motion picture censorship. In addition, examples of race-based censorship prominently displayed politicized or prejudiced censorship. Race-based censorship thus gave censorship a bad name.

The earliest confrontations between free-speech activists and civil rights censors occurred within a reform organization designed to uplift film in cooperation with the motion picture industry. This group, the National Board of Censorship—misnamed because it actually opposed state censorship—was a response to Protestant efforts to clean up motion picture theaters in the first decade of the twentieth century. In New York City the strongest voices for motion picture reform came from Protestant reformers, who had been campaigning for stricter enforcement of the bans on Sunday theatrical shows. The Episcopal canon William S. Chase and Reverend F. M. Foster, a Presbyterian, for example, founded the Interdenominational Committee for the Suppression of Sunday Vaudeville in New York City.[7] To many reformers, the popularity of motion pictures seemed to contribute to the physical and moral corruption of young people. The movies, after all, showed crimes and sexual scenes. Some worried that young girls were in particular danger in the theater from male viewers who would proposition them. The mayor of New York City, George McClellan, surprised even critics of motion pictures when he revoked the licenses of all movie theaters in the city—550 in total—in 1908. McClellan was worried that the storefront nickelodeons endangered their working-class and immigrant audiences by teaching them how to commit crimes, alienating children from families, and loosening sexual morality. Reformers wondered if the dangers of "nickel madness" would spread.

To guard against further government interference, the Motion Picture

Patents Company, a coalition of the largest film manufacturers, collaborated with the People's Institute, an educational and reform organization in operation since 1897. The institute set up a voluntary censorship board to review films prior to exhibition in New York City in 1909. Even prior to this partnership, the institute had focused on motion pictures, within the context of broadening and improving leisure options for the working class. Motion pictures, according to its reformers, could offer a positive alternative to the saloon, help educate all citizens, and heal social divides.[8] As opposed to the standard middle-class critique of movies as a threat to morality, the founder of the People's Institute, Charles Sprague Smith, "appreciated some of the possibilities the cinema offered for creating a more democratic culture and for easing, if not erasing, the distinction between the masses and the classes."[9] In these ways, these Progressive reformers felt essentially "optimistic" about motion pictures.[10]

The central idea of the National Board of Censorship was to improve motion pictures through the cooperation between reformers and the motion picture industry. The social reformers who staffed the board favored this type of collaboration because they felt it aligned the interests of the public, the reformers, and the movie producers: If the board could express true public opinion, moviemakers would deliver better films to make more money. The board believed motion pictures would become a valuable public forum; as such, they deserved the same respect as the press.[11] In 1913, for example, the board asserted that it would not censor "the news element or the element of public discussion in motion pictures, many of which are now made for propagandist purposes."[12] Movie producers and exhibitors agreed to support the board's work because they believed it would be more flexible and more consistent than the jigsaw puzzle of state and city censorship that was emerging around the country. The People's Institute believed the voluntary board would be "less corrupt" and more rational than politicians.[13] And the institute intended the board to represent "as broad a public as possible," as opposed to local censorship boards.[14] In particular, the board touted its own impartiality as an improvement to the flaws of the state censorship boards, which could not avoid prejudice because of their small size: "It is physically impossible . . . for a small group to be free from special prejudices or from viewing the pictures from the standpoint of certain groups or classes of the community. A disinterested expression of public opinion is hard to obtain from such a small official group."[15]

John Collier, the first chair of the National Board of Censorship, was particularly concerned about upholding "broadmindedness and liberality," instead of responding to special-interest groups, in the board's work.[16] A social worker who had served as the civic secretary of the People's Institute since 1908, Collier believed that nickelodeons built neighborhood community and exposed fans to a wider world. Movies were an asset to be cultivated for the social good, not a moral danger to be condemned.[17] In particular, Collier resisted the political pressure to "censor controversial items from films (e.g., polygamy in Utah)."[18]

The board's aspiration to represent national consensus proved contradictory in several ways. Although the board rejected official censorship because it could not accurately represent the public, it collaborated with several state and municipal censorship boards. For example, when a minority group protested against a particular film, the national board sometimes refrained from a decision but encouraged the group to seek a ban from the local censorship authorities. In addition, it professed for a democratic system of molding the movies, yet it also claimed that the movie-going public needed assistance in creating this positive public forum. Thus, it cast its staff and volunteer censors as expert authority figures.[19]

Another contradiction was between the board's commitment to serving the general public and its concern for vulnerable moviegoers who needed special protection. The board's understanding of vulnerable viewers involved not just age, although the question of children in the audience was by far the most widely discussed issue; race, gender, and religion also defined weakness. Unlike other reformers who sought to censor motion pictures from the child's perspective, the National Board of Censorship acknowledged the child in the audience but refused to censor from that standard alone. In 1911 it announced that it was not "possible to confine motion pictures to those themes which are entirely proper to discuss in the presence of children."[20] A few years later it clarified that with children and adults mixed together in the audience, the board would have to be flexible, taking children "into consideration," yet refusing to "judge films exclusively from the standpoint of children."[21]

The board moved further away from protection when Frederic Howe replaced John Collier as head of the board in 1912. Under Collier, the board had announced its ideal of protecting the vulnerable—"the young persons, immigrants, family groups, the formative and impressionable section of our cities."[22] In contrast, when Howe took over the board, he expressed a more adamant commitment to free speech, regardless of anyone's need for protection. He thought the attempts to suppress pictures "for the child, the woman, the weak and the immigrant" were examples of unjustified "class legislation."[23]

Howe's free-speech commitment, however, could not steer the National Board of Censorship clear of controversies surrounding the call to protect racial and religious minorities, as well as the working class. Between 1911 and 1914, the board debated films that seemed to endanger special groups—women and labor unionists, as well as religious and racial minorities. These controversial films included the well-known struggle over the white slavery movies, which raised concerns about child viewers, as well as about the safety of women. Many of these movies dealt with the representation of Mormons, Jews, and African Americans, and they were often social-problem films created by progressive filmmakers. Like muckraking journalists and realist painters and authors who exposed greed, poor working conditions, and corruption, these filmmakers hoped their art would reform society. The board's debates over these films exposed a core problem in its philosophy: it sought national consensus (the "public mind") but also sympathized with groups that claimed films hurt them. As a result, the board dealt with these controversial films inconsistently: faced with films that ridiculed Jews, it advised moviemakers to avoid anti-Semitism, but it made actual cuts to films dealing with Mormons and African Americans. It also sidestepped the most insistent protest groups by referring films to local censorship boards. By marginalizing divisive films about race and religion as "local" anomalies, the board thus tried to retain its identity as a democratic, free-speech organization while placating civil rights censors at the same time. Consensus censorship remained elusive.[24]

The National Board of Censorship had faced several years of controversy over the representation of minority groups before it addressed *The Birth of a Nation* in 1915. In 1911 the board debated a film about the arrest of John and James McNamara, two labor activists accused of bombing the *Los Angeles Times*, the country's most prominent anti-union newspaper.[25] The American Federation of Labor tried to help the brothers' defense by producing a film that offered a "true and correct representation" of the bombing.[26] *A Martyr to His Cause* portrays John McNamara as a hardworking, loyal citizen; employers are depicted as lawless and cruel.[27] The historian Steven Ross describes it as more radical than other movies in this genre.[28] After some debate, the National Board of Censorship passed the film. One member of the general committee objected to passing such a divisive picture with the trial still underway. "An unfinished process at law is before the public," explained Thomas Slicer, a member of the general committee. "I am not willing in a smouldering conflagration to add anything except water."[29] Labor leader Samuel Gompers pressured the review committee to pass the film, with visits and a telegram. In the end, other members of the committee outvoted Slicer, and the board passed the film.

The next set of controversial films involved the representation of Mormons and Jews. In January 1912, the governor of Utah wrote to the board to complain after the censoring committee had passed *A Victim of the Mormons*. The General Committee agreed to reexamine the picture as a "court of appeals" for the smaller censoring committee.[30] It suggested a few cuts and then deferred instead to local censors, explaining that it had "been frequently called upon [to] inspect pictures which contained elements offensive to some special interest or to some section of the country or some particular group of people." The board was, however, unsympathetic to these pleas because any realistic film or any film dealing with a "social problem is likely to be objectionable to some person or group." Then it added, "The Board always views with disfavor pictures which give gratuitous offense to adherents of religious creeds." It suggested cuts of "excessively brutal" scenes, but would not further condemn the film.[31] It ultimately felt that it could not reject the movie because it addressed an issue of public debate— polygamy in the United States and Europe—which it held to be "within the field of legitimate discussion." Because it was part of relevant public debate, the board said it would not forbid the film on the grounds of "offense to a religious sect."[32] It reminded citizens that local censors could still regulate movies to suit their particular constituencies, acknowledging that Utah and other states might rightfully suppress *A Victim of the Mormons*.[33]

Similar to Mormon complaints about harmful movies, the Anti-Defamation League lobbied the board in 1913 to adopt a policy against films that "defamed" Jews—depicting the Jew as a "thief, a blackmailer, a fire-bug, a defaulter, a violator of the public trust, a money-shark, or some other type of scoundrel."[34] In the ADL's 1915 annual report, it stated that it had sought a broader policy—a ban on films that tended to "arouse prejudice" against any religious group.[35] Although Jews supported this inclusive proposal, the correspondence to the National Board of Censorship focuses on anti-Semitism exclusively, and the ADL also emphasized that the "Jews more than any other people, resent exhibitions of this character."[36] The board did not approve either of the requests. Instead, it circulated a memo to motion picture manufacturers as a "suggestion," urging the

> inadvisability of pictures unnecessarily cartooning or rather lampooning Jews ... We wish to advise you that ... there is a strong movement developing to banish such caricaturing of the Jew from the film screens. The National Board recognizes that each nationality has its own peculiar characteristics, which are a legitimate field for comedy and satire. The Board, however, believes that where such comedy and satire has a libelous effect and shows malice, and tends to give an erroneous impression of a respected portion of our citizenship, that it should take action either by making eliminations or condemning a picture in toto.[37]

The board later reported that many had "complied with our request."[38] The ADL, however, was displeased with the board's complacency.

A few months after the ADL began to lobby the National Board of Censorship, the board faced a new controversy: white slavery films. It handled many of these similarly: it defended films as a discussion of social problems, tried to balance concern for a "vulnerable" part of the audience (in this case, children) with its free-speech stance, and often abdicated to local censorship authorities. Public concern with prostitution accelerated in 1908 with the publication of an exposé about white slavery in Chicago; a white slavery novel, *The House of Bondage*, became a best seller two years later; and Broadway showcased two plays about prostitution in 1910—*The Lure* and *The Fight*. White slavery films soon followed in 1913. The board was divided about how to handle these films, with some members hoping that these motion pictures could serve as a vehicle for educating society about a pernicious social problem, despite the sexual nature of the films.[39] In October of 1913 the National Board of Censorship reviewed its first white slavery film, *The Traffic in Souls*. One of its censoring committees passed the film, but the general committee, acting as an appeals court, then reviewed it. The discussion of the film at the October 27, 1913, meeting shows the board leaders' differing views. Mrs. Simkovitch expressed concern for the child spectator: "A large number of the attendants at the picture shows who will see this picture will be children. [I] would not care to have any children see this picture because it would not make a good impression on the child's mind." The advisory secretary, Orrin Cocks, who often favored censorship, added regional variation in taste to the concern for children: "The majority of the people in the United States hesitate to speak of these things and they would not like this picture. Children in the towns . . . did not know about the organization of the business."[40] John Collier, however, argued that small towns did "know about this thing" and that exposure of the problem might help small-town girls resist the lure of urban prostitution. The chairman, Frederic Howe, helped sway the group in favor of the film when he concluded that airing the film would diminish the crime when "every body knows all about it."[41] The general committee passed the film by a vote of six to two, after suggesting minor alterations.

The board condemned the next film involving prostitution, *Inside the White Slave Traffic*, for its sensationalistic, detailed scenes of brothel life devoid a moral lesson. In addition, the producer had angered the board by releasing the movie without its approval. However, some on the board agreed with prominent reformers and feminists, such as Inez Milholland Boissevain, who defended the film for offering an honest, public discussion of sex, as opposed to embarrassment and silence.[42] Howe stuck by his earlier position in relation to *The Traffic in Souls*—that the film, however controversial, was educational. After the producer, Samuel London, made revisions and persisted in his attempt to win board approval, the latter decided to suspend judgment of the film; it defined the picture as a special release and left censorship decisions up to local communities.[43]

After the controversies surrounding the board's approval of the white slavery films, it issued a statement about its approach to films about prostitution in the "Special Bulletin on Social Evil" in February 1914. It did not reject all white slavery films; rather, it disapproved only of those films that encouraged sexual titillation and "morbid curiosity."[44] A few months later, in May, the board issued a more comprehensive revision of its standards to address race, religion, and sexuality in film. All these films proved problematic because they challenged the board's desire to represent a composite audience (or the typical viewer) and to uphold film as an arena of public discussion. The revised standards exposed and tried to solve the board's problems with racial and religious ridicule. Instead of focusing on a "particular audience," it would judge films in relation to the "composite audience."[45] It held that motion pictures would educate the public about "historical situations, scientific truths, [and] industrial questions."[46] Yet in relation to race and religion, the board modified this principle: "It is clear that when treatment of a race is unduly libelous, the question of censorship is raised. Now all these prejudices and different points of view make it inexpedient to pass upon pictures in a purely rational manner according to certain principles theoretically conceived. Through the force of circumstances the Board is compelled to steer a middle course in an effort to adhere as closely as possible to the rationally conceived principles for which it stands, and yet pay sufficient regard to popular prejudice."[47] The board thus acknowledged a gap between its abstract values and the prejudice among audiences. It is not entirely clear what the authors meant by "popular prejudice," but it is a less complimentary way to talk about citizens' beliefs than "popular opinion," which the board used in other cases. Prejudice suggests a narrow, partial viewpoint; thus, the board presented its solution to cases where a vocal minority objected to a film: Apply the central values of assessment (defend movies as educational and political dialogue and do not favor any subgroup) but consider censorship in the cases of a minority group's uproar over libelous films.

In this context, the board faced the most explosive film yet, *The Birth of a Nation*. Prior to its Los Angeles premiere, the National Board of Censorship had initially passed the film unanimously in January 1915.[48] When the NAACP learned of the approval, it persuaded Howe to review the film a second time on March 1, 1915. The general committee again approved the film, but this time with a divided vote (15-8) and with several cuts, including the elimination of the scene implying the rape of a white woman. It defended the decision by stating that it could only judge a film based on "public morals," not historical accuracy or the creation of sympathies against one set of characters. The board speculated that the movie would "aggravate serious social questions," but it refused to act on that basis because the story had already circulated as a novel and a play. The board called an additional meeting on March 12 to review the revised film. After small alterations, it passed *The Birth of a Nation*. Howe dissented from the majority, arguing that the film would "lead to race trouble" and perhaps murder.[49] But he also said: "My theory of the Board is an organization to fight where necessary to uphold public opinion."[50] How could public opinion be upheld when there seemed to be such widespread disagreement about the film? In earlier controversies, Howe had defended films as a source of information and valuable political debate. Often in the minority, he usually urged the board to pass controversial movies. But he reversed this course with debate swirling around *The Birth of a Nation*.[51]

Dissatisfied with the outcome, the NAACP lobbied for an African American to be on the board: "To have moving pictures . . . used to outrageously misrepresent and caricature them with the approval of the Board of Censorship indicates that colored membership is needed on the Board."[52] In each case, the board rebuffed the NAACP. It argued that its view of *The Birth of a Nation* was well represented on the board, and it refused to help the NAACP, because the civil rights organization "intended to work for legalized censorship."[53] It also defended its position by referring to its alignment with public opinion, as measured by similar decisions about cuts at the censorship boards in Pennsylvania, Ohio, and Chicago. The national board thus both objected to censorship and looked to state censorship as affirmation of its controversial decisions. It was an incoherent position.

While African Americans were displeased with the board's decision to pass *The Birth of a Nation*, the Anti-Defamation League charged that the board had been unfair in its treatment of Jews and African Americans because it overlooked Jewish caricature but demanded modifications to *The Birth of a Nation*.[54] The ADL reported that Orrin Cocks had rebuffed early Jewish lobbying by asking why the Jew "should be any more sensitive than the negro, the Chinaman, the Irishman or the Italian."[55] The ADL was correct in some ways. The board had approved, without alteration, the films that the Chicago board was censoring for their misrepresentation of Jews, including *The Fatal Wedding*. The national board insisted that it could only handle the matter in an "advisory way" with producers and distributors, and did not cut or reject films that Jews criticized.[56]

The ADL intensified its lobbying of the National Board of Censorship when it heard about Griffith's plans for a new film, *Intolerance*. Griffith expressed his anger at the critics of *The Birth of a Nation* in *Intolerance*, which presented scenes of "hatred and intolerance, through all the ages"—including the fall of Babylon, the crucifixion of Christ, and the massacre of the Huguenots in the sixteenth century.[57] Griffith portrayed Jews as "Christ Killers," reinforcing predominant anti-Semitic attitudes. After the ADL met with Griffith, he agreed to delete some scenes and revise the crucifixion scene.[58] But the ADL did not rely exclusively on negotiations with Griffith. It also corresponded with the National Board of Censorship. It questioned the board's refusal to "censor pictures from the standpoint of any particular race, creed, people or religious belief." The ADL wondered, "Would the Board . . . pass without examination of any kind of film in which there appeared a scene showing Jesus stoned and beaten by Jews, and being crucified through the machinations of Jews." William McGuire, the board's executive secretary, responded that the board would not pass such a picture because it would be "libelous against the Jewish race as a race." But he stepped back from broader censorship of Jewish characters—cases in which the villain happens to be Jewish. "A villain . . . must belong to some race," he reasoned, adding that it was not always the case that a "Jewish villain was a villain because he was a Jew."[59]

In the years surrounding *The Birth of a Nation*, the National Board of Censorship tried to "represent the people," despite conflicts over class, sexuality, race, and religion, and it tried to strengthen its anticensorship stance, despite acknowledging that some films, particularly racist films, were too dangerous to exhibit.[60] It established a framework for dealing with the conundrum of defamatory films: it refrained from assessing historical accuracy and would not single out a particular people or region to protect from harm, except to suggest cuts or to appeal to local censors. In 1916 the board changed its name to the National Board of Review to underscore its opposition to undemocratic censorship, and it announced that it was involved in review and public service, not "a kind of bureaucratic blue pencil that works in secret and enforces its decisions on the public without ever giving the public a chance to decide for itself."[61]

As the board struggled over its standards and over *The Birth of a Nation* in particular, it confronted a new obstacle: the Supreme Court's endorsement of motion picture censorship in *Mutual Film Corporation v. Industrial Commission of Ohio* (1915). The Mutual Film Corporation had begun its campaign against motion picture censorship in 1914. It attacked censorship in Pennsylvania, Chicago, Kansas, and, most famously, in Ohio.[62] Its early arguments focused primarily on property rights, including violations of the Fourteenth Amendment's due process clause. But as the company's case against the Ohio board progressed, free speech became a more prominent argument, though still in combination with an emphasis on a the need for a more open market for movie commerce.[63] Mutual lawyers argued that motion pictures deserved the same First Amendment protection as the press ("the spreading of knowledge and the molding of public opinion"), that the Ohio board interfered with interstate commerce, and that it followed vague standards.[64] The Supreme Court unanimously ruled in favor of Ohio's censorship board. In the Court's opinion, Justice Joseph McKenna explained that movies, theater, or the circus did not deserve First Amendment protection because of their possible "evil" uses. Local communities thus had the right to police these kinds of performances. According to the

Court, movies were "a business, pure and simple"—not part of the press.[65] Frederic Howe decried the Court's affirmation of government interference with political debates: "Should the State pass upon the desirability of the portrayal of labor questions, of Socialism, the Industrial Workers of the World, and other insistent issues crowding to the fore?"[66]

The Mutual decision opened the door to further state and municipal censorship. Maryland launched a state censorship board in 1916 and Missouri (1919) and New York (1921) followed suit. Yet free-speech activists also achieved key victories. They defeated a state-wide referendum on censorship in Massachusetts, and they also stopped the establishment of federal censorship. As the motion picture industry explored new ways of organizing itself—to control film content and resist censorship—free-speech advocates gained ground, particularly in response to government censorship during World War I. The battles over local, state, and federal censorship after the Mutual decision disclose how motion picture manufacturers and free-speech activists focused on race-based censorship as an example of prejudice in censorship. Race-based provisions were particularly vulnerable in the face of free-speech claims, even when new censorship regulations ultimately succeeded.

As the web of censorship grew across the country, leading Protestant reform organizations, such as the Woman's Christian Temperance Union, pushed for federal censorship. Legislators introduced and debated federal censorship bills in 1914, 1916, 1926, and 1934. All failed. The hearings in 1914 and 1916 focused on democracy and censorship, debating whether the public could directly represent its taste as it bought tickets and whether any censorship board could adequately represent a diverse community. In this context, the power of racial minorities to censor movies indeed proved controversial. It is not surprising, then, that the debates about whether (or how) censors could truly represent the people led both sides back to questions about movies with controversial racial and religious themes that aroused vocal protests. Racial and religious politics informed the motivations of the Protestant leaders who backed the bills, and the central controversies over race-based censorship—*The Merchant of Venice* and *The Birth of a Nation*—were prominent examples of the perils of censorship in the testimony at the hearings. With several of his films at the center of censorship firestorms, Griffith was a leading figure in the growing free-speech coalition that fought federal censorship in these hearings.

The 1914 and 1916 hearings before the House of Representatives Committee on Education focused on the same bill for federal motion picture censorship, and they occurred on either side of the Mutual decision and *The Birth of a Nation* controversy. In 1914 Reverend Wilbur F. Crafts, a Methodist minister who was one of the founders of the International Reform Bureau, drafted a federal bill to censor motion pictures. Canon William Sheafe Chase, also a leader of the International Reform Bureau, joined Crafts in lobbying for federal legislation. Both had been critical of motion pictures and the National Board of Censorship's ineffectiveness, particularly of its favorable treatment of the industry that supported it. The bill in 1914 (HR 14805) proposed five federal censors, appointed by the president, to license "every film submitted to it and intended for entrance into interstate commerce, unless it finds that such a film is obscene, indecent, immoral, or depicts a bull fight or a prize fight or is of such a character that its exhibition would tend to corrupt the morals of children or adults or incite to crime."[67] Senator Hoke Smith from Georgia introduced the federal censorship bill in the Senate and Representative Dudley Hughes, also from Georgia, brought forth a similar bill in the House of Representatives.[68] In 1914, the Education Committee unanimously endorsed the Federal Motion Picture Commission, but the bill did not make it out of Congress to the president's desk. So the same bill was introduced two years later, again with the backing of Crafts and Chase, the leading advocates of federal censorship.

These two men believed in the federal regulation of film to protect the nation from un-American and immoral influences, which they often identified specifically as Jewish and African American pressure. Crafts argued that the authority of a small censorship board was a better alternative to the concentrated power of Jewish movie moguls. He argued that the country needed "effective control . . . over these Jews to prevent their showing such pictures as will bring them the greatest financial returns, irrespective of the moral injury they inflict upon the people."[69] Chase blamed "Hebrew" theater owners for the corruption of American morals in his 1921 book, *Catechism on Motion Pictures,* in which he described the defeat of the Massachusetts movie censorship referendum as evidence of "the political influence of the movie trust, composed of five or six New York Jews, over the Massachusetts voters."[70] It was not anti-Semitism alone that shrouded the advocacy for federal censorship; Crafts also expressed anxiety about African American crime. In his opening remarks at the 1916 hearing, Crafts looked back on his successful lobby for the Sims Act (barring fight films and targeting the African American champion Jack Johnson) and stated that this was his proudest moment: "It would have been worth while to have lived if only to save my country from being flooded with pictures of a negro indicted for white slavery and a white man voluntarily standing on the same brutal level, which, but for that law, would have been shown all over the country as a brace of heroes."[71]

At both hearings, the free-speech coalition advanced two core arguments: that censorship was undemocratic (or un-American) and that motion pictures were like the press and thus deserved First Amendment protection. At the first hearing in 1914, Walter Seligsberg, Griffith's lawyer, portrayed censorship as an autocratic process in which the censors "know what is good for you, the censored"; he also believed movies were part of the press: "The term 'press' is a broad and all-inclusive term."[72] Opponents of censorship also argued for direct representation—or the public as censors. Free-speech advocates, the motion picture producers, and the reformers on the National Board of Censorship emphasized that by appealing to public tastes, they were trusting citizens to act as their own censors.[73] P. A. Powers, an employee of Universal Film, explained, "We have to conform to . . . what the public wants."[74] The public did not need censors because the audience voted directly on movie standards by attending or not attending. In this way, the movie-going audience was a "plebiscite at the box office," according to the historian Anne Morey.[75]

Supporters of censorship challenged this "rhetoric of democracy"—that the audience expressed the community's standards and desires—by claiming that movie men were autocrats who manipulated a childlike audience.[76] Chase argued, "To-day the pictures exhibited publicly are arbitrarily forced upon the people by a few people who are influenced by the morality of the theater-going public in order to attract and increase the door receipts."[77] Horace Towner, a U.S. representative from Iowa, suggested that the federal censorship panel was actually a better way to represent the public will. "The representatives of the people should protect the people."[78] But J. W. Binder, a free-speech proponent who represented film exhibitors, manufacturers, and distributors, remained doubtful: "Through a commission of five people?"[79] Thus the debates over federal censorship focused on the characteristics of the audience and on whether or not audience tastes needed to be represented or regulated by censors.

While proponents of censorship emphasized the need to protect the vulnerable viewer, "the youngest and most ignorant," the defenders of free speech described the audience as intelligent and discerning. The pro-censorship side emphasized the vulnerable child spectator, and the "riffraff" in the audience. Chase held that children needed protection because they would "imitate" what they saw, but he broadened this notion of protection to include the wider audience as well.[80] Chase said expert federal censorship was necessary because the "ordinary citizen" was vulnerable to "frauds, cheats, and various kinds of injurious deceits. . . . licensing [was] necessary in order to protect the public."[81] In contrast, Seligsberg objected to the characterization of the movie audience as weak or impoverished: "You are dealing with something . . . that is patronized by people in all walks of life, and they are people whose judgment is keen."[82]

The ability of a censorship board to represent the nation emerged as another key question in these hearings. Much of the debate in 1914 and 1916 focused on which system—the National Board of Censorship or the proposed federal censorship board—would be the best system for regulating movies. The supporters of federal censorship criticized the National Board of Censorship as a misnomer: it did not represent the nation at all. Instead, it represented only New York; and, worse yet, it represented the movie interests.[83] In 1914, Seligsberg tried to defend the board: "I do not object to it seriously, because it is voluntary, because we can control the abuse of it. We are free to criticize it. Although in our relationship to it we are strangers."[84] The chairman was not convinced. "Now, you not only cooperate with them, but you furnish all the money to pay the expenses of that board of censors."[85] Similarly, at the 1916 hearing, one of the congressmen on the panel asked Reverend Cranston Brenton, the chair of the National Board of Censorship, "For whom are you speaking?" Brenton answered that the national board spoke "primarily for the public. Ours is a public service and is so recognized by the people."[86] Walter Erwin, the head of a film distribution company, worried that a small committee of five federal censors would become "warped" or "arbitrary."[87] The national board, on the other hand, was a larger group of volunteers who worked "without fear or favor . . . [not] malice, spite or jealousy."[88]

The witnesses who warned against undemocratic federal censorship returned to racial minorities as examples of problematic censors. The controversies surrounding *The Merchant of Venice* and *The Birth of a Nation* proved that censorship was irregular and political. African American and Jewish attempts to censor films to protect themselves made for particularly evocative examples because they fit the category of small pressure groups that often had a local or regional perspective, as well as a political agenda.

They were a sign of national fracture and political pressure. Free-speech advocates, in general, criticized instances in which "very small minorities" undertook censorship.[89] Similarly, Edward Moree, of the New York State Conference of Mayors, noted the dangers of politicized censorship and the difficulty of a national board's ability to negotiate the differences between "city and country, North and South, the white and black and the foreigner, the intellectual and the ignorant, the young and the mature."[90]

Chicago's censorship of the movie *The Merchant of Venice* exemplified partial or biased censorship in the 1914 hearing. Seligsberg, who represented the Mutual Film Corporation in its case against Ohio's state censorship board, pointed to the censorship of *The Merchant of Venice* as a "humorous incident"—an egregious example of inconsistency and political pressure bearing on a censor's decision. Although a film version of *The Merchant of Venice* had already been granted a permit earlier, Funkhouser had revoked the permit, largely in response to Jewish pressure. Seligsberg claimed he was "currying favor with the Hebrews in Chicago."[91] Later, Jews were uncertain about their attack on a "classic" text and pushed to have the license approved.[92]

In 1916 Jewish censorship was less prevalent in the hearings, but it still provided two negative examples for free-speech advocates. J. W. Binder, a representative of the Motion Picture Board of Trade of America, which had formed the previous year to combat censorship, pointed to the example of the Jewish mayor of Cincinnati, who refused to allow a movie because it reflected poorly on "the character of the Hebrews."[93] The mocking stories about the Jewish attack on *The Merchant of Venice* may have caused some Jewish leaders to revise their history in the 1916 hearing. The only discussion of the Anti-Defamation League presented a false history that erased the organization's commitment to censorship. Rabbi A. H. Simon explained that Jews had transformed the derogatory representation of Jews in motion pictures through pressure on producers, not through censorship.[94] He held that it was more dignified to protest directly to producers than to grovel to federal censors: "I had rather go to the citizenship of the country and say to the men as citizens, as men who are earning their living in their respective ways, 'We had rather have you do this thing voluntarily.'"[95] His scenario overlooked the ADL's commitment to censorship and also neglects his own support for state censorship two years earlier. He supported the Anti-Defamation League in 1914, when it called for a censorship board in

Washington, D.C., with the goal of preventing the "odious portrays of any creed or race" in motion pictures. Backers referred to the Chicago example as the model.[96]

Whereas the testimony in the 1914 hearings often referred to Jewish objections to *The Merchant of Venice*, the 1916 hearings considered African American efforts to suppress *The Birth of a Nation*. Four opponents of federal censorship used *The Birth of a Nation* as their main example of politicized censorship, and of the motion picture's similarity to the press. Moree described the black protesters as "demagogues" who encouraged riots: "What would have been the attitude of a national board appointed by a President who was particularly anxious to placate the negro vote?"[97] *The Birth of a Nation* presented the "truth"—however unpleasant it might be—much as did the press. It was a historical, educational, and artistic movie—an alternative to the "slap stick" and the "sentimental," according to Griffith's telegram to the proceedings.[98] In 1916 Martin Littleton, an attorney for Griffith, argued that because *The Birth of a Nation* was accessible only to a ticket-buying public, the government should not censor it for any minority group. An offended group could just choose not to attend. To illustrate this point, he told the story of New York City mayor William Gaynor passing through a park and seeing a play by the Irish Players, which sometimes aroused the "resentment of the Irish."

> If any man were to try and show a picture out in this park where everyone must pass and must see it . . . and that picture offended the decent notions of any race of people . . . I would exterminate him, because this is a public place. . . . But when a man takes a show and puts it inside a building and locks the doors and puts up the box office window . . . the question then arises, how far must the Government penetrate into the regions of that particular place to conserve the morals and the decency of the community?[99]

With the exception of a play in an open public venue, Littleton saw no validity in the Irish and African American protests against particular productions. Littleton thus set up a common strategy for free-speech activists: compare movies to the press and point to the illegitimacy of racial censorship. After decrying the efforts to censor *The Birth of a Nation*, Littleton defended movies in general because they analyzed "mercilessly the public questions, social controversies, religious disputes, and all of the purposes and motives and passions of mankind."[100] Thus, race-based censorship signaled minority interests run amok, not censorship serving the public good. And *The Birth of a Nation*, in particular, showed the political and educational relevance of motion pictures.

The symbol of race-based censorship proved to be as malleable as it was evocative, as proponents of censorship used controversies over racially inflammatory films to back federal censorship. Three witnesses, for example, referred to *The Birth of a Nation* as a reason to have federal censorship. Kate Barrett, a reformer, pleaded for censorship on "another ground than moral grounds . . . That is, upon political grounds" to prevent the United States from becoming a nation of "disjoined people of many races and many tongues."[101] She referred specifically to *The Birth of a Nation* as breaking up national unity. The only representative of the main groups lobbying for race-based censorship was Reverend A. C. Garner, a founding member of the Washington, D.C., chapter of the NAACP. Garner, not a leading national figure in the struggle against *The Birth of a Nation*, presented an argument that varied somewhat from the standard NAACP message about the film. He supported the suppression of Jack Johnson's fight films and *The Birth of a Nation* because they "would not be very good for the amicable relations of the two races," and he described *The Birth of a Nation* as a provocation to violence against African Americans.[102] But he also emphasized the moral weakness of blacks, particularly African American children, because of their poor environment. He explained, "If the white people need good pictures, the black people need them much more, because we are most likely to be surrounded with evil influences and more likely to be carried away by anything that is bad."[103] The NAACP traditionally emphasized that the African American viewer was vulnerable to white violence or might be aroused to fight against the whites as a result of the insulting play, but these repercussions did not result from African Americans' moral weakness.

In 1916, the free-speech coalition expanded. Eight people spoke against the bill in 1914; all were associated with the motion picture industry (as exhibitors, editors of industry publications, or lawyers for the studios) or with the National Board of Censorship.[104] Two years later, this anticensorship coalition expanded to twenty-one advocates who offered testimony at the hearing. For six late nights in the middle of January in 1916, this group challenged the club women, Protestant leaders, and crime-prevention experts who backed the bill. In the lively, sometimes raucous, hearing, the opponents did not seem discouraged by the recent Mutual decision backing motion picture censorship; in fact, they may have felt recommitted and better prepared than in 1914. By 1916, Binder had assembled a diverse group to protest federal censorship: film manufacturers, exhibitors and distributors, as well as newspaper editors, religious leaders, and free-speech activists unaffiliated with the industry. The opponents sometimes teased the supporters of censorship. When Crafts said that movies were more harmful than plays or books because viewing *Hamlet* would not make him violent but watching a Wild West movie would, J. Stuart Blackton, the president of Vitagraph, quipped, "We need a pre-publicity censorship, not for motion pictures, but to be applied to such men as Dr. Crafts." The audience laughed.[105] Late in the hearings, Binder interrupted Walter Laidlaw, who represented the Federation of Churches, when Laidlaw recalled an incident in which a boy in the audience had tried to murder someone after seeing a lynching on film. Binder interjected: "I just want you to give the name and address in the case you just cited." When Laidlaw said he did not know, Binder lamented, "Nobody ever does." To emphasize his point, he reached out and gave Laidlaw his card and asked him to please try to find out the information about the case.[106]

The new members of the free-speech coalition in 1916 included John D. Bradley, a representative of the Free Thought Federation and the Secular League. Describing movies as the "food of the mind," Bradley compared them to the press and to literature.[107] He was particularly concerned about the religious basis of censorship, claiming that the proposed bill would ban movies that demeaned religion but not movies that ridiculed "free thought" or "atheism."[108] Bradley, in addition, criticized the Catholic effort to have anti-Catholic publications banned from the postal service. He wondered why elected officials would leave censorship in the hands of religion if it was concerned with dampening racial prejudice. He referred to the early testimony of "two colored clergymen" who advocated censorship to lessen racial prejudice. Bradley did not trust churches to help end racism, when religious texts have been the "bulwark of race prejudice."[109] "Would it not be well," he asked, "to begin the censorship for the prevention of race prejudice with this basic and primary cause?"[110] In February 1915 he appeared before the House Committee on the Post Office and Post Roads to oppose a bill expanding the scope of postal censorship beyond sexual themes to include scurrilous and libelous texts; it was directed at the *Menace* and the *Yellow Jacket*, among other anti-Catholic publications.[111] Bradley defended the marketplace of ideas in which "every man who has an idea is constantly invited to the platform" and argued that the bill would not even accomplish its goal; instead it would increase "antagonism" against and controversy surrounding Catholics.[112]

The Catholic campaign to suppress anti-Catholic publications intensified at the same time as the 1916 congressional hearing on federal motion picture censorship. This Catholic effort, like Jewish and African American censorship drives, aimed to protect a minority group from defamation, but the Catholic effort was grounded in religion, not race. Just a few weeks before Bradley's testimony, in a U.S. District Court in Missouri, editors of the anti-Catholic magazine, the *Menace*, stood trial for obscenity, though the obscenity charge covered up Catholic complaints about the magazine's "sexualized anti-Catholic rhetoric"—including lurid stories about young women held hostage in convents and priests' seductive questions in confessionals.[113] In this case, the most prominent thus far, the defendants claimed that their material was already readily available in other published sources and also made strong First Amendment claims. When the *Menace* was acquitted, its staff celebrated the victory of freedom of the press and the defeat of Catholic "conspiracy" and intrusion into American institutions.[114]

The Knights of Columbus had pressed libel and obscenity cases against the *Menace* and other anti-Catholic publications for several years already. In 1914, the Knights of Columbus established the Commission on Religious Prejudices, which worked to counter anti-Catholicism through education, such as through pamphlets that celebrated Catholic contributions to the nation, and through legal censorship. The historian Christopher Kauffman has described it as the Catholic "anti-defamation league."[115] Catholics took swift action against the anti-Catholic press in this campaign against "Protestant bigotry."[116] The commission, along with the American Federation of Catholic Societies, encouraged legal action. There were several successful criminal libel cases against anti-Catholic publications like the *Silverton Journal* between 1911 and 1914, but anti-Catholic papers usually avoided libel charges by refraining from identifying particular Catholic priests or nuns. The commission criticized the limits of libel law because it did not cover societies or organizations. In 1916, Father Francis Rossman won a libel suit against the *Menace* in one of the rare instances in which the publication mentioned a priest by name. The commission thus sought other ways of fighting the magazines. When the United States entered World War I in April of 1917, it decided to disband a few months later. To show its effectiveness, the commission pointed to a drop in anti-Catholic publications and a decline in anti-Catholic bills in state legislatures In addition, it believed that the war would dissolve religious prejudice—"fear and suspicion."[117] The termination of this commission silenced one more voice that had supported group libel legislation.

The 1916 bill to establish a system of federal motion picture censorship seemed to be on its way to victory when Carl Laemmle and other movie men visited President Woodrow Wilson to make their case against motion picture censorship. Wilson announced that he opposed the bill because he "could not see how censorship could be considered safe since it was so largely a matter of taste, environment and prejudice." What some found acceptable, he often found shocking.[118] The so-called Hughes bill never came up for a vote in the House.

The reformers who sought federal censors waited a decade (1916–26) before another hearing on national motion picture censorship. The period marked a crucial transition in the history of film and censorship. Under increased scrutiny because of a series of scandals, Hollywood turned to stricter self-censorship schemes, and government censorship of motion pictures also expanded. The civil rights and nationalist groups that had backed a broad ban on racial ridicule also disintegrated; in their place, Catholic leaders joined with Hollywood to uphold sexual morality and, when they did consider defamation, focused on stopping insults to Catholics, not racial minorities.

After World War I, scandals within Hollywood propelled calls for more censorship and revived criticism of the National Board of Review. In 1918 the General Federation of Women's Clubs withdrew its support for the National Board of Review and focused instead on expanding state censorship. Three years later, the *Brooklyn Eagle* published a report on the board, revealing that its industry financing led to leniency with controversial films.[119] In addition, critics charged that Cecil B. DeMille's films placed an unhealthy emphasis on sex and undermined the moral code. In his 1919 *Male and Female*, Gloria Swanson, as Lady Mary, seems to be nude as she leaves her bathtub and walks to her bed.[120] At the 1926 federal hearings on movie censorship, Rev. Clifford Gray Twombley also criticized Swanson's offscreen immorality. "'Glorious Gloria' ... is represented as the ideal of American womanhood ... and she has been divorced four times, I believe."[121] Throughout the 1920s, Hollywood stars were entangled in scandals involving divorce, drugs, and murder. In 1920 screen darling Mary

Pickford divorced her husband and quickly married Douglas Fairbanks. One year later, actress Virginia Rappe died at a party hosted by the popular film comedian Roscoe "Fatty" Arbuckle.

State and city censorship expanded in response to Hollywood's multiple scandals. West Virginia established state movie censorship in 1919, as did New York in 1921 and Virginia in 1922. But a statewide referendum of motion picture censorship in Massachusetts was defeated—the only time the public had been invited to endorse or reject motion picture censorship. The setback for censors in Massachusetts stemmed the tide elsewhere as well. Many other attempts at censorship were introduced in state and local governments, but most did not pass or were ruled invalid if they did. Connecticut, one of the exceptions, set up a state censorship board in 1923, but it proved short-lived.[122] The city of Wichita, Kansas, similarly passed an ordinance in 1923 specifically designed to suppress *The Birth of a Nation*. It banned films that depicted "prize fighting or tended to create section strife or race prejudice."[123] But the Eighth Federal District Court in Kansas City struck down the law. One study found that, after 1922, all forty-five bills outlining prior restraint censorship were rejected by state legislatures.[124]

Civil rights censorship declined during this period, as many of the new censorship boards did not include any kind of racial considerations in their standards. New York State's new censorship commission, for example, did not evaluate a film's tendency to increase racial prejudice, though West Virginia's new statute banned any film "calculated to result in arousing the prejudice . . . or one race or class of citizens against any other race or class of citizens."[125] In Pennsylvania, the "ridicule of any sect (religious or otherwise)," which was one of its standards in 1915, did not appear to be a factor in the censors' decisions in 1917. In the 1917 annual report, the Pennsylvania board did not consider insults to religious or racial groups a reason to alter or reject a film, although it did report preventing or reconstructing films that disparaged the country or national allies.[126] The race-based censorship that remained was much different than the Irish, Jewish and African American efforts to protect themselves. Southern states, for example, stopped any film related to the "race question" or any film that challenged white supremacy or segregation.

Self-censorship in the motion picture industry also became more organized between 1916 and 1926. In response to rising calls for censorship, the National Association of the Motion Picture Industry (NAMPI), founded by producers in 1916, issued a guide to the items most likely to be censored by local and state boards. This document, published in 1921, clarified the "thirteen points" that movie producers should avoid to placate censors, save money by avoiding "re-editing" films in response to censors' cuts, and improve their reputation. The NAMPI seems to have blended the standards of censorship from boards across the country. The "Thirteen Points," did not reject racial ridicule or miscegenation, but the guide did hold the line on the ridicule of any religious officials, including priests and rabbis, and of any religious belief. There was no enforcement of the "Thirteen Points," however, and the points failed to bring any substantive changes to motion picture content.

In 1922 movie producers set up the Motion Picture Producers and Distributors of America (MPPDA) to stop censorship. The producers hired Will Hays, the postmaster general for President Harding and a leading Republican, to run the new organization. Hollywood leaders hoped that Hays, an elder in the Presbyterian Church, would help mend the relationship between Hollywood and the Protestant churches. Hays worked on publicity for the industry and lobbied against censorship bills, while he also sought a way to control the content of motion pictures. He appointed Jason Joy as the director of the new Studio Relations Council. Joy surveyed censorship boards across the country to determine the main censors' objections, as well as the most popular complaints from pressure groups. This report then formed the basis of a new formula for motion picture production: a list of "Don'ts and Be Carefuls" was circulated in 1927. "The offense to any nation, race or creed" was a don't, as was "ridicule of the clergy." In addition, the list forbade "miscegenation (sex relationships between the white and black races)."[127] When the industry revised its self-censorship scheme in the coming years, however, racial ridicule disappeared, while the prohibitions on sacrilege and miscegenation remained.

In the decade leading up to the federal hearing in 1926, Catholic influence on motion picture content grew. The Catholic Church became an outspoken opponent of state censorship and an ally of Hollywood's plans for self-regulation. After World War I, Catholics were increasingly concerned about motion pictures but disagreed about how to proceed. Some Catholics were early supporters of federal censorship, but most distrusted government regulation. Charles McMahon, the head of the National Catholic Welfare Conference (NCWC), which began as a Catholic advocacy organization during World War I dedicated to protecting the faith of Catholic servicemen, blacklisted dangerous films and also tried to produce its own positive movies. Catholic interest in the movies coalesced as Hollywood was focusing more on staving off government regulation with new voluntary censorship codes. Hays relied on Catholic support when he campaigned against censorship in Massachusetts in a statewide referendum. McMahon helped Hays at the last minute by writing an editorial supporting Hay's new reform efforts in the NCWC *Bulletin*. Massachusetts residents resoundingly defeated the measure; the Irish Catholic vote had been significant in its defeat.[128]

Hays thus set out to win the allegiance of Catholic leaders who were seeking a broader role in American reform movements. For example, he continued to solidify his relationship with McMahon and Rita McGoldrick in the 1920s. The NCWC's Motion Picture Committee began to issue a monthly bulletin of approved films. McGoldrick, of the International Federation of Catholic Alumnae (IFCA), also published a list of approved films through the IFCA—known as "white lists." It advised Catholic schools about appropriate films but declined to blacklist movies because that could arouse curiosity about illicit topics. As McGoldrick's influence grew, eclipsing McMahon and the NCWC, she joined the National Board of Review (NBR), where she reviewed films for both the NBR and the IFCA. Her dual role sometimes proved problematic. Her supervisor at the NBR accused her staff of being "overzealous."[129] Hays paid for the production and mailing of the IFCA publications, which he valued as cheap publicity for films, as well as McGoldrick's tours, in which she spoke out against the censorship of Hollywood.[130] The more Protestant critique Hays faced, the more he relied on Catholic supporters like McGoldrick.

This shift in the leadership of motion picture reform parallels a transformation of Irish American identity from the ethnocentrism and nationalist militancy of the early twentieth century to a "pan-ethnic, American Catholicism" after World War I. Instead of a commitment to Irish nationalism, the Irish American community blended Catholic and American allegiances with an ongoing appreciation for Irish culture. The war against Germany was one knock against Irish American nationalism, but the following civil war in Ireland proved a "devastating blow."[131] Irish nationalism died away after the Anglo-Irish Treaty of 1921 ended the Anglo-Irish war. The leading ethnocentric organizations, like the AOH and the Gaelic League, lost membership but survived because of the efforts of a "tired and divided group of warriors."[132] Enthusiasm for Gaelic sports teams and Gaelic language study declined. At the same time, the number of Catholic immigrants from outside of Ireland, such as Italy and Poland, increased significantly, and Irish Catholics cooperated more with these groups. Catholic and Protestant tension became more intense, but religious affiliation did not replace ethnic identities. By the 1920s, in Worcester, Pennsylvania, for example, Irish, French Canadians, Poles, and Lithuanians were the prominent Catholic groups, while the Protestant groups were the Swedish and the Yankees.[133] The Knights of Columbus emerged as the dominant Irish organization, attracting American-born upwardly mobile Irish Americans, but also welcoming non-Irish Catholics. The Catholic Church became more centralized and more conservative in the early twentieth century and nurtured a defensive Catholic militancy. Angry about a variety of insults, Catholics worked to mitigate the perceived dangers of non-Catholic institutions (such as Protestant colleges and the YMCA) and to rebut anti-Catholic discrimination and anti-Catholic stereotypes. New Catholic organizations, such as the Catholic Women's Club, became popular, just as parish membership rose.[134] Espousing American patriotism and a militant defense of American Catholicism, the Knights took a leading role in defending Catholicism from a variety of attacks, including from the Ku Klux Klan.[135] In these ways, a militant Catholic mind-set replaced the aggressive Irish nationalist perspective that had driven the campaign against the Stage Irish. The new logic underpinning censorship was religious militancy, not race pride and nationalism.

In the 1926 federal hearing the Catholic witnesses argued against federal censorship. McGoldrick claimed that state censorship was ineffective political control; she favored partnerships with production companies to make better films. The federal censorship of movies, she warned, would be like a "standardized religion."[136] The NCWC also registered its disapproval of federal censorship. McMahon compared federal censorship in the name of protecting children to the proposal to make public school attendance compulsory for all children in Oregon, which was rejected by the United States Supreme Court. Chief Justice Taft had written, "Those who nurture [the child] and direct his destiny have the right, coupled with the high duty, to recognize him and prepare him for additional obligations."[137] Catholics, although they had earlier tried to use the law to stop anti-Catholic material, did not want to align themselves with Protestant censors in Prohibition or blue laws, which they perceived as anti-Catholic.[138]

Unlike the earlier proposals for federal movie censorship, in 1926, race-based censorship was included in the standards of the proposed federal commission. The 1926 bill was more specific than the proposals from a decade earlier. The bill empowered federal commissioners to deny a license to any film that contained "anything which holds up to scorn any race, nation, sect, or religion." The bill also included NAMPI's "thirteen points." Chase had included these full standards of the bill in his 1921 book *Catechism on Motion Pictures in Inter-state Commerce*. The thirteen points focused primarily on sex and crime, including "persons scantily dressed," "an illicit love affair which tends to make virtue odious," and "the use of narcotics." The thirteen points also forbade any incidents that offended religious beliefs or "ridicule ministers, priests, rabbis or recognized leaders of any religious sect."[139] Witnesses commented only briefly on the inclusion of race and religion in the bill. Loring Black of New York requested of Chase, "I think you ought to limit the language of this so that there would be no question of controversial subjects coming up in any way, like racial topics or religious topics." Chase simply affirmed that it was.[140]

Although the proposed legislation would have outlawed racial and religious defamation, race-based censorship was not a topic in the hearings. The lobbying for race-based censorship seems to have been on the decline. Opponents to federal censorship did not refer to any examples of censorship of racial ridicule to prove the dangers of state control. Nor did any proponents of the bill argue for censorship to decrease racial prejudice. The ban on racial ridicule was in the text, but the intensity surrounding this issue had dissipated. The African American and Jewish civil rights groups did not participate in creating the framework for the bill.

Around 1917 the NAACP had begun to wind down its funding of legal efforts to stop *The Birth of a Nation*. In December 1916, for example, Du Bois encouraged African Americans to reject censorship and instead put forth their own "drama, poetry, music and pageant" to rebut slander like Griffith's film.[141] The NAACP headquarters turned down the Cincinnati local's request for funding its legal battle against *The Birth of a Nation* in 1917. NAACP leader Roy Nash explained, "[the] Association feels that it has already spent all that it can afford vs. Birth of a Nation."[142] By 1919 and 1920 the NAACP turned its focus more toward the explosion of race riots, in Chicago and Arkansas in 1919, for example. At this time, *The Birth of a Nation* did not appear as often in NAACP publications.

Officials from the NAACP renewed their attack on *The Birth of Nation* in the early 1920s as a way to challenge the second Ku Klux Klan, but at the same time, they became involved in the free-speech cause. The Ku Klux

Klan reemerged around 1915, after the lynching of Leo Frank and after the success of *The Birth of a Nation*. William J. Simmons led the Klan revival, based in Atlanta. The Klan and *The Birth of Nation* provided publicity for each other. Klansmen demonstrated in the streets ahead of film showings in some cities and, in other cases, ushers in movie theater wore Klan uniforms. In 1924 the Klan in Chicago showed the film to large audiences for two weeks. *The Birth of a Nation* seems to have been one early factor in the expansion of the Klan, which reached its peak of approximately 5 million members in the mid-1920s.[143] The NAACP had reached out to new allies, including the Knights of Columbus, which weighed in against the movie in Boston. The historian Melvyn Stokes suggests that Irish Catholic Boston was alarmed by *The Birth of Nation*, because it associated the film with the Klan's anti-Catholicism in the 1920s.[144]

When NAACP members demonstrated against *The Birth of a Nation* in New York City, they became proponents of free speech after officials stopped their protest.[145] Before the movie was scheduled to open in May 1921 in New York City, the NAACP again argued that the film was fueling the Klan and then organized a peaceful picket in which African American veterans of World War I joined African American women in distributing leaflets in front of the Capitol Theatre. The protesters were arrested for violating a city ordinance against throwing, casting or distributing "any handbill . . . or other advertising material . . . in or upon any public place." The NAACP appealed the suspended sentence, asserting that the arrests violated freedom of speech. Judge Alfred Talley backed the NAACP and held that the law was only intended to prevent the littering of advertising material. He defended free speech in his decision: "It would be a dangerous and un-American thing to sustain an interpretation of a city ordinance which would prohibit the free distribution by a body of citizens of a pamphlet setting forth their views against what they believed to be a movement subversive of the rights as citizens."[146]

The efforts to stop *The Birth of a Nation* increasingly required elaborate justifications in the face of the NAACP's commitment to free speech. *The Birth of a Nation*, according to Du Bois in 1922, was a "special case." African Americans did not have the money or opportunity to respond to the film, which he identified as "vicious" propaganda, not art. He concluded that it is "dangerous to limit expression, and yet, without some limitations civilizations would not endure."[147] But Du Bois embraced the politicization of African American art: "I do not care a damn for any art that is not propaganda."[148] Du Bois's free speech position was thus complicated and contradictory. For him, all art was propaganda, but the racist propaganda of *The Birth of a Nation* was not art. He defended the freedom of expression, but held censorship was necessary to create an equal marketplace of ideas. In 1931 the NAACP officer William Pickens wrote to Walter White about ACLU pressure in a similar way:

> Some people, like the honest officials of American Civil Liberties Union [*sic*], object to our opposition to performances of "The Birth of a Nation," on the ground that we are interfering with freedom of organization and of speech,—and that "The Birth of a Nation" should have the same rights as other shows and theatricals. . . . This objection to our attitude assumes what is not true: that we look upon "The Birth of a Nation" as an ordinary, legitimate theatre performance. We do not: we regard it as a treacherous, dangerous attack on the minority people who do not have "equal representation," in said theatres and performances. . . . We believe in the freedom of the stage, and screen, but we do not believe in mob-incitement and dangerous race-hate taking advantage of the theatre in order to claim immunity. . . . The difference between our attitude and that of others equally honest, is that we do not regard "The Birth of a Nation" as a legitimate theatrical performance or an honest endeavor in "Art."[149]

In this way, NAACP officials, including Du Bois, stated their support for artistic freedom and the freedom of the press but held that *The Birth of a Nation* was exempt from either.

During World War I, Irish nationalists also became free-speech activists. Irish nationalists in the United States responded to World War I first by supporting Germany and assailing the pro-British press, then reluctantly backing the American war effort while urging President Woodrow Wilson to support Irish independence as part of his international goals of national self-determination.[150] During World War I, Irish nationalists were embroiled, then, in debates about their patriotism: key Irish newspapers were censored as violations for treason and the government also intervened to stop some Irish nationalists' speeches, such as John Devoy's address to the Clan na Gael in Roxbury, Massachusetts.[151] The U.S. postmaster general banned several editions of the *Irish World*, the *Freeman's Journal*, and the *Gaelic American* in 1918 for violations of the Espionage Act of 1917 and the Sedition Act of 1918. Irish nationalists responded by asserting their

Americanism in many ways. They emphasized that their papers had not criticized the United States, but England. They denounced the "unjust suppression" and demanded no "special favors"—"only justice."[152] They also connected other censorship decisions to their own persecution. The *Gaelic American* printed a federal judge's decision backing the censorship of *The Spirit of '76* because it depicted British atrocities during the Revolutionary War. The judge justified censorship to prevent the incitement of "hatred of England."[153] As a result, Irish nationalists became outspoken defenders of "Free Speech," particularly as it related to the "Irish Cause."[154] Censorship of mail and movies, they argued, served the "British oligarchy and the maintenance of English rule in Ireland."[155]

Central Jewish organizations also turned away from legal responses to anti-Semitism. In 1920, the ADL announced that it was no longer concerned with motion picture censorship and that, instead, it negotiated with producers regarding motion pictures with Jewish content.[156] At around the same time, Louis Marshall and the American Jewish Committee rejected lawsuits as a response to Henry Ford's anti-Semitic diatribes in the *Dearborn Independent*, which Ford had purchased in 1918. The first article maligning the "International Jew" had appeared in 1920, and the series of anti-Semitic articles concluded in January 1922. The articles attacked individuals, like Julius Rosenwald, Bernard Baruch, and Louis Marshall, and also alleged a Jewish conspiracy in finance.[157] The *Dearborn Independent* adapted and affirmed *The Protocols of the Elders of Zion*, a fraudulent set of minutes from a supposed meeting of Jews plotting to control global finance and politics.[158] Instead of pursuing court battles, the AJC and other major organizations worked together to publish a pamphlet discrediting *The Protocols* ("The Protocols': Bolshevism and the Jews") and circulated petitions protesting the *Dearborn Independent*. The ADL emphasized its extensive publicity work to "develop sound public opinion" in the 1926 *B'nai B'rith Manual*. It circulated thousands of copies of ex-president Taft's essay on anti-Semitism and proclaimed that the general public now simply ignored the *Dearborn Independent*.[159]

Although Marshall and the AJC had pioneered the ban on defamatory advertising in New York in the first decade of the twentieth century, they turned away from litigating anti-Semitism unless it impinged on Jewish civil rights, which Ford's publications did not. At first, Marshall and his colleagues referred to the series in the *Dearborn Independent* as a "libel upon an entire people," and he supported the idea of group libel in theory and even tried to get group libel law (which would have banned the libel of "those belonging to any race, religious denomination, sect or order against whom in whole or in part as a class a malicious publication is directed") passed in New York.[160] Yet in the end he decided not to support the attempts to pass new group libel laws or to modify existing libel law. He realized that existing First Amendment jurisprudence recognized primarily individual libel, with First Amendment advocates focused on political dissent, not the insulting speech in the newspaper. He described the "technical difficulties" with proceeding with any group libel law.[161] In addition, Marshall and his peers at the AJC did not want to discuss Jewish traits or accomplishments on Ford's terms; this could create a public controversy that they could not contain.[162] Instead, they decided that Marshall should quietly urge newspapers to support a future boycott of Ford. Their moderate approach would, hopefully, prove that they were worthy of equal citizenship and respect.[163] The ADL pursued group libel law more aggressively, but still did not succeed in trying to ban the newspaper in many Midwestern cities. Cincinnati, as well as some other cities, passed an ordinance banning the circulation of any "inflammatory" publication.[164] In the Michigan legislature, the ADL lobbied for a "general libel" bill that would have banned the *Dearborn Independent* because of its anti-Semitism, but this failed.

Group libel laws were under fire from the new free-speech organization—the ACLU—which protested against many of these ordinances. The ACLU, in 1921, attacked Ford's "ignorant and hateful propaganda against the Jews," but it also opposed all efforts to censor the *Dearborn Independent*: "Every view, no matter how ignorant or harmful we may regard it, has a legal and moral right to be heard."[165] In addition, the ACLU challenged the NAACP when it lobbied the postmaster general, Will Hays, to keep Ku Klux Klan literature out of the mail. The organization's codirector, Albert DeSilver, explained to the NAACP: "We do not think that it is ever good policy for an organization interested in human liberty to invoke repressive measures against any of its antagonists."[166]

The emboldened free-speech movement also found more agreement among the judiciary. Federal judges in Pittsburgh, Cleveland, Toledo, and Detroit struck down group libel ordinances in those cities.[167] When officials arrested merchants for selling a Klan publication, the *Fiery Cross*, in Detroit in 1923, the Klan got an injunction stopping future action against the paper.[168] When Cleveland officials banned the *Dearborn Independent* based on an ordinance suppressing publications "calculated to excite scandal and having a tendency to create breaches of the peace," that paper got an injunction. The judge ruled against any prior restraint of publications, held that the publication was not "indecent, obscene, or scandalous," and suggested that it was anti-Semitic to assume that Jews would be aroused to violence because of the publication.[169] The growing disfavor for group libel is also apparent in *Drozda v. State* (1920) in which a Texas criminal appeals court reversed the conviction of a Bohemian-language newspaper for libeling Bohemians as a group. The court held that there was confusion about what the precise translation of the text should be, but also expanded its decision to undermine the criminalization of group libel in general: "A man who scurrilously attacks the Smiths, Johnsons, Jones, or the Jews, Gentiles or Syrians . . . could not be successfully hauled into court and convicted of libel of any particular person, unless there be something in such article which by fair interpretation thereof to bring into disrepute some particular person or persons." *Drozda*, therefore, narrowed the crime of defamation to cases in which particular individuals had been identified—or in which colloquium could be established.[170]

By the 1930s, advocacy groups recognized the difficulty of prosecuting group libel cases. They increasingly worried about First Amendment protests against the cases, realized that effective enforcement of the laws was uncertain (as just one person on a jury could thwart the case), and saw that a courtroom was often a theatrical stage, with the racist defendant as the star (and a martyr for First Amendment causes). Trials often became "sounding boards" for whether or not the defendant's racist claims were "true," as true statements were not libel. In 1935, B'nai B'rith, for example, still held that group libel should be an exception to the First Amendment, but realized that the interpretation of libel statutes as applying only to individuals "forms an insurmountable obstacle in bringing before the bar of justice one of the lowest types of malefactors."[171] In 1936, Robert Edmondson was arrested in New York City for his anti-Semitic pamphlets. Many Jewish organizations, including the American Jewish Congress, praised Mayor Fiorello LaGuardia for issuing the arrest warrant. Prior to the trial, however, the American Jewish Congress withdrew its support for the case. It argued instead that the best answer to bigotry was "a campaign of education fostered by all groups."[172]

Although the major civil rights groups turned against race-based censorship and courts withdrew their support for it, state and municipal boards continued to use race in their censorship decisions, but often outside of the framework established by the civil rights censors. Censors in Virginia and Maryland eliminated images that challenged white supremacy, depictions of interracial contact, the negative portrayal of whites, and any racial themes deemed controversial. In 1924, for example, Maryland censors cut many scenes from *Birthright*, a film by the African American director Oscar Micheaux which traced the story of a northern black man, Peter, who opens a school in the South. Censors cut scenes that depicted any unfair treatment of African Americans, as well as references to miscegenation, including a scene in which a black woman described white men: "They don't care. We are just nigger women. They make you feel—Naked."[173] Many northern censorship boards did not refer to race in their standards, but they still periodically censored films for racist or anti-Semitic themes. In 1928, New York State's Motion Picture Division made cuts to *City without Jews* because of censors' perception of anti-Semitism: it held that communities needed to "welcome all races and creeds" to be successful.[174]

Race-based censorship had thus caught the attention of a group of well-organized and outspoken free-speech advocates who saw racial themes in films as inherently political topics. Movie producers and free-speech activists identified motion pictures as sources of information and political suasion, like the press. At the same time, the definition of racial harm contracted to a question of violence. The ADL and NAACP advocacy for race-based censorship declined, and the Irish were less likely to identify themselves as a race any more, while Catholics campaigned for the reform of sexual morality in film and the positive portrayal of Catholics. In these ways, the multiracial commitment to race-based censorship collapsed and debates about immorality and entertainment again converged on sexuality—or immorality in the narrow sense.

CONCLUSION

The Jazz Singer, the first feature film with sound, premiered in 1927. Starring Al Jolson as a cantor's son who chooses a stage career instead of his family's rigid Jewish tradition, *The Jazz Singer* is famous both for its technological innovation and Jolson's emotional blackface scenes. These blackface performances highlight both cross-racial affinity and exploitation. Jolson's forlorn songs seemed to express some sympathy with African American pain: the performer had a strong African American fan base that linked him to Bert Williams, and he was known for his "cross-racial conviviality" with African American artists in the 1920s.[1] But the blackface tradition also mocked and marginalized African Americans. The arc of *The Jazz Singer*, in particular, depicts a Jewish performer's upward mobility through the use of blackface in an entertainment industry that did not offer similar opportunities for African Americans. Jakie Rabinowitz escapes from his Jewish past and woos his Gentile girlfriend through his blackface masquerade. As the historian Michael Rogin states, *The Jazz Singer* "facilitates the union not of black and white but of gentile and Jew."[2]

The Jazz Singer marks a milestone for Jewish–African American relations in entertainment, but it is just one piece of a bigger puzzle of film controversy based on religion and race in 1927.[3] In this remarkable year, Irish Catholic protesters attacked two movies—*The Callahans and the Murphys* (MGM) and *Irish Hearts* (Warner Brothers)—for insulting the Irish race and the Catholic religion. At the same time, Jewish leaders battled against *The King of Kings*, while Catholics praised the film. Also in 1927, Hollywood producers introduced a new self-regulation scheme—the "Don'ts and Be Carefuls"—which included a ban on racial ridicule, but it was soon replaced by the Production Code, which did not cover racial ridicule. In 1927, progressive race-based censorship was weak but cantankerous, usually drowned out by Catholic censorship of sacrilege and sexual immorality. While the Irish benevolent societies, like the Ancient Order of Hibernians, still mustered an assault on two movies for insulting their race, Catholic organizations focused on the insult to the Catholic religion; both Irish and Catholic protests attacked Jews as anti-Christian conspirators. Thus the multiracial landscape of censorship in earlier decades had turned into a bifurcated religious battleground in 1927.

On December 4, 1926, the *Gaelic American* announced that a film version of *McFadden's Row of Flats*—the "notorious caricature on the Irish race"— was in production. The short article reminded readers that, a little more than twenty years before, proud Irishmen had driven the play from the theaters.[4] Familiar alarm bells went off in the Irish American community. Half a year after news of the *McFadden's Row of Flats* production broke, in the summer of 1927, Irish Americans protested two new films, *The Callahans and the Murphys* and *Irish Hearts*. The Callahans and the Murphys, who live across from each other in Goat Alley, spar throughout the film. But Callahan's daughter, Ellen, falls in love with Murphy's son, Dan, who is a bootlegger. Their tenement apartment has bugs and lacks indoor plumbing. Catholic symbols mark the sets, and several scenes show them drunk and disorderly, including a raucous St. Patrick's Day picnic that ends with arrests. Many of the complaints resembled the critique of *McFadden's Row of Flats*, particularly the focus on the image of Irish women.[5] The Irish American protesters claimed that Mrs. Callahan and Mrs. Murphy were portrayed as "apes."[6] Other complaints focused on the carousing of these drunken Irish mothers at a St. Patrick's Day outing.[7] Objections to *Irish Hearts* also focused on the depiction of a poor Irish girl, Mary McAvoy, who fights so much that she ends up with two black eyes.[8] Although *The Callahans and the Murphys* and *Irish Hearts* reminded many of the Stage Irishwoman from earlier in the century, Irish protesters would soon find that the context of 1927 differed immensely from 1903.

Whereas Irish nationalists had dominated the campaign against the Stage Irish two decades earlier, Catholic leaders joined the attack on these films in 1927. Irish and Catholic were clearly overlapping categories, but organizations representing the Catholic Church played a distinctive role in the protests in 1927. They emphasized the defense of the Catholic reputation, not a defense of the Irish race.[9] The National Board of Review (previously the National Board of Censorship) passed *The Callahans and the Murphys* with little comment, and several state censorship boards endorsed it with minor alterations. But Irish American activists and Catholic leaders referred to a "medley of offense" to the Irish race and to the Catholic religion.[10] Charles McMahon of the National Catholic Welfare Conference explained that the movie was an "outrage against [the Irish American] race and ...

religion." But he also went a step further to claim that the anti-Catholicism was more damaging (a "hideous defamation") than the "crass caricature" of the Irish race.[11] Exasperated with the mounting protests, MGM believed that McMahon's dual arguments against "the Irish race as well as the Irish religion" indicated that no editing would satisfy him.[12]

To quell the protests, MGM asked Rita McGoldrick, of the International Federation of Catholic Alumni, and Father John Kelly, of the Catholic Theater Guild, to review the film. They suggested cutting all mentions of Catholicism, all images of the crucifix, and changing the picnic to something other than a St. Patrick's Day celebration. Irish Catholic pressure also forced several censorship boards to reconsider their earlier approvals. The New York State Motion Picture Commission rescreened the movie in August of 1927 and then cut scenes of drunkenness, the fight at the picnic, and a caterpillar on a salad, among others.[13] The New York state censors then responded to John T. Kelly, of the American Irish Vigilance Committee, to say that they could not cut any further, or stop the film as a whole, because "this picture [was] found not to fall within prohibitions of the statute." The state censors suggested protesters work to amend the law in the legislature.[14] Irish activists then turned to a familiar style of protest—direct action—which they referred to as "the only real remedy."[15] On August 24, 1927, one spectator stood up during *The Callahans and the Murphys* and shouted down the film. A similar protest erupted the following night. At another showing, Irish spectators threw a stink bomb. They also disrupted movie houses featuring *Irish Hearts*. The *Gaelic American* bragged that all Loew's theaters in New York had to have police protection.[16] As a result, theater owners withdrew the film from several cities, including Cincinnati, Washington, D.C., and Bridgeport, Connecticut.[17] The mayor stopped the film in Bayonne, New Jersey.[18]

After the New York State Board of Censors explained that it had no power to ban or further modify *The Callahans and the Murphys*, Irish Catholic activists tried to amend New York City law to include a prohibition of films that "disparaged any race, creed or nationality."[19] The debates surrounding the proposed amendment, which died in committee, resembled earlier efforts to expand race-based censorship, as some of the same organizations and activists, such as the United Irish American Societies and Thomas Tuite, backed the amendment and some of efforts to "vindicate the Irish" were also familiar.[20] The failure of the Irish proposal also shows the change in the climate for race-based censorship since the first decade of the twentieth century; by 1927, it was more difficult to defend race-based censorship. The suggested amendment protected any race, creed, or nationality, offering "equal protection to all nationalities and creeds."[21] But this inclusive rhetoric was quickly overshadowed by emphatic anti-Semitism in the struggle over *The Callahans and the Murphys* and *Irish Hearts*, which were both produced by Jewish companies—MGM and Warner Brothers, respectively. Irish Catholic protesters referred to the Jewish film producers as a "disgrace to their race," throughout the campaign, consistently identifying their foes as Jews who spread "propaganda against Christian ideals."[22] "When an illiterate East Side Jew through his genius for accumulating money can control the American movie industry," vented one Irish American critic, "the time has come for Americans to save themselves from the demoralization brought on the movie industry by men who have not a single noble or decent idea in their minds."[23] The Irish Catholic protesters were frustrated with Will Hays, the Protestant leader in charge of administering Hollywood's self-regulation schemes, but identified him as merely the Christian front representing his "Jewish employers" in the background.[24]

As the New York aldermen were debating in October, Catholic leaders in Philadelphia also spoke out strongly against the film. Cardinal Dougherty of Philadelphia, as well as the Philadelphia archdiocese, demanded a recall of the film. On October 24, 1927, MGM finally relented; it withdrew the film. The studio's written explanation of its decision appeared in Catholic newspapers across the country.[25] On the one hand, the outcome seems familiar: the Irish had again succeeded with practical censorship but, on the other hand, the complaints against the film were about the images of the Irish and of Catholicism. Not only had the critique shifted to include negative images of Catholicism but the true power to control representation was moving into the hands of Catholic leaders who backed and enforced Hollywood's new self-regulation scheme.

Around the same time, religious controversy was brewing over *The King of Kings*, a dramatization of the life of Jesus. MGM's surrender in the battle over *The Callahans and the Murphys* shaped the negotiations over *The King of Kings* in many ways. The Motion Picture Producers and Distributors of America (MPPDA), a trade association which had been established in 1922 to regulate motion pictures before their release, hoped to avoid a protracted period of protest, and Jewish leaders may have hoped to score a similar achievement for themselves. Anticipating criticism from religious groups, the director Cecil DeMille had consulted with Protestant, Catholic, and Jewish leaders while making the film. Reverend George Reid, who served on the Federal Council of Churches, represented Protestants; Father Daniel Lord, a Chicago-born Jesuit, represented Catholics; and Rabbi Edgar Magnin represented Jews. DeMille made concessions to his religious advisors. For example, at Lord's request, he eliminated a "sensual kiss" involving Mary Magdalene.

When *The King of Kings* premiered on April 15, 1927—Good Friday—at the Gaiety Theatre in New York City, it quickly emerged that Jews had not been placated by DeMille's work with several rabbis behind the scenes. Various Jewish leaders objected to *The King of Kings* because of the portrayal of Jews as "Christ-killers" and the portrayal of Caiaphas, the high priest, as a Shylock stereotype. Some Jewish critics argued that even though the myth that Jews killed Jesus had a long history and was dramatized at the Passion Play in Oberammergau every ten years, *The King of Kings* proved particularly dangerous because it could reach millions of movie fans.[26] Rabbi Stephen Wise criticized the depiction of Caiaphas, whom DeMille presented as a greedy and corrupt leader who felt Jesus was getting in the way of his profits. Wise wrote that Caiaphas conformed to the "present conception of an East European peasant of the Jew caring for revenue and revenue only." He was a cheap "Shylock."[27] DeMille in return cut some of the troublesome scenes and promised to include a foreword that absolved Jews for the death of Jesus.

The protests over *The King of Kings* reinforced the religious schisms of the debate over *The Callahans and the Murphys*. Rita McGoldrick was not pleased with the cuts made in *The King of Kings* to appease Jews. Although she was sensitive to insults to Catholics, she resented the B'nai B'rith's ongoing critique of the film. She tracked the Jewish campaign and urged Catholic leaders to drum up further support for the film in cities seeing Jewish protests[28] In 1928 she described her opposition to the Jewish "effort to stop this sympathetic story of Christ."[29] The Jewish attack on the film intensified in late October, after MGM recalled *The Callahans and the Murphys*.[30] If Catholics could win the cancellation of *The Callahans and the Murphys*, perhaps Jews wanted to win an unequivocal victory as well. Several rabbis accused liberal Christians of tacitly endorsing the film. Rabbi Israel Goldstein, for example, repeatedly pleaded for Christian allies in his critique of *The King of Kings*.

As rabbis publically complained about the film, the B'nai B'rith was working behind the scenes to shape Jewish images in Hollywood. To head off public protests from religious and racial minorities, the MPPDA sought advisory relationships with "large, representative" bodies, which would negotiate with the MPPDA prior to a film's release. On November 22, 1927, the B'nai B'rith announced that it was the "official consultant" to the organization of film producers on films with Jewish characters and themes.[31] B'nai B'rith's success, however, proved controversial among Jewish groups. Rabbi Wise, who had previously worked with B'nai B'rith in negotiations with DeMille, devoted a sermon to attacking *The King of Kings* at the Free Synagogue, which met in Carnegie Hall, and other rabbis criticized the film in print and in speaking engagements. Wise turned against B'nai B'rith because he believed the organization was trying to silence the protests against the film. Wise's American Jewish Congress did not shy away from direct confrontation and disdained B'nai B'rith moderation and elitism. B'nai B'rith, in turn, argued that a public outcry made the film more profitable and would perhaps identify Jews in the public mind as critics of the "Christian Bible."[32]

After the battle over *The King of Kings*, different religious groups took stock of their victories and disappointments. They competed with each other and overshadowed other racial minorities as they vied to control content on screen. Irish American protesters did not amend New York City's censorship law to include racial insults, but Irish and Catholic activists succeeded in suppressing *The Callahans and the Murphys*. *The King of Kings* survived with Catholic support, despite Jewish opposition. A B'nai B'rith committee became an official consultant on Jewish-themed films only, while Catholics continued to work with the Hollywood bureaucracy to set standards for all films, not just movies depicting Catholics.[33] Protestant ministers and the MPPDA worked together closely during the production of *The King of Kings*, but their relationship quickly deteriorated when it failed to be as popular as predicted and when negotiations for a formal relationship between a Protestant movie watchdog group and the MPPDA broke down.[34] By 1930, the MPPDA was thus ready to work closely with the Catholic Church.

The year 1927 also proved important for the revision of Hollywood's self-regulation; Catholics played a central role in this transition. The "Don'ts and Be Carefuls," a weak system set up in 1927, gave way just three years later to Hollywood's new Production Code. In 1927, Jason Joy, the head of the Studio Relations Committee, had studied the cuts of censorship boards throughout the country, held conferences with civic groups nationwide, and then worked with Irving Thalberg, of MGM, to synthesize all the common rules for censorship from city, state, and international boards. This list, known as the "Don'ts and Be Carefuls," included crime (such as drug use, murder, and brutality), sexuality (such as white slavery, venereal disease, and sexual perversion), and "ridicule of the clergy." Race relations were included on the list in two ways: Miscegenation was the fifth don't and willful offense to any nation, race, or creed was the eleventh and final one. Joy kept the list up to date by visiting censorship boards throughout the year.[35] The "Don'ts and Be Carefuls," however, did not receive widespread support from motion picture studios, which submitted less than 20 percent of their films to Joy's office. As a result, censorship boards continued to cut material covered on the list. Official censors would cut when studios were unwilling to act. Reformers, in turn, doubted the industry's sincerity about reform. One critic described how the code really worked: "If you can't be good, be careful."[36]

McGoldrick's decisions in *The Callahans and the Murphys* case helped position her as a powerful and credible ally in Hays's campaign to improve Hollywood's reputation. Under intense pressure from Protestant reformers, who attacked him as a puppet of movie producers busy turning the United States into a "brothel house," Hays turned to Catholic leaders for support.[37] In particular, he began to build an alliance with McGoldrick, who had testified against federal censorship in the 1926 congressional hearing and had refused to join the campaign against *The Callahans and the Murphys*. She was loyal to Hays and his system of industry regulation.[38] The IFCA's Motion Picture Bureau published a list of approved films. Printed in twenty-one Catholic newspapers as well as two major metropolitan papers, this list circulated among more than five thousand groups in the United States.[39] The standards of the IFCA were strict: it rejected 49 percent of the films it reviewed in 1929.

By late 1929, as criticism of the film industry continued to grow, Hays considered an overhaul of the "Don'ts and Be Carefuls." He relied on his network of Catholic allies for the task of improving the self-censorship code. Chicago Catholics played a prominent role in the revision of Hollywood's standards. Cardinal George Mundelein had organized the Eucharistic Congress in 1926, partly as a response to a Ku Klux Klan parade in 1925. Close to a million Catholics from the United States and Europe gathered for the event in Chicago. Martin Quigley, a Catholic-educated publisher of the *Exhibitors Herald* who had also served on the Chicago Motion Picture Commission, worked closely with Fox film studio to film the Eucharistic Congress. Then Joseph Breen, the congress's public relations director, sent the film to Catholic schools and groups throughout the country. Charles Pettijohn, the MPPDA lawyer, began talking to Cardinal Mundelein in Chicago about the possibility of withdrawing his support for the city's censorship board. In return, Pettijohn promised to follow the Catholic Church's moral guidelines. Mundelein then conferred with Father FitzGeorge Dineen, who had served on the Chicago Board of Censorship. Dineen disparaged the Hollywood proposal as vague and unrealistic. Still alarmed at the immorality of Hollywood films, Dineen started discussions with Quigley about how to improve the "Don'ts and Be Carefuls." They brought Father Daniel Lord into the discussions because of his experience with *The King of Kings*. In 1930 Lord pulled their notes together into the Motion Picture Production Code, which outlined the moral basis for regulation as well as the specific themes and images to avoid.

Racial ridicule almost completely disappeared in the Production Code, but a conservative ban on miscegenation remained. The code prohibited the words "Chink, Dago, Frog, Greaser, Hunkie, Kike, Nigger, Spig, Wop, Yid." This list, under the category "Profanity," is one remnant of the bans on racial ridicule. The Production Code ruled out any religious ridicule and also banned the disparagement of other nations. These components— profanity, religious and national insults—left out race. But the Production Code did not simply diminish the significance of race. It retained the ban on miscegenation, which had been added to the "Don'ts and Be Carefuls." The historian Susan Courtney concludes that the Hays office added the miscegenation ban to Lord's draft of the code. One Production Code Administration (PCA) official later recalled that Quigley was "infuriated that we could not treat a picture dealing with miscegenation."[40] With the miscegenation ban, Hays responded to prevalent complaints from the public. Around the time of the code's creation, many states passed antimiscegenation statutes, not just in the South but in the West as well. The PCA was vigilant in rejecting scripts and scenes depicting sexual attraction between black and white characters (although the PCA was never clear in its definition of black and white races). Hays's comment in 1927 informed the PCA through the 1940s: He noted it was "inadvisable always to show white women in scenes with negroes where there is any inference of miscegenation or social relationship."[41] Censors from the PCA pressured Universal to withdraw *Imitation of Life* (1934), because it featured a light-skinned African American woman, Peola, who passes for white. Peola worried censors because her light skin tone suggested miscegenation in her lineage. Although censors corresponded extensively about *Imitation of Life*, they eventually passed the film without explaining their decision.[42]

To enforce the Production Code, Catholic leaders established the Legion of Decency in 1933 as a pressure group. It decided on lists of forbidden films, circulated the lists throughout the country, and organized boycotts of theaters that showed the films on the list. The Legion of Decency merged with the IFCA to create a rating system with four levels, and the IFCA agreed to supply a list of condemned films. With its headquarters in New York City, the legion depended on the allegiance of individual bishops who in fact had varying levels of enthusiasm for it.[43] Nevertheless, the Legion of Decency was in step with the PCA; by 1938, it rarely condemned any film having PCA approval. Why did Catholics succeed as national censors when other minority groups in the past had failed to represent the country's morals? First, the Legion of Decency brought immense practical power to bear on the moral debates surrounding motion pictures. Although Catholics made up about 20 percent of the population in 1930, the number of Catholics was much higher in large cities. In places like Boston and Chicago, the Catholic population made up nearly half of the city; their boycotts could thus disrupt a film's success. Their influence also filled a gap vacated by Protestants who were divided by their own scandals related to their efforts to shape Hollywood. Second, Catholics actually gained the backing of other religious groups. Despite anti-Catholic sentiment, other religious groups also disliked the films that the Legion of Decency condemned. The Catholic Church found non-Catholic allies who shared an antimodern critique of American popular culture.[44] Often criticized for being only a Catholic effort, the Legion cultivated (and sometimes exaggerated) support from Protestants and Jews.[45]

If racial ridicule declined in the revision of Hollywood's internal systems of censorship, it reappeared in new debates about "group libel" during and after World War II. Group libel laws gained support largely because of concerns about the Nazi racism.[46] In 1942 David Riesman, then a legal scholar, wrote a series of essays in support of the restriction of racial and religious defamation. Riesman argued that fascists exploited civil liberties to undermine democracy and create racial and religious schisms in society.[47] In 1943, Massachusetts passed a group libel law that outlawed "any false, written or printed material with the intent to maliciously promote hatred of any group of persons in the common wealth because of race, color or religion."[48] Rhode Island's legislature passed a group libel bill in 1944, but the governor vetoed it. In 1952, the Supreme Court upheld an Illinois group libel law, initially passed in 1917 to stop *The Birth of a Nation*. Several cities—such as Chicago, Houston, and Denver—had group libel laws. Citing the rise of anti-Semitic materials in the mail, the American Jewish Congress lobbied Congress, in 1943 and 1944, to pass a law banning "defamatory . . . statements . . . [based on] race or religion" from the U.S. mail.[49] The ACLU opposed the law, along with the NAACP, the Anti-Defamation League, and the American Jewish Committee. The bill thus failed, as did other efforts to restrict hate speech at the federal level.[50]

Group libel did not take hold in the middle of the twentieth century because minority groups' complaints about harmful speech seemed dangerously divisive and intolerant. Free-speech activists warned against fractures in American society and against any hint of totalitarian censorship similar to Nazi book burning. For example, one critic complained about "the arrogance of a minority in using its power to control and even persecute the majority."[51] In a so-called town-hall debate in 1949, Morris Ernst, an attorney for the ACLU, debated other lawyers and scholars about whether minority pressure groups infringed on freedom of speech in a democracy. A year earlier, the Anti-Defamation League had protested against a U.S. tour of a British film version of *Oliver Twist*; it lobbied the Motion Picture Association of America (MPAA, formerly the MPPDA) to stop the film. The PCA would not approve the movie because it insulted a religious group. Ernst decried Jewish, Catholic, and African American threats to "editors, broadcasters and movie moguls." Reminding his audience about the harms of Nazi state controls, Ernst asked, "What if Negro or Catholic groups thought it bad to have this program go on the air tonight?"[52] On the other hand, Henry Epstein, an attorney affiliated with the Anti-Defamation League, identified the pressure from minority groups as self-protection, referring to the Holocaust when he warned that John Milton's ideas about truth and tolerance of hateful speech did not save "six million dead Jews."[53] Harmful stereotypes like Uncle Remus and Fagin were not incidental; they buttressed the "exploiters, the restrictors, and the segregators."[54] Protests against racial and religious ridicule deserved First Amendment protection: Negroes, Jews, and Catholics had the right to "exercise such forms of persuasion and influence as are available to them."[55] Although the debate revealed that minority groups remained active in trying to control their representation in popular culture, this forum also shows the remarkable distance from the Irish, Jewish, and African American protests of the early twentieth century. In the 1949 forum, the pressure groups carefully separated their activity from state censorship and defended it within the same free-speech framework outlined by the civil libertarians.

In 1949, when his opponents declared that pressure groups had the right to voice their public opinion, Ernst suggested that these minorities did much more than talk: he pressed his opponents to disclose the "techniques of pressure of the Catholic groups."[56] He would have been satisfied with several movie controversies in the late 1940s that exposed the Legion of Decency's reach into government authority. As group libel withered and ACLU proponents cast doubt on all pressure groups, the MPAA and the ACLU searched for test cases to challenge the constitutionality of motion picture censorship. The MPAA tried to fight censorship and appease NAACP critics at the same time by attacking southern censors' bans on movies that questioned white supremacy. Although race-based censorship lingered in motion picture censorship, it was most prominent in southern censorship boards, which censored material that they believed would disrupt white supremacy. In 1927, Lloyd Binford became chairman of the Memphis's censorship board and presided over two decades of race-based censorship to protect an "Old South perspective on race relations."[57] In 1945 he banned *Brewster's Millions* for presenting "too much familiarity between the races" and, two years later, *Annie Get Your Gun* because its roles for African Americans were "too big."[58] When Binford censored *Curley* in 1947 because it featured social equality among school children, the black press, the producers of *Curley*, and others mocked his overzealousness as a throwback to the Civil War.[59] *Colliers*, for example, contrasted Binford's outlandish censorship with the Legion of Decency's responsible lobbying of Hollywood.[60] The ACLU worked with United Artists, which produced *Curley*, to challenge Memphis's conservatism in court.

As the *Curley* case was winding through appeals, other examples of southern censorship of racial equality also caught the attention of motion picture producers who sought test cases to overturn *Mutual v. Ohio* (1915). The MPAA also took legal action against Atlanta's suppression of *Lost Boundaries* in 1949 and Marshall, Texas's ban of *Pinky*, also in 1949; the censorship of these films was tied to their depiction of African Americans passing as white.[61] Critics recognized that these films addressed serious racial problems and challenged racial inequality in the United States. Although the Supreme Court refused to hear the appeals related to *Curley* and *Lost Boundaries*, the MPAA still held out hope that the *Pinky* case, *Gelling v. Texas*, would be the Supreme Court test case to overturn the Mutual decision. But, as *Gelling* proceeded through the court system, a new film aroused a firestorm of debate.

Produced in Italy in 1947, *The Miracle*, a dramatization of a Federico Fellini story about the virgin birth, opened in New York City on December 12, 1950.[62] When the Mary figure, Nanny, realizes she is pregnant, a nun scolds her for her sin, unwilling to believe in a miracle. Villagers mock her. On the one hand, the film criticized how contemporary society would treat the virgin birth. On the other hand, some observers believed it ridiculed Catholic beliefs. The New York State censors approved *The Miracle* twice in 1949, once without English subtitles and then with subtitles. The board had the power to ban sacrilegious films, but it did not see *The Miracle* as a violation of that provision. When the film opened in New York City in 1950, the Legion of Decency condemned it and pressed to have the New York City licenser, Edward McCaffrey, pressure theaters to stop showing the film. McCaffrey followed through, threatening movie theaters with revoking their licenses if they screened the film.[63] The New York Supreme Court held that McCaffrey did not have the power to stop *The Miracle*; only the state censorship board could ban films. Catholics picketed theaters showing *The Miracle*, but ticket sales were high and many critics praised the film's artistry. So Catholics searched for another way. They forced the New York State Censorship Board to review the film for a third time in 1951. At this point the board found that *The Miracle* was sacrilegious because it tied Christianity to licentiousness and drunkenness.[64]

With the backing of the ACLU, Joseph Burstyn, who was in charge of distributing *The Miracle*, fought censorship through the New York state court and then took the case all the way to the Supreme Court. In his legal battle he argued that motion picture censorship constituted prior restraint and thus violated the First Amendment, that the ban on sacrilege violated the separation of church and state, and that the standards of censorship violated the due process clause of the Fourteenth Amendment because they were too vague.[65] In a unanimous opinion, Justice Tom Clark overturned the Mutual precedent, holding that for-profit entertainment could not be separated from the communication of information or the press. Clark wrote, "We conclude that expression by means of motion pictures is included within the free speech and free press guaranty of the First and Fourteenth Amendments." He also concluded that sacrilege was too vague, leaving open the possibility of more narrowly defined censorship in other areas, namely, obscenity.[66] Historians note the restraint of the decision as well as the pioneering and unanimous expansion of First Amendment protection amid the repressions of the Cold War.[67] Following further censorship cases that loosened the definition of obscenity, most states abandoned their motion picture censorship boards in the 1960s; only Maryland, with a revised statute, censored films until 1981.

It is fitting that race-based censorship was the understudy in the drama leading to the end of motion picture censorship because the censorship of racial ridicule had long served as a problematic example of the censors' interference with political messages and the prejudiced viewpoint of a censor. Although questions about sexuality and crime usually overshadowed the debates over race and censorship, race-based censorship constituted a significant effort to expand the definitions of morality and decency to include fair depictions of all races. Binford's bigoted censorship was a far cry from the Irish, Jewish, and African American activists of the early twentieth century who tried to make racism "immoral" in their critique of American popular entertainment. But Binford's racist views raised similar concerns about whether or not a minority should gain cultural authority. The expansion of the First Amendment in the twentieth century thus swept away race-based motion picture censorship, along with the government's prior restraint of films.

The cluster of censorship struggles in 1927, the town-hall debate about Jewish, Catholic, and "Negro" pressure groups in 1949, and the multiple test cases of motion picture censorship in the late 1940s and early 1950s show that a wide, comparative framework works best for understanding any minority group's protest against harmful representations. The configurations changed during the twentieth century—the Irish melted into a Catholic pressure group and Jews rejected racial identity—but a competitive tension remained. These groups perpetually reacted to each other and to past injuries, not just to the texts in print, on stage, or on the screen. While some of the reasons for choosing particular targets remain mysterious, it is clear that the groups did not mobilize against particular plays and movies because of the texts alone.

Throughout the twentieth century, multiple minority groups undertook similar efforts to control representation to ensure visibility, equality, and safety in American democracy as First Amendment protection expanded and limited their tactics. Race-based censorship of motion pictures was no longer a weapon in their arsenal. But government control of hate speech remained, though in new venues—outside of vaudeville and movie theaters. Federal law, for example, requires the regulation of harassing speech (that creates a "hostile environment") in the workplace and at colleges and universities, although these provisions are increasingly raising First Amendment concerns.[68] In the late 1980s, colleges and universities responded to a rise of racist incidents on campus with new regulations on hate speech. The University of Michigan, for example, passed a hate speech code in 1989, after students found handbills announcing "open hunting season" on African Americans and after a students unfurled a Ku Klux Klan uniform from a dormitory window. Michigan's rule disciplined students who engaged in "any behavior, verbal or physical, that stigmatizes or victimizes an individual on the basis of race, ethnicity, religion, sex, sexual orientation, creed, national origin, ancestry, age, marital status, handicap or Vietnam-era veteran status."[69] The U. S. District Court, Eastern District, overturned Michigan's policy because it found the rules to be vague and overly broad; the judge noted that universities could not restrict speech just because it was "offensive" to "large groups of people."[70] Although the campus hate speech codes from the late-1980s did not survive judicial review, a new wave of regulations has emerged because of expanded interpretations of Title VI and Title IX of the Civil Rights Act of 1964 to include "hostile environment" provisions similar to the proscription of "hostile work environment" as a form of sexual harassment under Title VII. Title VI holds that colleges and universities receiving federal funds must take steps to prevent a "racially hostile environment," while Title IX requires educational institutions that accept federal money to provide an environment free of sexual harassment.[71] Critics of these policies argue that freedom of speech, not censorship, has been a powerful weapon against racism and sexism, that the regulation of hate speech does not reach the root causes of racism or sexism, and that hate speech codes could be turned against civil rights activists. Remnants of the debates over the regulation of racial ridicule are thus evident in the debates over campus rules about hostile educational environments—the new frontier in hate speech regulation.[72]

This book began with an early-twentieth-century reformer's dire warning against motion pictures as the "devil's melting pot." It is fitting to end in 1949, when Morris Ernst offered a different model of the multicultural nation and the danger of censorship: "I love the symphony of people. I am fearful of the people who go [in] back of the symphony leader and take out some of the notes."[73] From melting pot to symphony, from *Rebecca's Wedding Day* (1914) to *The King of Kings* (1927), from racial ridicule to group libel and hate speech, the central tension between equality and freedom of expression, between the protection of groups and the rights of individuals, animates this twentieth-century dilemma.

Notes

INTRODUCTION

1. Dr. Julian Morgenstern, "A Review of Jewish Events," *B'nai B'rith News*, May/June 1910, 21.

2. Fred Gresham, "Race Men Oppose Showing The Nigger," *Chicago Defender*, May 15, 1915, 7. Gary, Indiana, and Tucson, Arizona, censored the film. "The 'Nigger' Barred by Act of Council," *Chicago Defender*, August 28, 1915, 1; and "Mr. Griffith Killed in Gary," *Chicago Defender*, July 24, 1915, 4. W. E. B. Du Bois linked *The Birth of a Nation* to the high number of lynchings. Du Bois to Walter White, [1922], folder: "Films and Plays, Birth of a Nation, 1922." C-301, National Association for the Advancement of Colored People Records, Manuscript Reading Room, Library of Congress (hereafter NAACPR).

3. "Opinion of Commissioner Joseph Levenson on Protest Filed by the National Association for the Advancement of Colored People" (1922), folder "Motion Picture Commission," box 12, Governor Miller Correspondence, New York State Archives.

4. McElya, *Clinging to Mammy*, 116–59; Johnson, "'Ye Gave Them a Stone.'"

5. "Gaelic Notes," *Irish World*, August 13, 1904, 8.

6. Pennsylvania State Board of Censors of Motion Pictures (Harrisburg), "Report for the Week Ending December 24, 1915," file "ADL: Motion Pictures," B'nai B'rith International Archives, Jacob Rader Marcus Center, American Jewish Archives (formerly held at the B'nai B'rith Klutznick National Museum; hereafter BBIA). On this document, held in the ADL's files, *Reproduction of the Fall of Warsaw* and *The Immigrant* are both marked with an "X."

7. "Villifiers of the Irish Race," *Irish World*, August 26, 1899, 9.

8. "Stage Irishwoman Is Speedily Suppressed," *Gaelic American*, December 6, 1919, 4.

9. Russell, *Indianapolis Freeman*, April 2, 1904, quoted in Sampson, *The Ghost Walks*, 314–15.

10. See Diner, *In the Almost Promised Land*; Melnick, *A Right to Sing the Blues*; Greenberg, *Troubling the Waters*; Goldstein, *The Price of Whiteness*; Harrison-Kahan, *The White Negress*; and Jacobson, *Whiteness of a Different Color*.

11. Bornstein, *The Colors of Zion*.

12. Jacobson, *Special Sorrows*, 184–88.

13. Nelson, *Irish Nationalism*, 43–50.

14. Goldstein, *The Price of Whiteness*, 92–93.

15. Gaines, *Uplifting the Race*, 100–104.

16. Kenny, "Race, Violence and Anti-Irish Sentiment," 375.

17. Gross, *What Blood Won't Tell*, 17; Rogin, *Blackface, White Noise*.

18. Report Book o, 252, Keith/Albee Collection, Special Collections, The University of Iowa, Iowa City (hereafter KAC); Report Book 16, 123, KAC.

19. Report Book o, 297; Report Book 12, 250, KAC. In 1909, a Boston theater manager noted that a comedian had "discarded his former Hebrew make up. . . . My personal opinion is that the change improves his act very much as he gets away from the old stereotypical style" (Report Book 10, 48, KAC).

20. Report Book o, 335, KAC.

21. "To Hebrew Comedians," New Evening Post, January 9, [1909], Envelope 2528 "Joe Welch," Robinson Locke Theatre Collection, Billy Rose Theatre Division, New York Public Library for the Performing Arts, Dorothy and Lewis B. Cullman Center (hereafter BRTD). See also J. Rosamond Johnson's editorial in New York Age: "Noting that the play McFadden's Flats had several years earlier been halted by the protests of Irish Americans incensed by the drama's stereotyping of their ethnic group, Johnson calls for the city's 100,000 African Americans to stand united against a film that misrepresents and vilifies them" (quoted in Oliver and Walker, "James Weldon Johnson's 'New York Age' Essays," 5). Another example also puts these three groups together: "The German dialect of the theatre world is at least as old as the Irish brogue. The Swedish dialect put into the mouths of serving maids and sailor men makes a long chapter of stage lingo. Italian hand-organ men are famous butts. Who has not seen the overdrawn stage Frenchman—the "frog-eater"? In how many plays have the Yankees been held up to ridicule? What of the thick and drawling Englishman who stalks as the chief form of humor on many histrionic boards? The Southern Brigadiers? The negro minstrels? The Jews? The types which have suffered in this manner at the hands of the comedy writers almost fill the catalogue of humanity" ("The Fate of the Stage Irishman," editorial, New York Sun, [c. March 27, 1903], the McFadden's Row of Flats clipping file, BRTD). The Irish World noted, in 1903, that Jews would follow Irish protests: "The Jews have suffered equally, and it would surprise no one if impersonators of their race were soon treated in the same way" ("Thanks to the Irish Societies," Irish World, April 11, 1903, 12). In his response to Birth of a Nation, Lester Walton, theater critic for the New York Age, wrote that the racism of filmmakers would have been stopped if the Jews and Irish had been the maligned (Cripps, Slow Fade to Black, 57). See also "Jottings," American Israelite, March 2, 1917, 7; "Libeling Nations on the Stage," American Israelite, February 8, 1917, 7; and "News and Views: Fighting the Irish Caricature and Stage Jew," American Israelite, March 17, 1910, n. p. One article in the African American newspaper, the Washington Bee, noted the overlapping political goals of the three racial groups: "The Jews in America have made friends for the Jews in Russia. . . . Our Irish-American friends only last week raised $100,000 to the cause of the Irish in their native land" ("Report of L. G. Jordan," Washington Bee, November 10, 1906, 5).

22. "The Stage Jew," B'nai B'rith News, October 1910, 17.

23. "Limitations of Caricature," Irish World, April 11, 1903, 12. In this article the author seems to support other Jewish stereotypes such as the "tendency to display." See also "Thanks to the Irish Societies," Irish World, April 11, 1903, 12.

24. "Hooted Off the Stage," Gaelic American, February 2, 1907, 5. Both African American and Irish protesters went out of their way to identify the Jewish theater managers who booked controversial films, such as The Birth of a Nation. One protester wrote to

the NAACP about *The Birth of a Nation*: "It is almost useless to say that it is a house under Jewish control which is bringing it, that they have money and that we are in for a real fight" (Letter to Mary Childs Nerney, August 31, 1915, folder: "Films and Plays, Birth of a Nation, October 1915," C-300, NAACPR). Another account blamed the Irish for the insulting impersonations of African Americans: "The Irishman is touched to the quick at the slightest reference to his own. . . . It is well known that many, if not most, of the so-called black-face artists upon the stage are and always have been of Irish lineage" ("Things Pertinent and Impertinent," clipping, n.d., file: "Irish Stereotypes on Stage," Harvard Theatre Collection, Houghton Library, Harvard University, hereafter HTC). See also "Decision of Federal Judge in California," *Gaelic American*, February 2, 1918, 1; "Gaelic Notes," *Irish World*, April 11, 1903, 8; "Gaelic Notes," *Irish World*, April 28, 1906, 7.

25. "Protect Citizens from Insult," *Gaelic American*, December 16, 1911, 4. On October 18, 1914, *L'Italia* urged Italians to protest a movie that had negative images of Italians. See Jaret, "The Greek, Italian, and Jewish American Ethnic Press," 52.

26. Chauncey Yellow Robes, "The Menace of the Wild West Shows," *Quarterly Journal of the Society of American Indians* (July–September 1914), quoted in Kasson, *Buffalo Bill's Wild West*, 164. Yellow Robes was a reformer who advocated the assimilation of Indians; he disapproved of Wild West shows because they perpetuated "tribal habits and customs."

27. *New York World*, November 30, 1913, 1; and *Iowa City Journal*, November 4, 1913, 1, quoted in Moses, *Wild West Shows and the Images of American Indians*, 240.

28. "'Chinks' Mob Movie Theater," *Motography*, September 23, 1916. "Forest Park Theater," *Forest Leaves*, October 6, 1916, 13. Leaders of New York City's Chinatown also protested against the depiction of Chinese characters wielding knives in *The Tong Man* in 1919. See Haenni, *The Immigrant Scene*, 179–80.

29. Irish protesters noted the "indulgent German community" when they criticized a play, *The Belle of Avenue A*, which had negative portrayals of Irish and German women. The German woman, according to the Irish critics, was "reduced to the depths of the gutter whense she literally swam in beer" ("Stage Irishman War," *Irish World*, January 10, 1903, 8). See also "Gaelic Notes," *Irish World*, January 10, 1903, 8.

30. Chamber of German-American Commerce, Inc. to The National Board of Censorship of Motion Pictures, October 21, 1914, folder: "Ordeal." National Board of Review of Motion Pictures Manuscripts and Archives Division, New York Public Library, Humanities and Social Sciences Library (hereafter NBR).

31. Distler discusses Irish, German, and Jewish "racial comics" and notes that the German type disappears during World War I, without any German campaign against it ("Exit the Racial Comics." 251–52).

32. Kazal, *Becoming Old Stock*, 273. See also his entire chapter 5. He notes that German Catholics did not use the language of race (119).

33. Prell, *Fighting to Become Americans*.

34. Greenberg, *Troubling the Waters*, 3.

35. For descriptions of the Stage Irishman, see Curtis, *Apes and Angels*, and Barrett, *The Irish Way*, 157–94.

36. Miller, *Emigrants and Exiles*, 498.

37. Couvares, "'The Good Censor,'" 234.

38. Hate speech expresses "hatred or prejudice based on race, religion, gender or some other social grouping," according to Nadine Strossen (Strossen, "Hate Speech and Pornography," 449). See also Matsuda, Lawrence, Delgado, and Crenshaw, *Words That Wound*; Haupt, "Regulating Hate Speech"; Maitra and McGowan, eds., *Speech and Harm*.

39. Title VII of the Civil Rights Act of 1964 outlaws a "hostile work environment" as a type of sexual harassment (along with quid pro quo sexual harassment in which a supervisor demands sex in exchange for rewards in the job). Speech that is "severe or pervasive" enough to create a hostile work environment constitutes sexual harassment. See *Harris v. Forklift Systems, Inc* (1993) in Heumann and Church, *Hate Speech on Campus*, 21–22; MacKinnon, *Only Words*.

40. Sunstein, *Democracy and the Problem of Free Speech*, xvi. See also Lewis, *Freedom for the Thought We Hate*.

41. Sunstein, *Democracy and the Problem of Free Speech*, 20.

42. MacKinnon, *Only Words*, 71 Rebecca Brown argues that liberal disdain for hate speech is not hypocrisy but a manifestation of comprehensive liberalism, in which the state commits to a particular moral good, without necessarily remaining neutral. In particular, within the context of unequal power relations, a comprehensive liberal approach may require more state intervention to attain equality and individual autonomy ("Confessions of a Flawed Liberal").

43. Benjamin Hooks, quoted in Nadine Strossen, "Hate Speech and Pornography."

44. Strossen, "Hate Speech and Pornography"; "Brief Amici Curiae of Feminist Anti-Censorship Taskforce."

45. Young, *Justice and the Politics of Difference*, 158. Ingram, *Group Rights*, 15. Hayward and Watson, "Identity and Political Theory."

46. Ingram, *Group Rights*, 15.

47. Stromquist, *Reinventing "The People,"* 8. See also Diffee, "Sex and the City."

48. Stromquist discusses efforts to purify democracy (*Reinventing "The People,"* 67–69). See also Gilmore, *Who Were the Progressives?*

49. Connolly, *The Triumph of Ethnic Progressivism*, 8. Connelly elaborates that Progressivism can best be defined by what it was not—partisan. Stromquist argues that, while one central part of the Progressive movement emphasized class harmony when it identified "the people," a more radical group of Progressives articulated an "alternative reform vision" based on class struggle (*Reinventing "The People,"* 3, 9). See also Rodgers, *Contested Truths*; Dawley, *Changing the World*; Selig, *Americans All*; Higham, *Strangers in the Land*; Lissak, *Pluralism and Progressives*.

50. Selig, *Americans All*, 8. See also Rich, *Transcending the New Woman*; Petit, *The Men and Women We Want*; Mizruchi, *The Rise of Multicultural America*.

51. Connelly, *The Triumph of Ethnic Progressivism*, 11.

52. Graber, *Transforming Free Speech*, 76. See also Rabban, *Free Speech in Its Forgotten Years*; and Blanchard, "The American Urge to Censor."

53. Graber, *Transforming Free Speech*, 82.

54. Ibid., 76

55. Ibid., 91, 93.

56. Schiller, "Free Speech and Expertise." In the Red Scare following World War I

and the Bolshevik Revolution of 1917, Attorney General A. Mitchell Palmer investigated possible communist conspiracies and deported thousands of radicals. Some historians claim that the scope of repression during this period spurred an outcry over the necessity of freedom of speech for a vital democracy.

57. Rabban, *Free Speech in Its Forgotten Years*, 72.

58. Ibid., 70.

59. Schiller, "Free Speech and Expertise," 3. See also Barbas, "How the Movies Became Free Speech."

60. Friedman, *Prurient Interests*, 4.

61. Griffith, *The Rise and Fall of Free Speech*, 12.

62. Ibid., 24. His pamphlet also cited a newspaper column warning readers that if *The Birth of Nation* was barred, then *The Merchant of Venice* could also be censored, for insulting a "relatively small element of the public" (*Rhode Island Westerly Sun*, as quoted in Griffith, *The Rise and Fall of Free Speech*, 39, 40).

63. Griffith, *The Rise and Fall of Free Speech*, 20.

64. Irish protesters bragged that their violent action had put one play, *McFadden's Row of Flats*, under "practical censorship" ("Reform it Altogether," *Irish World*, April 11, 1903, 12). Kibler, "The Stage Irishwoman"; Kibler, "Pigs, Green Whiskers, and Drunken Widows."

65. Roger Lane, in addition, refers to an article in the *New York Evening Journal* in which a reader noted that the *Journal* had already stopped using "sheenie," so should now stop using "coon" (*William Dorsey's Philadelphia and Ours*, 30).

66. Strum, *When the Nazis Came to Skokie*, 62. The other ordinances set a high insurance requirement and banned military uniforms.

67. *Beauharnais v. Illinois* (1952), in Heumann and Church, *Hate Speech on Campus*, 85.

68. Jones, *Human Rights*, 85 n. 153.

69. Lewis, *Freedom for the Thought That We Hate*, 49.

70. Strum, *When the Nazis Came to Skokie*, 101.

71. *Collin v. Smith* (1978), in Heumann and Church, *Hate Speech on Campus*, 107.

72. "Observations by Our Man about Town," *Moving Picture World*, May 22, 1915, 1250.

CHAPTER ONE

1. Onkey, "'A Melee and a Curtain.'" See also Onkey, *Blackness and Transatlantic Irish Identity*. Boyle, "Low Life and High Jinks." Boyle describes the relationship between African Americans and Irish shifted between rancorous and harmonious (38). See also Barrett, *The Irish Way*, 164-5.

2. Smith, "Blacks and Irish on the Riverine Frontiers"; Lott, *Love and Theft*, 46-48

3. Roediger, *Wages of Whiteness*, 116. Lott, *Love and Theft*, 96–97.

4. Roediger, *Wages of Whiteness*, 118. For more on the diverse targets of ridicule in the minstrel show, see Mahar, *Behind the Burnt Cork Mask*.

5. *Christy's Panorama Songster*, 79, quoted in Saxton, *The Rise and Fall of the White Republic*, 176

6. Rogin, *Blackface, White Noise*, 53. For critiques of Rogin, see Diner, "Trading Faces"; Rosenberg, "Rogin's Noise"; and Itzkovitz, "Passing Like Me."

7. Cockrell, *Demons of Disorder*, 199. Lott, *Love and Theft*, 94-96

8. Lott, *Love and Theft*, 94.

9. *Harper's New Monthly Magazine*, June 1889, 135. See also Nowatzki, "Paddy Jumps Jim Crow." For more on the Irish background of minstrel stars, see Moloney, "Irish-American Popular Music," 383.

10. Lavitt, "First of the Red Hot Mamas."

11. Melnick, *A Right to Sing the Blues*, 111.

12. Alexander, *Jazz Age Jews*, 150.

13. An article in the Jewish press in 1928 remarked, "It is a notable thing that at least three of the most popular makers of music on the American stage should be Jewish boys, two of whom blacken their faces and sing Negro 'Mammy' songs while the third has written many songs in the Negro dialect" (*Forward*, October 1928, quoted in Melnick, *A Right to Sing the Blues*, 178). See also Alexander, *Jazz Age Jews*. Eddie Cantor, Al Jolson, and Irving Berlin comprised this trio.

14. Barrett, *The Irish Way*, 164–65.

15. Dumont, *The Yellow Kid Who Lives in Hogan's Alley*, 7.

16. [Gus Hill], *McFadden's Row of Flats: A Farcical Review in Three Acts*, [1903?]. Annenberg Rare Book and Manuscript Library, University of Pennsylvania, Philadelphia.

17. Barrett, *The Irish Way*, 162. Williams, *'Twas Only an Irishman's Dream*, 168–72. Moloney, "Irish-American Popular Music," 389.

18. Romeyn, *Staging the Self in Immigrant New York*, 138–40. See also Koger, "A Critical Analysis of Edward Harrigan's Comedy." Barrett notes the "prejudice . . . and fascination with urban diversity" in Harrigan's plays (*The Irish Way*, 162).

19. Dormon, "Ethnic Cultures of the Mind."

20. Onkey, *Blackness and Transatlantic Irish Identity*, 69. Eagan, "I Did Imagine."

21. Onkey, "'A Melee and a Curtain'"; Romeyn, *Street Scenes*, 136–38.

22. Onkey, *Blackness and Transatlantic Identity*, 76. See also Barrett, *The Irish Way*, 76.

23. "Jottings," *American Israelite*, May 19, 1910, 1. Barrett, *The Irish Way*, 166-67. See also Kibler, *Rank Ladies*, 55–57.

24. Merwin, *In Their Own Image*, 22.

25. Distler, "The Rise and Fall of the Racial Comics," 81; Romeyn, *Street Scenes*, 134–36.

26. Merwin, *In Their Own Image*, 20. Welch, in 1916, noted his Irish relatives—Murphy, Callahan, and Flanagan. He bragged that he marched in St. Patrick's Day parades and liked corn beef and cabbage, but he did not get to play Irish parts ("Joe Welch Objects," *New York Telegraph*, clipping, April 10, 1916, Envelope 2528, BRTD).

27. *American Israelite*, August 20, 1908, 5; "Jottings," *American Israelite*, March 31, 1910, 1. A B. Seelenfreund, Grand Secretary of B'nai B'rith, "objected to the portrayal of the Jew as a pawnbroker and an incendiary and said that such plays as 'The Melting Pot' had done more to injure the race than the lampoons of low comedy" ("To Boycott the Stage Jew," *New York Times*, April 25, 1913, 3).

28. "Caricaturing the Jews," *American Israelite*, August 25, 1910, 4; "Abolish Jewish Caricature," *New York Times*, March 26, 1912, 9.

29. Distler, "Exit the Racial Comics." See also Curtis, *Apes and Angels*; Dormon, "Ethnic Cultures of the Mind"; Kibler, "Rank Ladies, Ladies of Rank"; and Forker, "The Use of the 'Cartoonist's Armoury.'"

30. "The Stage Irishman Knocked Out," *Irish World*, January 7, 1905, 1. Several months later, some Irish activists also criticized the Ancient Order of Hibernians branch of Pittsfield, Massachusetts, for showing *The Finish of Bridget McKeen*.

31. Kibler, "Rank Ladies, Ladies of Rank," 72–73. See also Knobel, "A Vocabulary of Ethnic Perception"; Wittke, "Immigrant Theme on the American Stage"; Williams, "Green Again"; Flynn, "Screening the Stage Irishman."

32. Kibler, "The Stage Irishwoman."

33. Report Book 12, 105, KAC, quoted in Snyder, *The Voice of the City*, 111; see also Merwin, *In Their Own Image*, 21.

34. Snyder, "Irish in Vaudeville"; Barrett, *The Irish Way*, 170. In addition, Al Dubin, the son of Russian Jewish immigrants, wrote the sentimental tribute to the Irish homeland, "'Twas Only an Irishman's Dream," along with the Irishman John O'Brien, in 1916.

35. Harry Jolson, as told to Alban Emley, *Mistah Jolson*, 83–84, quoted in Merwin, *In Their Own Image*, 22. John T. Kelly usually presented a stock Irish character; but when he impersonated a Chinese character, he spoke with an Irish accent (Distler, "The Rise and Fall of the Racial Comics," 115). Another performer, Barney Reynolds, offered "Dutch, Irish, and Negro Dialect" (clipping, October 15, 1877, Tony Pastor Scrapbook, MWEZ + n.c. 4547, BRTD).

36. Report Book 8, 121, KAC. Kibler, *Rank Ladies*, 116–18; and Nasaw, *Going Out*, 57-61

37. Report Book 2, 37, KAC.

38. "White patrons only want to see [me] portray the antebellum 'darkey.'" (*Variety*, December 14, 1907, quoted in Sotiropoulos, *Staging Race*, 192).

39. George Walker, "Bert and Me and Them," *New York Age*, December 24, 1908, 4.

40. Ernest Hogan, "All Coons Look Alike to Me" (1896), University of Mississippi Digital Collections, Archives and Special Collections.

41. Sotiropoulos, *Staging Race*, 42–43.

42. Ibid.

43. One drama critic called him one of the "less serious exponents of the Niagara Movement" (*Indianapolis Freeman*, October 10, 1903, quoted in Sotiropoulos, *Staging Race*, 77).

44. Russell, *Indianapolis Freedman*, June 22, 1907, quoted in Sampson, *The Ghost Walks*, 407–8.

45. Marks, *They All Sang*, 91.

46. Rogin, *Blackface, White Noise*, 55. See also Nasaw, *Going Out*, and Sotiropoulos, *Staging Race*.

47. Jacobson, *Whiteness of a Different Color*, 78–79. For another account of some Jewish leaders' protests over the U.S. government's on-going racial classification of Jews, see Goldstein, *The Price of Whiteness*, 105-8.

48. Nelson, *Irish Nationalists*, 9–10; Barrett and Roediger, "In between Peoples," 10. See also Fields, "Whiteness, Racism, and Identity"; Roediger, *Wages of Whiteness*, 133, 146. Eric Arneson and Eric Foner emphasize that all European immigrants were "free

white persons" in terms of naturalization law (Arneson, "Whiteness and the Historian's Imagination"; Foner, "Response to Eric Arneson," 57). See also Miller, *Emigrants and Exiles*, 533; Guterl, *The Color of Race*, 74–77.

49. *New York Times*, July 17, 1863, 4, quoted in Jacobson, *Whiteness of a Different Color*, 54–55.

50. Goldstein, *The Price of Whiteness*, 18–20, 31. Around the turn of the twentieth century, some anthropologists defined Jews as Oriental, not European (Rogoff, "Is the Jew White?").

51. Ibid., 40.

52. *Watson's Magazine*, January 1915, quoted ibid., 43.

53. Goldstein, *The Price of Whiteness*, 19, 21; Nelson, *Irish Nationalists*, 45–54.

54. Ibid., 21.

55. Nelson, *Irish Nationalists*, 43. Guterl, *The Color of Race*, 5–10.

56. Jacobson, *Whiteness of a Different Color*, 95.

57. Kenny, *The American Irish*, 181.

58. Goldstein, *The Price of Whiteness*, 88–89. See also "Is There a Jewish Race?" *American Israelite*, January 21, 1909, 8.

59. Ibid., 102–8;

60. Perlmann, *Ethnic Differences*, 43; Miller, *Emigrants and Exiles*, 511.

61. Barrett, *The Irish Way*, 6.

62. Richard Jensen, "'No Irish Need Apply'"; Kenny, *Making Sense of the Molly Maguires*.

63. Jensen, "'No Irish Need Apply.'" Kerby Miller writes, "The image of the Irish-American as exile was extremely useful in holding together the increasingly disparate and contented Irish-American community" (*Emigrants and Exiles*, 554).

64. Meagher, *Inventing Irish America*, 103; Miller, *Emigrants and Exiles*, 511

65. Miller, *Emigrants and Exiles*, 496. In Providence, there was only modest economic improvement before 1925, when less than one in five households was headed by a white-collar worker (Perlmann, *Ethnic Differences*, 44).

66. Jensen, "'No Irish Need Apply'"; Barrett, *The Irish Way*, 115.

67. Barrett, *The Irish Way*, 108–9.

68. Perlmann, *Ethnic Differences*, 46; Miller, *Emigrants and Exiles*, 499; Barrett, *The Irish Way*, 113–15.

69. Miller, *Emigrants and Exiles*, 535.

70. "United Irish American Societies," *Gaelic American*, March 18, 1911, 5. Another critique of the lack of Irish dancing at community events: Why do they relegate "these dances to a reeking subcellar.... Simply because they have become so American?" ("Gaelic Notes," *Gaelic American*, December 12, 1903, 8). See Miller, *Emigrants and Exiles*, 511.

71. Miller, *Emigrants and Exiles*, 495–99.

72. Ibid., 534.

73. Meagher, *Inventing Irish America*, 264–65.

74. Kelleher, "Maternal Strategies."; Meagher, "Sweet Good Mothers and Young Women out in the World."

75. "The Irish Declaration of Independence," *Puck*, May 9, 1883, quoted in Urban, "Irish Domestic Servants," 275.

76. Sorin, *A Time for Building,* 34–37; Diner, *In the Almost Promised Land,* 3–16.

77. Ibid., 152; Diner, *In the Almost Promised Land,* 15.

78. Higham, *Strangers in the Land,* 161.

79. Greenberg, *Troubling the Waters,* 31; Sorin, *A Time for Building,* 170.

80. Sorin, *A Time for Building,* 174.

81. Prell, *Fighting to Become Americans,* 23–25. On the vulgarity and boorishness of Eastern European Jews, see, "The Real Danger," *American Israelite,* August 27, 1908, 7.

82. Greenberg, *Troubling the Waters,* 33. See also Cohen, *Encounter with Emancipation,* 327.

83. Goldstein, *The Price of Whiteness,* 63.

84. Wells, "Lynch Law," *The Reason Why,* 32.

85. Quoted in Reed, *Black Chicago's First Century,* 374. See also Cooks, "Fixing Race"; Rudwick and Meier, "'Black Man in the White City.'"

86. Kelley, "Right to Ride," 349. Welke, *Recasting American Liberty.*

87. Baldwin, *Chicago's New Negroes,* 39–40. See also Greenberg, *Troubling the Waters,* 17–20.

88. Baldwin, *Chicago's New Negroes,* 40.

89. Greenberg, *Troubling the Waters,* 18.

90. Ibid., 18.

91. Gaines, *Uplifting the Race,* 75.

92. Ibid., 90.

93. Higham, *Strangers in the Land,* 247.

94. Ibid., 208–9.

95. Ibid., 212.

96. Diner, "The Encounter between Jews and America," 247–48.

97. Woeste, "Insecure Equality."

98. Baldwin, *Henry Ford and the Jews,* 80.

99. Dumenil, *The Modern Temper,* 236.

100. Miller, *Emigrants and Exiles,* 541.

101. Nelson, "Irish Americans, Irish Nationalism, and the 'Social' Question," 156-57.

102. Barrett, *The Irish Way,* 97–98.

103. Bornstein, *The Colors of Zion,* 88. See also Mishkin, *The Harlem and Irish Renaissances.*

104. The Marcus Garvey and Universal Negro Improvement Association Papers, 58, quoted in Bornstein, *The Colors of Zion,* 100.

105. Nelson, *Irish Nationalists,* 48–49, 121–47.

106. Gaines, *Uplifting the Race,* 11.

107. Rutkoff and Scott, *Fly Away,* 80. "Irish nationalism was perhaps the quickest to take hold and the most prolific in its organizational expression" (Jacobson, *Special Sorrows,* 24). Matthew Guterl also explains: "With its numerous Race Conventions and its sponsorship of the IRB [Irish Republican Brotherhood] revolution, Irish American nationalism had become the standard by which all other subversive nationalisms in the United States were to be judged" (Guterl, "The New Race-Consciousness," 332).

108. Guterl, "The New Race-Consciousness," 330.

109. "Dedication of UNIA Liberty Hall," in The Marcus Garvey and Universal

Negro Improvement Association papers, 472, quoted in Guterl, "The New Race-Consciousness," 330.

110. When Garvey reflected on the Irish and race in 1920, he saw differences in the two trajectories, arguing that the Irish struggle "is not a matter of injustice done because of race. . . . [We] cannot say that Ireland's fight is just like ours" (Guterl, "The New Race-Consciousness," 337).

111. Du Bois to D. J. Bustin, March 30, 1921, W. E. B. Du Bois Papers, quoted in Guterl, "The New Race-Consciousness," 336.

112. Sorin, *A Time for Building*, 223.

113. Bornstein, *The Colors of Zion*, 93

114. Michael Davitt, *Within the Pale*, 86, quoted in Jacobson, *Special Sorrows*, 17.

115. Greene, "A Chosen People in a Pluralist Nation," 162.

116. Miller, *Emigrants and Exiles*, 449-50; Meagher, *Inventing Irish America*, 250-52.

117. "The Star Spangled Banner," *Gaelic American*, July 22, 1916, 7.

118. Greenberg, *Troubling the Waters*, 39. See Kallen, "Democracy versus the Melting Pot."

119. Greene, "A Chosen People in a Pluralist Nation," 176.

120. Diner, "The Encounter between Jews and America," 9.

121. Greenberg, *Troubling the Waters*, 33–36. Rogow, *Gone to Another Meeting*.

122. Korelitz, "'A Magnificent Piece of Work,'" 182.

123. Greenberg, *Troubling the Waters*, 36.

124. Booker T. Washington, "Interesting People—Bert Williams," *American Magazine* (September 1910), quoted in Gaines, *Uplifting the Race*, 77. See also Greenberg, *Troubling the Waters*, 24-5.

125. "Exit the Stage Irishman," *Gaelic American*, March 2, 1907, 8.

126. "Libeling Nations on Stage," *American Israelite*, February 8, 1917, 7. B'nai B'rith leaders objected to racial ridicule because it "tends to narrowness and prejudices that are, to say the least, un-American" ("Race Insults," *B'nai B'rith News*, October 1910, 17). Irish leader Edward McCrystal, explained, "It makes no difference what the race is that is selected for contumely, the mere fact that any people are decried is wrong" ("Irish Rise against Caricatures," clipping, March 28, 1903, clipping file: "McFadden's Row of Flats," BRTD).

127. "Truckling to Colored Voters," *Lancaster Intelligencer*, November 13, 1906, 5.

128. Sylvester Russell, *Indianapolis Freeman*, April 4, 1904, quoted in Sampson, *The Ghost Walks*, 292.

129. Clark, "Urban Blacks and Irishmen," 16; Roediger, *Wages of Whiteness*, 134.

130. Douglass, *My Bondage, My Freedom*, 98. See also Jenkins, "'Beyond the Pale'"; Roediger, *Wages of Whiteness*, 134.

131. Roediger, *Wages of Whiteness*, 134.

132. Meagher, *The Columbia Guide to Irish American History*, 214.

133. *New York Tribune*, May 11, 1850, quoted in Wittke, *The Irish in America*, 125.

134. Schneider, *Boston Confronts Jim Crow*, 163.

135. Wittke, *The Irish in America*, 130. See also Shankman, "Black on Green."

136. Shankman, "Black on Green."

137. Ibid., 296.

138. Clark, "Urban Blacks and Irishmen," 19, 24; Miller, *Emigrants and Exiles*, 524, 525.

139. O'Donnell, "Hibernians versus Hebrews." O'Donnell argues that historians have exaggerated the anti-Semitism of this incident. See another description of Irish violence against Jews in "An Anti-Irish Calumny," *Irish World*, October 7, 1899, 10.

140. Barrett, *The Irish Way*, 44-45.

141. Barrett and Roediger, "The Irish and the 'Americanization' of the 'New Immigrants,'" 9.

142. Roediger, *Wages of Whiteness*, 145.

143. Eric Arneson, arguing against "whiteness" scholars, holds that the Irish were defending their economic status as whites. Whiteness had a concrete economic benefit, considering white "occupational monopolies" and "how municipal employment was reserved for whites, and how legalized segregation ensured white workers access to public resources" ("Whiteness and the Historians' Imagination," 12). Irish fought African Americans bitterly over jobs, largely because blacks were least able to defend themselves against violence. This job competition, according to Roediger, does not explain Irish racism fully (*Wages of Whiteness*, 147).

144. Arneson, "Whiteness and the Historians' Imagination," 12.

145. Roediger, *Wages of Whiteness*, 143.

146. Meagher, *The Columbia Guide to Irish American History*, 223.

147. Greenberg, *Troubling the Waters*, 16. See also Lewis, "Parallels and Divergences," and Diner, *In the Almost Promised Land*.

148. Ibid., 46.

149. *New York Age*, May 18, 1889, quoted in Foner, "Black-Jewish Relations," 360.

150. "Hotel Affronts Senator's Sister," *New York Times*, May 18, 1907, 1; "Apology to Mrs. Frank," *New York Times*, May 23, 1907, 1; "Bill to Protect Jews in Hotels," *New York Times*, May 24, 1907, 2.

151. Higham, *Strangers in the Land*, 161.

152. "Colonial Theater Refuses Colored Gentlemen—Fined," *Chicago Defender*, June 11, 1910, 1. See Kibler, *Rank Ladies*, 35; Nasaw, *Going Out*.

153. Goldstein, *The Price of Whiteness*, 69–70; Goldstein notes that those Jews who had achieved the most assimilation, like Felix Adler, an ethical culturalist who had rejected Judaism, were often the most sympathetic to African Americans, perhaps because such a connection mitigated the "emotional trauma of the assimilation process" (*Price of Whiteness*, 70). Others, like Joel Spingarn, also followed this path from Judaism to ethical culture and civil rights. Reform Rabbis, who emphasized universalism, were the second group, according to Goldstein, to establish links between the Jewish community and African Americans.

154. Goldstein, *The Price of Whiteness*, 75.

155. Ibid., 72.

156. Ibid.

157. *Jewish Daily Forward*, July 7, 1903, 1, quoted in Goldstein, *The Price of Whiteness*, 81.

158. Washington, *The Future of the American Negro*, 66, quoted in Foner, "Black-Jewish Relations," 361.

159. Foner, "Black-Jewish Relations," 362; Goldstein, *The Price of Whiteness*, 64–66.

160. *Public* (Chicago), August 22, 1903, 307–8, quoted in Goldstein, *The Price of Whiteness*, 65.

161. Sorin, *A Time for Building*, 167; Moore, *B'nai B'rith*, 107.

162. Levy, "'Is the Jew a White Man?" 213–14; Dinnerstein, *The Leo Frank Case*.

163. Brownlow, *Behind the Mask of Innocence*, 378–79.

164. Levy, "'Is the Jew a White Man?'" 219. The *Chicago Defender* wrote that Frank had forgotten the plight of "HIS PEOPLE" in Eastern Europe and instead espoused racism in calling Conley a "BLACK BRUTE" (May 9, 1914, and December 12, 1914). See Levy, "Is the Jew a White Man?" 217.

165. *Boston Jewish Advocate*, December 12, 1913, quoted in Levy, "'Is the Jew a White Man?'" 219; Melnick, *A Right to Sing the Blues*, 5–6.

166. Levy, "Is the Jew a White Man?" 216.

167. *Chicago Defender*, May 9, 1914, and December 12, 1914, quoted in Levy, "Is the Jew a White Man?" 217–18.

168. "The Governor and the Mob," *American Israelite*, July 8, 1915, 5.

169. Diner, *In the Almost Promised Land*, 96–97.

170. Ibid., 130; Lewis, "Parallels and Divergences."

171. Diner, *In the Almost Promised Land*, 20.

172. "Anti-Defamation League," *B'nai B'rith News*, October 1913, 1; Greenberg, *Troubling the Waters*, 36.

CHAPTER TWO

1. *Boston Pilot*, 1878, as quoted in Flynn, "Ethnicity after Sea-Change," 36; "Pat Rooney in Trouble: Unappreciative Irishmen in Scranton Make the Comedian's Life a Burden," *New York Times*, March 10, 1884, 4. See Granshaw, "'What Do Ye Allow a Baboon Like That on the Stage For?'" 70–94.

2. I use David Grimsted's definition of a riot: "Incidents where a number of people work together to enforce their will immediately, by threatening or perpetrating injury to people or property outside of legal procedures but without intending to challenge the general structure of society" ("Rioting in Its Jacksonian Setting," 365). In this way, Grimsted excludes criminality and social revolution from rioting.

3. "The Theatre Doors Shut," *New York Times*, April 30, 1887, 1. See also Clark, *Erin's Heirs*, 147.

4. "Irish Blood Aroused," *New York Times*, April 29, 1887, 1; "A Row up at M'Caulls," *North American*, April 29, 1887.

5. "The Theatre Doors Shut," *New York Times*, April 30, 1887, 1.

6. "Dr. Peter McCahey Dead," *Gaelic American*, October 28, 1916, 2. See also "Societies Raise Funds to Defend Irishmen," *Public Ledger*, April 4, 1903, 2.

7. "The Stage Irishman Insult," *Irish World*, July 18, 1903, 8.

8. "The 'Stage Irishman' Must Go," *Irish World*, February 9, 1907, 5. Protesters also referred to McAvoy as the "typical green-whiskered stage Irishman" ("Barred Dan McAvoy's Show," *Irish World*, February 23, 1907, 5).

9. "The Stage Irishman Again," *National Hibernian*, January 15, 1904, 4.

10. "Attacks Stage Irishman at Church Performance," *Gaelic American*, December 20, 1919, 4.

11. As Lucy McDiarmid explains, the Irish nationalists in Philadelphia did not seem to care about details of the production, for they did not wait for the "objectionable" parts of the play to launch their protests. But they were inspired by previous uprisings—in Dublin in 1907 and in other American cities in 1911 and 1912. Irish activists in Philadelphia, she notes, would have "felt shamed" if they did not respond as aggressively to the play as their allies had in Dublin or New York City ("The Abbey and the Theatrics of Controversy," 65). See also McDiarmid, *The Irish Art of Controversy*.

12. The *Brooklyn Eagle* reported that sixteen members of the Volunteer Irish Patriots' Brigade launched the protest at the Orpheum Theatre. The Volunteers, organized in 1895, were closely linked with the Clan na Gael ("Irish Patriots Held," *Irish World*, February 9, 1907, 5, reprinted from the *Brooklyn Eagle*). See also "The Sixty-Ninth Scheme," *New York Times*, March 1, 1898, 1.

13. "Another Stage Insult," *Irish World*, May 16, 1903, 12.

14. "Issue Protests," *Daily News* (Denver), October 13, 1902, 2. The historian Timothy Meagher notes that the AOH in Worcester, though officially neutral in nationalist debates, "strongly supported revolutionary nationalism" in the late 1890s and early 1900s (*Inventing Irish America*, 257).

15. Onkey, "'A Melee and a Curtain,'" 6. See also Dorman, "Ethnic Cultures of the Mind."

16. Townsend had published stories about children in immigrant ghettoes in the 1890s, such as *Chimmie Fadden* in 1895; the new name of the comic strip seems to have come from Townsend's stories about Chimmie Fadden. The historian Kerry Soper argues that the popularity of the Yellow Kid is based on the characters' appeal both to native-born and immigrant audiences, because the Yellow Kid was not a simplistic "ethnic scapegoat." According to Soper, the image of the Irish in the comic strips of the 1890s was more sympathetic than earlier political cartoons; the Irish in the Yellow Kid cartoons were "wise fools," not dirty animals ("From Swarthy Ape to Sympathetic Everyman and Subversive Trickster," 277).

17. "Columbia Theatre: 'McFadden's' etc." October 26, 1897, *McFadden's Row of Flats* clipping file, BRTD.

18. [Hill], *McFadden's Row of Flats*, 17.

19. I believe the undated script is Gus Hill's production because its plot matches the description of Hill's play in New York City in 1897 ("People's—McFadden's Row of Flats," *New York Dramatic Mirror*, October 9, 1897, 16). The characters are identical, including the "Yellow twins"—Alex and George—played in 1897 by Curtis and Harry Speck. Mark Winchester notes that the Speck Brothers became a "key part of Hill's McFadden's Row of Flats" ("Cartoon Theatricals from 1896 to 1927," 94). It also seems likely that a copy of a script representing the most controversial production of the play would have been preserved. The *McFadden's Row of Flats* text should not be considered a definitive guide to what actually occurred on stage. The play had a loose plot, interspersed with vaudeville acts, and Hill's production was also revised during its long run. Characters' names changed—from Bud Taggem to Jacob Baumgartner, for example—and some stage directions were dramatically altered. The program for

Hill's production of *McFadden's Row of Flats* at the Academy of Music in Washington, D.C., on November 29, 1899, lists "Bud Taggem" instead of Jacob Baumgartner. See *McFadden's Row of Flats* Program, November 20, 1899, *McFadden's Row of Flats* Folder, Theater Division, Free Library, Philadelphia. The script cited in this essay indicates that Kerrigan, the police officer, wheels Mrs. Murphy on stage in a wheelbarrow, but reviews of the controversial play in New York City and Philadelphia refer to a donkey pulling Mrs. Murphy on stage in a cart. The script indicates Mrs. Murphy—"maudlin drunk"—throws a drink at McSwatt, trips over her own robe and confesses, "It isn't the first time my feet were tangled up." ([Hill], *McFadden's Row of Flats*, 14.) Although this script does not exactly match the live performance of the play in New York City and Philadelphia, it is still useful to consider this text, along with published reviews and the protesters' complaints to reconstruct the productions as closely as possible.

20. "Play Mobbed by Irishmen," *New York Sun*, March 28, 1903, 1, clipping, *McFadden's Row of Flats* clipping file, BRTD.

21. "Play Mobbed by Irishmen," *New York Sun*, March 28, 1903, 1, clipping, *McFadden's Row of Flats* clipping file, BRTD.

22. Ibid. The *Irish American*, a more moderate Irish American paper than the *Gaelic American*, noted that the central organizations were the Clan na Gael, the AOH, and the Greater New York Irish Athletic Association ("Purging the Stage," *Irish American*, April 4, 1903, 4).

23. "Play Mobbed by Irishmen."

24. "Gaelic Notes," *Irish World*, April 11, 1903, 8.

25. "Put the Blame for Riot on Irish Societies," *Public Ledger*, April 1, 1903, 2.

26. The play appeared at the National Theatre (March 28–April 2, 1898), the Auditorium (February 27–March 4, 1899), the People's Theatre (March 20–March 25, 1899), the Auditorium (November 6–11, 1899), the People's Theatre (November 27–December 2, 1899), and again the National Theatre (April 15–20, 1901, and March 3–8, 1902). See Philadelphia Theatre Index at the Free Library, Philadelphia.

27. "Reform It Altogether," *Irish World*, April 11, 1903, 12.

28. "Irishmen Pelt Actors with Eggs," *Public Ledger*, March 31, 1903, 1.

29. "The scene that was egged in New York, in which Mrs. Murphy, who is styled the Queen of the Flats, drives on stage seated in a cart drawn by a donkey, passed off without so much as a hiss" ("Irishmen Pelt Actors with Eggs," *Public Ledger*, March 31, 1903, 1).

30. Ibid.

31. "McFadden's Flats Quiet," *New York Times*, April 7, 1903, 9.

32. "Reform It Altogether," *Irish World*, April 11, 1903, 12. A few months later, in a debate over another cartoon theatrical, *Happy Hooligan*, the *Irish World* again explained that "a matter of shaving off green whiskers has little or nothing to do with the case. The Stage Irishman must go, with or without whiskers" ("Gaelic Notes," *Irish World*, May 9, 1903, 8).

33. "Gaelic Notes," *Irish World*, April 4, 1903, 8.

34. "Gaelic Notes," *Irish World*, April 11, 1903, 8.

35. "Piloting McFadden's Flats," *Gaelic American*, May 5, 1906, 5. A few months later, the *Irish World* noted that that smell of ancient eggs "hangs round [the play] still. Pro-

tests against the play in New Haven and Paterson were "not quite effective in either place," according to the report ("Gaelic Notes," *Irish World*, April 21, 1906, 7).

36. *McFadden's Row of Flats* is mentioned in the discussions of the Russell Brothers. See "Irish Patriots Held," *Irish World*, February 9, 1907, 5.

37. "Vaudeville Stage—The Irish Servant Girls," unidentified clipping, June 16, 1896, Tony Pastor Scrapbook, MWEZ+n.c. 4547, BRTD.

38. "Vile Stage Attack on Irish Womanhood," *Gaelic American*, February 9, 1907, 1. See Maschio, "Ethnic Humor and the Demise of the Russell Brothers"; Distler, "Exit the Racial Comics"; Flynn, "How Bridget Was Framed."

39. "More Trouble for the Russells," *New York Dramatic Mirror*, February 9, 1907, 18; "New Stage Censorship," *Brooklyn Eagle*, January 26, 1907, 4. Further description of the act is in "The Stage Irishwoman," *Irish World*, February 23, 1907, 4.

40. "Hooted Off the Stage," *Gaelic American*, February 2, 1907, 5. Tuite was the secretary of the United Irish American Societies, which seems to have been dominated by the Clan na Gael ("The Russells Rebuked," *Gaelic American*, March 16, 1907, 2). In 1912 Tuite reported to the UIAS about a deported Irish girl; he claimed that she was deported for having only "$20 required by immigration law" not for immorality ("Irish American Societies," *Gaelic American*, October 15, 1912, 2).

41. "Irishmen Hiss Actors," *New York Dramatic Mirror*, February 2, 1907, 17; "Chase It from the Stage," *Irish World*, February 9, 1907, 4.

42. "Vile Stage Attack on Irish Womanhood," *Gaelic American*, February 9, 1907, 1.

43. "Irish Patriots Held," *Irish World*, February 9, 1907, 5.

44. Twenty-two protesters were originally removed from the theater, but six were released at the police station when they could not be positively identified as participants in the riot ("More Trouble for the Russells," *New York Dramatic Mirror*, February 9, 1907, 18).

45. Distler, "Exit the Racial Comics," 251.

46. "Gaelic Notes," *Irish World*, April 4, 1903, 8.

47. "Thanks to the Irish Societies," *Irish World*, April 11, 1903, 12. For "indulgent Germans," see "Stage Indecency Suppressed," *Gaelic American*, March 30, 1907, 8.

48. "Vile Attack on Irish Womanhood," *Gaelic American*, February 9, 1907, 1.

49. Meagher, *Inventing Irish America*, 243.

50. Emmons, *The Butte Irish*, 117. Kerby Miller concludes, "The Irish-American bourgeoisie tended to be morbidly sensitive to real or imagined threats to their tenuous grasp on respectability" (*Emigrants and Exiles*, 498). William H. A. Williams argues that the "most powerful force driving the change in their image was the Irish-American community's search for respectability" (*'Twas Only an Irishman's Dream*, 1996, 203). Thomas J. Rowland argues that the Ancient Order of Hibernians campaigned against the Stage Irish as part of their "quest for respectability," but he does not mention that the protests were often disorderly. See Rowland, "Irish American Catholics and the Quest for Respectability," 7. John P. Harrington also agrees with this view: "[The Irish] could openly protest what they felt slowed an accelerating rate of assimilation and accomplishment" (*The Irish Play on the New York Stage*, 61).

51. "The Stage Irishman," *Irish World*, April 21, 1906, 8. See Miller, *Emigrants and Exiles*, 496–98.

52. Prior to 1886, Ford supported a variety of radical causes, including land reform, civil rights for African Americans, and socialism. Other Irish nationalists, such as John Devoy, believed that Ford's support for a wide range of domestic protests watered down his Irish nationalism. After 1886 Ford became increasingly reformist and tied to "respectability." Edited by Patrick Ford, the *Irish World* had a circulation of 125,000 by the 1890s, while the *Gaelic American*, published by the rival nationalist and Clan na Gael leader John Devoy, reached only 30,000 by 1913. Before 1886 Ford supported a variety of radical causes, including civil rights for African Americans, but he became more conservative in the late 1880s and increasingly concerned with "respectability" (Rodechko, *Patrick Ford and His Search for America*, 50).

53. Rodechko, *Patrick Ford and His Search for America*, 204–7

54. Harrington, *The Irish Play on the New York Stage*, 60.

55. The author in the *Irish World* elaborated: "Violence and disorder is never to be countenanced, but if it could be justified, there seems to be an occasion in these vile plays" ("Purging the Stage," *Irish American*, April 4, 1903, 4); "Rioters Who Need Suppression," *New York Times*, February 2, 1907, 8.

56. Meagher, *Inventing Irish America*, 243.

57. Wilentz, *Chants Democratic*, 258.

58. Levine, *Highbrow/Lowbrow*, 64–68. See also McConachie, "Pacifying American Theatrical Audiences."

59. Kasson, *Rudeness and Civility*, 231.

60. "Under Arrest, Irish Players Triumph in Criticized Playboy," *North American*, January 18, 1912, 1.

61. Gilje, *Rioting in America*, 123–30.

62. Barrett and Roediger, "The Irish and the 'Americanization' of the 'New Immigrants"; Way, "Evil Humors and Ardent Spirits"; Rosenzweig, *Eight Hours for What We Will*; Meagher, *Inventing Irish America*; Kenny, *Making Sense of the Molly Maguires*; Kelleher, "Class and Catholic Irish Masculinity in Antebellum America."

63. Barrett and Roediger, "The Irish and the "Americanization" of the 'New Immigrants," 9.

64. "Mr. Gibbs on the Stage Irishman," *Irish World*, March 14, 1903, 8. The author dismissed the critics of hissing in the theaters as "do nothings."

65. "'Stage Irishman' War," *Irish World*, January 10 1903, 8.

66. "Gaelic Notes," *Irish World*, March 23, 1907, 7; "Stage Indecency Suppressed," *Irish World*, March 30, 1907, 8. In Ballyhaunis, Ireland, Gaelic League members disrupted the theater when "Judy O'Trot"—a drunken Irish woman—appeared on the stage. ("Didn't Suit Ballyhaunis," *Gaelic American*, March 31, 1906, 6). The *Irish World* also commended the "self-respecting Irish American," Edward McLaughlin, for demonstrating in the theater against a play. After his action, the "objectionable part was cut out" ("Give Him No Quarter," *Irish World*, January 7, 1905, 4). One Irishman was ejected when he objected to "The Mick Who Threw a Brick" in 1900 ("Our Gaelic World," *Irish World*, July 14, 1900, 9).

67. "Smashed the Caricature," *Gaelic American*, December 17, 1910, 4.

68. "Maude and His Thugs," *Gaelic American*, February 9, 1907, 5.

69. "The Stage Irishman Insult," *Irish World*, July 18, 1903, 8. An actress was also

driven off the stage when she unfurled the Union Jack ("British Flag Hissed," *Irish World*, February 24, 1900, 5).

70. "The Stage Irishman Hunted from Butte," *Gaelic American*, December 30, 1905, 1.

71. "The Stage Irishman Hunted from Butte," *Gaelic American*, December 30, 1905, 8. Similarly, the *Irish World* pointed out that there was no disorder or violence when the Butte's AOH and the Robert Emmet Literary Association kept the Dreamland Burlesquers from appearing at a local theatre ("Gaelic Notes," *Irish World*, January 27, 1905, 7).

72. "Home Rule in Dim Future," *Gaelic American*, January 19, 1907, 8.

73. Hutchinson, *The Dynamics of Cultural Nationalism*, 16. He dispels four myths about cultural nationalism, including the conflation of political and cultural nationalism and the notion that cultural nationalism is primarily linguistic (8–9). Una Bromell has pointed out that the death of Parnell was a key factor, though not the only one, in the rise of cultural nationalism ("The American Mission," 18). See also Jacobson, *Special Sorrows*, 30.

74. Clark, *Erin's Heirs*, 147.

75. Bromell, "The American Mission," 23.

76. Higham, *Strangers in the Land*, 170.

77. Bromell, "The American Mission," 120. During his 1905–6 tour of the United States, Hyde reported that he tried to dispel the anxieties of "wealthy" Irish men and women who were "afraid that we were somehow against the Parliamentarians" (Bromell, "The American Mission," 146).

78. Miller, *Emigrants and Exiles*, 535.

79. Clan na Gael correspondence from this period indicates that 726 Spruce Street was a Clan location. William Crossin wrote to Daniel Cohalan from the Irish American Club at 726 Spruce Street in Philadelphia on January 24 and 26, 1902 (Folder 27 "Correspondence—Clan na Gael, 1900–1904," Box 2, Daniel F. Cohalan Papers, American Irish Historical Society, New York). Clark notes that the Irish American Club was "controlled by the Clan na Gael" (*Erin's Heirs*, 164).

80. Clark, *Erin's Heirs*, 147; "Societies Raise Funds to Defend Irishmen," *Public Ledger*, April 4, 1903, 2.

81. "Societies Raise Funds to Defend Irishmen," *Public Ledger*, April 4, 1903, 2. The remaining three were Michael Mooney, Robert Grogen, and John P. Gibbs. See the Clan list of delegates, 1903, Minute Book, Irish American Club, Box 1, folder 9, Dennis Clark Papers, Historical Society of Pennsylvania, Philadelphia.

82. "Bad Eggs Showered on Stage Performers," *Public Ledger*, March 31, 1903, 6.

83. I was able to identify the occupations for nine of the eighteen arrestees; of these nine, six were semiskilled or unskilled. Four laborers, a driver, and a finisher were arrested, but only two skilled workers were arrested—a stonemason and a cooper— along with a low-white-collar worker, a grocer.

84. Meagher, *Inventing Irish America*, 243. Meagher refers mainly to AOH membership, but he notes that many people were members of both organizations. Meagher notes that the Clan na Gael drew on "immigrant, lower-class Irish" (*Inventing Irish America*, 243).

85. Clark, *The Irish in Philadelphia*, 136.

86. Clark, *Erin's Heirs*, 149.

87. Miller, *Emigrants and Exiles*, 541.

88. Clark, *The Irish Relations*, 121; Golway, *Irish Rebel*, 178. Golway writes, "The Clan, by 1900, was prepared to resume its place at the center of the international conspiracy to win Ireland's freedom" (*Irish Rebel*, 178). The Clan reunited in 1900, and three years later Devoy began to publish the *Gaelic American*, which covered the campaign against the Stage Irish with great enthusiasm.

89. Dennis Clark notes Ryan's election as president of the UILA in 1908 (*Erin's Heirs*, 161).

90. "Irish Patriots Held" (originally from the *Brooklyn Eagle*), *Irish World*, February 9, 1907, 5. Another article offered a similar explanation of the Gaelic League as a leader in the attack on the Russell Brothers. See "Chase It from the Stage," *Irish World*, February 9, 1907, 4. See also W. B. "Bat" Masterson, "Russells Were Assaulted by Professional Irishmen," February 3, 1907, clipping, clipping file "Russell," Harvard Theatre Collection, Houghton Library, Harvard University (hereafter HTC).

91. "Irish Patriots Held," *Irish World*, February 9, 1907, 5.

92. Masterson, "Russells Were Assaulted by Professional Irishmen," February 3, 1907, clipping, clipping file: "Russell," HTC. Although the United Irish American Societies, the network of Irish groups behind the protests against the Russell Brothers, officially denied any "particular form of Irish National movement," the Gaelic League and Clan na Gael seemed to dominate this group. In 1910 a member of the United Irish League, a moderate nationalist group, was defeated in an election and the Clan na Gael survived an attempt to push it out of the UIAS. The Clan na Gael was supported by the Irish Volunteers, Sinn Fein, and the Gaelic League, along with a substantial number of AOH members ("Irish American Societies Stand Firm," *Gaelic American*, May 4, 1910, 1). See also "Disruptionists Are Again Defeated," *Gaelic American*, June 18, 1910, 1.

93. One critic noted that the Clan na Gael members "were full of fight and must find relief in some manner or other" (Masterson, "Russells Were Assaulted by Professional Irishmen," February 3, 1907, clipping, clipping file "Russell," HTC).

94. Meagher, *Inventing Irish America*, 243.

95. Emmons, *The Butte Irish*, 144. Kerby Miller notes that in 1893, a Philadelphia AOH had a slight majority of working-class members, "a substantial number of whom were unskilled laborers" (*Emigrants and Exiles*, 534).

96. Meagher, *Inventing Irish America*, 252. Miller notes that Irish American laborers became involved in nationalism because of a "proletarian culture of masculinity which exalted physical force as a means of redressing or revenging both personal and communal injuries" (*Emigrants and Exiles*, 550).

97. Brundage, "In Time of Peace, Prepare for War," 332.

98. Rosenzweig, *Eight Hours for What We Will*, 74.

99. Meagher, *Inventing Irish America*, 252.

100. "Irish-American's Protest," *New York Times*, April 5, 1903, 27. For another defense of violence, see "Stage Irishwoman," *Irish World*, February 23, 1907, 4; and "Gaelic Notes," *Irish World*, April 4, 1903, 8.

101. "Keep Up the Good Work," *Irish World*, April 25, 1903, 12.

102. "Gaelic Notes," *Irish World*, April 4, 1903, 8.

103. In 1907, James C. Lynch, a past president of the Gaelic League of New York, explained that Gaelic League members "first thought that it would be best to go about this in a quiet manner." But Lynch and other leaders explained that stronger action was necessary to overcome the resistance of theater managers; they announced that the protesters had "the hearty approval of every Irish American in the United States who retains a trace of race pride" ("Irish Patriots Held," *Irish World*, February 9, 1907, 5). Overall, the rioters were "doing their duty"; they were "determined men," defending the "honor" of the race ("Philadelphia Irishmen Doing Their Duty," *Irish World*, April 4, 1903, 12). See also "Fight It Down," *Irish World*, May 2, 1903, 4; and "The Stage Irishman Must Go," *Irish World*, February 9, 1907, 5.

104. "The Stage Irishman," *Irish World*, April 4, 1903, 4.

105. "Chase It from the Stage," *Irish World*, February 9, 1907, 4.

106. On St. Patrick's Day and the Fourth of July, for example, rowdiness was respectable among the working-class Irish (Rosenzweig, *Eight Hours for What We Will*, 78).

107. Clark, *Irish Relations*, 114–15.

108. Ibid., 121.

109. "Clan na Gael War on Irishmen," *Irish World*, July 12, 1902, 4. John F. Finerty led a UILA celebration in Chicago, where one speaker stated the desire for Ireland's "full and complete independence" but added that "armed resistance to English rule is to-day impossible" ("Ireland's Day in Chicago," *Irish World*, August 30, 1902, 5). Then, in July 1902, at an AOH conference in Denver, the Clan na Gael tried to use its influence within the AOH to force a formal condemnation of the United Irish League. John Redmond's supporters lashed out at the Clan for creating "malignant factionalism" among Irish American nationalists ("Malignant Factionalism," *Irish World*, October 18, 1902, 2).

110. O'Day, *Irish Home Rule*, 196.

111. "Land Ahead for Ireland," *New York Times*, February 22, 1903, 4. On March 17, the *Irish Times* printed a transcript of Parliament in which Redmond asked, "When the Irish Land Bill will be introduced?" Mr. Balfour answered, March 25, 1903 ("The Irish Land Bill," *Irish Times*, March 17, 1903, 6).

112. "Irish-Americans on the Irish Land Bill," *Irish World*, April 11, 1903, 2.

113. "The Fraud Land Bill," *Gaelic American*, October 3, 1903, 4; O'Day, *Irish Home Rule*, 197.

114. "Irish Americans on the Irish Land Bill," *Irish World*, April 11, 1903, 2.

115. "Irish Rise against Race Caricatures," [March 28, 1903], clipping, *McFadden's Row of Flats* Clipping File, BRTD.

116. The historian Declan Kiberd concluded that the protests in late January were a "curious quirk of Irish theatrical history." See Kiberd, *Synge and the Irish Language*, 250–51. The *Gaelic American*, in addition, discussed protests against Gerhart Hauptmann's play, *Die Jungfern vom Bischofsberg*, in Berlin during the same week as the protests in New York and Dublin. This was a "world-wide revolt against vicious plays" ("To Purify the Stage," *Gaelic American*, May 4, 1907, 3).

117. *Sinn Fein*, February 2, 1907, 2.

118. Kiberd, *Synge and the Irish Language*, 119.

119. *Freeman's Journal*, January 29, 1907, 7, quoted in Kilroy, *The Playboy Riots*, 15.

120. "Gaelic Notes," *Irish World*, March 23, 1907, 7. A San Francisco conflict over *The Belle of Avenue A* followed closely, in March 1907.

121. The *Gaelic American* reported on the "first pantomime of the season" at the Abbey Theatre on January 5, 1907. This seems to be a reference to protests against productions at the Abbey. "For a National Drama," *Gaelic American*, January 5, 1907, 6.

122. Gregory, *Our Irish Theatre*, 178.

123. Kilroy, *The Playboy Riots*, 10. Specific complaints related to women include the "case of the publican going off to a wake and requesting a strange young man whom he had not seen before to take care of his house and his daughter" ("J. M. Synge Dead," *Gaelic American*, April 10, 1909, 2). See also "Yeats' Anti-Irish Campaign," *Gaelic American*, November 18, 1911, 4.

124. Kilroy, *The Playboy Riots*, 7.

125. The *National Hibernian* wrote that "she, or rather he, for the character was usually taken by the ugliest specimen of manhood that could be found, represented all that was loathsome about the race" ("The Death of the Stage Irishman," *National Hibernian*, July 15, 1906, 7).

126. "San Francisco Irishmen," *Gaelic American*, April 6, 1907, 2. See also "Boston Irishmen Protest," *Gaelic American*, November 4, 1911, 10.

127. "Gaelic Notes," *Irish World*, April 11, 1903, 8. Another protester noted such "an Irishwoman as never was seen in real life" ("Gaelic Notes," *Irish World*, April 4, 1903, 8). See also "Stunning Blow for the Stage Irishman," *Gaelic American*, April 20, 1907, 1.

128. "Gaelic Notes," *Irish World*, January 27, 1905, 4.

129. Outcault, "Hogan's Alley," *New York World*, May 3, 1896; reprinted in Blackbeard, *R. F. Outcault's The Yellow Kid* (cartoon no. 18). The Yellow Kid throws as snowball at her in "Signs of Snow," *New York Journal*, January 2, 1898; reprinted in Blackbeard, *R. F. Outcault's The Yellow Kid* (cartoon no. 99). Outcault, "McFadden's Row of Flats," November 1 and 8, 1896, *New York Journal*; reprinted in Blackbeard, *R. F. Outcault's The Yellow Kid* (cartoon nos. 44 and 45).

130. Outcault, "McFadden's Row of Flats," *New York Journal*, November 1 and 22, 1896; reprinted in Blackbeard, *R. F. Outcault's The Yellow Kid* (cartoon nos. 44 and 49).

131. "Rhode Island," *National Hibernian*, June 15, 1906, 5.

132. "Stage Indecency Suppressed," *Gaelic American*, March 30, 1907, 8.

133. "Didn't Suit Ballyhaunis," *Gaelic American*, March 31, 1906, 6.;"Gaelic Notes," *Irish World*, February 16, 1907, 7. The *Irish World* noted an offensive Irish woman with her "whiskey bottle" in May 1904 ("The Stage Irishman in Brockton," *Irish World*, May 7, 1904, 8). Drunken Irish women are mentioned in "The Stage Irishwoman," *Gaelic American*, September 17, 1910, 4. See also Kibler, "The Stage Irishwoman."

134. "Gaelic Notes," *Irish World*, April 18, 1903, 8.

135. [Hill], *McFadden's Row of Flats*, 7.

136. Ibid.

137. Ibid.

138. Ibid.

139. Ibid., 23.

140. Diner, *Erin's Daughters*, 113.

141. Ibid.

142. Rosenzweig, *Eight Hours for What We Will*, 43, 63.

143. "The Stage Irishwoman," *Irish World*, February 23, 1907, 4.

144. "Stage Indecency Suppressed," *Gaelic American*, March 30, 1907, 8. *McFadden's Row of Flats* stirred up controversy mainly because of the "indecency" of the female characters: "These actresses give an exhibition of feminine disregard for modesty that would bring a blush in a Coney Island dance hall" ("An Orgy of Indecency," *Irish World*, April 11, 1903, 12).

145. "Vile Stage Attack on Irish Womanhood," *Gaelic American*, February 9, 1907, 1; "Chase It from the Stage," *Irish World*, February 9, 1907, 4.

146. Amy Leslie, *Detroit News*, September 10, 1913, quoted in Ullman, *Sex Seen*, 59.

147. "Chase the Beast!" *Irish World*, February 23, 1907, 5.

148. "Stunning Blow for the Stage Irishman," *Gaelic American*, April 20, 1907, 1.

149. "Gaelic Notes," *Irish World*, April 11, 1903, 8. In 1910 the *Gaelic American* was similarly outraged over the appearance of the Stage Irishwoman because it attacked the "most cherished treasure of the Irish people . . . the matchless purity and unsullied virtue of our womanhood" ("Stage Indecency Suppressed," *Gaelic American*, March 30, 1907, 8).

150. Kelleher, "Gender Shapes Ethnicity," 151; Moloney, *American Catholic Lay Groups*, 94–95.

151. Kelleher, "Gender Shapes Ethnicity," 153–54. Even anti-Catholic and anti-Irish critics "grudgingly admitted that Irish women 'preserve the abstinence from sexual vice which distinguishes them so honourably at home" (Diner, *Erin's Daughters*, 116).

152. Diner, *Erin's Daughters*, 116.

153. "Irish Rise against Race Caricatures," [March 23 1903], clipping, *McFadden's Row of Flats* clipping file, BRTD.

154. "Hibernians and the Stage Irishman." *National Hibernian*, March 15, 1903, 1. "Gaelic Notes," *Irish World*, September 3, 1904, 8. This complaint referred to a picture postcard on which "Paddy, wearing a plug hat and carrying a shillalay, is leading a fat pig, presumably to the market, but the rope, instead of being tied around the pig's foot, is tied to its tail." An 1830 satire on the Irish, *The Irish Stew*, depicted people and pigs eating out of the same tub (Malcolmson and Mastoris, *The English Pig*, 8).

155. L. Perry Curtis Jr. writes that cartoonists of the early twentieth century often portrayed the Irish as a "hardy pig" (*Apes and Angels*, 57).

156. Way, "Evil Humors and Ardent Spirits," 1404.

157. *Judge's*, September 1901, quoted in Dormon, "Ethnic Stereotyping in American Popular Culture," 492. More broadly, Ireland had been known as Muck Inis in Gaelic or "Hog Island." See Smith, "'I Have Been a Perfect Pig,'" 135.

158. Malcolmson and Mastoris, *The English Pig*, 44.

159. "Put Blame for Riot on Irish Societies," *Public Ledger*, April 1, 1903, 2.

160. "Irish Societies Welcome German Fleet," *Gaelic American*, June 15, 1912, 1. Another protest focused on a postcard with an "Irish girl with a pig in her arms" ("Good Work in Seattle," *Gaelic American*, April 2, 1910, 3). See also "The Stage Irishman Again," *Irish World*, March 3, 1906, 7.

161. "Fouling Their Own Nests," *Gaelic American*, December 3, 1904, 3.

162. "Anti-Irish Caricatures," *Irish World*, May 25, 1901, 5. *The Finish of Bridget McKeen*

(Edison, 1901), Motion Picture, Broadcasting, and Recorded Sound Division, Library of Congress. Another film with a similar plot was *How Bridget Made the Fire*.

163. Murphy, "Bridget and Biddy," 159.

164. Diner, *Erin's Daughters*, 89. Whereas few Italian or Jewish women arrived in the United States alone, many single Irish women migrated, often lured by the assurances of domestic work year-round. Italian and Jewish women rejected the degradation of positions in domestic service and sought out less lucrative positions in manufacturing, but Irish women favored the higher wages of domestic service. In Massachusetts in 1906, teachers were the only group of female workers who earned more money than domestic servants. See also Lynch, *The Irish Bridget*, xvii–xviii.

165. Urban, "Irish Domestic Servants," 264.

166. D. W. Cahill, *Metropolitan Record*, 1860, quoted in Dudden, *Serving Women*, 66.

167. Lynch, *The Irish Bridget*, 72.

168. Urban, "Irish Domestic Servants," 274–75.

169. Murphy, "Bridget and Biddy," 156. Murphy calls the large muscular domestic servant in Opper's cartoons a "violent . . . household tyrant" (16).

170. Urban, "Irish Domestic Servants," 272.

171. "Death of the Stage Irishman," *National Hibernian*, July 15, 1906, 7. See also Murphy, "Bridget and Biddy."

172. "Gaelic Notes," *Irish World*, May 23, 1903, 8. In 1906, Irish protested against an illustration, "Everybody Works But Father" ("Gaelic Notes," *Irish World*, April 21, 1906, 7).

173. "Gaelic Notes," *Irish World*, December 9, 1905, 7; and "Insult the Irish Again," *Gaelic American*, May 7, 1904, 5. In both of these cases, Irish nationalists were outraged that Irish patrons seemed to enjoy the acts, first in St. Peter's Church entertainment, and later in a Manhattan Catholic church's amusements. See also "A Vile Production," *Irish World*, March 9, 1907, 7. In general, critics noted the Stage Irishwoman's lack of femininity. In 1906 the *Irish World* complained about this description of an Irish woman in *McClure's* magazine: "She had the arm of a butcher—short, but powerful—and a body of the same build" ("Gaelic Notes," *Irish World*, March 23, 1906, 7).

174. Winchester, "The Yellow Kid and the Origins of Comic Book Theatricals," 54. See Soper, "From Rowdy, Urban Carnival to Contained Middle-Class Pastime"; and Soper, "From Swarthy Ape to Sympathetic Everyman and Subversive Trickster."

175. "Fouling Their Own Nests," *Gaelic American*, December 3, 1904, 3. For other examples of cross-dressing, see "Irish Plays by Amateurs," *Gaelic American*, March 10, 1906, 3; "Irish Caricature," *Irish World*, March 30, 1901, 5; and the controversies over Kate Elinore's gender in Kibler, "Rank Ladies, Ladies of Rank."

176. "Irish-American's Protest," *New York Times*, April 5, 1903, 27. In 1905, protesters in Butte turned against the Dreamland Burlesquers and sought the arrest of the performers for "creating or maintaining a nuisance." They decided not to "molest the female members of the company, but to arrest the male members" ("The Stage Irishman Hunted from Butte," *Gaelic American*, December 30, 1905, 8).

177. McDevitt, "Muscular Catholicism." See also Cairns and Richards, "'Woman' in the Discourse of Celticism," 43–47; Kelleher, "Class and Catholic Irish Masculin-

ity in Antebellum America"; Hickman and Walter, "Deconstructing Whiteness: Irish Women in Britain."

178. "A Gross Insult to Irishmen and Catholics," *National Hibernian*, April 15, 1905, 4. For similar war rhetoric, see "Fight It Down," *Irish World*, May 2, 1903, 4; and "Gaelic Notes," *Irish World*, March 31, 1906, 7.

179. There is little evidence of women participating in the theater disturbances. Mrs. Ellen Jolly, active in the Ladies Auxiliary of the Ancient Order of Hibernians, did protest against the Stage Irishwoman on a few occasions. See "Rhode Island," *National Hibernian*, June 15, 1906, 5.

180. "Gaelic Notes," *Irish World*, February 16, 1907, 7.

181. Urban, "Irish Domestic Servants," 280.

182. The temptations of the American metropolis undermined Irish leaders' trust in the self-control of their brethren, and some reformers set up programs for the protection of Irish immigrant women from prostitution and premarital pregnancies. Moloney, *American Catholic Lay Groups*, 97–100.

183. Mary Sarsfield Gilmore, "Woman's Page," *Irish World*, October 7 1905, 11; "Another Danger for Emigrant Girls," *Irish World*, December 14, 1907, 11.

184. "The Woman's Movement," *Irish World*, January 12, 1909, 11.

185. For more on the comparison of Irish working women and Irish mothers, see Meagher, "Sweet Good Mothers and Young Women out in the World."; and Moloney, *American Catholic Lay Groups*.

186. "Gaelic Notes," *Irish World*, February 16, 1907, 7.

187. "Russell Brothers Reply," *Irish World*, February 16, 1907, 2. Another example of the use of motherhood in the debate occurs in "Gaelic Notes," *Irish World*, March 31, 1906, 7.

188. "Chase It from the Stage," *Irish World*, February 9, 1907, 4.

189. Ap Hywel, "Elise and the Great Queens of Ireland," 26, 29. See also Banerjee, *Muscular Nationalism*.

190. Ryan, "Traditions and Double Moral Standards." Ryan and other historians have pointed out that this dilemma was not unique to Irish nationalism. See also Thapar, "Women as Activists."

191. Ap Hywel, "Elise and the Great Queens of Ireland," 25. W. B. Yeats, paraphrased by David Kiely, expresses the link between Irish women's morality and Irish nationalism: "Certain people have objected to Mr Synge's play because Irish women, being more chaste than those of England and Scotland, are a valuable part of our national argument" (Kiely, *John Millington Synge*, 124). Historians have also pointed out that Synge's disobedient and desiring women violated the familialism that held rural life together in Ireland and that such an insult to the ideology of small tenant farmers threatened the nationalist coalition (Cairns and Richards, "Reading a Riot," 229–30).

192. Ap Hywel, "Elise and the Great Queens of Ireland," 24–25.

193. "To the Men Who Put an End to the Vile Production," *Irish World*, April 4, 1903, 12.

194. Kenny, *The American Irish*, 194–95.

195. Doorley, *Irish-American Diasporic Nationalism*, 40; Miller reports a peak membership of 275,000 (*Emigrants and Exiles*, 542).

196. Barrett, *The Irish Way*, 253–55; Doorley, *Irish-American Diasporic Nationalism*, 40.

197. "Boston Men Indignant," *Gaelic American*, January 20, 1917, 1–2. See also "Protest Vigorously against Insulting Picture," *Gaelic American*, January 13, 1917, 5.

198. "Propagandist Picture Getting Punctured," *Gaelic American*, January 27, 1917, 2; "Whom the Gods Destroy Being Destroyed," *Gaelic American*, January 20, 1917, 2.

199. "Propagandist Picture Getting Punctured," *Gaelic American*, January 27, 1917, 2.

200. "Philadelphians See New Irish Drama," *Gaelic American*, May 5, 1917, 7.

201. "An Insulting Irish Play," *Gaelic American*, September 22, 1917, 2. See also "The 'Irish Play' Again," *Gaelic American*, September 29, 1917, 4.

202. French, "Irish-American Identity," 241–42.

203. Ibid., 288.

204. "'Kathleen Mavourneen' Provokes Theatre Riot," *Gaelic American*, February 28, 1920, 4; "Protest Stops 'Kathleen Mavourneen' in Bayonne," *Gaelic American*, November 8, 1919, 6.

205. "'Stage Irishwoman' Is Speedily Suppressed," *Gaelic American*, December 6, 1919, 6.

CHAPTER THREE

1. Gregory, *Our Irish Theatre*, 185.

2. These findings counter David Nasaw's conclusion in *Going Out*: "Other ethnic groups had some success in banning tasteless and offensive slurs, but African Americans could not threaten a boycott (they were too small an audience to matter), take direct action, or exert much political pressure" (59). Lady Augusta Gregory notes that censorship officials decided not to intervene with *Playboy of the Western World* in Boston, Providence, New Haven, New York City, Washington, or Philadelphia. Newspapers reported that New Haven censors cut lines, but this appears to have been a mistake. The censor was actually watching *The Shewing Up of Blanco Posnet*, according to Gregory (*Our Irish Theatre*, 187). For more on *The Playboy*'s escape from state censorship, see Murphy, "The Reception of Synge's *Playboy* in Ireland and America."

3. Stokes, *D. W. Griffith's The Birth of a Nation*, 35–47.

4. Johnson, *Sisters in Sin*, 14–16.

5. "Mayor Will See Play for Himself," *Hartford Courant*, December 5, 1906, 13.

6. Blackstone, *Of Public Wrongs, Commentaries on the Laws of England*, 150–51, quoted in Horowitz, *Rereading Sex*, 40.

7. Horowitz, *Rereading Sex*, 377–78.

8. Rabban, *Free Speech in Its Forgotten Years*, 137.

9. "Suppress the Clansman," *Washington Post*, September 26, 1906, 6.

10. *State v. McKee*, 73 (Conn. 18 (1900), quoted in Rabban, *Free Speech in Its Forgotten Years*, 142.

11. Rabban, *Free Speech in Its Forgotten Years*, 144.

12. "Free Speech a Nuisance," *New York Times*, December 27, 1914, C2.

13. Rabban, *Free Speech in its Forgotten Years*, 119.

14. Budke, "Addressing the 'Offense of Public Decency,'" 207.

15. "Negroes Hot after Clansman," *New York Tribune*, December 21, 1905, 8; see also "Mayor Will See Play for Himself," *Hartford Courant*, December 5, 1906, 13.

16. "Even Smalley Slaps It," *Gaelic American*, February 17, 1912, 2.

17. "The Clansman Denounced," *Freeman*, January 6, 1906, 6.

18. Budke, "Addressing the 'Offense of Public Decency.'"

19. Johnson, "*Zaza*," 224.

20. Johnson, *Sisters in Sin*, 15.

21. Friedman, *Prurient Interests*, 98.

22. Johnson, *Sisters in Sin*, 60.

23. Houchin, *Censorship of the American Theatre*, 42.

24. Ibid., 41.

25. Ibid.

26. Ibid., 48.

27. Friedman, *Prurient Interests*, 20. Katie Johnson notes that her most enthusiastic support came from women (*Sisters in Sin*, 63).

28. Harrington, *The Irish Play on the New York Stage*, 34.

29. Houchin, *Censorship of the American Theater*, 53.

30. Ibid., 55.

31. Friedman, *Prurient Interests*, 20.

32. Houchin, *Censorship of the American Theater*, 46.

33. Friedman, *Prurient Interests*, 95.

34. Ibid., 147, 5

35. "Censored Plays Often Succeed," *Chicago Daily Tribune*, June 16, 1907, 15.

36. "Against 'The Clansman,'" *New York Times*, December 25, 1906, 7.

37. "Censored Plays Often Succeed," *Chicago Daily Tribune*, June 16, 1907, 15.

38. Williams, "Versions of Uncle Tom," 119.

39. "Against 'The Clansman,'" *Baltimore Sun*, October 7, 1906, 2. See also "'The Clansman' and 'Uncle Tom's Cabin,'" *Baltimore Sun*, October 29, 1906, 7.

40. Stokes, *D. W. Griffith's "The Birth of a Nation,"* 37.

41. Waller, *Main Street Amusements*, 45. The Kentucky law banned "any play that is based upon antagonism between master and slave, or that excites racial prejudice" (Grieveson, *Policing Cinema*, 63; also see Williams, *Playing the Race Card*).

42. Waller, *Main Street Amusements*, 45.

43. Ibid., 44.

44. *Lexington Leader*, January 18, 1906, 4, quoted in Waller, *Main Street Amusements*, 165.

45. "Negroes Fight Clansman," *Des Moines Register and Leader*, February 5, 1911, 1. Brown was active in other fights over race and representation. In 1911 he objected to *The Nigger*, a play by Edward Shelton, because it increased "antipathy for the negro race" ("Police Can't Stop Play at Princess," *Des Moines Register and Leader*, March 23, 1911, 1). In 1918 Brown corresponded with a Des Moines newspaper editor about capitalizing "Negro," "which has been adopted as the name of a Race of people." Lowercase type suggested disrespect, according to Brown. The editor agreed to change the practice (S. Joe Brown to W. E. Battenfield, November 20, 1918, folder "Des Moines, Iowa,

1916–1934," box G–68, Branch Files, NAACP Records, Manuscript Division, Library of Congress, Washington, D.C. [hereafter NAACPR]). See Jack Lufkin, "Brown, Samuel Joe," *Biographical Dictionary of Iowa*.

46. "Negroes against the Clansman," *Des Moines Register and Leader*, March 1, 1907, 6.

47. Ibid.

48. "The Hissing of The Clansman," *Atlanta Constitution*, October 22, 1905, B5.

49. "The Damning of Dixon" *New York Age*, October 19, 1905, 7.

50. "Dixon's Play Stirs Wrath of Columbia," *Atlanta Constitution*, October 16, 1905, 1.

51. "The Clansman" *Macon Telegraph*, October 22, 1905, 4.

52. "The Clansman in Syracuse," *Hartford Courant*, January 3, 1906, 7.

53. Nahshon, "The Pulpit to the Stage," 10.

54. Ibid., 23–24.

55. "A Protest from a Hebrew," *New York Times*, November 5, 1894, 8.

56. Grusd, *B'nai B'rith*, 140.

57. "Resents Jewish Caricatures," *New York Times*, April 4, 1910, 8.

58. Inscoe, "The Clansman on Stage and Screen," 139.

59. "Casualties of the Clansman," *New York Age*, November 16, 1905, 2.

60. "Hiss Dixon and Play," *New York Tribune*, October 16, 1905, 1.

61. *News and Observer* October 5, 1905, quoted in Inscoe, "The Clansman on Stage and Screen," 146.

62. "Mr. Dixon's Press Agent," *Macon Morning Telegraph*, January 7, 1906, 4. Another [Dr. Broughton] explained that the "negro ever is hard to see a lesson; he gives way to passion and if such insane agitations of passion continue unchecked, it will be the ruin of the negro and the disgrace of the whites" ("Dr Broughton Talks of Dixon," *Atlanta Constitution*, November 6, 1905, 7). See also "Talk of War on Whites at Negro Conference," *New York Times*, October 10, 1906, 16.

63. "They Don't Want to See Play," *Atlanta Constitution*, October 1, 1906, 5.

64. W. E. Gonzalez, "The Clansman Denounced," Letter to the Editor, *New York Times*, January 2, 1906, 8.

65. "The Clansman Condemned," *Atlanta Constitution*, reprinted in *Baltimore Afro-American*, November 17, 1906, 4.

66. "Is the Negro a Man?" *Iowa State Bystander*, 1906, quoted in Everett, *Returning the Gaze*, 62

67. "Casualties of the Clansman," *New York Age*, November 16, 1905, 2.

68. Crowe, "Racial Massacre in Atlanta," 152.

69. Ibid., 153.

70. Daniel, *Standing at the Crossroads*, 60.

71. Stokes, *D. W. Griffith's "The Birth of a Nation,"* 51.

72. Pete Daniel concludes that "irresponsible newspapers, politics, and . . . even a play" contributed to the Atlanta riot (*Standing at the Crossroads*, 59).

73. "The Clansman Tabooed," *Washington Post*, September 25, 1906, 1; "No Clansman in Birmingham," *Atlanta Constitution*, September 27, 1906, 7; "They Don't Want to See Play," *Atlanta Constitution*, October 1, 1906, 5. "With the Atlanta horror yet fresh in the public mind . . . its production . . . in this city is . . . perilous to public peace" ("Wants Clansman Barred," *Baltimore Sun*, October 4, 1906, 2).

74. Henry Bass won, on the Republican ticket, a seat in the general assembly—the first African American state legislator in Pennsylvania—in 1910, after losing four years earlier when he ran as an independent (Smith, "'Asking for Justice and Fair Play,'" 173–75).

75. "The Clansman Affair," *Wilmington Evening Journal*, November 1, 1906, 4.

76. "Dixon Blames Politics," *Bulletin*, October 26, 1906, clipping, scrapbook 126, William H. Dorsey Manuscript Collection, Leslie Pinckney Hill Library, Cheyney University of Pennsylvania (hereafter Dorsey).

77. "Truckling to Colored Voters," *Lancaster Intelligencer*, November 13, 1906, 5. The Philadelphia case was also explained as electioneering: "Last year the mayor refused to stop the play. It is nearer election now—and the Mayor grows smaller as he grows older" ("The Stopping of The Clansman, *Bulletin*, November 1, 1906, clipping, scrapbook 126, Dorsey).

78. Cripps, *Slow Fade to Black*, 55. "The play is not new to Philadelphia, having been given here last season, but as a dramatic production its crudities are as noticeable as ever. In fact, its bid for popular favor seems to be entirely based upon an appeal to race prejudice" ("The Clansman—Walnut," *Philadelphia Record*, October 23, 1906, clipping, scrapbook 126, Dorsey).

79. Lane, *William Dorsey's Philadelphia*, 180–81. Part of the coalition of clergy around Mossell, Reverend W. H. Heard, born and raised in the South, brought a case against the Interstate Commerce Commission after he had been ejected from a railroad car in 1887. The ICC ruled that railroads had to provide separate cars for anyone excluded from first class travel.

80. Haller, "Recurring Themes," 288. Pfeifer, *Lynching Beyond Dixie*.

81. Downey, "The 'Delaware Horror.'"

82. "3000 Negroes Start Riot to Stop Play They Dislike," *North American*, October 23, 1906, clipping, scrapbook 126, Dorsey.

83. "Riot of Negroes over Class Play Halted by Police," *Record* (Philadelphia), October 23, 1906, clipping, scrapbook 126, Dorsey.

84. Ibid.

85. "3000 Negroes Start Riot to Stop the Play They Dislike," *North American*, October 23, 1906, clipping, scrapbook 126, Dorsey. The crowd outside was described as a "swaying mass of negroes [that] blocked both Walnut and Ninth Streets." Protesters in the crowd shouted out their claim that the play portrayed the negro as a "beast of the jungle." ("Negro Mob Causes Trouble at Theatre" *Public Ledger*, October 23, 1906, 1.)

86. "3000 Negroes Start Riot trying to Stop Play They Dislike" *North American*, October 23, 1906, clipping, scrapbook 126, Dorsey.

87. "A Premium on Mob Law," *Public Ledger*, November 2, 1906, clipping, scrapbook 126, Dorsey; "Extra! Mayor Prohibits Clansman Being Played." *Evening Bulletin*, October 23, 1906, clipping, scrapbook 126, Dorsey; "The Clansman Gets a Black Eye," *Afro-American Ledger*, October 27, 1906, 1. See also "Mayor Stops Play: Negroes Win Fight against 'Clansman," *North American*, October 24, 1906, clipping, scrapbook 126, Dorsey. In this article Mossell argues that the crowd was "not an unruly mob."

88. "Weaver Closes Clansman after Hearing Protest," *Philadelphia Inquirer*, October 24, 1906, clipping, scrapbook 126, Dorsey.

89. Ibid.

90. "Mayor Stops Play," *North American*, October 24, 1906, clipping, scrapbook 126, Dorsey.

91. "Court Scores Dixon," *Baltimore Sun*, October 26, 1906, 2.

92. "To Enjoin Mayor in Theatre Case," October 25, 1906, clipping, scrapbook 126, Dorsey.

93. "Race Play Barred," *Washington Post*, October 26, 1906, 1.

94. "To Enjoin Mayor in Theatre Case," October 25, 1906, clipping, scrapbook 126, Dorsey.

95. Ibid.

96. Ibid.

97. Ibid.

98. Ibid.

99. Schultz, "Group Rights, American Jews."

100. *Woodrow v. Duffy* (1914), *Pennsylvania County Court Reports* (1915), 641, 642.

101. Des Moines Ordinance, no. 1423, March 1907, folder "Films and Plays: *Birth of a Nation*, May 1915," C-300, NAACPR.

102. Murphy, "The Reception of Synge's Playboy in Ireland and America," 521; Harrington, *The Irish Play on the New York Stage*.

103. "Stamp Out the Atrocious Libel," *Gaelic American*, October 14, 1911, 4. "There are things more important even than Art or Literature. Among these are Truth and Fairness. Do these plays present a truthful and fair portrayal of life and conditions in Ireland?" ("Sombre and Repulsive," *Gaelic American*, October 28, 1911, 2).

104. "Obdure and Art in Drama," *Gaelic American*, October 21, 1911, 4.

105. "Riot in Theatre over an Irish Play," *New York Times*, November 27, 1911, 3.

106. "Irish Players Well Received in Boston," *Gaelic American*, September 30, 1911, 10.

107. "Stamp Out the Atrocious Libel," *Gaelic American*, October 14, 1911, 4; "Yeats' Anti-Irish Campaign," *Gaelic American*, November 18, 1911, 4. Another editorial criticized Synge for presenting Irish women as "brazen strumpets" ("The Playboy Must Be Suppressed," *Gaelic American*, October 28, 1911, 4). Another description complained that the women in the play "do all the amorous boasting" ("Yeats' Anti-Irish Campaign," *Gaelic American*, November 18, 1911, 4). See also McDevitt, "Muscular Catholicism"; Cairns and Richards, "'Woman' in the Discourse of Celticism."

108. "Irishmen Will Stamp Out the Playboy," *Gaelic American*, October 14, 1911, 1.

109. "Boston Gives It the Cold Shoulder," *Gaelic American*, October 21, 1911, 1. Paula Kane notes a tension between Irish Catholic nationalists who protested against the play and the Irish Protestant leaders of the Abbey Theatre (Kane, "'Staging a Lie'").

110. "Boston Gives It the Cold Shoulder," *Gaelic American*, October 21, 1911, 1.

111. Ibid.

112. "Irishmen Will Stamp Out the Playboy," *Gaelic American*, October 14, 1911, 11.

113. "Yeats Cables Tale of Glorious Victory," *Gaelic American*, November 4, 1911, 10.

114. Ibid., 1.

115. Ibid.

116. "O'Schaunessy, George Francis," *Biographical Dictionary of the U.S. Congress*.

117. "Playboy Given with Change, Management Says," *Providence Evening Bulletin*, November 1, 1911, 1.

118. The local Providence paper noted that "the protestants intimated that were the play produced there might be trouble in the theatre" ("Protest against Irish Players Made to Commissioners," *Providence Evening Bulletin*, October 30, 1911, 1).

119. "Protests of No Avail," *Gaelic American*, November 11, 1911, 8.

120. "Riot in Theatre over an Irish Play," *New York Times*, November 28, 1911, 1.

121. Jeremiah O'Leary, "An Irish-American's View," *Gaelic American*, December 16, 1911, 3.

122. "Riot in Theater over Irish Play," *New York Times*, November 27, 1911, 1.

123. *New York Times*, November 28, 1911, quoted in Gregory, *Our Irish Theatre*, 281.

124. "Censorship by Missiles," *Christian Science Monitor*, January 19, 1912, 16. The *New York Times* described the style of protest as "particularly Irish" ("The Playboy Row," *New York Times*, November 29, 1911, 10).

125. "Under Arrest, Irish Players Triumph in Criticized Playboy," *North American*, January 18, 1912, 9.

126 "New York's Protest against a Vile Play," *Gaelic American*, December 2, 1911, 1.

127. Ibid.; "Playboy Dead as Nail in a Door," *Gaelic American*, December 9, 1911, 1.

128. "Playboy Dead as Nail in a Door," *Gaelic American*, December 9, 1911, 1; "Lady Gregory's Moral Victory, Moryah," *Gaelic American*, November 11, 1911, 4.

129. "Yale Students Wreck Stage; Riot Frightens Gaby Deslys." *Chicago Tribune*, November 19, 1911, 2. See Kibler, "Freedom of the Theatre."

130. "Probing Arrest of Men at Yale," *Boston Daily Globe*, November 20, 1911, 9.

131. Gregory, *Our Irish Theatre*, 187–88.

132. "Protesters Were Right," *Gaelic American*, December 16, 1911, 3.

133. *New York Sun*, November 29, 1911, quoted in Gregory, *Our Irish Theatre*, 283.

134. "M'Adoo's Report," *Gaelic American*, December 16, 1911, 5.

135. Ibid.

136. "Nullifies Order to Stop 'Playboy'" *Chicago Tribune*, February 1, 1912, 19.

137. "First Performance in Chicago of 'The Playboy of the Western World: No Riots," *Chicago Daily Tribune*, February 7, 1912, 13.

138. "Philadelphia Spanks the Playboy," *Gaelic American*, January 20, 1912, 7.

139. "Cops Throw Out 29; Check 'Playboy' Riot," *North American*, January 16, 1912, 1.

140. Ibid. The *North American* reported that a currant cake hit an actor, but no "solid vegetables" were thrown ("Play Is Again Halted by Riots, Police Arrest 14," *North American*, 17 January 1912, 6).

141. "Lady Gregory's Inane Talk," *Gaelic American*, January 27, 1912, 4.

142. "Real Comedy Off the Stage," *Gaelic American*, January 27, 1912, 4.

143. "Play Is Halted by Riots, Police Arrest 14," *North American*, January 17, 1912, 6.

144. "Philadelphia Spanks the Playboy," *Gaelic American*, January 20, 1912, 1.

145. "Pennsylvania Air Bad for 'Playboy,'" *Gaelic American*, January 27, 1912, 7.

146. Ibid., 1.

147. "Censorship by Missiles," *Christian Science Monitor*, January 19, 1912, 16.

148. "Irish Players in Comedy Court," *Philadelphia North American*, January 20, 1912, quoted in Gregory, *Our Irish Theatre*, 293.

149. "Pennsylvania Air Bad for Playboy," *Gaelic American*, January 27, 1912, 1.

150. "Irish Players in Comedy Court," *Philadelphia North American*, January 20, 1912, quoted in Gregory, *Our Irish Theatre*, 293.

151. "To Enjoin Mayor in Theatre Case," October 25, 1906, clipping, scrapbook 126, Dorsey.

152. "Censorship by Unanimous Consent," *Chicago Tribune*, January 31, 1912, 8.

153. Houchin, *Censorship of the American Theatre*, 83.

154. Erdman, "Jewish Anxiety in 'Days of Judgment,'" 51. See also Warnke, "*God of Vengeance*."

155. Harry Weinberger to Roger Baldwin, June 28, 1924, folder 3, box 24, Harry Weinberger Papers, Yale University, Manuscript and Archives (hereafter HWP).

156. Harry Weinberger to Dr. Samuel Schulman, March 29, 1923, folder 5, box 25, HWP.

157. Quoted in Erdman, "Jewish Anxiety in 'Days of Judgment,'" 63.

158. Weinberger to Schulman, March 26, 1923, folder 5, box 25, HWP.

159. Schulman to Weinberger, March 28, 1923, folder 5, box 25, HWP.

160. Weinberger to Schroeder, September 26, 1924, folder 5, box 25, HWP.

161. Rabban, *Free Speech in Its Forgotten Years*, 48–49.

162. Rabban, *Free Speech in Its Forgotten Years*, 49.

163. Schroeder, *Free Speech for Radicals*, 63. See Rabban, *Free Speech in Its Forgotten Years*, 60.

164. Schroeder, *Free Speech for Radicals*, 27.

165. Walker, *In Defense of American Liberties*, 82. Leigh Ann Wheeler explains that, between 1873 and 1935, "few would have considered the possibility that the First Amendment might embrace motion pictures; and fringe radicals had a fairly uncontested monopoly on the notion of a 'right' to sexual expression" (*Against Obscenity*, 7).

166. Houchin, *Censorship of the American Theatre*, 89.

167. Ibid., 90.

168. Weinberger to Roger Baldwin, September 26 (25?), 1924, folder 3, box 24, HWP.

169. Weinberger to Theodore Schroeder, October 1, 1924, folder 5, box 25, HWP. On September 25, 1924, Weinberger wrote to Baldwin: "Suppose someone, for instance, having listened to your experiences during the war and believing that your views should be propagandized in the form of a play strongly visualized it, and then actually wrote it as a play. It would be very clear that that play would be an expression of your ideas verbal and pictorial" (folder 3, box 24, HWP).

170. Weinberger to Baldwin, August 21, 1925, folder 3, box 24, HWP.

171. Baldwin to Weinberger, September 29, 1924, folder 3, box 24, HWP.

172. Baldwin to Weinberger, October 1, 1924, folder 3, box 24, HWP. In this letter Baldwin admitted that, in the *God of Vengeance* case, the "issue of morality has been somewhat complicated by the religious issue."

173. Weinberger to Baldwin, October 1, 1924, folder 3, box 24, HWP.

174. Theodore Schroeder to Roger Baldwin, October 3, 1924, box 14, Theodore Schroeder Collection, Morris Library, Southern Illinois University, Carbondale, Illinois.

175. Rabban, "The Free Speech League," 76, 55.

176. Chafee, *Freedom of Speech*, 170.

177. Ibid., 171.

178. Ibid., 175.

179. Ibid., 203.

180. Schroeder, *Free Speech for Radicals*, 27.

CHAPTER FOUR

1. Jessye E. McClain (?) to Mary Childs Nerney, April 15, 1915, folder, "Films and Plays: Birth of a Nation, April 1915," C-300, NAACPR.

2. *Block v. City of Chicago, 87 N. E. 1011, 239, Ill.* (1909). Several scholars repeat only this limited summary of the law. See Baldwin, *Chicago's New Negroes*, 98. See Lindstrom, "'Almost Worse than the Restrictive Measures.'"

3. Turner, "The City of Chicago." ·

4. The ADL, for example, emphasized its effort to restore "the good name of the Jew" (*Report of the Anti-Defamation League*, [1915], 41 BBIA).

5. Scholars underestimate the significance of the ADL in fighting the Stage Jew. John P. Roche, for example, argues that the ADL challenged studios in 1915 and 1916, two years after their advocacy actually began (*The Quest for the Dream*, 92-95). Patricia Erens, in addition, argues incorrectly that "*Intolerance* became the first successful attempt on the part of Jewish agencies to police the image of the Jew on the American screen" (*The Jew in American Cinema*, 72).

6. Higham, *Strangers in the Land*, 161.

7. "Hotel Affronts Senator's Sister," *New York Times*, May 18, 1907, 1.

8. Cohen, *Not Free to Desist*, 3.

9. Norris Waldman, *Nor by Power*, 154, quoted in Jacob Sable, "Some American Jewish Organizational Efforts," 142.

10. Sable, "Some American Jewish Organizational Efforts," 151, 152.

11. Ibid., 228.

12. 1895 *New York Laws* Chapter 1042, quoted in Friss, "Blacks, Jews, and Civil Rights," 73.

13. Friss, "Blacks, Jews, and Civil Rights Law," 75–77.

14. Ibid., 81.

15. Gurock, "The 1913 New York State Civil Rights Act," 96; Sable, "Some American Jewish Organizational Efforts," 191; Schultz, "Group Rights, American Jews, and the Failure of Group Libel Laws."

16. New York State Legislature, Senate, An Act to Amend Chapter 1042, S. R. 1791, May 23, 1907, 1-4, quoted in Gurock, "The 1913 New York State Civil Rights Act," 96.

17. Friss, "Blacks, Jews, and Civil Rights Law," 87. See also "Editorial," *American Israelite*, July 30, 1908, 4. In this editorial, the author noted a placard that read: "No Jews or dogs or tuberculosis patients."

18. Louis Marshall to Martin Saxe, June 3, 1907, box 1576, American Jewish Archives, quoted in Friss, "Blacks, Jews, and Civil Rights Law," 87.

19. "Publicity Bureau of District No. 6 Resent Affront to Jews," *B'nai B'rith News*, October 1908, 5. After the law was passed, Julian Morgenstern, a reform rabbi, criticized

the law as an imposition on individual freedom: "I believe it to be a natural and inherent right of the individual to determine just whom he does like and wishes to associate with . . . I have never invited a negro [sic] to dine with me, and probably will never do so. . . . I believe I have a constitutionally legal right to select my own social associates, and if I feel this way with regard to the negro [sic], then I must accord the same right to the anti-Semite" (Julian Morgenstern, "Self Protection of Self-Assertion," *B'nai B'rith News*, May 1913, 41, quoted in Gurock, "The 1913 New York State Civil Rights Act," 107).

20. Friss, "Blacks, Jews, and Civil Rights Law in New York," 88.

21. "The Thing Must Stop," *Jewish Comment*, May 31, 1907, 122, quoted in Gurock, "The 1913 New York State Civil Rights Act," 98.

22. Max Heller, "Regulating the Summer Hotel," *American Israelite*, May 30, 1907, 4, quoted in Gurock, "The 1913 New York State Civil Rights Act," 100.

23. Oppenheim, *The American Jewish Year Book*, (1918), 381. A. C. Stein introduced an early version in 1915, and the governor also vetoed the bill (*American Jewish Year Book* [1916], 363, for mention of the veto). The Colorado legislature passed a law against discriminatory hotel advertising in 1917 (*American Jewish Year Book* [1917], 237). Livingston noted various bills introduced in state legislatures to prevent the "public dissemination by hotels and kindred institutions of literature discriminatory of any sect or nationality" ("President's Message," ADL, Report of Proceedings of Grand Lodge No. 2, International Order of B'nai B'rith 65th Meeting, Cincinnati, 20 May 1917, Series B, BBIA).

24. Schultz, "Group Rights, American Jews." The B'nai B'rith reported that "even more drastic legislation" had passed in Minnesota. Cohon, *B'nai B'rith Manual*, 367. See also Konvitz and Leskes, *A Century of Civil Rights*, 169.

25. Konvitz and Leskes, *A Century of Civil Rights*, 169. When the ADL referred back to the New York Civil Rights Law, it referred only to the outlawing of advertisements of a "discriminatory policy." "Summer Resort Discrimination," *Anti-Defamation League Bulletin*, no. 3 [1915?] 1. folder 10, box 2, David Philipson Collection, Jacob Rader Marcus Center, American Jewish Archives (hereafter cited as Philipson).

26. *Report of the Anti-Defamation League Together with Principles of League and Correspondence* (International Order of B'nai B'rith 1915), 32, BBIA. The ADL explained that it was not motivated by "any desire to compel the reception of Jews in such hostelries" (*Report of the Anti-Defamation League* [1915], 43, BBIA). When the AJC evaluated the new law in 1915, the committee reported violations only of the advertising ban: the offenders "have uniformly destroyed their illegal letter-heads and folders and abandoned their advertisements and conformed to the law" (Jacobs, *The American Jewish Yearbook*, 372).

27. Gurock, "The 1913 New York State Civil Rights Act," 110, 111.

28. Turner, "City of Chicago," 581.

29. Theodore Bingham, "Foreign Criminals in New York," *North American Review* (1908), 383–84, quoted in Sable, "Some American Jewish Organizational Efforts," 186. See also George Kibbe Turner, "Daughters of the Poor," *McClure's* (November 1909): 45–61.

30. A sympathetic reply to Bingham explained, "When he does speak of the criminals amongst us he goes out of his way, as it seems to us, to inject a considerable amount

of venom and prejudice into his remarks on the Russian Hebrews. He points out that their crimes are mainly against property" ("Crime in New York," *American Hebrew and Jewish Messenger*, September 4, 1908, 419). See also "White Slave Traffic," *American Israelite*, November 26, 1908, 1.

31. Goren, *New York Jew and the Quest for Community*, 36. Regarding the reports of Jewish crime, the *American Israelite* commented, "The respectable Jews of New York are deeply chagrined at the radically changed conditions" ("Charity in the Metropolis," *American Israelite*, November 19, 1908, 4).

32. Sorin, *A Time for Building*, 84.

33. Goren, *New York Jews and the Quest for Community*, 143. See also Alexander, *Jazz Age Jews*.

34. *Tageblatt*, September 3, 1908, 4, quoted in Goren, *New York Jews and the Quest for Community*, 28. The *Tageblatt* accused the *American Hebrew*, which represented the Americanized Jewish community, of ignoring the seriousness of the Bingham report and attacking East Side Jews instead (*Tageblatt*, September 14, 1908, 4; quoted in Goren, *New York Jews*, 29–30).

35. Goren, *New York Jews and the Quest for Community*, 26.

36. Ibid., 28.

37. Goren, *New York Jews and the Quest for Community*, 137-38. See also Sorin, *A Time for Building*, 214–18.

38. Sable, "Some American Jewish Organizational Efforts," 188.

39. Minutes of the Executive Committee, AJC, November 7, 1908, quoted in Sable, "Some American Jewish Organizational Efforts," 189.

40. Jacobs, *American Jewish Year Book* (1915), 380.

41. Goren, *New York Jews and the Quest for Community*, 143.

42. Ibid., 135.

43. "Caricaturing the Jews," *American Israelite*, August 25, 1910, 4; "Abolish Jewish Caricature," *New York Times*, March 26, 1912, 9.

44. Quoted in Roche, *Quest for the Dream*, 93.

45. Carr, *Hollywood and Anti-Semitism*, 52.

46. Ibid., 34.

47. Sarna, *American Judaism*, 195. See also Sorin, *Tradition Transformed*, 128.

48. The committee began to pressure textbook publishers to remove sectarian items from their books in 1908, defeating an Oklahoma proposal to make Bible reading compulsory in 1909, and then it battled against Sunday rest laws.

49. S. N. Deinard, "The Merchant of Venice in Our Public Schools," *B'nai B'rith News*, January 1909, 5.

50. Frisch et al., *Year Book of the Central Conference of American Rabbis*, vol. 21, 86, Jacob Rader Marcus Center, American Jewish Archives (hereafter AJA); "Forbes-Robertson on Shylock," *American Israelite*, January 15, 1914, 4. While some felt that Shakespeare's sympathies were with Shylock, others, like S. N. Deinard, writing in the *B'nai B'rith News*, wrote that "I know what villain now means. [Shylock is] the blackest villain, an unscrupulous, usurious, vindictive, bloodthirsty fiend" ("The Merchant of Venice in Our Public Schools," *B'nai B'rith News*, January 1909, 5).

51. On the crucifixion comparison, see "Forbes-Robertson on Shylock," *American*

Israelite, January 15, 1914, 4; and "Christian Attitudes toward Jews," *American Israelite*, January 4, 1912, 5. For a typical debate about *The Merchant of Venice*, see "Shakespeare's Merchant of Venice," *B'nai B'rith News*, June 1909.

52. Frisch et al., *Year Book of the Central Conference of American Rabbis, vol. 21*, 86, AJA

53. Adler, *American Jewish Year Book (1916)*, 87. A Louisiana rabbi persuaded the superintendent of his local schools to remove *The Merchant of Venice* and substitute another text (Oppenheim, *American Jewish Year Book (1918)*, 151).

54. Schneiderman, *American Jewish Year Book* (1919), 137.

55. Morgenstern, Lefkowitz, and Philipson, *Year Book of the Central Conference of American Rabbis*, vol. 19, 88, AJA.

56. Marx, Morgenstern, and Heller, *Year Book of the Central Conference of American Rabbis, vol. 20*, 109, AJA.

57. Ibid., 110. They also distributed accurate accounts of holy days to the press and tried to cancel the "requirement in many High Schools of the reading of *The Merchant of Venice*."

58. Frisch et al., *Year Book of the Central Conference of American Rabbis*, vol. 21, 79, AJA; "Abolish Jewish Caricature," *New York Times*, 26 March 1912, 9.

59. Tobias Schanfarber, "News and Views," *American Israelite*, October 20, 1910, 5.

60. Guttmacher and Rosenau, *Year Book of the Central Conference of American Rabbis*, vol. 14, 140, 153, AJA. The CCAR was concerned about any public display disrupting "unity of common citizenship into opposing factional creeds and sects" (152).

61. Marx, Morgenstern, and Heller, *Year Book of the Central Conference of American Rabbis*, vol. 20, 77–78, AJA. A B'nai B'rith member in Mobile, Alabama, wrote to a local theater manager, Gaston Neubrik, to complain about a Jewish pawnbroker— "Goldstein"—in the play, *Lost—24 Hours*. Neubrik responded, "Being a Jew myself, I never like or want to see the race caricatured and I am sincerely sorry that it unpleasantly occurred in this house" ("Caricaturing the Jew," *B'nai B'rith News*, October 10, 1908, 2). For another discussion of Jewish pawnbrokers, see "Pawnbroker's Daughter," *American Israelite*, July 3, 1913, 7.

62. "Jottings," *American Israelite*, September 22, 1910, 7.

63. Morgenstern, "A Review of the Month," *B'nai B'rith News*, September 1911, 11.

64. "More Stage Jew," *American Israelite*, August 5, 1909, 6; "Columbus and the Jews," *American Israelite*, July 18, 1912, 1. See also "The Jews and Modern Capitalism," *American Israelite*, December 15, 1913, 1.

65. "Acting Off the Stage," *American Israelite*, December 19, 1912, 4. Another writer similarly claimed, "It is a well-known fact that were it not for Jews' support there would be neither grand opera nor symphony orchestras in the United States and outside of vaudeville shows . . . there would be very few theatres" (*American Israelite*, February 1, 1912, 4).

66. *American Israelite*, August 24, 1916, 4. Considering Lubin's power, the *American Israelite* concluded that "the production of these offensive pictures can be stopped, but it can be done only by holding up to scorn the Jew who for profit permits his fellow Jews to be slandered" (*American Israelite*, August 24,1916, 4).

67. "Caricaturing the Jew," *B'nai B'rith News*, October 10, 1908, 2 The *American Israelite* also responded to charges that Jews controlled the mail-order business: "The

unfairness of the thing becomes apparent when we stop to consider that among the mail order houses there is but one that is known to be controlled by Jews, that is the Sears-Roebuck Co., at Chicago, whose head is fast gaining the reputation of being one of the greatest philanthropists of the country" (*American Israelite*, March 5, 1914, 4). In another case, the *American Israelite* claimed that Jewish managers could not be credited with the moral elevation or decay of the American stage: "They [Jewish managers] and their Christian contemporaries are merely the product of the times. The manager that does not select his plays with an eye on the box office does not exist" ("Acting Off the Stage," *American Israelite*, December 19, 1912, 4). Another article decried overgeneralizations in many different cases: "Not every German is an advocate of the open beer saloons on Sunday, nor do all Irishmen drink whiskey. All Jews are not in the clothing business, nor are all Catholics priest-ridden. Judging any class en masse is an exhibition of stupid prejudice" (*American Israelite*, October 15, 1914, 4).

68. "Report of the President of District Grand Lodge No. 6," May 17, 1908, quoted in Mantel, "The Anti-Defamation League of B'nai B'rith," 15. Moore, *B'nai B'rith*, 105.

69. Quoted in Moore, *B'nai B'rith*, 105.

70. Ibid., 106.

71. Rogow, *Gone to Another Meeting*; Golomb, "The 1893 Congress of Jewish Women"; Korelitz, "A Magnificent Piece of Work"; Gabaccia, *From the Other Side*, 82–83.

72. Council of Jewish Women, *Proceedings of the Fifth Triennial Convention*, 229.

73. Ibid., 225.

74. *Program of Work of the Council of Jewish Women Seventh Triennial Period, 1911–1914*, 116. National Council of Jewish Women Nearprint, box 1, AJA.

75. Dinnerstein, *The Leo Frank Case*, 74–76; Moore, *B'nai B'rith*107–8.

76. Cohen, *Not Free to Desist*, 29.

77. Moore, *B'nai B'rith*, 108; Dinnerstein, *The Leo Frank Case*.

78. "Anti-Defamation League," *B'nai B'rith News*, October 1913, "Conventions and Printed Materials, 1907–1917," series B, BBIA. See also Moore, *B'nai B'rith*, 108.

79. Ibid. See also Roche, *The Quest for the Dream*, 24.

80. Morgenstern, *Central Conference of American Rabbis: Twenty-Fifth Anniversary Convention*, vol. 24, 133, AJA.

81. Council of Jewish Women, *Official Report of the Ninth Triennial Convention*, 149. The NCJW was nevertheless proud of being "the only organization of women . . . cooperating with this league" (149).

82. *Moving Picture World*, April 18, 1914, 337; Brownlow, *Behind the Mask of Innocence*, 377.

83. "To the Producers of Motion Pictures," October 26, 1915, NBR.

84. Sable, "Some American Jewish Organizational Efforts," 242–44.

85. Louis Marshall to JH Stolper, July 12, 1916, Schiff Papers, AJA, quoted in Sable, "Some American Jewish Organizational Efforts," 196.

86. Moore comments that the only example of ADL censorship was its support for bans on anti-Semitic advertising and that it "rarely looked to legal remedies" (*B'nai B'rith*, 109). See also Sable, "Some American Jewish Organizational Efforts," 243; Roche, *The Quest for the Dream*, 95-97. Sable describes the ADL as a "vigorous" supporter of censorship, but mainly emphasizes protests against *The Merchant of Venice*.

87. "Founding Statement," *B'nai B'rith News*, October 1913, 1. The ADL targeted *The Master Cracksman* and *In the Clutches of Gangsters* in 1914. See *Motion Picture Bulletin*, no. 7 (September 3, 1914) and *Motion Picture Bulletin*, no. 9 (November 5, 1914). All from folder 10, box 2, Philipson.

88. *Report of the Anti-Defamation League* (1915), 6, BBIA.

89. *Report of the Anti-Defamation League* (1915), 13, BBIA. The ADL's survey is in appendix #4 of the 1915 report.

90. Kellogg, *NAACP*; Meier and Bracey, "The NAACP as a Reform Movement"; Carle, "Race, Class and Legal Ethics."

91. Kellogg, *NAACP*, 15.

92. Ibid., 58–59.

93. Ibid., 19.

94. Walling, "Race War in the North," quoted in Kellogg, *NAACP*, 11.

95. "The Task for the Future," *NAACP Ninth Annual Report* (1919), 80.

96. "Propaganda," *NAACP Fourth Annual Report* (New York, 1914), 15. In 1914 Spingarn similarly concluded: "Publicity is the breath of life to a movement whose main object is to alter public opinion" ("Report of the Chairman of the Board of Directors," *NAACP Fifth Annual Report* [1914], 5).

97. "Opinion: Insulting Terms," *Crisis*, January 1914, 126. See also "Veiled Insults," *Crisis*, April 1914, 287.

98. Lester Walton to the Associated Press, April 21, 1913, box 7, folder 1, Lester Walton Papers, Schomburg Center, New York Public Library (hereafter LWP).

99. Walton recounts the lack of progress in his letter to the New York Board of Education in 1916 (Walton to Honorable William G. Willcox, President of the New York City Board of Education, May 15, [1916], box 7, folder 1, LWP). It is significant that Willcox declined to raise the issue with the board. Walton was particularly critical of the *New York Times*: in 1918, he wrote to the newspaper about its "painful distinction" between "negroes" and "Chinamen" in a recent editorial (Lester Walton to the Editor of the *New York Times*, October 13, 1918, box 7, folder 1, LWP). See also "Negro," *Crisis*, December 1914.

100. ADL Appendix No. 16: "Note on the Word 'Jew,'" *Report of the Anti-Defamation League*, 1915, 80, 81, BBIA.

101. *Report of the Anti-Defamation League* (1915), 20, BBIA. See Sable, "Some American Jewish Organizations," 254–55.

102. The ADL explained that it had reached "many minds [which] would have been poisoned by the defamation"; the work ahead was arduous, though, because the "prejudice which distorts the public mind is the result of centuries of animosity." *Report of the Anti-Defamation League* (1915), 37, BBIA.

103. In 1909 Adolf Kraus, then president of B'nai B'rith, wrote to the manager of the Associated Press: "If A. B., a nonJew, commits a crime, the Associated Press dispatches furnish the public with the news without any reference as to whether he is a Methodist, a Catholic or whatever Christian denomination he may belong to. If, however, A. B. happens to be a Jew, then almost invariably the news item informs us that A. B. a Jew, etc., committed an offense. Is there any reason for making such a distinction?" ("A Step Forward," *American Israelite*, January 14, 1909, 5). The AP seems to have agreed to

Kraus's proposal, but other groups noted that the issue remained unresolved for newspapers in general. At the 1910 CCAR convention, the Committee on Church and State recommended that "whenever the word Jew is applied in the local press to malefactors, members of the Conference protest against this manifest injustice." Marx, Morgenstern and Heller, *Year Book of the Central Conference of American Rabbis*, vol. 20, 110, AJA.

104. "The Vigilance Committee: A Call to Arms," *Crisis*, May 1913, 28.

105. "Jack Johnson," *Crisis*, December 1912, 72.

106. "The Work of the Association's Branches," *NAACP Ninth Annual Report*,(1919) 68.

107. "The Gall of Bitterness," *Crisis*, February 1912, 153.

108. "Social Uplift," *Crisis*, March 1912, 9.

109. "Opinion," *Crisis*, September 1912, 233. In 1914, Du Bois noted that "all that we have, except Negro melody, is imitation" ("Negro Art," *Crisis*, May 1914, 17). See also "Opinion," *Crisis*, April 1913, 276.

110. Sylvester Russell, *Indianapolis Freeman*, quoted in Sampson, *The Ghost Walks*, 316.

111. Lester Walton, "Two Stage Forces," *New York Age*, December 24, 1908, 6–7; Lester Walton, "The Motion Picture Industry and the Negro," *New York Age*, June 5, 1913, quoted in Everett, *Returning the Gaze*, 29.

112. Castronovo, "Beauty along the Color Line."

113. "National Association for the Advancement of Colored People," *Crisis*, July 1913, 144.

114. Carle, "Race, Class, and Legal Ethics."

115. "Colored Folk in Theatres," *Crisis*, May 1912, 20; In August 1913, the *Crisis* referred to the New York branch's success in several other theater segregation cases ("Courts," *Crisis*, August 1913, 167).

116. Carle, "Race, Class, and Legal Ethics."

117. An African American man won $50 and court costs in his lawsuit against a California theater that refused to allow him to sit on the first floor. The *Crisis* bragged that this was the "first time that the owner or manager of a place of public amusement has been punished in southern California for violating the civil rights laws of the state" ("Courts," *Crisis*, September 1912, 221). See also "Courts," *Crisis*, January 1912, 100; "The Ghetto," *Crisis*, May 1914, 12; "Courts," *Crisis*, July 1914, 115.

118. Zangrando, *The NAACP Crusade against Lynching*, 31.

119. Waldrep, *African Americans Confront Lynching*, 67. Kellogg also concluded that "publicity following investigation was the most frequently used weapon in the fight against lynching" (Kellogg, *NAACP*, 214).

120. "Accomplishments," *NAACP First Annual Report* (1911), 8.

121. Lester Walton, "The Degeneracy of the Motion Picture Theatre," *New York Age*, August 5, 1909, quoted in Everett, *Returning the Gaze*, 20. Several years later, the association's focus on lynching expanded; it established a Committee on Anti-Lynching Programme in 1916, following the resurgence of the Ku Klux Klan, the glorification of the Klan in *The Birth of a Nation*, and the lynching of Leo Frank, which became a national case that outraged NAACP leaders. The NAACP combined its traditional publicity work with a new campaign for a federal anti-lynching law. In 1918, the NAACP backed two Republicans—Leonidas Dyer (of Missouri) and Merrill Moores (of Indi-

ana) to put forward an antilynching bill, which held that members of a mob could be prosecuted at the federal level for a capital crime, and that officials who did not protect the victim from lynchers could be fined and imprisoned. Although the NAACP succeeded in getting the bill through both the House and Senate, it never won passage of a federal antilynching law.

122. *Lexington Herald*, March 13, 1906, 5, quoted in Waller, *Main Street Amusements*, 45. See also Marshall, "The 1906 Uncle Tom's Cabin Law."

123. Strub, "Black and White and Banned All Over," 687.

124. Streible, "The History of the Boxing Film," 243.

125. 52nd Congress, 2nd session, Chapter 263, quoted in Streible, "The History of the Boxing Film,", 243–44.

126. *Congressional Record*, 62nd Congress, 2nd Session, July 1, 1912, quoted in Streible, "The History of the Boxing Film," 247.

127. Streible, "The History of the Boxing Film," 247.

128. Chenery, "The Guide Post," *Record Herald* [Chicago], quoted in Stokes, *D. W. Griffith's "The Birth of a Nation*," 133.

129. Lennig, "Myth and Fact," 123.

130. "Sixth Annual Report," *Crisis*, March 1916, 251. Nerney wrote that "all forms of censorship are dangerous to the free expression of art [but if a censorship board already existed] it was our right and our duty to see that this body acted with fairness and justice" (Nerney to "Our Branches and Locals," April 19, 1915, NAACPR, quoted in Cripps, *Slow Fade to Black*, 58).

131. Friedman, *Prurient Interests*, 145, 140–41.

132. *Report of the Anti-Defamation League* (1915), 5, BBIA.

133. James Weldon Johnson, "Uncle Tom's Cabin and the Clansman," quoted in Everett, *Returning the Gaze*, 69.

134. Oliver and Walker, "James Weldon Johnson's 'New York Age' Essays," 5.

135. "Hotel Advertisement Bill/Motion Picture Legislation" [1914], file: "ADL: Motion Pictures," BBIA. (This collection was previously held at the B'nai B'rith Klutznick National Jewish Museum). This document lists the legislative sessions for fourteen states; at this point, the ADL was preparing to lobby all fourteen to pass both bills.

136. *Report of the Anti-Defamation League* (1915), 54, BBIA.

137. Ibid., 7.

138. "ADL Bulletin" No. 3 [1915–16?] folder 10, box 2, Philipson. In 1914 the ADL lobbied the District of Columbia to establish a board of censors that would ban insulting portrayals of any "creed or race" ("Film and Stage Rule," *Washington Post*, March 10, 1914, 4).

139. "An Act" [1914], file: "ADL Motion Pictures," BBIA.

140. Goldstein, *The Price of Whiteness*, 88–89.

141. Ibid.

142. Ibid., 89.

143. MacGregor, "Official Censorship Legislation," 166–68. In 1913, Ohio created the Ohio Board of Censors as part of the Industrial Commission. Kansas gave its superintendent of public instruction the power to censor motion pictures in 1913, and in 1917 established the Kansas Board of Review.

144. *Executive Committee Report*, ADL, Chicago, November 1914, quoted in Sable, "Some American Jewish Organizational Efforts," 248. A letter from Columbia University to the ADL in December 1913 refers to the ADL's bill "regulating the censorship of moving pictures films" (J. P. Chamberlain to Anti-Defamation League, December 15, 1913, file: "ADL Motion Pictures," BBIA).

145. "Film stories or scenes holding up to ridicule and reproach races, classes or other social groups will be disapproved as well as the irreverent and sacrilegious treatment of religious bodies or other things held to be sacred. The materialization of the figure of Christ may be condemned" (quoted in Saylor, "The Pennsylvania State Board of Censors," 15). Later the word "race" dropped out, but still seems to be included in the category. See the list of Pennsylvania's censorship standards including the ban on ridicule of "any sect (religious or otherwise)" (*Pennsylvania State Board of Censors of Motion Pictures Rules and Standards* [1915], 15; "Censor Board Lays Down Standards" *Motography*, December 18, 1915, 1293). See also Saylor, "Pennsylvania State Board of Censors," 14–15. Similarly, Kansas's general rules included: "Ridicule of any religious sect or peculiar characteristics of any race of people will not be approved." Ohio banned movies with "national, class or racial hatred" (The 1962 *International Motion Picture Almanac*, quoted in Carmen, *Movies, Censorship, and the Law*, 178). See also *Motion Picture Censors' and Reviewers' Manual* (1934). It lists Maryland, Pennsylvania, and Portland as banning racial ridicule in motion pictures.

146. "Censor Board Standards," *Film Year Book, 1922–1923*, 338–39. "Anti-Jewish Defamation League" [*sic*] lobbied the Maryland Board to make many cuts from films based on that rule, according to the board in 1922. Letter to Governor Albert C. Ritchie 1922, Papers of the Maryland Board of Censors, State Archives of Maryland, Annapolis. See Smith, "Patrolling the Boundaries of Race," 277.

147. Haberski and Wittern-Keller, *The Miracle Case*, 27; Robinson, "In the Year 1915."

148. Bernstein, *Screening a Lynching*, 17.

149. Ibid., 20.

150. Atlanta barred any Frank films that included images of the lynching or the funeral. Censors explained that they were acting after "prominent officials and citizens complained to us about the pictures, and declared that their being run would be a lack of consideration for the feelings of many people in Atlanta" ("Atlanta Bars Frank Pictures," *Moving Picture World*, September 11, 1915, 1858). See also Bernstein, *Screening a Lynching*, 19.

151. "Leo Frank Pictures Barred," *Moving Picture World*, October 9, 1915, 304.

152. "No Frank Films in Spokane," *Moving Picture World*, September 11, 1915, 1860.

153. Bernstein, *Screening a Lynching*, 19. The movie was also banned in Louisville, Kentucky. See *Moving Picture World*, April 27, 1915, 1952, quoted in Brownlow, *Behind the Mask of Innocence*, 378–79. In May of 1915, while Frank's case was under appeal, Kansas City prohibited all pictures related to the case because the city did not allow movies that exploited "famous criminal cases." The Kansas City censors noted that recent Frank pictures had depicted the "negro" as the murderer ("Kansas Censors Willard," *Moving Picture World*, May 29, 1914, 1458).

154. "Rejected, 1910–1930," box 72, Chicago Board of Motion Picture Censor Re-

cords (CMPCB), Illinois Regional Archive Depository, Northeastern Illinois University, Chicago.

155. "Movie on Frank Case Forbidden by City Censors" *Chicago Tribune*, May 23, 1915, 1.

156. A newsreel by *Gaumont News* showed Frank's hanging body. Bernstein, *Screening a Lynching*, 19. See Brownlow, *Behind the Mask of Innocence*, 378–79.

157. "Moving Picture Shows Freed from Offensive Characterization," *American Israelite*, December 2, 1915.

158. *Moving Picture World*, September 18, 1915, 2126, quoted in Brownlow, *Behind the Mask of Innocence*, 379. Minutes of the Executive Committee Meeting, AJC, September 20, 1915, American Jewish Committee Archives, quoted in Sable, "Some American Jewish Organizational Efforts," 14. Some accounts do not mention Jewish pressure. See "Police Bar Frank Pictures," *Moving Picture World*, September 18, 1915, 2026.

159. See Wood, *Lynching and Spectacle*, 148. The efforts to censor both movies in St. Louis are covered in articles on the same page in the *Moving Picture World*, September 18, 1915, 2024.

160. *Indianapolis Freeman*, August 28, 1915, 4, quoted in Sampson, *Blacks in Black and White*, 156. See also Melnick, *Black-Jewish Relations*.

161. Robinson, "In the Year 1915."

162. Mary Childs Nerney to Mr. S. P. Keeble, Cleveland NAACP, April 9, 1915, NAACPR.

163. "Country Given New Kind of Negro," *Evansville Courier*, December 11, 1915, clipping, folder: "Films and Plays—Birth of a Nation, December 1915." C-301, NAACPR.

164. Mary Childs Nerney to Rabbi Rudolph Coffee, June 7, 1915, folder: "Films and Plays—Birth of a Nation, June 1–10, 1915," C-300, NAACPR.

165. *New York News-Courier*, March 31, 1915, quoted in Schickel, *D. W. Griffith*, 285–86; Diner, *In the Almost Promised Land*, 134.

166. *Indianapolis Freeman*, August 28, 1915, 4, quoted in Sampson, *Blacks in Black and White*, 156.

167. Wood, *Lynching and Spectacle*, 164–65.

168. Everett, *Returning the Gaze*, 63

169. "Fighting Race Calumny," *Crisis*, June 1915, 88. The *Crisis* also reprinted the direct question, posed by a critic of *The Birth of a Nation*: "Is lynching Negroes immoral?" The answer, for this author, was, regrettably, that the anti-Negro features of film affirmed lynching ("Opinions," *Crisis*, June 1915, 71).

170. "The Birth of a Nation" and "Lynching," *Crisis*, June 1915, 69–72. Anna Everett recounts many other examples in *Returning the Gaze*, 103.

171. "Negro Protest Stops Film Play," *Public Ledger*, August 14, 1915, quoted in Stokes, *D. W. Griffith's "The Birth of a Nation,"* 159.

172. Nerney to W. L. Sledge, September 8, 1915, folder, "Films and Plays—Birth of a Nation, September 1915," C-300, NAACPR.

173. Stokes, *D. W. Griffith's "The Birth of a Nation,"* 154. Griffith got an injunction and the movie's run continued in Philadelphia. The judge said, "their [negroes'] judgement should not be the rule as many spoken plays could be criticized by other races because of reflections on race and nationality" ("Court Lifts Ban upon 'The Birth of a Nation,'"

Philadelphia *North American*, September 5, 1915, 13, quoted in Fleener-Marzec, *D. W. Griffith's The Birth of a Nation*, 114.

174. Malcolm Davis to Mary Childs Nerney, n. d., folder: "Films and Plays—Birth of a Nation—undated," C-301, NAACPR.

175. In 1921, James Weldon Johnson wrote of a protest in which the demonstration "was not to create violence but to protest against the kind of violence to which 'The Birth of a Nation' gives rise, [so] that the NAACP took action" ("Statement by James W. Johnson," May 7, 1921, folder: "Films and Plays—Birth of a Nation—1921," C-301, NAACPR).

176. *Epoch v. Davis*, quoted in Fleener-Marzec, *D. W. Griffith's The Birth of a Nation*, 122.

177. "Dr. Krauskopf and Motion Pictures Censorship," *Jewish Exponent*, June 25, 1915, 8.

178. Kansas censored a newsreel of Frank's lynching in 1915. And, in December 1915, Kansas also banned Griffith's film because it presented African Americans as negative characters and encouraged racial hatred. In addition, it found the film sexually suggestive, historically inaccurate, and likely to cause sectional strife ("Birth of a Nation Rejected by State Movie Censors," *Topeka Daily Capital*, January 25, 1916, quoted in Butters, *Banned in Kansas*, 85–86).

179. "The New Governor, Eliminations," folder 4, box 4, Pennsylvania State Board of Censors (Motion Pictures), RG 22, Pennsylvania State Archives, Harrisburg, Pennsylvania (hereafter PSBC). Two years later the board also cut "nigger" from *Jim Bludso*.

180. "Pennsylvania State Board of Censors (Motion Picture), List of Condemnations and Eliminations, Week Ending December 24, 1915," file: "ADL: Motion Pictures," BBIA.

181. Saylor, "The Pennsylvania State Board of Censors (Motion Pictures)"; folder 1, "Movie censorship, outgoing correspondence, 1915–1920," box 2, Ellis Paxson Oberholtzer Papers, Historical Society of Pennsylvania, Philadelphia.

182. "Phoenix, Ariz., Commission Is Censor Board," *Chicago Defender*, June 19, 1915, 4.

183. "An Ordinance to Prohibit the Exhibition of Any Moving Picture Likely to Cause Ill-Feeling between the White and Black Races," June 8, 1915, C-300, NAACPR, quoted in Fleener-Marzec, *D. W. Griffith's The Birth of a Nation*, 330.

184. "Tacoma City Ordinance No. 6178," August 12, 1914, C-300, NAACPR, quoted in Fleener-Marzec, *D. W. Griffith's The Birth of a Nation*, 330.

185. "St. Paul," *Appeal*, November 6, 1915, 4, quoted in Fleener-Marzec, *D. W. Griffith's The Birth of a Nation*, 331. Wichita's 1923 ordinance also included only "race."

186. Fleener-Marzec, *D. W. Griffith's The Birth of a Nation*, 330–31.

187. Ibid., 109.

188. "The Clansman," *Western Outlook*, quoted in Fleener-Marzec, *D. W. Griffith's The Birth of a Nation*, 111–12.

189. Mary Childs Nerney to W. L. Sledge, September 8, 1915, folder: "Films and Plays—Birth of a Nation, September 1915," C-300, NAACPR.

190. *Nixon Theatre Company v. Joseph Armstrong*, folder 1, box 10, PSBC. Fleener-Marzec notes that four judges rejected the idea that *Birth of a Nation* should be censored because of racial stereotypes (*D. W. Griffith's Birth of a Nation*, 109–18).

191. *McCarthy v. Chicago* (1915), 2, file: "Birth of a Nation," NBR. See also Fleener-Marzec, *D. W. Griffith's The Birth of a Nation*, 113.

192. "Protests against 'Birth of a Nation,'" *Baltimore Ledger*, August 7, 1915, 1, quoted in Fleener-Marzec, *D. W. Griffith's The Birth of a Nation*, 240. In St. Paul police would not intervene because the law called for the suppression of movies that were "immoral or obscene," not racially insulting. Protesters then charged that the entire film was immoral, and won several cuts from the film. See exchange about St. Paul, including letter to Nerney, August 31, 1915, in "Films and Plays—Birth of a Nation, October 1915," C–300, NAACPR.

193. Joseph Prince Loud to Miss Nerney, April 15, 1915, folder, "Films and Plays—Birth of a Nation April 1915," C–300, NAACPR.

194. Fleener-Marzec, *D. W. Griffith's The Birth of a Nation*, 234.

195. "Judge Refuses to Stop 'Birth of a Nation' Film," *Boston Evening Globe*, April 21, 1915, 2, quoted in Fleener-Marzec, *D. W. Griffith's The Birth of a Nation*, 108.

196. Ibid.

197. Lennig, "Myth and Fact," 126.

198. Cripps, *Slow Fade to Black*, 59.

199. Fleener-Marzec, *D. W. Griffith's The Birth of a Nation*, 222.

200. Weinberger, "The Birth of a Nation and the Making of the NAACP." See also Sullivan, *Lift Every Voice*, 49–50.

201. Cripps, *Slow Fade to Black*, 66.

202. Zangrando, *The NAACP Crusade against Lynching*, 41.

203. Ibid., 35.

204. Moore, *B'nai B'rith*, 102, 114.

CHAPTER FIVE

1. Earlier laws censored prize-fighting films, but they did not address films broadly. See Orbach, "Prizefighting and the Birth of Movie Censorship."

2. The Chicago Municipal Code of 1922, quoted in Jowett, "Moral Responsibility and Commercial Entertainment," 4. Kraus is identified as the author of the law in the *Chicago Motion Picture Commission Report* (1920). Kraus served on this commission, which convened in 1918. See Haberski, "Reel Life, Reel Censorship," 14.

3. *Chicago Motion Picture Commission Report*, 98. The founding Chicago censors interpreted the law as the protection of many races. One censor explained: "Are all the Jews Shylocks or money grubbers? Are all Irishmen drunkards or wife beaters? Are all Germans pot-bellied beer drinkers? Are all negroes razor wielders or chicken stealers? Rather than instill in the child mind, or even the adult mind a stronger dislike he may already have toward those of different nationality, race or creed, let us portray the Jew, Irishman, German, negro and others at their best" ("What a Censor Thinks of It," *Motography*, March 7, 1914, 168). Sergeant Jeremiah O'Connor, the first police officer in charge of motion picture censorship, explained that Chicago censors "have to be absolutely free from prejudice as to race and religion, for no nationality will be debased, nor a monkey made of a priest, minister or other representative of any religious teaching" (Mabel Condon, "How the Chicago Censor Board Works," *Motography*, March 15, 1913, 197).

4. *Hearings before the Committee on Education* (1914), 100.

5. Lindstrom, "Getting a Hold Deeper in the Life of the City," 10. By 1908 the number of licensed nickelodeons in Chicago reached 320. The trend dramatically increased to 606 in 1913, after which the number of nickelodeons declined, giving way to larger movie palaces. See also Luckett, *Cinema and Community*. Luckett notes that Chicago censorship was particularly important because the city was the distribution hub for movies in the Midwest and the West (*Cinema and Community*, 19).

6. McCarthy, "Nickel Vice and Virtue," 40.

7. Rabinovitz, *For the Love of Pleasure*, 122–32.

8. Lindstrom, "'Almost Worse Than the Restrictive Measures,'" 100.

9. Rabinovitz, *For the Love of Pleasure*, 131.

10. "Film Shows Busy; Panic Stops One," *Chicago Tribune*, April 15, 1907, 1, 4.

11. Lindstrom, "'Almost Worse Than the Restrictive Measures,'" 103; McCarthy, "Nickel Vice and Virtue," 38; and Uricchio and Pearson, *Reframing Culture*, 36–38.

12. Lindstrom, "'Almost Worse Than the Restrictive Measures,'" 95-98. Rabinovitz, *For the Love of Pleasure*, 134–35.

13. Rabinovitz, *For the Love of Pleasure*, 122–32. Couvares, "The Good Censor."

14. *Jake Block et al. vs. The City of Chicago* (1909), in *Reports of Cases at Law and in Chancery Argued and Determined in the Supreme Court of Illinois*, (1909), 258.

15. McCarthy, "Nickel Vice and Virtue," 46–47. Luckett argues that the period from 1913 to 1917 is the period of highest visibility for the censorship board; this corresponds, roughly, to Jewish involvement (*Cinema and Community*, 171).

16. Lewis Jacobs writes, "In 1914 the movie business was at a turning point in its development" (*Rise of American Film*, 160).

17. Gabler, *An Empire of Their Own*, 59.

18. May, *Screening Out the Past*, 169.

19. Ibid., 63.

20. Gabler, *An Empire of Their Own*, 59.

21. Ibid.

22. Erens, *The Jew in American Cinema*, 37; Friedman, *Hollywood's Image of the Jew*, 19.

23. Patricia Erens suggests that that traditional "scheming merchant" was not punished in early comedies because "men like Sigmund Lubin and Gilbert Anderson and others were themselves Jews" (*The Jew in American Cinema*, 37). The historian Lester Friedman concludes: "How could L. B. Mayer or Jack Warner not treat a movie that portrayed a significant aspect of his life or racial history differently from a picture about black sharecroppers?" (*Hollywood's Image of the Jew*, 9). See also Cripps, "The Movie Jew as an Image of Assimilation," 191. Friedman explains: "Unlike films about other American minorities, movies with Jews were often scrutinized by one segment of that minority group with the power to decide how the entire group would be presented to society as a whole" (*Hollywood's Image of the Jew*, 3).

24. Sorin, *Tradition Transformed*, 64.

25. Gems, "Sport and the Forging of a Jewish-American Culture,"15; Mazur, "Jewish Chicago," 264.

26. Sorin, *Tradition Transformed*, 22.

27. Sinai executive board minutes, September 28, 1885, quoted in Mazur, "Jewish Chicago," 270.

28. Sorin, *Tradition Transformed*, 25.

29. Mandel, in 1900, was the second vice president of the National Council of Jewish Women. Purvin, also involved in the NCJW, was the daughter of German immigrants ("Jennie Franklin Purvin, 1873–1958," *Jewish Women: A Comprehensive Historical Encyclopedia*, Jewish Women's Archive, JWA.org); Hannah Solomon was the first president of the NCJW ("Hannah Greenbaum Solomon, 1858–1942," *Jewish Women's Archive*, JWA.org).

30. "Jews Join War on Theater," *Chicago Tribune*, April 5, 1913, 3.

31. "Gallery of Local Celebrities," *Chicago Tribune*, August 12, 1900, 51. For another example of Jewish support for Mayor Harrison, see Skinner, "Henry Horner," 160. Kraus is described as a staunch Democrat in *Prominent Democrats of Illinois*, 358–59.

32. Moore, *B'nai B'rith*, 102–3; Cutler, *The Jews of Chicago*, 164–65.

33. Kraus, *Reminiscences and Comments*, 177.

34. Anderson, "Prostitution and Social Justice," 208; see also Kraus, *Reminiscences and Comments*, 178.

35. Kraus, *Reminiscences and Comments*, 178.

36. Barnes, "The Story of the Committee of Fifteen," 146. The Committee took a controversial stand against segregating vice, favoring instead the complete repression of prostitution.

37. Anderson, "Prostitution and Social Justice," 217.

38. Vande Haar, "Harvey Ingham."

39. "Will Be Riots Here—Dixon," *New York Times*, September 24, 1906, 2; "Drama Inspires Negro Lynching," *Chicago Tribune*, October 30, 1905, 4; "The Rights of Playwrights," *Chicago Tribune*, October 27, 1906, 10.

40. Mack and Pam nominated Eva Loeb for the "Jewish" spot on the civilian censorship board. And Pam joined Kraus on the Jewish jury for *The Merchant of Venice*.

41. "Social Workers to Censor Shows," *Chicago Tribune*, May 3, 1907, 3.

42. Nancy Reis, "In the World of Jewish Womanhood," *Reform Advocate*, April 8, 1916, 265.

43. Kraus, Israel Cowan, Philip Stein, and Mrs. Herman Landauer protested the proposal to change the censorship board from ten citizens to three, appointed by the mayor ("Shot at Censors Rouse Protest," *Chicago Tribune*, March 4, 1914, 3).

44. Hannah Solomon represented "women's clubs" on the Chicago Motion Picture Commission in 1920.

45. "Funkhouser as Morals Guardian," *Chicago Tribune*, March 21, 1913, 2.

46. "A Prudish Old Maid," *Motography*, December 13, 1913, 418.

47. "Funkhouserism," *Motography*, February 7, 1914, 89; the extreme censorship, according to movie producers, was making Chicago a "laughing stock" ("Chicago Kills and Cutouts," *Motography*, August 1, 1914, 160).

48. Funkhouser sought out businessmen to "arrive at a standard of censorship for motion pictures" ("'Animal Dances' Called Danger," *Chicago Tribune*, October 17, 1913, 8); and members of the Chicago Woman's club viewed Funkhouser's cuts approvingly on January 28, 1914 ("Women Indorse Maj. Funkhouser's Movie 'Cut Outs,'" *Chicago*

Tribune, January 29, 1914, 15); "Police Censors Unchanged," *Motography*, May 3, 1913, 332.

49. "Motion Picture Bulletin," no. 10, November 6, 1914, folder 10, box 2, Philipson.

50. *Report of the Anti-Defamation League* (1915), 9, BBIA.

51. "Women Oppose Film O.K. on 'Twilight Sleep,'" *Chicago Tribune*, April 4, 1915, 12; "Favoritism Over, Funkhouser Says," *Chicago Tribune*, March 13, 1914, 3.

52. "Urge Good Shows as Blow to Vice," *Chicago Tribune*, February 9, 1914, 5.

53. Funkhouser remembers February 1914. See *Chicago Motion Picture Commission Report*, 83.

54. "Picks 5 Women as Film Censors," *Chicago Tribune*, February 17, 1914, 1.

55. James McQuade, "Chicago Letter," *Moving Picture World*, March 7, 1914, 1245.

56. Funkhouser seems to be remembering incorrectly. The civilian board had not yet been formed at this point. It was established in mid-February 1914.

57. *Chicago Motion Picture Commission Report*, 86.

58. "Bars Film Ridiculing Jews," *Chicago Tribune*, January 24, 1914, 3.

59. Ibid.

60. "Film Manager Flails Censor," *Chicago Tribune*, February 1, 1914, 10.

61. James McQuade, "Chicago Letter," *Moving Picture World*, March 7, 1914, 1245.

62. *Anti-Defamation League Bulletin*, no. 2, folder 10, box 2, Philipson. The movie was denied a permit in Chicago on January 23, 1914 (*Report of the ADL* [1915], 45–46, BBIA).

63. "Film Manager Flails Censor," *Chicago Tribune*, February 1, 1914, 10.

64. "Women Support Funkhouser in Censorship of Films," *Chicago Tribune*, January 9, 1914, 9; see also "Women Indorse Maj. Funkhouser's Movie 'Cut Outs,'" *Chicago Tribune*, January 29, 1914, 15.

65. "Women Censors See Twelve Reels; Indorse Two Cuts," *Chicago Tribune*, February 20, 1914, 1.

66. "Citizens Bar Slave Film," *Chicago Tribune*, March 11, 1914, 3. She also represented "club women" when she lobbied the major to uphold the ban on *Twilight Sleep* ("Women Oppose Film O.K. on 'Twilight Sleep,'" *Chicago Tribune*, April 4, 1915, 12). Solomon also supported movie censorship not always as a Jewish woman, but as a representative of the Woman's City Club ("Blame Cutouts on Law, Not Him, The Major Says," *Chicago Tribune*, November 24, 1917, 5).

67. *Chicago Motion Picture Commission Report*, 82.

68. Friedman, *Prurient Interests*, 129.

69. Ibid. Similarly, in 1911 the Los Angeles Board of Censorship included five members. One had to appointed by the Board of Education and Civic League, "an organization of women interested in prevention of immorality" ("Board of Censors," *Los Angeles Times*, June 21, 1911, I12).

70. "Kansas Women Will Censor All Films," *Christian Science Monitor*, April 6, 1917, 8. See also James McQuade, "Chicago Letter," *Moving Picture World*, March 7, 1914, 1244.

71. Grieveson, *Policing Cinema*, 101; "Facts and Comments" *Moving Picture World*, January 31, 1914, 519.

72. James McQuade, "Chicago Letter," *Moving Picture World*, February 21, 1914, 959. Critics also accused him of catering to the "suffragette vote" ("Funkhouserism," *Motography*, February 7, 1914, 89).

73. "Philip Stein, Former Superior Court Judge, Dies; Career Notable," *Chicago Tribune*, December 26, 1922, 17.

74. "'Movie' Censors Learning Fast," *Chicago Tribune*, February 19, 1914, 3.

75. James McQuade, "Chicago Letter," *Moving Picture World*, March 7, 1914, 1245.

76. "Women Censors See Twelve Reels; Endorse Two Cuts," *Chicago Tribune*, February 20, 1914, 1.

77. *Report of the Anti-Defamation League* (1915), 9, BBIA.

78. ADL Executive Committee Letter, January 27, 1914, *Report of the Anti-Defamation League* (1915), 46, BBIA.

79. The ADL referred to both movies in *Anti-Defamation League Bulletin*, no. 2 (1914?), 1, folder 10, box 2, Philipson; James McQuade, "Chicago Letter," *Moving Picture World*, March 14, 1914, 1389; "'September Morn' Copper Goes Back to Street Duty," *Chicago Tribune*, February 28, 1914, 9.

80. "Growing Menace of Chicago Censors," *Motography*, October 3, 1914, 461.

81. "Motion Picture Section—City of Chicago," November 27, 1918, in *Chicago Motion Picture Commission Report*, 183.

82. "Motion Picture Bulletin," no. 8, in *Report of the Anti-Defamation League* (1915), 46, BBIA. This bulletin describes the Chicago Board of Censors' rejection of *The Master Cracksman* in August 1914.

83. "Motion Picture Bulletin," no. 6 (June 10, 1914) in *Report of the Anti-Defamation League* (1915), 11, 19, 50, BBIA. *Great Mysteries of New York* was censored on January 29, 1915, because the picture showed methods of criminals, gruesome scenes of violence, drugging a woman and leading her to a criminal life, without teaching any moral lesson. In 1921 Chicago also rejected *The Winning Hand* because it contained a series of lawless acts and makes a hero of a criminal ("Rejected, 1910–1930," box 72, CBMPC).

84. "Growing Menace of Chicago Censors," *Motography*, October 3, 1914, 459. The rejection is from September 2, 1914.

85. "Motion Picture Bulletin," no. 7, (September 3, 1914), folder 10, box 2, Philipson. *In the Clutches of Gangsters* was also denied a permit in Chicago in November 1914. The ADL objected to the film because it "contained two criminal characters—the worst in the gang—who were described, and intended to represent, men of the Jewish faith" ("Motion Picture Bulletin," no. 9 [November 5, 1914], folder 10, box 2, Philipson). The ADL also complained to the Majestic Motion Picture Company about its movie, *The Surgeon's Experiment*, in which the "fence" is "made up as a Jew, and indulges in the mannerisms and idiosyncracies usually coupled with impersonations of a Jewish pawnbroker on the burlesque stage" (Leon Lewis to Majestic Motion Picture Co., June 20, 1914, in *Report of the Anti-Defamation League* [1915], 59, BBIA). The ADL report alleged that the censors also objected to the misrepresentation of Jews, but there is no evidence of this in the censor files ("Rejected, 1910-1930," box 72, CBMPC).

86. "Major Funkhouser, Must We Take Samson to a Barber Shop?" *Chicago Tribune*, February 15, 1914, 6.

87. "Mister Funkhouser, Do You Realize What a Big Man You Are?" *Chicago Tribune*, February 18, 1914, 8.

88. Laemmle described "the awful spectacle presented here on Thursday when he invited an audience composed wholly of Jews to witness Shakespeare's immortal clas-

sic, "The Merchant of Venice," and in effect said to them "If *you* think it's all right, I'll let the *rest* of Chicago see it" ("Funkhouser's Cry of 'Wolf!' Fools the Villagers," *Chicago Tribune*, February 20, 1914, 8).

89. "Funkhouser's Cry of 'Wolf!' Fools the Villagers," *Chicago Tribune*, February 20, 1914, 8.

90. Ibid.

91. "Major Funkhouser, Must We Take Samson to a Barber Shop?" *Chicago Tribune*, February 15, 1914, 6.

92. ADL Executive Committee to Carl Laemmle, March 12, 1914, file: "ADL: Motion Pictures," BBIA.

93. "Funkhouser Denounced," *Motography*, February 7, 1914, 97.

94. "Funkhouserism," *Motography*, February 7, 1914, 90.

95. "Urge Good Shows as Blow to Vice," *Chicago Tribune*, February 9, 1914, 5.

96. "Rejected, 1910–1930'," box 72, CBMPC. *Motography* reported a rejection from July 8, 1914: "*His Trade* [Lubin] Permit refused because picture is a reflection on the Jewish race by showing how Jewish glazier gives boys balls to break windows within in order to secure business" ("Weird Stunts of Our Censor Board" *Motography*, August 1, 1914, 152).

97. "Motion Picture Bulletin," no. 10 (November 6, 1914), folder 10, box 2, Philipson.

98. *Report of the Anti-Defamation League* (1915), 11, BBIA.

99. "Motion Picture Bulletin," no. 10 (November 6, 1914), folder 10, box 2, Philipson.

100. *Anti-Defamation League Bulletin*, no. 2, folder 10, box 2, Philipson.

101. *Report of the Anti-Defamation League* (1915), 61–62, BBIA.

102. *Anti-Defamation League Bulletin*, no. 2, folder 10, box 2, Philipson.

103. "'September Morn' Copper Goes Back to Street Duty," *Chicago Tribune*, February 28, 1914, 9.

104. McQuade, "Chicago Letter," *Moving Picture World*, March 14, 1914, 1389.

105. "Rejected, 1910-1930," box 72, CBMPC.

106. "Weird Stunts of Our Censor Board," *Motography*. August 1, 1914, 153.

107. *A Bicycle Bug's Dream* was also banned on August 7, 1914, because it reflected poorly on a minister ("Rejected, 1910–1930," box 72, CBMPC). For other cuts, see "Censors Slash Doubtful Film," *Chicago Tribune*, February 21, 1914, 3; "September Morn Copper Goes Back to Street Duty," *Chicago Tribune*, February 28, 1914, 9.

108. "Pertinent Story in Headlines," *Chicago Defender*, March 7, 1914, 1.

109. "States Theatre Displays Vile Race Pictures," *Chicago Defender*, May 30, 1914, 1.

110. "'Hit the Nigger' New Film Insult," *Chicago Defender*, February 28, 1914, 1.

111. Stewart, *Migrating to the Movies*, 121.

112. *Chicago Defender*, January 29, 1910, quoted in Spear, *Black Chicago*, 122–23.

113. Reed, *The Chicago NAACP*, 43.

114. "Representation Everywhere," *Chicago Defender*, February 21, 1914, 4.

115. "Race Still Has No Representative on Film Censor Board," *Chicago Defender*, March 14, 1914, 1.

116. Spear, *Black Chicago*, 64. See also Baldwin, *Chicago's New Negroes*, 125; and Regester, "Black Films, White Censors."

117. "Growing Menace of Chicago Censors," *Motography*, October 3, 1914, 461.

118. "Funkhouser to Preach at Institutional Church," *Chicago Defender*, April 18, 1914, 1. African American groups, such as the Appomattox Club, worked to get an African American on the censorship board ("Frank Hamilton to Stir Up Civic Committee," *Chicago Defender*, March 14, 1914, 4).

119. "Bowling Appointed Movie Picture Censor," *Chicago Defender*, March 20, 1915, 1; "Race Again Has Member on Censor Board," *Chicago Defender*, May 8, 1915, 1. One activist lobbied the New York governor to include an African American on the censorship board in 1921: "[He] is of the Colored race which has suffered cruel misrepresentation in many moving pictures. . . . But some might ask, Why a colored man on the Board. Would not a white man serve justice just as well? The answer is 'A white man might see the danger in a picture submitted and then again he might not: but a colored man would put his finger on it at once" (Thomas O'Keefe, Pastor, Church of St. Benedict the Moor to Honorable Nathan Miller, April 7, 1921, Miller Central Subject and Correspondence Files, Box 9, folder Motion Picture Legislation, Motion Picture Division, New York State Archives [hereafter NYMPD]). See also Charles W. Anderson to Gov Miller, April 1, 1921, folder: "Motion Picture Legislation," box 9, NYMPD.

120. "Mayor's Wife O.K.'s Birth of a Nation Obnoxious Movie,' *Chicago Defender*, April 3, 1915, 1. Mrs. Harrison later denied her role in this process. See James McQuade, "Chicago Letter," *Moving Picture World*, May 22, 1915, 1264. See also Ross, "D. W. Griffith v. City Hall."

121. James McQuade, "Chicago Letter," *Moving Picture World*, April 10, 1915, 219.

122. "Mayor's Wife O.K.'s Birth of a Nation Obnoxious Movie," *Chicago Defender*, April 3, 1915, 1.

123. Kitty Kelly, "Flickerings from Film Land," *Chicago Tribune*, June 5, 1915, 14.

124. James McQuade, "Chicago Letter," *Moving Picture World*, June 26, 1915, 2079.

125. James McQuade, "Chicago Letter," *Moving Picture World*, June 12, 1915, 1758; James McQuade, "Chicago Letter," *Moving Picture World*, May 29, 1915, 1416.

126. James McQuade, "Chicago Letter," *Moving Picture World*, June 26, 1915, 2079.

127. James McQuade, "Chicago Letter," *Moving Picture World*, June 12, 1915, 1758.

128. Ibid., 1759.

129. Kitty Kelly, "Emotion Rocked Crowd Watches Birth of a Nation," *Chicago Tribune*, June 6, 1915, A1.

130. *McCarthy v. Chicago*, qtd. in Marzec, *D. W. Griffith's The Birth of a Nation*, 113.

131. Scott, "'Black Censor,' White Liberties," 226.

132. Reed, *The Chicago NAACP*, 41.

133. *House Debates* (1915), 269, quoted in Scott, "Black 'Censor,' White Liberties," 229.

134. "Jews Wage Battle on Stage Caricature," *Chicago Tribune*, September 3, 1913, 9. See also Scott, "Black 'Censor,' White Liberties," 234–36.

135. Scott, "Black 'Censor,' White Liberties," 235.

136. "Illinois Film Men Urge Governor to Veto Censor Law," *Motion Picture News*, July 10, 1913, 63; "Illinois Censor Bill hearing," *Motion Picture World*, July 10, 1915, 287.

137. Scott, "Black 'Censor,' White Liberties," 236.

138. "Movie Censor Chief 'Jumped' over Two Women," *Chicago Tribune*, March 17, 1916, 13. In this case, the mayor criticized Funkhouser for showing movie "cut outs"

to members of the Anti-Cruelty Society. For descriptions of Mayor Thompson, see Luckett, *Cinema and Community*, 173, 198.

139. "Plan New Move to Cut Powers of Funkhouser," *Chicago Tribune*, April 22, 1916, 14.

140. "Film Censors May Lose Jobs; Fixers Foiled," *Chicago Tribune*, April 13, 1917, 12. The article reported that Harry Igel, "a city hall 'negotiator' for several big film companies," had very friendly dealings with the new board.

141. Ibid. *Motography* reported a decline in Funkhouser's power as well, noting that the mayor, the mayor's wife, and the mayor's secretary had issued their own permits ("Chicago's New Administration," *Motography*, April 24, 1915, 651).

142. "Steffen Moves to Curb Power of Funkhouser," *Chicago Tribune*, September 25, 1917, 15.

143. Ross, "D. W. Griffith v. City Hall," 28.

144. Alsace, "Rejected, 1910–1930," box 72, CMPCB. In 1915 Funkhouser was accused of suppressing a film—*It's a Long Way to Tipperary*—because it was not neutral toward Germany. It featured two Irishmen fighting the Germans ("Is Funkhouser a German?" *Motography*, February 6, 1915, 192).

145. *Life Photo Film Corporation v. Bell* (1915) in *The Miscellaneous Reports: New York (State) Superior Court*, 471.

146. *Ibid.*, 472–73.

147. Several years later, Judge Baker, of the U.S. Circuit Court of Appeals, concluded that a censor must consider "all the public," not merely the young and foolish. He overturned Funkhouser's decision to ban *The Spy* ("Our Film Censorship," *Chicago Tribune*, March 11, 1918, 8).

148. Mae Tinee, "Proceeding to Censor the Censor," *Chicago Tribune*, July 3, 1917, 14; "Citizen Censors Approve 'Little American' Film," *Chicago Tribune*, July 10, 1917, 9.

149. "Censorship of Movies a Farce, Aldermen Told," *Chicago Tribune*, November 21, 1917, 12.

150. "Blame Cutouts on Law, Not Him, the Major Says," *Chicago Tribune*, November 24, 1917, 5. The *Chicago Tribune* also turned against Funkhouser, referring to his decisions as "rampage[s]" and identifying some censored films as "timid, trite, and tiresome" (Mae Tinee, "Yo Ho! And the Censor Is on Rampage Again," *Chicago Tribune*, August 24, 1917, 10). "Barred Film Is So Mild Court Assails Censor," *Chicago Tribune*, February 20, 1917, 15. The columnist Mae Tinee was particularly hostile to Funkhouser. In another article she called for Funkhouser to "rub the sleepy seeds from his eyes" ("Proceeding to Censor the Censor," *Chicago Tribune*, July 3, 1917, 14).

151. Ross, "D. W. Griffith v. City Hall," 30.

152. "Eliminating Maj Funkhouser," *Chicago Tribune*, May 11, 1918, 6.

153. "Civic Leaders Decry Attack on Funkhouser," *Chicago Tribune*, May 27, 1918, 17.

154. "Censorship Not Factor in Case against Major," *Chicago Tribune*, May 29, 1918, 9. Funkhouser was dismissed on August 1, 1918.

155. Ross, "D. W. Griffith v. City Hall," 37.

156. Baldwin, *Chicago's New Negroes*, 144–45.

157. *Report of the Anti-Defamation League* (May 1920), 47, BBIA.

158. "Strangers Beware," (Rejected, 1910–1930), box 72, CMPCB.

159. "The Birth of a Nation's Rebellion against Censorship" *Motography*, June 5, 1915, 922.

CHAPTER SIX

1. Griffith, *The Rise and Fall of Free Speech*, 26.

2. *Report of the Anti-Defamation League* (1915), 6, BBIA.

3. *Federal Motion Picture Commission Hearings* (1916), 43.

4. "The Moving Picture and the National Character," 317, quoted in Butters, *Banned in Kansas*, 11.

5. Devoted to "politicizing the content of his movies," Griffith was, according to the historian Steven Ross, a "progressive filmmaker" who used "true" historical events to teach moral lessons about class, race, and religion (Ross, *Working-Class Hollywood*, 39). Nancy Rosenbloom describes him as "socially conscious" ("From Regulation to Censorship," 371).

6. Wertheimer, "Mutual Film Reviewed"; Jowett, "'A Capacity for Evil.'"

7. Czitrom, "The Politics of Performance," 23.

8. Rosenbloom, "In Defense of the Moving Pictures," 42.

9. Ibid., 47.

10. Rosenbloom, "From Regulation to Censorship," 372.

11. Rosenbloom, "In Defense of the Moving Pictures," 52–53.

12. *Report of the National Board of Censorship* (1913), 9. The board encouraged local officials, a mayor or police officers, to forbid "any film which may ... offend some local standard which the National Board could not ... have taken into account" (*Report of the National Board of Censorship* [1913], 13).

13. Friedman, *Prurient Interests*, 32.

14. Rosenbloom, "In Defense of the Moving Pictures," 47.

15. *Report of the National Board of Censorship* (1914), 10.

16. National Board of Censorship, *The Policy and Standards of the National Board of Censorship of Motion Pictures, Revised May 1914*, 5.

17. Rosenbloom, "In Defense of the Moving Pictures," 47.

18. Feldman, *National Board of Censorship (Review)*, 62.

19. Friedman, *Prurient Interests*, 33.

20. *Report of the National Board of Censorship* (1911), 24.

21. *Report of the National Board of Censorship* (1914), 5.

22. Feldman, *The National Board of Censorship*, 41

23. National Board of Censorship, *The Question of Motion Picture Censorship*, 6–11.

24. Couvares, "The Good Censor," 245.

25. Ross, *Working-Class Hollywood*, 93.

26. Ibid.

27. Ibid., 94.

28. Ibid.

29. Minutes of the Special Meeting of the General Committee, October 7, 1911, folder: "General Committee, Reports of Special Review Meetings, 1911–1914," box 121, NBR.

30. Minutes of the special meeting of the General Committee, January 31, 1912 (*A Victim of the Mormons*), folder "General Committee Minutes of Special Review Meetings, 1911–1914," box 121, NBR.

31. Minutes of the meeting of the Executive Committee of the Board of Censorship, January 24, 1912, folder "Executive Committee, Minutes and Reports 1909–1915," box 118, NBR.

32. "Suggested Wording for Statement by Board of Censorship with Reference to the Mormon Picture," folder "Committee Papers, 1909–1915," box 118, NBR.

33. Ibid.

34. Anti-Defamation League to John Collier, January 15, 1913, box 15, NBR.

35. *Report of the Anti-Defamation League* (1915), 7, BBIA.

36. Anti-Defamation League to John Collier, January 15, 1913, box 15, NBR.

37. "To Manufacturers of Motion Pictures," n.d., box 15, NBR.

38. Executive Secretary, National Board of Censorship, to Sarah Kendall, November 27, 1914, folder, "Evangeline-Fatal Wedding," box 104, NBR.

39. As the historian Nancy Rosenbloom concludes, "Obscenity and crime-for-crime's sake ranked at the top of the list of problems to be eliminated" ("From Regulation to Censorship," 311).

40. "Record of the meeting held at the Universal Film Co," October 27, 1913, folder "General Committee, Reports of Special Review Meetings, 1911–1914," box 121, NBR.

41. Ibid.

42. *New York Times*, February 4, 1914, 8, quoted in Friedman, *Prurient Interests*, 50.

43. Stamp, "Moral Coercion," 51. See also Diffee, "Sex and the City."

44. *New York Herald*, December 22, 1913, 5, quoted in Stamp, "Moral Coercion," 55.

45. National Board of Censorship, *The Policy and Standards of the National Board of Censorship, Revised May 1914*, 8. It emphasized that it sought the viewpoint of the "typical American" (11).

46. *Report of the National Board of Censorship* (1914), 11.

47. National Board of Censorship, *The Policy and Standards of the National Board of Censorship, Revised May 1914*, 14.

48. Couvares, "The Good Censor," 234. See also Grieveson, *Policing Cinema*, 194.

49. Fleener-Marzec, *D. W. Griffith's The Birth of a Nation*, 359.

50. "Censor Board Splits on Dixon's Clansman Film," *New York World*, March 24, 1915; and "Clansman Is Kicked Out of New York," *Chicago Defender*, March 27, 1915, 1, quoted in Fleener-Marzec, *D. W. Griffith's The Birth of a Nation*, 360.

51. Rosenbloom, "From Regulation to Censorship," 387.

52. NAACP to Rev. Charles MacFarland, quoted in Fleener-Marzec, *D. W. Griffith's The Birth of a Nation*, 360.

53. Ibid., 361.

54. *Report of the Anti-Defamation League* (1915), 7, BBIA.

55. Ibid.

56. Executive Secretary, National Board of Censorship, to Sarah Kendall, November 27, 1914, box 104, folder "Evangeline—Fatal Wedding," NBR.

57. Sklar, *Movie-Made America*, 61

58. Erens, *The Jew in American Cinema*, 72–73.

59. W. D. McGuire to Leon Lewis, January 20, 1915, (Regional Correspondents), folder "Regional Correspondents: Illinois, Abingdon-Chicago, 1914–1931," box 54, NBR.

60. Feldman, *National Board of Censorship*, 112

61. National Board of Review, press release, March 29, 1916, quoted in Feldman, *National Board of Censorship*, 112. Note the continuation of this pattern of handling controversial films with *A Mormon Maid* in 1917. In that case, the national board advocated suppression of the film in Utah, but it also officially passed the film with minor changes and rebuffed the complaints of the governor of Utah and of Joseph Smith, the head of the Church of Jesus Christ of the Latter-Day Saints. The board also advised Smith and Governor Bamberger that they could stop the film locally through "ordinary police regulation" (H. E. Ellison to D. W. Griffith, March 5, 1917, folder "Mormon Maid," box 105, NBR; William McGuire to Theodore Mitchell, March 5, 1917, folder "Mormon Maid," box 105, NBR.

62. See, for example, *Buffalo Branch, Mutual Film Corporation v. Breitinger*, 250 Pa. 225, 95 A. 433 (1915) and *Mutual Film Corporation v. City of Chicago*, 224 F. 101 (USCCA Ill. 1915).

63. Wertheimer, "Mutual Film Reviewed," 178.

64. *Mutual Film Corporation v. Ohio Industrial Commission*, 236 U. S. 230, U. S. Supreme Court (1915), 238, quoted in Black, *Hollywood Censored*, 16.

65. *Mutual Film Corporation v. Ohio Industrial Commission*, 238, quoted in Black, *Hollywood Censored*, 16; Jowett, "Moral Responsibility and Commercial Entertainment."

66. W. P. Lawson, "Do You Believe in Censors?" *Harper's Weekly*, January 23, 1915, 88, quoted in Black, *Hollywood Censored*, 17.

67. Grieveson, *Policing Cinema*, 189; Jowett, "'A Capacity for Evil,'" 70.

68. Feldman, *National Board of Censorship (Review)*, 67.

69. Chase, *Catechism on Motion Pictures*, 13. See Jowett, "'A Capacity for Evil.'"

70. *Hearings before the Committee on Education on H. R. 4094 and H. R. 6233* (1926), 398. See also Chase, *Catechism of Motion Pictures*, 160. William Chase, the main advocate of federal motion picture censorship, adhered to a "quieter anti-Semitism" than his colleague Crafts, according to the historian Frank Couvares ("The Good Censor," 134).

71. *Federal Motion Picture Commission Hearings* (1916), 8–9.

72. Motion Picture Commission, *Hearings before the Committee on Education* (1914), 111, 99.

73. *Federal Motion Picture Commission Hearings* (1916), 23.

74. Ibid., 24.

75. Morey, *Hollywood Outsiders*, 130.

76. Martin Littleton, an attorney who worked for D. W. Griffith, stated that "the corrective force of public opinion [was] the fire and flame of every democracy" (*Federal Motion Picture Commission Hearings* [1916], 256).

77. *Federal Motion Picture Commission Hearings* (1916), 169.

78. Ibid., 25.

79. *Federal Motion Picture Commission Hearings* (1916), 25. At one point, members of the House Committee debated with a witness about the possibility of electing, rather

than appointing, the federal board: "Do you seriously mean to have a commission which represents the real effective democratic idea of the country, or do you mean to set up a standard of morals that would be away above everybody?" (ibid., 186).

80. *Hearings before the Committee on Education* (1914), 6.

81. Ibid., 132.

82. Ibid., 121. Seligsberg also held that the working-class viewer was a respectable "everyman" (ibid., 121).

83. Feldman, *National Board of Censorship*, 92.

84. *Hearings before the Committee on Education* (1914), 103.

85. Ibid., 103.

86. *Federal Motion Picture Commission Hearings* (1916), 48.

87. Ibid., 57.

88. Ibid. His example of the problems of representing the entire public in censorship is the case of Jews complaining about *The Locked Door*, which depicted a Jewish sweatshop owner as responsible for the deaths of a hundred workers in the Triangle Shirtwaist Fire. Hundreds of Jews wrote to complain about the film, according to Erwin. Groups like this could unfairly pressure politicians to censor films—any censorship board would be "subject to influence" (ibid., 58).

89. Ibid., 51.

90. Ibid., 63.

91. *Hearings before the Committee on Education* (1914), 96.

92. One editorial against federal censorship used the case of *The Merchant of Venice* as an example of censorship's inherent bias: "What we apply as a standard of exclusion is our own moral susceptibilities, not the other man's. . . . If we are to have any other censorship than public opinion and the criminal law, it should be local and adjusted to the variety of American life and social condition" ("No Jews among These Censors," *Chicago Tribune*, July 4, 1914, 6).

93. *Federal Motion Picture Commission Hearings* (1916), 21.

94. The ADL "wrote to all of the movie manufacturers of the country asking them that they do not traduce the Jewish character and the Jewish religion; and that they do not hold us up to ridicule" (ibid., 144).

95. Ibid., 145.

96. "Film and Stage Rule," *Washington Post*, March 10, 1914, 4.

97. *Federal Motion Picture Commission Hearings* (1916), 62.

98. Ibid., 124.

99. *Federal Motion Picture Commission Hearings* (1916), 254. He explained that the legal battles over *The Birth of Nation* in New York City resulted only in innocuous editing, which "to the minds of the many [made] no difference" (*Federal Motion Picture Commission Hearings* [1916], 255).

100. Ibid., 256.

101. Ibid., 90.

102. Ibid., 100.

103. Ibid. Following Garner, Reverend J. Milton Waldron, a Baptist minister from the nation's capital, expressed concern about the images of mob violence in movies like *The*

Birth of a Nation. "I say it is right to kill a man if he has done anything worthy of death, but that the killing ought to be done by the law, by the legally constituted authorities and not by mobs or individuals" (*Federal Motion Picture Commission* [1916], 100).

104. The coalition consisted of W. Stephen Bush (the editor of *Moving Picture World*), Rev. William Carter, Frederic Howe and Orrin Cocks (of the National Board of Censorship), Walter Seligsberg (the lawyer for Reliance, Mutual, and Majestic film corporations), Fulton Brylawski, Aaron Brylawski (motion picture exhibitors), and Jacob Schechter (of Universal Film Manufacturing).

105. *Federal Motion Picture Commission* (1916), 116. Earlier in the hearings the audience applauded when one congressman proposed that movies and newspapers were similar (69).

106. Ibid., 191. At one point, when one congressman asked Crafts why crime could be shown in newspapers, but not in movies, the audience burst into "applause" (ibid., 69).

107. Ibid., 208.

108. Ibid., 211.

109. Ibid., 213.

110. Ibid., 213–14.

111. *Hearing before the Committee on the Post Office and Post Roads* (1915), 5.

112. Ibid., 49.

113. Nordstrom, *Danger at the Doorstep*, 2.

114. Ibid., 184–85.

115. Ibid., 156.

116. "Protestants and Roman Catholics: A Suggestion," *Christian Register*, January 7, 1915, 150.

117. Kauffman, *Faith and Fraternalism*, 202.

118. "President against Censorship," *Moving Picture World*, October 21, 1916, 371, quoted in Feldman, *National Board of Censorship (Review)*, 110. See also Butters, *Banned in Kansas*, 100–101.

119. Black, *Hollywood Censored*, 29–30.

120. Ibid., 28.

121. *Proposed Federal Motion Picture Commission* (1926), 29.

122. Louisiana passed a motion picture censorship law in 1935, but it did not set up a board. Rhode Island also passed a law in 1938 (Randall, *Censorship of the Movies*, 16–17).

123. "Wichita Kansas Bars 'Birth of a Nation,'" Press Release, June 8, 1923, NAACPR, quoted in Fleener-Marzec, *D. W. Griffith's The Birth of a Nation*, 116.

124. Randall, *Censorship of the Movies*, 17. See also Ernst and Lorentz, *Censored*.

125. Undated report by J. C. Gilmer, Charleston, West Virginia, quoted in Stokes, *D. W. Griffith's "Birth of a Nation,"* 230.

126. *Report Pennsylvania State Board of Censors, for the Year Ending November 30, 1917*, 8–9. See also Saylor, "The Pennsylvania State Board of Censors," 14–15.

127. Moley, *The Hays Office*, 240.

128. Walsh, *Sin and Censorship*, 28.

129. Ibid., 33.

130. Ibid., 51.

131. Emmons, *The Butte Irish*, 405.

132. Ibid., 407; Meagher, *Inventing Irish America*, 272.

133. Meagher, *Inventing Irish America*, 284–87.

134. Ibid., 334–35.

135. Ibid., 352–53.

136. *Proposed Federal Motion Picture Commission* (1926), 31.

137. Ibid., 236.

138. Couvares, "The Good Censor," 140.

139. *Proposed Federal Motion Picture Commission* (1926), 7.

140. Ibid., 136.

141. Du Bois, *Independent* (December 1915), 76, quoted in Weinberger, "The Birth of a Nation," 91.

142. William Stevenson to Roy Nash, March 19, 1917, Branch Files—Cincinnati, NAACPR, quoted in Burns-Watson, "The Birth of a Nation and the Death of a Board," 59. See also W. White to E. Covington, Apr. 22, 1924, "Films and Plays—*Birth of a Nation*, 1924," C-302, NAACPR.

143. Stokes, *D. W. Griffith's "Birth of a Nation,"* 235.

144. Ibid., 238.

145. Ibid., 236.

146. Judge Alfred Talley, November 3, 1921, folder "Films and Plays: *Birth of a Nation*, 1921," C-301, NAACPR. See also Gevenson, *Within Our Gates*, 95.

147. Memorandum from W. E. B. Du Bois to Walter White [1922?], folder "Films and Plays–*Birth of a Nation*, 1922," C-301, NAACPR.

148. Du Bois, "Criteria for Negro Art," *Crisis*, October 1926, quoted in Woodley, "In Harlem and Hollywood," 18.

149. Memorandum from William Pickens to Walter White, n.d. [1931?], folder, "Films and Plays—*The Birth of a Nation*, 1931," C-302, NAACPR.

150. French, "Irish-American Identity, Memory, and Americanism," 260.

151. "Brands Them as Liars," *Gaelic American*, December 1, 1917, 1.

152. "Want 'Gaelic America' Suppressed," *Gaelic American*, November 17, 1917, 4.

153. "Decision of a Federal Judge in California," *Gaelic American*, February 2, 1918, 1; "The 'Gaelic American' and the Mails," *Gaelic American*, February 3, 1918, 4.

154. "The False Charge of Treason," *Gaelic American*, September 22, 1917, 4.

155. "Is the 'Gaelic American' to Be Crushed?" *Gaelic American*, July 13, 1918, 1.

156. Cohon, *B'nai B'rith Manual*, 362.

157. Woeste, "Insecure Equality," 883.

158. Schultz, "Group Rights, American Jews," 101–3.

159. Cohon, *B'nai B'rith Manual*, 370.

160. Louis Marshall to Governor Nathan Miller, February 21, 1921, quoted in Schultz, "Group Rights, American Jews,"104. Some also tried to get the postmaster general to ban publications that advertised the *Dearborn Independent*. See also Rosenstock, *Louis Marshall*, 167–69.

161. Letter from Louis Marshall to Adolf Kraus, April 2, 1921, quoted in Schultz, "Group Rights, American Jews," 103.

162. Woeste, "Insecure Equality," 888. See also Rosenstock, *Louis Marshall*, 167. Marshall concluded: "We, of all people, cannot afford to rest under the imputation that we are prepared to proceed with a policy of suppression."

163. Rosenstock, *Louis Marshall*, 169–70. Other Jewish leaders favored a libel suit against Ford under existing statutes. Despite Marshall's lack of encouragement, prominent Jewish citizens brought three lawsuits against Ford. The most important was by Herman Bernstein, an editor whom Ford had identified as an international spy in the *Dearborn Independent*. Marshall opposed Bernstein's lawsuit against Ford, for individual libel, but he privately helped in the case. None of the three cases was successful, although Ford did have to spend some time and money fighting the charges.

164. Walker, *Hate Speech*, 20.

165. ACLU form letter, March 28, 1921, NAACPR, quoted ibid., 20.

166. Walker, *Hate Speech*, 23. Hays rejected the NAACP request, as he had most other requests to censor any political literature.

167. Schultz, "Group Rights, American Jews," 104. See also Walker, *Hate Speech*, 21.

168. Jackson, *The Ku Klux Klan in the City*, 131–32.

169. *Dearborn Publishing Co. v. Fitzgerald*, 271 F. 479, 480 (N. D. Ohio 1921), quoted in Schultz, "Group Rights, American Jews," 106.

170. Jones, *Human Rights*, 97; Tanenhaus, "Group Libel."

171. Fourteenth Convention, *B'nai B'rith Proceedings* (1935), 201, quoted in Schultz, "Group Rights, American Jews," 111.

172. In this case, the American Jewish Congress joined with the American Jewish Committee to reject group libel prosecutions. Brief for the American Jewish Committee on Religious Rights and Minorities, the American Jewish Committee, the American Jewish Congress and the Human Relations Committee of the National Council of Jewish Women (American Jewish Committee Archives, Legal Briefs, 1938), quoted in Schultz, "Group Rights, American Jews," 123. See also Dov Flisch, "The Libel Trial of Robert Edward Edmundson."

173. "Maryland Eliminations Bulletin, Week Ending January 26, 1924," quoted in Smith, "Patrolling the Boundaries of Race," 280.

174. Naidus, "City without Jews," 37.

CONCLUSION

1. Musser, "Why Did Negroes Love Al Jolson and The Jazz Singer?" 210. See also Rogin, *Blackface, White Noise*.

2. Rogin, *Blackface, White Noise*, 79.

3. For a discussion of film developments in 1927 outside of these controversies, see Brownlow, "Annus Mirabilis."

4. "'McFadden's Flats,' Vile Play, Filmed," *Gaelic American*, December 4, 1926, 1.

5. In February 1928, as part of the same set of protests, Irish observers also complained about the depiction of an impoverished Irish woman in *Mother Machree* ("Bill to Curb Indecent Movies Has Not Been Introduced in New York State Legislature," *Gaelic American*, February 25, 1928, 1). They also criticized *Finnegan's Ball* at the same time ("Irish Race Target in Another Film, 'Finnegan's Ball,'" *Gaelic American*, September 3, 1927, 21).

6. "Irish Close Ranks to Put an End to Film Slanders," *Irish World*, October 29, 1927, 1.

7. The "intoxication scenes" involving Mrs. Callahan and Mrs. Murphy were eliminated by many censorship boards ("Eliminations," folder "Callahans and Murphys," Production Code Administration Records, Margaret Herrick Library, Academy of Motion Picture Arts and Sciences, Beverly Hills, California [hereafter PCA]).

8. "'Irish Hearts': A Coarse and Vile Caricature of the Irish Is Being Shown in New York," *Gaelic American*, February 11, 1928, 1.

9. Catholic protesters then turned their attention to *The Garden of Allah*, in which a monk in Algeria leaves the church to marry a woman who does not know of his past. After she learns the truth, she convinces him to return to the church. McGoldrick worked closely with the producers of *The Garden of Allah* to avoid the uproar surrounding *The Callahans and the Murphys*. She arranged for a preview of the film with powerful Catholic clergy and then published an IFCA endorsement of *The Garden of Allah* in Catholic newspapers around the country (Walsh, *Sin and Censorship*, 50).

10. "Producers of Vile Photoplays Which Caricature the Irish Refuse to Withdraw Them," *Gaelic American*, August 6, 1927, 1. Observers noticed the activism of Catholic and Irish societies. See "Many Organizations in Drive against Sinister Propaganda," *Gaelic American*, August 13, 1927, 1.

11. Charles McMahon, "An Affront to Catholics," July 25, 1927, folder "Callahans and Murphys," PCA; Walsh, *Sin and Censorship*, 29.

12. E. J. Mannix to Jason Joy, August 10, 1927, folder "Callahans and Murphys," PCA.

13. W. D. Kelly, MGM, to James Wingate, Director Motion Picture Division, September 1927, Motion Picture Division, Filmscript Files, folder: Callahans and Murphys (#1673), New York State Archives.

14. Counsel to John T. Kelly, September 12, 1927, Motion Picture Division, Filmscript Files, folder: "Callahans and Murphys (#1673), New York State Archives. Irish protests continued through the fall, but MGM refused to make any additional cuts. The company screened the film for representatives of Irish American organizations of New York City; they gathered and seemed to enjoy the film, according to studio representatives, but continued their defiant stance against the picture (Walsh, *Sin and Censorship*, 40).

15. "Rotten-Egg the Stage Irishman," *Gaelic American*, August 6, 1927, 4.

16. Walsh, *Sin and Censorship*, 42. "Loew's Theaters under Police Guard," *Gaelic American*, September 3, 1927, 1.

17. Walsh, *Sin and Censorship*, 43.

18. "Film Trust Wars on Christian Ideals," *Gaelic American*, September 10, 1927, 1.

19. Ibid., 43.

20. "Racial Films Fight Will Go to Albany," *New York Times*, October 29, 1927, 4.

21. "Film Men Absent at Censor Hearing," *New York Times*, October 1, 1927, 21.

22. "The M'Kee Ordinance Is Still Held Up by General Welfare Committee of Board of Aldermen," *Gaelic American*, December 17, 1927, 1; "Jewish Film Firms War on Irish Race," *Gaelic American*, August 13, 1927, 1. See also "Caricaturing Irish Race and Catholic Church," *Gaelic American*, August 20, 1927, 1. Stephen Carr confirms the anti-Semitism in this incident. See *Hollywood and Anti-Semitism*, 76–82.

23. "Concerted Move of Jewish Film Producers to Belittle Irish Race and Catholic Practices," *Gaelic American*, September 7, 1927, 2.

24. "Widespread Indignation against Pictures Caricaturing Irish Race and Catholic Church," *Gaelic American*, August 20, 1927, 1. They noted that the Episcopal Bishop William T. Manning, of New York, saw the film as part of a "world-wide concerted attack . . . upon Christ's standards of sexual morality and marriage." See also "New York State Censorship of Films a Joke," *Gaelic American*, September 24, 1927, 1; "NY 'World' Joins Jew Picture Firms in War on Irish," *Gaelic American*, August 20, 1927, 2.

25. Walsh, *Sin and Censorship*, 44.

26. Herman, "'The Most Dangerous Anti-Semitic Photoplay,'" 15–16.

27. Wise to Alfred M. Cohen, November 9, 1927, Wise Papers, American Jewish Historical Society, quoted in Herman, "'The Most Dangerous Anti-Semitic Photoplay,'" 16. Maltby, "The King of Kings and the Czar of All Rushes."

28. Walsh, *Sin and Censorship*, 54.

29. Rita McGoldrick to "Catholic Priests and Schools," June 22, 1928, Record #5-0804, MPPDA Digital Archive, Flinders University, Adelaide, South Australia.

30. Herman, "'The Most Dangerous Anti-Semitic Photoplay,'" 15.

31. Ibid., 19.

32. Ibid.

33. Ibid., 22.

34. Romanowski, *Reforming Hollywood*, 71–73; Maltby, "The King of Kings and the Czar of All Rushes."

35. Walsh, *Sin and Censorship*, 47; Moley, *The Hays Office*, 63.

36. Walsh, *Sin and Censorship*, 47.

37. *Churchman*, September 7, 1929, quoted in Walsh, *Sin and Censorship*, 48.

38. Walsh, *Sin and Censorship*, 49.

39. Ibid., 50.

40. Courtney, *Hollywood Fantasies of Miscegenation*, 115. See also Francis Couvares, "So This Is Censorship."

41. Cited in Auster memo, March 13, 1934, *Imitation of Life* file, PCA, quoted in Courtney, *Hollywood Fantasies of Miscegenation*, 124.

42. Courtney, *Hollywood Fantasies of Miscegenation*, 146.

43. Black, *The Catholic Crusade*, 27.

44. Ibid., 101; Wittern-Keller and Haberski, *The Miracle Case*, 138.

45. Cadegan, "Guardians of Democracy or Storm Troopers," 261–62.

46. "Group Libel Laws: Abortive Efforts."

47. Riesman, "Democracy and Defamation: Control of Group Libel"; Riesman, "Democracy and Defamation: Fair Game and Fair Comment"; Riesman, "Democracy and Defamation: Fair Game and Fair Comment II."

48. Walker, *Hate Speech*, 82.

49. The American Jewish Congress, however, refused to back the criminal libel prosecution of Robert Edmondson, for his anti-Semitic pamphlets, in 1937. See Schultz, "Group Rights, American Jews."

50. In "Group Libel Laws," the author notes that all federal group libel laws were

defeated between 1935 and 1949. Eight states had criminal libel laws, but most of these had very lax prosecutions (225).

51. John Hanes Holmes, "Sensitivity as Censor," *Saturday Review* (February 1949), folder 12 (miscellaneous, 1949), box 757, American Civil Liberties Union Records, Princeton University (hereafter ACLUR). Gleason, "Minorities (Almost) All."

52. "Should Minority Groups Exercise Censorship over Books and Films," *Town Meeting* (May 10, 1949), 9, folder 12, box 757, ACLUR.

53. Ibid., 7.

54. Ibid., 21.

55. Ibid., 7.

56. Ibid., 15.

57. Strub, "Black and White and Banned All Over," 686. See also Dowdy, "Censoring Popular Culture." For a discussion of race-based censorship in another southern state, Virginia, see Smith, "Patrolling the Boundaries of Race."

58. "'Brewster's Millions' Is Banned in Memphis," *New York Times*, April 7, 1945, and "Censor Binford Says No to 'Annie Get Your Gun,'" *Memphis Press-Scimitar*, September 29, 1947, quoted in Strub, "Black and White and Banned All Over," 689, 690.

59. Strub, "Black and White and Banned All Over," 691.

60. *Colliers*, May 6, 1950, quoted in Cadegan, "Guardians of Democracy," 262.

61. McGehee, "Disturbing the Peace"; and Patton, "White Racism/Black Signs"; Courtney, *Hollywood Fantasies of Miscegenation*.

62. Black, *The Catholic Crusade*, 91.

63. Ibid., 94.

64. Ibid., 97.

65. Wittern-Keller and Haberski, *The Miracle Case*, 97. See also Black, *Catholic Crusade*, 98.

66. Ibid., 113–14.

67. Ibid., 117–18.

68. See, for example, Oshige McGowan, "Certain Illusions about Speech"; Volokh, "What Speech Does 'Hostile Work Environment' Harassment Law Restrict?"; and Earle and Cova, "The Collision of Rights and a Search for Limits."

69. Shiell, *Campus Hate Speech on Trial*, 17–19.

70. *Doe v. University of Michigan*, (1989), quoted in Shiell, *Campus Hate Speech on Trial*, 73.

71. The Office for Civil Rights explains, "Harassing conduct (e.g., physical, verbal, graphic, or written) that is sufficiently severe, pervasive or persistent so as to interfere with or limit the ability of an individual to participate in or benefit from the services, activities or privileges provided by the University creates a racially hostile environment" (U.S. Department of Education, Office for Civil Rights, Racial Harassment Guidance [1994], Berkeley Office for the Prevention of Harassment and Discrimination, http://ophd.berkeley.edu/policies-procedures/hostile-environment).

72. Earle and Cava, "The Collision of Rights and a Search for Limits"; Shiell, *Campus Hate Speech on Trial*.

73. "Should Minority Groups Exercise Censorship over Books and Films," *Town Meeting* (May 10, 1949), 15, folder 12, box 757, ACLUR.

Bibliography

MANUSCRIPT COLLECTIONS

Albany, New York
  New York State Archives
    Governor Nathan Miller Central Subject and Correspondence Files
    Motion Picture Division (Commission) Records
Annapolis, Maryland
  Maryland State Archives
    Maryland Motion Picture Censors
Cambridge, Massachusetts
  Harvard University Law School
    Special Collections
    Motion Picture Censorship: Scrapbooks and Pamphlets
  Harvard University Library
    Harvard Theatre Collection
Carbondale, Illinois
  Southern Illinois University, Morris Library Special Collections
    Theodore Schroeder Papers
Cheyney, Pennsylvania
  Cheyney University, Leslie Pinckney Hill Library
    William Dorsey Collection
Chicago, Illinois
  Northeastern Illinois University, Ronald Williams Library
    Illinois Regional Archive Depository
      Chicago Board of Motion Picture Censors Records
Cincinnati, Ohio
  Jacob Rader Marcus Center of the American Jewish Archives
    B'nai B'rith District 2 Collection
    B'nai B'rith International Archives
    Anti-Defamation League Papers
    Central Conference of American Rabbis Papers
    David Philipson Collection
    National Council of Jewish Women Nearprint File
Harrisburg, Pennsylvania
  Pennsylvania State Archives
    Records of the Department of Education
      State Board of Censors (Motion Picture)

Iowa City, Iowa
    University of Iowa Library, Special Collections
        Keith/Albee Collection
Los Angeles, California
    Margaret Herrick Library
        Motion Picture Association of America
            Production Code Administration Records
New Haven, Connecticut
    Yale University Library
        Harry Weinberger Papers
New York, New York
    American Irish Historical Society
        Daniel F. Cohalan Papers
    New York Public Library
        Manuscript and Archives Division
            National Board of Review of Motion Pictures Records
        Schomburg Center for Research in Black Culture
            Lester Walton Papers
    The New York Public Library for the Performing Arts, Dorothy and Lewis B.
            Cullman Center
        Billy Rose Theatre Division
        Robinson Locke Theatre Collection
Philadelphia, Pennsylvania
    Historical Society of Pennsylvania
        Dennis Clark Papers
        Ellis Oberholtzer Manuscript Collection
Princeton, New Jersey
    Princeton University Library
        American Civil Liberties Union Records
Villanova, Pennsylvania
    Villanova University Library
        Joseph McGarrity Collection
Washington, D. C.
    Library of Congress
        Manuscript Reading Room
            National Association for the Advancement of Colored People Records
        Motion Picture, Broadcasting and Recorded Sound Division

NEWSPAPERS AND MAGAZINES

American Israelite
B'nai B'rith News
Chicago Daily Tribune
Chicago Defender
Crisis

Des Moines Register and Leader
Gaelic American
Irish World and American Industrial Liberator
Jewish Exponent
Motion Picture World
Motography
National Association for the Advancement of Colored People Annual Reports
National Hibernian
New York Age
New York Times
North American (Philadelphia)
Public Ledger
Washington Bee

ARTICLES AND BOOK CHAPTERS

Anderson, Eric. "Prostitution and Social Justice: Chicago, 1910–1915." *Social Science Review* 48.2 (June 1974): 203–28.

Ap Hywel, Elin. "Elise and the Great Queens of Ireland: Femininity as Constructed by Sinn Fein and the Abbey Theatre, 1901–1907." In *Gender in Irish Writing*, edited by David Cairns and Toni O'Brien Johnson, 23–39. Philadelphia: Open University Press, 1991.

Arnesen, Eric. "Whiteness and the Historian's Imagination." *International Labor and Working Class History* 60 (Fall 2001): 3–32.

Barbas, Samantha. "How Movies Became Free Speech." *Rutgers Law Review* 64 (Spring 2012): 1–73.

Barnes, Clifford W. "The Story of the Committee of Fifteen of Chicago." *Journal of Social Hygiene* 4 (1918): 145–56.

Barrett, James, and David Roediger. "Inbetween Peoples: Race, Nationality, and the 'New Immigrant' Working Class." *Journal of American Ethnic History* 16.3 (Spring 1997): 4–44.

———. "The Irish and the 'Americanization' of the 'New Immigrants' in the Streets and in the Churches of the Urban United States, 1900–1930." *Journal of American Ethnic History* 24.4 (Summer 2005): 4–33.

Blanchard, Margaret. "The American Urge to Censor: Freedom of Expression versus the Desire to Sanitize Society—From Anthony Comstock to 2 Live Crew." *William and Mary Law Review* 33.3 (1992): 741–841.

Bornstein, George. "The Colors of Zion: Black, Jewish, and Irish Nationalisms at the Turn of the Century." *Modernism/modernity* 12.3 (2005): 369–84.

"Brief Amici Curiae of Feminist Anti-Censorship Taskforce, et al., in *American Booksellers Association v. Hudnut*." *University of Michigan Journal of Law Reform* 21 (Fall 1987/Winter 1988): 69–136.

Brown, Rebecca A. "Confessions of a Flawed Liberal." *Good Society* 14.1/2 (2005): 30–34.

Brownlow, Kevin. "Annus Mirabilis: The Film in 1927." *Film History* 17.2/3 (2005): 168–78.

Brundage, David. "In Time of Peace, Prepare for War: Key Themes in the Social Thought of New York's Irish American Nationalists, 1900–1916." In *The New York Irish*, edited by Ronald Bayor and Timothy Meagher, 321–34. Baltimore: Johns Hopkins University Press, 1996.

Cadegan, Una. "Guardians of Democracy or Cultural Storm Troopers? American Catholics and the Control of Popular Media, 1934–1966." *Catholic Historical Review* 87.2 (April 2001): 252–82.

Cairns, David, and Shaun Richards. "'Woman' in the Discourse of Celticism: A Reading of *A Shadow of the Glen*." *Canadian Journal of Irish Studies* 13.1 (June 1987): 43–60.

Carle, Susan. "Race, Class, and Legal Ethics in the Early NAACP (1910–1920)." *Law and History Review* 20.1 (Spring 2002): 97–146.

Castronovo, Russ. "Beauty along the Color Line: Lynching, Aesthetics, and *The Crisis*." *PMLA* 121 (October 2006): 1443–59.

Chris, Cynthia. "Censoring Purity." *Camera Obscura* 27.1 (2012): 97–125.

Clark, Dennis. "Urban Blacks and Irishmen: Brothers in Prejudice." In *Black Politics in Philadelphia*, edited by Miriam Ershkowitz and Joseph Zikmund II, 15–30. New York: Basic Books, 1973.

Cooks, Bridget. "Fixing Race: Visual Representations of African American Fairgoers, World's Columbian Exposition, Chicago 1893." *Patterns of Prejudice* 41.5 (November 2007): 435–65.

Couvares, Francis. "The Good Censor: Race, Sex, and Censorship in the Early Cinema." *Yale Journal of Criticism* 7.2 (Fall 1994): 233–51.

———. "So This Is Censorship: Race, Sex, and Censorship in Movies of the 1920s and 1930s." *Journal of American Studies* 45 (August 2011): 581–97.

Cripps, Thomas. "The Movie Jew as an Image of Assimilation, 1903–1927." *Journal of Popular Film* 4.3 (1975): 190–207.

Crowe, Charles. "Racial Massacre in Atlanta September 22, 1906." *Journal of Negro History* 54.2 (April 1969): 150–73.

Czitrom, Daniel. "The Politics of Performance: Theater Licensing and the Origins of Movie Censorship in New York." In *Movie Censorship and American Culture*, edited by Francis Couvares, 16–42. Washington: Smithsonian Institution Press, 1996.

Diffee, Christopher. "Sex and the City: The White Slavery Scare and Social Governance in the Progressive Era." *American Quarterly* 57.2 (June 2005): 411–37.

Diner, Hasia. "The Encounter between Jews and America in the Gilded Age and Progressive Era." *Journal of the Gilded Age and Progressive Era* 11.1 (January 2012): 3–25.

———. "Trading Faces." *Common Quest* (Summer 1997): 40–44.

Dinnerstein, Leo. "Leo Frank and the American Jewish Community." *American Jewish Archive Journal* 20.2 (1968): 107–26.

Distler, Paul. "Exit the Racial Comics." *Educational Theatre Journal* 18 (October 1966): 247–54.

Dormon, James. "Ethnic Cultures of the Mind: The Harrigan-Hart Mosaic." *American Studies* 33.2 (Fall 1992): 21–41.

———. "Ethnic Stereotyping in American Popular Culture: The Depiction of American Ethnics in the Cartoon Periodicals of the Gilded Age." *Amerikastudien/ American Studies* 30.4 (1985): 489–507.

Dowdy, G. Wayne. "Censoring Popular Culture: Political and Social Control in Segregated Memphis." *West Tennessee Historical Society Papers* 55 (2001): 98–117.

Downey, Dennis. "The 'Delaware Horror': Two Ministers, a Lynching, and the Crisis of Democracy." In *Lynching beyond Dixie: American Mob Violence outside the South*, edited by Michael Pfeifer, 237–60. Urbana-Champaign: University of Illinois Press, 2013.

Earle, Beverly, and Anita Cava. "The Collision of Rights and a Search for Limits: Free Speech in the Academy and Freedom from Sexual Harassment on Campus." *Berkeley Journal of Employment and Labor Law* 18.2 (1997): 282–322.

Erdman, Harley. "Jewish Anxiety in 'Days of Judgement': Community Conflict, Antisemitism, and *The God of Vengeance* Obscenity Case." *Theatre Survey* 40.1 (1999): 51–74.

Erickson, Mary P. "'In the Interest of the Moral Life of Our City': The Beginning of Motion Picture Censorship in Portland, Oregon." *Film History* 22.2 (2010): 148–69.

Fields, Barbara. "Whiteness, Racism, and Identity." *International Labor and Working-Class History* 60 (October 2001): 48–56.

Flynn, Peter. "How Bridget Was Framed: The Irish Domestic in Early American Cinema, 1895–1917." *Cinema Journal* 50.2 (2011): 1–20.

———."Screening the Stage Irishman: Irish Masculinity in Early American Cinema, 1895–1907." *Moving Image* 12.2 (Fall 2012): 122–47.

Foner, Eric. "Response to Eric Arnesen." *International Labor and Working-Class History* 60 (2001): 57–60.

Foner, Philip. "Black-Jewish Relations in the Opening Years of the Twentieth Century." In *Strangers and Neighbors: Relations between Blacks and Jews in the United States*, edited by Maurianne Adams and John Bracey, 237–44. Boston: University of Massachusetts Press, 1999.

Forker, Martin. "The Use of 'Cartoonist's Armoury' in Manipulating Public Opinion: Anti-Irish Imagery in 19th-Century British and American Periodicals." *Journal of Irish Studies* 27 (2012): 58–71.

Friss, Evan. "Blacks, Jews, and Civil Rights Law in New York, 1895–1913." *Journal of American Ethnic History* 24.4 (Summer 2005): 70–99.

Gems, Gerald. "Sport and the Forging of a Jewish-American Culture: The Chicago Hebrew Institute." *American Jewish History* 83.1 (1995): 15–26.

Gleason, Philip. "Minorities (Almost) All: The Minority Concept in American Social Thought." *American Quarterly* 43.3 (September 1991): 392–424.

Golomb, Deborah Grand. "The 1893 Congress of Jewish Women: Evolution or Revolution in American Jewish Women's History." *American Jewish History* 70.1 (1980): 52–67.

Greene, Daniel. "A Chosen People in a Pluralist Nation: Horace Kallen and the

Jewish-American Experience." *Religion and American Culture: A Journal of Interpretation* 16.2 (2006): 161–94.

Grimsted, David. "Rioting in Its Jacksonian Setting." *American Historical Review* 77.2 (1972): 361–97.

"Group Libel Laws: Abortive Efforts to Combat Hate Propaganda." *Yale Law Journal* 61.2 (February 1952): 252–64.

Gurock, Jeffrey. "The 1913 New York State Civil Rights Act." *AJS Review* 1 (1976): 93–120.

Guterl, Matthew Pratt. "The New Race-Consciousness: Race, Nation, and Empire in American Culture, 1910–1925." *Journal of World History* 10.2 (September 1999): 307–52.

Haller, Mark. "Recurring Themes." In *The Peoples of Philadelphia: A History of Ethnic Groups and Lower Class Life, 1790–1940*, edited by Allen F. Davis and Mark Haller, 277–90. Philadelphia: University of Pennsylvania Press, 1998. First published in 1973 by Temple University Press.

Haupt, Claudia. "Regulating Hate Speech—Damned If You Do and Damned If You Don't: Lessons Learned from Comparing the German and U.S. Approaches." *Boston University International Law Journal* 23 (2005): 299–335.

Hayward, Clarissa, and Watson, Ron. "Identity and Political Theory." *Washington University Journal of Law and Policy* 33 (2010): 9–41.

Herman, Felicia. "'The Most Dangerous Anti-Semitic Photoplay in Filmdom': American Jews and *The King of Kings* (DeMille 1927)." *Velvet Light Trap* 46 (1999): 12–25.

Hickman, Mary, and Bronwen Walter. "Deconstructing Whiteness: Irish Women in Britain." *Feminist Review* 50 (1995): 5–19.

Inscoe, John. "The Clansman on Stage and Screen: North Carolina Reacts." *North Carolina Historical Review* 64.2 (April 1987): 139–61.

Itzkovitz, Daniel. "Passing Like Me: Jewish Chameleonism and the Politics of Race." In *Passing: Identity and Interpretation in Sexuality, Race and Religion*, edited by Maria Carla Sanchez and Linda Schlossberg, 38–63. New York: New York University Press, 2001.

Jaret, Charles. "The Greek, Italian, and Jewish American Ethnic Press." In *Immigrant Institutions: The Organization of Immigrant Life*, edited by George Pozzetta, 101–25. New York: Routledge, 1991.

Jenkins, Lee. "Beyond the Pale: Frederick Douglass in Cork." *Irish Review* 24 (Autumn 1999): 80–95.

Jensen, Richard, "'No Irish Need Apply': A Myth of Victimization." *Journal of Social History* 36.2 (Winter 2002): 405–29.

Johnson, James Weldon. "Uncle Tom's Cabin and the Clansman." In *Selected Writings of James Weldon Johnson*, vol. 1, edited by Sondra Kathryn Wilson, 12–13. New York: Oxford University Press, 1995.

Johnson, Joan Marie. "'Ye Gave Them a Stone': African American Women's Clubs, the Frederick Douglass Home, and the Black Mammy Monument." *Journal of Women's History* 17.1 (2005): 62–86.

Johnson, Katie. "Zaza: That 'Obtruding Harlot' of the Stage." *Theatre Journal* 54.2 (May 2002): 223–43.

Jowett, Garth. "'A Capacity for Evil': The 1915 Supreme Court Mutual Decision." *Historical Journal of Film, Radio, and Television* 9.1 (1989): 59–78.

———. "Moral Responsibility and Commercial Entertainment: Social Control in the United States Film Industry, 1907–1968." *Historical Journal of Film, Radio, and Television* 10.1 (1990): 3–31.

Kallen, Horace. "Democracy versus the Melting Pot: A Study of American Nationality." *The Nation* (February 18 and 25, 1915): 190–94, 217–20.

Kane, Paula. "'Staging a Lie': Boston Irish-Catholicism and the New Irish Drama." In *Religion and Identity*, edited by Patrick O'Sullivan. Irish World Wide Series, vol. 5. Leicester and New York: Leicester University Press and St. Martin's Press, 1996.

Kelleher, Patricia. "Class and Catholic Irish Masculinity in Antebellum America: Young Men on the Make in Chicago." *Journal of American Ethnic History* 28.4 (Summer 2009): 7–42.

———."Maternal Strategies: Irish Women's Headship of Families in Gilded Age Chicago." *Journal of Women's History* 13.2 (Summer 2001): 80–106.

Kelley, Blair L. M. "Right to Ride: African American Citizenship and Protest in the Era of *Plessy v. Ferguson*." *African American Review* 41.2 (Summer 2007): 347–56.

Kenny, Kevin. "Race, Violence, and Anti-Irish Sentiment in the Nineteenth Century." In *Making the Irish American: The History and Heritage of the Irish in the United States*, edited by J. J. Lee and Marion Casey, 364–80. New York: New York University Press, 2006.

Kibler, M. Alison. "'Freedom of the Theatre' and 'Practical Censorship': Two Theater Riots in the Early Twentieth Century." *Organization of American Historians Magazine of History* 24.2 (2010): 15–19.

———."Paddy, Shylock, and Sambo: Irish, Jewish, and African American Efforts to Ban Racial Ridicule on Stage and Screen." In *Culture and Belonging in Divided Societies: Contestation and Symbolic Landscapes*, edited by Marc Howard Ross, 259–80. Philadelphia: University of Pennsylvania Press, 2009.

———. "Pigs, Green Whiskers, and Drunken Widows: Irish Nationalists and the 'Practical Censorship' of *McFadden's Row of Flats* in 1902 and 1903." *Journal of American Studies* 42.3 (2008): 489–514.

———. "Rank Ladies, Ladies of Rank: The Elinore Sisters in Vaudeville." *American Studies* 38.1 (Spring 1997): 91–115.

———. "The Stage Irishwoman." *Journal of American Ethnic History* 24.3 (Spring 2005): 5–30.

Knobel, Dale. "The Vocabulary of Ethnic Perception: Content Analysis of the American Stage Irishman, 1820–1860." *Journal of American Studies* 15.1 (April 1981): 45–71.

Korelitz, Seth. "'A Magnificent Piece of Work': The Americanization Work of the National Council of Jewish Women." *American Jewish History* 83.2 (1995): 177–203.

Lavitt, Pamela Brown. "First of the Red Hot Mamas: 'Coon Shouting' and the Jewish Ziegfeld Girl." *American Jewish History* 87.4 (1999): 253–90.

Lennig, Arthur. "Myth and Fact: The Reception of *The Birth of a Nation*." *Film History* 16.2 (2004): 117–41.

Lewis, David Levering. "Parallels and Divergences: Assimilationist Strategies of Afro-American and Jewish Elites from 1910 to the Early 1930s." *Journal of American History* 71.3 (December 1984): 543–64.

Levy, Eugene. "'Is the Jew a White Man?' Press Reaction to the Leo Frank Case, 1913–1915." *Phylon* 35.2 (June 1974): 212–22.

Lindstrom, J. A. "'Almost Worse Than the Restrictive Measures': Chicago Reformers and the Nickelodeons." *Cinema Journal* 39.1 (Autumn 1999): 90–112.

Lufkin, Jack. "Brown, Samuel Joe." *The Biographical Dictionary of Iowa*. Iowa City: University of Iowa Press, 2009. Web. June 1, 2014.

MacGregor, Ford H. "Official Censorship Legislation." *Annals of the American Academy of Political and Social Science* 128 (November 1926): 163–74.

Maltby, Richard. "The King of Kings and the Czar of all Rushes: The Propriety of the Christ Story." In *Controlling Hollywood: Censorship and Regulation in the Studio Era*, edited by Matthew Bernstein, 60–86. New Brunswick: Rutgers University Press, 1999.

Mandle, W. F. "The I.R.B and the Beginnings of the G. A. A." *Irish Historical Studies* 20.80 (September 1977): 418–38.

Marshall, Anne. "The 1906 *Uncle Tom's Cabin* Law and the Politics of Race and Memory in Early-Twentieth-Century Kentucky." *The Journal of the Civil War Era* 1.3 (September 2011): 368–93.

Maschio, Geraldine. "Ethnic Humor and the Demise of the Russell Brothers." *Journal of Popular Culture* 26.1 (Summer 1992): 81–92.

Mazur, Edward. "Jewish Chicago: From Diversity to Community." In *Ethnic Frontier: Essays in the History of Group Survival in Chicago and the Midwest*, edited by Melvin Holly and Peter Jones, 263–92. Grand Rapids, Mich.: William Eerdman's Publishing, 1977.

McCarthy, Kathleen. "Nickel Vice and Virtue: Movie Censorship in Chicago, 1907–1915." *Journal of Popular Film* 5.1 (1976): 37–55.

McConachie, Bruce. "Pacifying American Theatrical Audiences." In *For Fun and Profit: The Transformation of Leisure into Consumptions*, edited by Richard Butsch, 47–70. Philadelphia: Temple University Press, 1990.

McDevitt, Patrick. "Muscular Catholicism: Nationalism, Masculinity, and Gaelic Team Sports, 1884–1916." *Gender and History* 9.2 (August 1997): 262–84.

McDiarmid, Lucy, "The Abbey and the Theatrics of Controversy, 1909–1915." In *A Century of Irish Drama: Widening the Stage*, edited by Stephen Watt, Eileen Morgan, and Shakir Mustafa, 57–71. Bloomington: Indiana University Press, 2000.

McEwan, Paul. "Lawyers, Bibliographies, and the Klan: Griffith's Resources in the Censorship Battle over *The Birth of a Nation* in Ohio." *Film History* 20.3 (2008): 357–66.

McGehee, Margaret. "Disturbing the Peace: *Lost Boundaries*, *Pinky*, and Censorship in Atlanta, Georgia, 1949–1952." *Cinema Journal* 46.1 (2006): 23–51.

Meagher, Timothy. "Sweet Good Mothers and Young Women out in the World: The Roles of Irish American Women in Late Nineteenth and Early Twentieth Century

Worcester, Massachusetts." *U.S. Catholic Historian* 5 (Summer/Fall 1986): 352–43.

Meier, August, and John Bracey Jr. "The NAACP as a Reform Movement, 1909–1965: 'To Reach the Conscience of America.'" *Journal of Southern History* 59.1 (February 1993): 3–30.

Meier, August, and Elliott Rudwick. "Black Man in the 'White City': Negroes and the Columbian Exposition." *Phylon* 26.4 (1965): 354–61.

Moloney, Mick. "Irish-American Popular Music." In *Making the Irish American: History and Heritage of the Irish in the United States*, edited by J. J. Lee and Marion Casey, 381–405. New York: New York University Press, 2006.

Murphy, Maureen. "Bridget and Biddy: Images of the Irish Servant Girl in Puck Cartoons, 1880–1890." In *New Perspectives on the Irish Diaspora*, edited by Charles Fanning, 154–75. Carbondale: Southern Illinois University Press, 2000.

Musser, Charles. "Why Did Negroes Love Al Jolson and *The Jazz Singer*? Melodrama, Blackface, and Cosmopolitan Theatrical Culture." *Film History* 23.2 (2011): 196–222.

Nahshon, Edna. "The Pulpit to the Stage: Rabbi Joseph Silverman and the Actors' Church Alliance." *American Jewish History* 91.1 (2003): 5–27.

Naidus, Jeremy. "City without Jews." *New York Archives* 12.2 (Fall 2012): 37.

Nelson, Bruce. "Irish Americans, Irish Nationalism, and the 'Social' Question, 1916–1923." *boundary 2* 31.1 (2004): 147–78.

Nowatzki,, Michael. "Paddy Jumps Jim Crow: Irish Americans and Blackface Minstrelsy." *Eire-Ireland* 41.3/4 (2007): 162–84.

O'Donnell, Edward T. "Hibernians versus Hebrews? A New Look at the 1902 Jacob Joseph Funeral Riot." *Journal of Gilded Age and Progressive Era* 6.2 (April 2007): 209–25.

Oliver, Lawrence, and Terri Walker. "James Weldon Johnson's *New York Age* Essays on *The Birth of a Nation*' and the 'Southern Oligarchy.'" *South Central Review* 10.4 (Winter 1993): 1–17.

Onkey, Lauren. "'A Melee and a Curtain': Black-Irish Relations in Ned Harrigan's *The Mulligan Guard Ball*." *Jouvert* 4.1 (1999), http://english.chass.ncsu.edu/jouvert/v4i1/onkey.htm. April 30, 2014.

Orbach, Barak. "Prizefighting and the Birth of Movie Censorship." *Yale Journal of Law and the Humanities* 21 (Summer 2009): 251–304.

Oshige McGowan, Miranda. "Certain Illusions about Speech: Why the Free-Speech Critique of Hostile Work Environment Harassment Is Wrong." *Constitutional Commentary* 19.2 (2002): 391–452.

Patton, Cindy. "White Racism/Black Signs: Censorship and Images of Race Relations." *Journal of Communication* 45.2 (Spring 1995): 65–77.

Quinn, John F. "'Safe in Old Ireland': Frederick Douglass's Tour, 1845–1846." *Historian* 63. 3/4 (Spring/Summer 2002): 535–50.

Rabban, David M. "The Free Speech League, the ACLU, and the Changing Conceptions of Free Speech in American History." *Stanford Law Review* 45.1 (1992): 47–114.

Riesman, David. "Democracy and Defamation: Control of Group Libel." *Columbia Law Review* 42.5 (1942): 727–80.

———. "Democracy and Defamation: Fair Game and Fair Comment." *Columbia Law Review* 42.7 (1942): 1085–123.

———. "Democracy and Defamation: Fair Game and Fair Comment II: The United States." *Columbia Law Review* 42.8 (1942): 1282–318.

Robinson, Cedric. "In the Year 1915: D. W. Griffith and the Whitening of America." *Social Identities* 3.2 (June 1997): 161–93.

Rodechko, James. "An Irish-American Journalist and Catholicism." *Church History* 39.4 (1970): 524–40.

Rogoff, Leonard. "Is the Jew White?: The Racial Place of the Southern Jew." *American Jewish History* 85.3 (1997): 195–230.

Rosenberg, Joel. "Rogin's Noise: The Alleged Historical Crimes of *The Jazz Singer*." *Prooftexts* 22 (Winter/Spring 2002): 221–39.

Rosenbloom, Nancy. "From Regulation to Censorship: Film and Political Culture in New York in the Early Twentieth Century." *Journal of the Gilded Age and Progressive Era* 3.4 (October 2004): 369–406.

———. "In Defense of the Moving Pictures: The People's Institute, the National Board of Censorship, and the Problem of Leisure in Urban America." *American Studies* 33.2 (Fall 1992): 41–60.

Ross, Harris. "D. W. Griffith v. City Hall: Politics, Ethnicity, and Chicago Film Censorship." *Journal of the Illinois State Historical Society* 100.1 (Spring 2007): 19–40.

Rowland, Thomas J. "Irish-American Catholics and the Quest for Respectability in the Coming of the Great War, 1900–1917." *Journal of American Ethnic History* 15.2 (Winter 1996): 3–31.

Ryan, Louise. "Traditions and Double Moral Standards: The Irish Suffragists' Critique of Nationalism." *Women's History Review* 4.4 (1995): 487–503.

Sawyers, June Skinner. "Henry Horner." In *Chicago Portraits: New Edition*, edited by Judith Skinner Sawyers, 160. Chicago: Northwestern University Press, 2012.

Schiller, Reuel. "Free Speech and Expertise: Administrative Censorship and the Birth of the Modern First Amendment." *Virginia Law Review* 86.1 (February 2000): 1–102.

Schultz, Evan. "Group Rights, American Jews, and the Failure of Group Libel Laws, 1913–1952." *Brooklyn Law Review* 66 (Spring 2000): 71–146.

Scott, Ellen C. "Black Censor, White Liberties: Civil Rights and Illinois's 1917 Film Law." *American Quarterly* 64.2 (June 2012): 219–47.

Shankman, Arnold. "Black on Green: Afro-American Editors on Irish Independence, 1840–1921." *Phylon* 41.3 (1980): 284–99.

Smith, Christopher J. "Blacks and Irish on the Riverine Frontiers: The Roots of American Popular Music." *Southern Cultures* 17.1 (Spring 2011): 75–102.

Smith, Eric D. "'I Have Been a Perfect Pig': A Semiosis of Swine in 'Circe.'" *Joyce Studies Annual* 13 (Summer 2002): 129–46.

Smith, Eric Ledell. "'Asking for Justice and Fair Play': African American State Legislators and Civil Rights in Early Twentieth-Century Pennsylvania." *Pennsylvania History* 63.2 (Spring 1996): 169–203.

Smith, J. Douglas. "Patrolling the Boundaries of Race: Motion Picture Censorship and Jim Crow in Virginia, 1922–1932." *Historical Journal of Film, Radio, and Television* 21.3 (2001): 273–91.

Snyder, Robert. "The Irish and Vaudeville." In *Making the Irish American: The History and Heritage of the Irish in the United States*, edited by J. J. Lee and Marion Casey, 406–10. New York: New York University Press, 2006.

Soper, Kerry. "From Rowdy, Urban Carnival to Contained Middle-Class Pastime: Reading Richard Outcault's *Yellow Kid* and *Buster Brown*." *Columbia Journal of American Studies* 4.1 (2000): 143–81.

———. "From Swarthy Ape to Sympathetic Everyman and Subversive Trickster: The Development of Irish Caricature in America Comic Strips between 1890 and 1920." *Journal of American Studies* 39.2 (2005): 257–96.

Stamp, Shelley. "Moral Coercion; or, The National Board of Censorship Ponders the Vice Question." In *Controlling Hollywood: Censorship and Regulation in the Studio Era*, edited by Matthew Bernstein, 41–59. New Brunswick: Rutgers University Press, 1999.

Streible, Dan. "The History of the Boxing Film, 1894–1915: Social Control and Social Reform in the Progressive Era." *Film History* 3.3 (1989): 235–57.

Strossen, Nadine. "Hate Speech and Pornography: Do We Have to Choose between Freedom of Speech and Equality?" *Case Western Reserve Law Review* 46 (Winter 1996): 449–78.

Strub, Whitney. "Black and White and Banned All Over: Race, Censorship and Obscenity in Postwar Memphis." *Journal of Social History* 40.3 (2007): 685–715.

Tanenhaus, Joseph. "Group Libel." *Cornell Law Quarterly* 35.2 (Winter 1950): 261–302.

Thapar, Suruchi. "Women as Activists; Women as Symbols: A Study of the Indian Nationalist Movement." *Feminist Review* 44 (1993): 81–96.

Turner, George Kibbe. "The City of Chicago: A Study of the Great Immoralities." *McClure's Magazine* (April 1907): 575–92.

———. "Daughters of the Poor." *McClure's* (November 1909): 45–61.

Urban, Andrew. "Irish Domestic Servants, 'Biddy,' and Rebellion in the American Home, 1850–1900." *Gender and History* 21.2 (August 2009): 263–86.

Vande Haar, Dale. "Ingham, Harvey." *The Biographical Dictionary of Iowa*. Iowa City: University of Iowa Press, 2009. Web. June 1, 2014.

Volokh, Eugene. "What Speech Does 'Hostile Work Environment' Harassment Law Restrict?" *Georgetown Law Journal* 85 (February 1997): 627–48.

Warnke, Nina. "*God of Vengeance*: The 1907 Controversy over Art and Morality." In *Sholem Asch Reconsidered*, edited by Nanette Stahl, 56–70. New Haven: Yale University Press, 2004.

Way, Peter. "Evil Humors and Ardent Spirits: The Rough Culture of Canal Construction Laborers." *Journal of American History* 79.4 (March 1993): 1397–428.

Weinberger, Stephen. "*The Birth of a Nation* and the Making of the NAACP." *Journal of American Studies* 45.1 (February 2011): 77–93.

Wells, Ida B. "Lynch Law." In *The Reason Why the Colored American Is Not in the World's Columbian Exposition*, edited by Robert Rydell, 29–43. (Urbana: University of Illinois Press, 1999, originally published 1893).

Wertheimer, John. "Mutual Film Reviewed: The Movies, Censorship, and Free Speech in Progressive America." *American Journal of Legal History* 37.2 (April 1993): 158–89.

Williams, Linda. "Versions of Uncle Tom: Race and Gender in American Melodrama."
  In *New Scholarship from BFI Research*, edited by Colin MacCabe and Duncan
  Petrie. London: BFI Publishing, 1996.

Williams, William. "Green Again: Irish-American Lace-Curtain Satire." *New Hibernia
  Review* 6.2 (2002): 9–24.

Winchester, Mark D. "The Yellow Kid and the Origins of Comic Book Theatricals:
  1895–1898." *Theatre Studies* 37 (1992): 32–55.

Wittke, Carl. "The Immigrant Theme on the American Stage." *Mississippi Valley
  Historical Review* 39.2 (September 1952): 211–32.

Woeste, Victoria Saker. "Insecure Equality: Louis Marshall, Henry Ford and the
  Problem of Defamatory Antisemitism, 1920–1929." *Journal of American History* 91.3
  (December 2004): 877–905.

BOOKS

Adler, Cyrus, ed., *American Jewish Year Book, 1916–1917*. Philadelphia: Jewish
  Publication Society of America, 1916.

Alexander, Michael. *Jazz Age Jews*. Princeton: Princeton University Press, 2001.

Baldwin, Davarian. *Chicago's New Negroes: Modernity, the Great Migration, and Black
  Urban Life*. Chapel Hill: University of North Carolina Press, 2007.

Baldwin, Neil. *Henry Ford and the Jews: The Mass Production of Hate*. New York:
  Public Affairs, 2002.

Banerjee, Sikata. *Muscular Nationalism: Gender, Violence, and Empire in India and
  Ireland, 1914–2004*. New York: New York University Press, 2012.

Barrett, James. *The Irish Way: Becoming American in the Multiethnic City*. New York:
  Penguin, 2012.

Bernstein, Matthew. *Screening a Lynching: The Leo Frank Case on Film and Television*.
  Athens: University of Georgia Press, 2009.

Black, Gregory. *The Catholic Crusade against the Movies, 1940–1975*. Cambridge:
  Cambridge University Press, 1997.

———. *Hollywood Censored: Morality Codes, Catholics, and the Movies*. Cambridge:
  Cambridge University Press, 1994.

Blackbeard, Bill, ed. *R. F. Outcault's The Yellow Kid: A Centennial Celebration of the Kid
  Who Started the Comics*. Northampton, Mass.: Kitchen Sink Press, 1995.

Blackstone, William. *Of Public Wrongs*. Vol 4. of *Commentaries on the Laws of England*.
  Chicago: University of Chicago Press, 1979.

Bornstein, George. *The Colors of Zion: Blacks, Jews, and Irish from 1845 to 1945*.
  Cambridge: Harvard University Press, 2011.

Brownlow, Kevin. *Behind the Mask of Innocence*. New York: Knopf, 1990.

Butters, Gerald R. *Banned in Kansas*. Columbia: University of Missouri Press, 2007.

Carmen, Ira. *Movies, Censorship, and the Law*. Ann Arbor: University of Michigan
  Press, 1966.

Carr, Stephen. *Hollywood and Anti-Semitism: A Cultural History up to World War II*.
  Cambridge: Cambridge University Press, 2001.

Chafee, Zechariah. *Freedom of Speech*. New York: Harcourt, Brace, 1920.

Chase, William Sheafe. *Catechism on Motion Pictures in Inter-state Commerce*. New York: Lord's Day Alliance of the United States, 1922.

Church, Thomas, and Milton Heumann, eds. *Hate Speech on Campus: Cases, Case Studies, and Commentary*. Boston: Northeastern University Press, 1997.

Clark, Dennis. *Erin's Heirs: Irish Bonds of Community*. Lexington: University Press of Kentucky, 1991.

——. *The Irish in Philadelphia*. Philadelphia: Temple University Press, 1982.

——. *The Irish Relations: Trials of an Immigrant Tradition*. London: Associated University Presses, 1982.

Cockrell, Dale. *Demons of Disorder: Early Blackface Minstrelsy and Their World*. Cambridge: Cambridge University Press, 1997.

Cohen, Naomi. *Encounter with Emancipation: The German Jews in the United States, 1830–1914*. Philadelphia: Jewish Publication Society, 1984.

——. *Not Free to Desist: A History of the American Jewish Committee, 1906–1966*. Philadelphia: Jewish Publication Society, 1972.

Cohon, Samuel, ed. *B'nai B'rith Manual*. Cincinnati, 1926.

Connolly, James. *The Triumph of Ethnic Progressivism: Urban Political Culture in Boston, 1900–1925*. Cambridge: Harvard University Press, 1998.

Council of Jewish Women. *Official Report of the Ninth Triennial Convention*. Denver, Colo., 1920.

——. *Proceedings of the Fifth Triennial Convention*. Chicago: Toby Rubovitz, 1909.

Courtney, Susan. *Hollywood Fantasies of Miscegenation: Spectacular Narratives of Gender and Race*. Princeton: Princeton University Press, 2004.

Crenshaw, Kimberlé, Richard Delgado, Charles Lawrence, and Mari Matsuda. *Words That Wound: Critical Race Theory, Assaultive Speech, and the First Amendment*. Boulder, Colo.: Westview Press, 1993.

Cripps, Thomas. *Slow Fade to Black: The Negro in American Film, 1900–1942*. Oxford: Oxford University Press, 1993 (originally published in 1973).

Curtis, L. Perry, Jr. *Apes and Angels: The Irishman in Victorian Caricature*. Washington: Smithsonian Institution Press, 1979.

Cutler, Irving. *The Jews of Chicago: From Shtetl to Suburb*. Urbana-Champaign: University of Illinois Press, 1996.

Daniel, Pete. *Standing at the Crossroads: Southern Life in the Twentieth Century*. Baltimore: Johns Hopkins University Press, 1996.

Dawley, Alan. *Changing the World: American Progressives in War and Revolution*. Princeton: Princeton University Press, 2003.

Diner, Hasia. *Erin's Daughters in America: Irish Immigrant Women in the Nineteenth Century*. Baltimore: Johns Hopkins University Press, 1983.

——. *In the Almost Promised Land: American Jews and Blacks, 1915–1935*. Baltimore: Johns Hopkins University Press, 1995 (originally published in 1977).

Dinnerstein, Leonard. *The Leo Frank Case*. New York: Columbia University Press, 1968.

Doorley, Michael. *Irish-American Diasporic Nationalism: The Friends of Irish Freedom, 1916–1935*. Dublin: Four Courts Press, 2005.

Dudden, Faye. *Serving Women: Household Service in Nineteenth-Century America*. Middletown, Conn.: Wesleyan University Press, 1983.

Dumenil, Lynn. *The Modern Temper: American Culture and Society in the 1920s.* New York: Hill and Wang, 1995.

Dumont, Frank. *The Yellow Kid Who Lives in Hogan's Alley.* New York: Dewitt Publishing, 1897.

Emmons, David. *The Butte Irish: Class and Ethnicity in an American Mining Town, 1875–1925.* Urbana-Champaign: University of Illinois Press, 1989.

Erens, Patricia. *The Jew in American Cinema.* Bloomington: Indiana University Press, 1984.

Ernst, Morris, and Pare Lorentz. *Censored: The Private Life of the Movie.* New York: J. Cape and H. Smith, 1930.

Everett, Anna. *Returning the Gaze: A Genealogy of Black Film Criticism, 1909–1949.* Durham: Duke University Press, 2001.

Feldman, Charles. *The National Board of Censorship (Review) of Motion Pictures, 1909–1922.* New York: Arno Press, 1977.

Fleener-Marzec, Nickieann. *D. W. Griffith's The Birth of a Nation: Controversy, Suppression, and the First Amendment as It Applies to Filmic Expression, 1915–1973.* New York: Arno Press, 1980.

Friedman, Andrea. *Prurient Interests: Gender, Democracy, and Obscenity in New York City, 1909–1945.* New York: Columbia University Press, 2000.

Friedman, Lester. *Hollywood's Image of the Jew.* New York: Ungar, 1982.

Frisch, Ephraim, et al., eds. *Year Book of the Central Conference of American Rabbis.* Vol. 21. Cincinnati: Central Conference of American Rabbis, 1911.

Gabaccia, Donna. *From the Other Side: Women, Gender, and Immigrant Life in the U.S., 1820–1990.* Bloomington: Indiana University Press, 1994.

Gabler, Neal. *An Empire of Their Own: How the Jews Invented Hollywood.* New York: Crown Publishers, 1988.

Gaines, Kevin. *Uplifting the Race: Black Leadership, Politics, and Culture in the Twentieth Century.* Chapel Hill: University of North Carolina Press, 1996.

Gevinson, Alan. *Within Our Gates: Ethnicity in American Feature Films, 1911–1960.* Berkeley: University of California Press, 1997.

Gilje, Paul. *Rioting in America.* Bloomington: Indiana University Press, 1996.

Gilmore, Glenda, ed. *Who Were the Progressives? Readings.* Boston: Bedford/St. Martin's, 2002.

Goldstein, Eric. *The Price of Whiteness: Jews, Race, and American Identity.* Princeton: Princeton University Press, 2006.

Golway, Terry. *Irish Rebel: John Devoy and America's Fight for Ireland's Freedom.* New York: St. Martin's, 1998.

Goren, Arthur. *New York Jews and the Quest for Community: The Kehillah Experiment, 1908–1922.* New York: Columbia University Press, 1979.

Graber, Mark. *Transforming Free Speech: The Ambiguous Legacy of Civil Libertarianism.* Berkeley: University of California Press, 1991.

Greenberg, Cheryl. *Troubling the Waters: Black-Jewish Relations in the American Century.* Princeton: Princeton University Press, 2006.

Gregory, Lady. *Our Irish Theatre: A Chapter of Autobiography.* New York: G. P. Putnam's Sons, 1913.

Grieveson, Lee. *Policing Cinema: Movies and Censorship in Early Twentieth-Century America*. Berkeley: University of California Press, 2004.

Gross, Ariela J. *What Blood Won't Tell: A History of Race on Trial in America*. Cambridge: Harvard University Press, 2008.

Grusd, Edward. *B'nai B'rith: The Story of a Covenant*. New York: Appleton-Century, 1966.

Guterl, Matthew. *The Color of Race in America, 1900–1940*. Cambridge: Harvard University Press, 2001.

Guttmacher, Adolf, and William Rosenau, eds. *Year Book of the Central Conference of American Rabbis: Containing the Proceedings of the Convention Held at Louisville, June 26–30, 1904*. Vol. 14. Cincinnati: Central Conference of American Rabbis, 1904.

Haberski, Raymond, and Laura Wittern-Keller. *The Miracle Case: Film Censorship and the Supreme Court*. Lawrence: University Press of Kansas, 2008.

Haenni, Sabine. *The Immigrant Scene: Ethnic Amusements in New York, 1880–1920*. Minneapolis: University of Minnesota Press, 2008.

Harrington, John P. *The Irish Play on the New York Stage, 1874–1966*. Lexington: University Press of Kentucky, 1997.

Harrison-Kahan, Lori. *The White Negress: Literature, Minstrelsy, and the Black-Jewish Imaginary*. New Brunswick: Rutgers University Press, 2011.

Higham, John. *Strangers in the Land: Patterns of American Nativism, 1860–1925*. 2nd edition. New Brunswick: Rutgers University Press, 1963.

Horowitz, Helen. *Rereading Sex: Battles over Sexual Knowledge and Suppression in Nineteenth-Century America*. New York: Knopf, 2002.

Houchin, John. *Censorship of the American Theatre in the Twentieth Century*. Cambridge: Cambridge University Press, 2003.

Hutchinson, John. *The Dynamics of Cultural Nationalism: The Gaelic Revival and the Creation of the Irish Nation State*. London: Allen and Unwin, 1987.

Ingram, David. *Group Rights: Reconciling Equality and Difference*. Lawrence: University Press of Kansas, 2000.

Jackson, Kenneth. *The Ku Klux Klan in the City, 1915–1930*. New York: Oxford University Press, 1967.

Jacobs, Joseph, ed. *The American Jewish Yearbook, 1915–1916*. Philadelphia: Jewish Publication Society of America, 1915.

Jacobs, Lewis. *The Rise of the American Film: A Critical History*. New York: Harcourt, Brace, 1939.

Jacobson, Matthew Frye. *Special Sorrows: The Diasporic Imagination of Irish, Polish, and Jewish Immigrants in the United States*. Cambridge: Harvard University Press, 1995.

———. *Whiteness of a Different Color*. Cambridge: Harvard University Press, 1999.

Johnson, Katie. *Sisters in Sin: Brothel Drama in America, 1900–1920*. Cambridge: Cambridge University Press, 2006.

Jones, Thomas David. *Human Rights: Group Defamation, Freedom of Expression, and the Law of Nations*. The Hague: Kluwer Law International. 1998.

Kasson, John. *Rudeness and Civility: Manners in Nineteenth-Century Urban America*. New York: Hill and Wang, 1990.

Kasson, Joy. *Buffalo Bill's Wild West: Celebrity, Memory, and Popular History*. New York: Hill and Wang, 2000.

Kauffman, Christopher. *Faith and Fraternalism: The History of the Knights of Columbus, 1882–1982*. New York: Harper and Row, 1982.

Kazal, Russell. *Becoming Old Stock: The Paradox of German-American Identity*. Princeton: Princeton University Press, 2004.

Kellogg, Charles. *NAACP: A History of the National Association of the Advancement of Colored People*, Vol. 1. Baltimore: Johns Hopkins University Press, 1973.

Kenny, Kevin. *The American Irish*. Harlow, Essex, UK: Longman, 2000.

———. *Making Sense of the Molly Maguires*. Oxford: Oxford University Press, 1998.

Kiberd, Declan. *Synge and the Irish Language*. Totowa, N.J.: Rowan and Littlefield, 1979.

Kibler, M. Alison. *Rank Ladies: Gender and Cultural Hierarchy in American Vaudeville*. Chapel Hill: University of North Carolina Press, 1999.

Kiely, David. *John Millington Synge: A Biography*. New York: St. Martin's Press, 1994.

Kilroy, James, ed. *The Playboy Riots*. Dublin: Dolmen, 1971.

Konvitz, Milton and Theodore Leskes. *A Century of Civil Rights*. New York: Columbia University Press, 1961.

Kraus, Adolf. *Reminiscences and Comments: The Immigrant, the Citizen, a Public Office, the Jew*. Chicago: Toby Rubovits, 1925.

Lane, Roger. *William Dorsey's Philadelphia and Ours: On the Past and Future of the Black City in America*. New York: Oxford University Press, 1991.

Levine, Lawrence. *Highbrow/Lowbrow: The Emergence of Cultural Hierarchy in America*. Cambridge: Harvard University Press, 1988.

Lewis, Anthony. *Freedom for the Thought That We Hate: A Biography of the First Amendment*. New York: Basic Books, 2007.

Lissak, Rivka Shpak. *Pluralism and Progressives: Hull House and the New Immigrants, 1890–1919*. Chicago: University of Chicago Press, 1989.

Lott, Eric. *Love and Theft: Blackface Minstrelsy and the American Working Class*. Oxford: Oxford University Press, 1993.

Luckett, Moya. *Cinema and Community: Progressivism, Exhibition, and Film Culture in Chicago, 1907–1917*. Detroit: Wayne State University Press, 2013.

MacKinnon, Catharine A. *Only Words*. Cambridge: Harvard University Press, 1993.

Mahar, William. *Behind the Burnt Cork Mask: Early Blackface Minstrelsy and Antebellum American Popular Culture*. Urbana: University of Illinois Press, 1999.

Maitra, Ishani, and Kate McGowan, eds. *Speech and Harm: Controversies over Free Speech*. Oxford: Oxford University Press, 2012.

Malcolmson, Robert, and Stephanos Mastoris. *The English Pig: A History*. London: Continuum, 2003.

Marks, Edward. *They All Sang: From Tony Pastor to Rudy Vallee*. New York: Viking Press, 1934.

May, Lary. *Screening Out the Past: The Birth of Mass Culture and the Motion Picture Industry*. Chicago: University of Chicago Press, 1980.

McDiarmid, Lucy. *The Irish Art of Controversy*. Ithaca: Cornell University Press, 2005.

McElya, Micki. *Clinging to Mammy: The Faithful Slave in Twentieth-Century America*. Cambridge: Harvard University Press, 2007.

Meagher, Timothy. *The Columbia Guide to Irish American History*. New York: Columbia University Press, 2005.

———. *Inventing Irish America: Generation, Class, and Ethnic Identity in a New England City, 1880–1928*. Notre Dame, Ind.: University of Notre Dame Press, 2001.

Melnick, Jeffrey. *A Right to Sing the Blues: African Americans, Jews, and American Popular Song*. Cambridge: Harvard University Press, 1999.

———. *Black-Jewish Relations on Trial: Leo Frank and Jim Conley in the New South*. Jackson: University Press of Mississippi, 2000.

Merwin, Ted. *In Their Own Image: New York Jews in Jazz Age Popular Culture*. New Brunswick: Rutgers University Press, 2006.

Miller, Kerby. *Emigrants and Exiles: Ireland and the Irish Exodus to North America*. New York: Oxford University Press, 1988.

Mizruchi, Susan. *The Rise of Multicultural America: Economy and Print Culture, 1863–1915*. Chapel Hill: University of North Carolina Press, 2008.

Moley, Raymond. *The Hays Office*. Indianapolis: Bobbs-Merrill, 1945.

Moloney, Deirdre. *American Catholic Lay Groups and Transatlantic Social Reform in the Progressive Era*. Chapel Hill: University of North Carolina Press, 2002.

Moore, Deborah Dash. *B'nai B'rith and the Challenge of Ethnic Leadership*. Albany: State University of New York Press, 1981.

Morey, Anne. *Hollywood Outsiders: The Adaptation of the Film Industry, 1913–1934*. Minneapolis: University of Minnesota Press, 2003.

Morgenstern, Julian. *Central Conference of American Rabbis: Twenty-Fifth Anniversary Convention*. Vol. 24. Cincinnati: Central Conference of American Rabbis, 1914.

Morgenstern, Julian, David Lefkowitz, and David Philipson, eds. *Year Book of the Central Conference of American Rabbis: Containing the Proceedings of the Convention Held in New York City, November 9–16, 1909*. Vol. 19. Cincinnati: Central Conference of American Rabbis, 1910.

Moses, L. G. *Wild West Shows and the Images of American Indians, 1883–1933*. Albuquerque: University of New Mexico Press, 1996.

Motion Picture Commission, *Chicago Motion Picture Commission Report*. Chicago: House of Severinghaus, 1920.

Nasaw, David. *Going Out: The Rise and Fall of Public Amusements*. New York: Basic Books, 1993.

National Board of Censorship of Motion Pictures. *The Policy and Standards of the National Board of Censorship of Motion Pictures, Revised January 1915*. New York: National Board of Censors, 1915.

———. *The Policy and Standards of The National Board of Censorship of Motion Pictures, Revised May 1914*. New York: National Board of Censorship, 1914.

———. *Report of the National Board of Censorship*. New York: National Board of Censorship, 1911.

———. *Report of the National Board of Censorship*. New York: National Board of Censorship, 1914.

———. *The Question of Censorship*. New York: National Board of Censorship, 1914.

Nelson, Bruce. *Irish Nationalists and the Making of the Irish Race*. Princeton: Princeton University Press, 2012.

Nordstrom, Justin. *Danger at the Doorstep: Anti-Catholicism and American Print Culture in the Progressive Era*. Notre Dame, Ind.: University of Notre Dame Press, 2006.

O'Day, Alan. *Irish Home Rule, 1867–1921.* Manchester: Manchester University Press, 1998.

Onkey, Lauren. *Blackness and Transatlantic Irish Identity: Celtic Soul Brothers.* New York: Routledge, 2010.

Oppenheim, Samson. *The American Jewish Year Book, 1918–1919* Philadelphia: Jewish Publication Society of America, 1918.

Pearson, Roberta, and William Uricchio. *Reframing Culture: The Case of the Vitagraph Films.* Princeton: Princeton University Press, 1993.

Perlmann, Joel. *Ethnic Differences: Schooling and Social Structure among the Irish, Italians, Jews, and Blacks in an American City, 1880–1935.* Cambridge: Cambridge University Press, 1989.

Petit, Jeanne. *The Men and Women We Want: Gender, Race, and the Progressive Era Literacy Test Debate.* Rochester, N.Y.: University of Rochester Press, 2010.

Pfeifer, Michael, ed. *Lynching beyond Dixie: American Mob Violence outside the South.* Urbana-Champaign: University of Illinois Press, 2013.

Prell, Riv-Ellen. *Fighting to Become Americans: Assimilation and the Trouble between Jewish Women and Jewish Men.* Boston: Beacon Press, 1999.

Prominent Democrats of Illinois: A Brief History of the Rise and Progress of the Democratic Party of Illinois. Chicago: Democrat Publishing Co., 1899.

Rabban, David. *Free Speech in Its Forgotten Years.* Cambridge: Cambridge University Press, 1997.

Rabinovitz, Lauren. *For the Love of Pleasure: Women, Movies, and Culture in Turn-of-the-Century Chicago.* New Brunswick: Rutgers University Press, 1998.

Randall, Richard. *Censorship of the Movies: The Social and Political Control of a Mass Medium.* Madison: University of Wisconsin Press, 1968.

Reed, Christopher. *Black Chicago's First Century, 1833–1900.* Columbia: University of Missouri Press, 2005.

———. *The Chicago NAACP and the Rise of Black Professional Leadership, 1910–1966.* Bloomington: Indiana University Press, 1997.

Rich, Charlotte. *Transcending the New Woman: Multiethnic Narratives in the Progressive Era.* Columbia: University of Missouri Press, 2009.

Roche, John. *The Quest for the Dream: The Development of Civil Rights and Human Relations in Modern America.* New York: Macmillan, 1963.

Rodechko, James. *Patrick Ford and His Search for America: A Case Study of Irish American Journalism, 1870–1913.* New York: Arno Press, 1976.

Rodgers, Daniel. *Contested Truths: Keywords in American Politics since Independence.* Cambridge: Harvard University Press, 1998.

Roediger, David. *Wages of Whiteness: Race and the Making of the American Working Class.* Rev. ed. London: Verso, 2007.

Rogin, Michael. *Blackface, White Noise: Jewish Immigrants in the Hollywood Melting Pot.* Berkeley: University of California Press, 1996.

Rogow, Faith. *Gone to Another Meeting: The National Council of Jewish Women, 1893–1993.* Tuscaloosa: University of Alabama Press, 1993.

Romanowski, William. *Reforming Hollywood: How American Protestants Fought for Freedom at the Movies.* New York: Oxford University Press, 2012.

Romeyn, Esther. *Street Scenes: Staging the Self in Immigrant New York, 1880–1924*. Minneapolis: University of Minnesota Press, 2008.

Rosenstock, Morton. *Louis Marshall, Defender of Jewish Rights*. Detroit: Wayne State University Press, 1965.

Rosenzweig, Roy. *Eight Hours for What We Will: Workers and Leisure in an Industrial City, 1870–1920*. Cambridge: Cambridge University Press, 1985.

Ross, Steven J. *Working-Class Hollywood: Silent Film and the Shaping of Class in America*. Princeton: Princeton University Press, 1998.

Rutkoff, Peter, and William Scott. *Fly Away: The Great American Cultural Migrations*. Baltimore: Johns Hopkins University Press, 2010.

Sampson, Henry, ed. *The Ghost Walks: A Chronological History of Blacks in Show Business, 1865–1910*. Metuchen, N.J.: Scarecrow Press, 1988.

Sarna, Jonathan. *American Judaism: A History*. New Haven: Yale University Press, 2004.

Schickel, Richard. *D. W. Griffith: An American Life*. New York: Simon and Schuster, 1984.

Schneider, Mark R. *Boston Confronts Jim Crow, 1890–1920*. Boston: Northeastern University Press, 1997.

Schneiderman, Harry, ed. *American Jewish Year Book, 1919–1920* Philadelphia: Jewish Publication Society, 1919.

Schroeder, Theodore. *Free Speech for Radicals*. New York: Burt Franklin, 1969.

Selig. Diana. *Americans All: The Cultural Gifts Movement*. Cambridge: Harvard University Press, 2011.

Shiell, Timothy. *Campus Hate Speech on Trial*. 2nd edition. Lawrence: University Press of Kansas, 2009.

Sklar, Robert. *Movie-Made America: A Cultural History of American Movies*. New York: Random House, 1975.

Snyder, Robert. *The Voice of the City: Vaudeville and Popular Cultures in New York*. Oxford: Oxford University Press, 1989.

Sorin, Gerald. *A Time for Building: The Third Migration, 1880–1920*. Baltimore: Johns Hopkins University Press, 1992.

Spear, Allan. *Black Chicago: The Making of a Negro Ghetto, 1890–1920*. Chicago: University of Chicago Press, 1967.

Stewart, Jacqueline. *Migrating to the Movies: Cinema and Black Urban Modernity*. Berkeley: University of California Press, 2005.

Stokes, Melvyn. *D. W. Griffith's "The Birth of a Nation": A History of "The Most Controversial Motion Picture of All Time."* New York: Oxford University Press, 2007.

Stromquist, Shelton. *Reinventing "The People": The Progressive Movement, The Class Problem, and the Origins of Modern Liberalism*. Urbana: University of Illinois Press, 2006.

Strum, Philippa. *When the Nazis Came to Skokie: Freedom for Speech We Hate*. Lawrence: University Press of Kansas, 1999.

Sunstein, Cass. *Democracy and the Problem of Free Speech*. New York: Free Press, 1993.

Ullman, Sharon R. *Sex Seen: The Emergence of Modern Sexuality in America*. Berkeley: University of California Press, 1997.

Waldrep, Christopher. *African Americans Confront Lynching: Strategies of Resistance from the Civil War to the Civil Rights Era*. Lanham, Md.: Rowman and Littlefield, 2009.

Walker, Samuel. *Hate Speech: The History of an American Controversy*. Lincoln: University of Nebraska Press, 1994.

———. *In Defense of American Liberties: A History of the ACLU*. New York: Oxford University Press, 1990.

Waller, Gregory. *Main Street Amusements: Movies and Commercial Entertainment in a Southern City, 1896–1930*. Washington: Smithsonian Institution Press, 1995.

Walsh, Frank. *Sin and Censorship: The Catholic Church and the Motion Picture Industry*. New Haven: Yale University Press, 1996.

Washington, Booker T. *The Future of the American Negro*. New York: Negro Universities Press, 1899.

Welke, Barbara. *Recasting American Liberty: Gender, Race, Law, and the Railroad Revolution, 1865–1920*. Cambridge: Cambridge University Press, 2001.

Wheeler, Leigh Ann. *Against Obscenity: Reform and the Politics of Womanhood in America, 1873–1935*. Baltimore: Johns Hopkins University Press, 2004.

Wilentz, Sean. *Chants Democratic: New York City and the Rise of the American Working Class, 1788–1850*. Oxford: Oxford University Press, 1984.

Williams, William H. A. *'Twas Only an Irishman's Dream: The Image of Ireland and the Irish in American Popular Song Lyrics, 1800–1920*. Urbana: University of Illinois Press, 1996.

Wittern-Keller, Laura, and Raymond Haberski. *The Miracle Case: Film Censorship and the Supreme Court*. Lawrence: University Press of Kansas, 2008.

Wittke, Carl F. *The Irish in America*. New York: Russell and Russell, 1970.

Wood, Amy Louise. *Lynching and Spectacle: Witnessing Racial Violence in America, 1890–1940*. Chapel Hill: University of North Carolina Press, 2009.

Young, Iris Marion. *Justice and the Politics of Difference*. Princeton: Princeton University Press, 1990.

Zangrando, Robert. *The NAACP Crusade against Lynching, 1909–1950*. Philadelphia: Temple University Press, 1980.

UNPUBLISHED MATERIALS

Bromell, Una. "The American Mission: The Gaelic Revival and America, 1870–1915." Ph.D. thesis, Lehigh University, 1998.

Boyle, Sean Patrick. "Low Life and High Jinks: Race, Ethnicity, and Politics in Edward Harrigan's Mulligan Guard Plays, 1879–1883." Ph.D. diss., Rutgers, the State University of New Jersey, 2013.

Budke, Timothy. "Addressing the 'Offense of Public Decency': The Advent of Censoring Particular Dramas on the New York Stage, 1890–1905." Ph.D. diss., University of Missouri–Columbia, 1989.

Burns-Watson, Roger. "The Birth of a Nation and the Death of a Board: Race, Politics, and Film Censorship in Ohio, 1913–1921." M.A. thesis, University of Cincinnati, 2001.

Distler, Paul Antonie. "The Rise and Fall of the Racial Comics in Vaudeville." Ph.D. diss., Tulane University, 1963.

Flynn, Joyce. "Ethnicity after Sea-Change: The Irish Dramatic Tradition in Nineteenth-Century American Drama." Ph.D. diss., Harvard University, 1985.

French, John. "Irish-American Identity, Memory, and Americanism during the Eras of the Civil War and First World War." Ph.D. diss., Marquette University, 2012.

Granshaw, Michelle. "'What Do Ye Allow a Baboon Like That on the Stage For?' Protest, Irish-American Identity, and the Works of Harrigan, Hart, and Braham." M.A. thesis, University of Maryland, 2007.

Kelleher, Patricia. "Gender Shapes Ethnicity: Ireland's Gender Systems and Chicago's Irish Americans." Ph.D. diss., University of Wisconsin, 1995.

Lindstrom, J. A. "Getting a Hold Deeper in the Life of the City: Chicago Nickelodeons, 1905–1914." Ph.D. diss., Northwestern University, 1998.

Mantel, Thomas. "The Anti-Defamation League of B'nai B'rith." Honorst thesis, Harvard University, 1950.

Sable, Jacob. "Some American Jewish Organizational Efforts, 1906–1930." Ph.D. diss., Yeshiva University, 1964.

Saylor, Richard. "The Pennsylvania State Board of Censors (Motion Pictures)." M.A. thesis, Pennsylvania State University at Harrisburg, 1999.

Winchester, Mark. "Cartoon Theatricals from 1896 to 1927: Gus Hill's Cartoon Shows for the American Road Theatre." Ph.D. diss., Ohio State University, 1995.

GOVERNMENT DOCUMENTS

The Miscellaneous Reports: New York (State) Superior Court. Albany: James B. Lyon Co. Publisher, 1915.

Motion Picture Commission, Hearings before the Committee on Education, House of Representatives. 63rd Cong., 2nd sess., 1914. New York: Arno Press, 1978.

Pennsylvania County Court Reports. Vol. 42. Philadelphia: T. and J. W. Johnson, 1915.

Pennsylvania State Board of Censors (of Motion Pictures): Rules and Standards. Harrisburg, Pa.: William Stanley Ray, 1915.

Reports of Cases at Law and in Chancery Argued and Determined in the Supreme Court of Illinois, vol. 239. Bloomington: Isaac Newton Phillips, Reporter of Decisions, 1909.

U. S. Congress. House of Representatives. Hearing Before the Committee on the Post Office and Post Roads. 63rd Cong., 3rd sess., February 1, 1915. Washington: Government Printing Office, 1915.

U. S. Congress, House of Representatives. Federal Motion Picture Commission. Hearings before the Committee on Education on H.R. 456. 64th Cong., 1st sess., January 13–19, 1916. Washington: Government Printing Office, 1916.

U. S. Congress. House of Representatives, Committee on Education, Hearings before the Committee on Education on H. R. 4094 and H. R. 6233, Bills to Create a Commission to Be Known as the Federal Motion Picture Commission, 69th Cong., 1st sess., 1926. Washington: Government Printing Office, 1926.

Index

Illustrations are indicated by *italic* page numbers.

Carney, Henry, 65
Carr, Stephen, 124
Cartwright, James, 149
Casement, Roger, 42
Catechism on Motion Pictures in Inter-State Commerce (Chase), 196
Catholics, 190–91, 193–95, 203–6, 211, 275 (n. 9); and film censorship, 194, 204–7, 209–11, 214; and Germans, 7–8; and Irish, 194–95, 206
Catholic Theater Guild, 205
Catholic Total Abstinence Union, 35
Catholic Women's Club, 195
Catskill Mountains, 117
Central Conference of American Rabbis (CCAR), 117, 124–26, 152
Chafee, Zechariah, 114–15
Chase, William S., 172, 183, 184, 185, 196, 270 (n. 70)
Chicago, Ill.: African Americans in, 163–64; Anti-Defamation League in, 128, 155–56; *Birth of a Nation* in, 164–68; censorship bill in, 166–67; *The Frank Case* and, 139; Funkhouser in, 149, 155, 155–57, 155–59, 160, 167–69, 186, 267 (n. 150); Jews in, 151–52; Kraus in, 152–53; motion picture censorship law in, 147; nickelodeons in, 147–48, 261 (n. 5); *Playboy of the Western World* in, 106–7; women in, 154
Chicago Board of Censorship, 210
Chicago Defender (newspaper), 162–63, 164
Chicago World's Fair, 37–38, 43; African Americans and, 37–38; Jewish organizations and, 43
Chimmie Fadden (Townsend), 231 (n. 16)
Christy, George, 22
Citizen juries, in censorship, 154–61, 262 (n. 40)
Citizenship: of African Americans, 38, 44, 130; identity and, 168; minority groups and, 168; race and, 4
City Club of Chicago, 148
"City of Chicago, The" (Turner), 121–22
City without Jews (film), 202
Civil Rights Act of 1875, 118–19

Civil Rights Act of 1964, 216, 222 (n. 39)
Civil rights legislation, 100, 119–20, 250 (nn. 23, 25–26), 256 (n. 135)
Civil rights organizations, 43–44. *See also specific organizations*
Clan na Gael, 53, 64–68, 235 (nn. 79, 84); Irish assimilation and, 36; Irish independence and, 40; Irish nationalism and, 80, 198; *McFadden's Row of Flats* and, 56–57; *Playboy of the Western World* and, 108; Stage Irish and, 73, 75, 101, 236 (n. 88); United Irish American Societies and, 233 (n. 40), 236 (n. 92); United Irish League of America and, 237 (n. 109); Volunteer Irish Patriots and, 231 (n. 12)
Clansman, The (Dixon), 45, 94, 95; Atlanta race riots and, 83, 94–96; background of, 83; banning of, 83, 96, 98; *Birth of a Nation* and, 97, 100; Brown and, 90–91; censorship of, 88–100; free speech and, 112–13; Jews and, 91–92; Kraus and, 153–54; lynching and, 142; *Playboy of the Western World* vs., 101, 110; Silverman and, 91–92; Sulzberger and, 98–100; *Uncle Tom's Cabin* and, 89–90; violence and, 92–95
Clark, Tom, 214–15
Coastguard's Daughter, A (play), 69
Cobleigh, Rolphe, 142
Cockrell, Dale, 22
Cocks, Orrin, 177–78, 180, 271 (n. 104)
Cohalan, Daniel, 80, 235 (n. 79)
Cohen, Paul, 18–19
Cold War, 215
Collier, John, 173–75, 178
Collin, Frank, 17, 18
Collins, Patrick, 35
Collin v. Smith, 18–19
Colored Citizens Protection League, 85
Columbian Exposition, 37–38, 43
Comedy: African Americans and, 28; melee and, 21, 24–25; musical, 2, 23–25, 28; racial, 29, 30–33, 221 (n. 31); satire and, 177; Stage Irish and, 29; Stage Jew and, 6, 26, 157; in vaudeville, 25
Comic strips, 55–56, 76–77, 231 (n. 16)

Commission on Religious Prejudices (Knights of Columbus), 41

Committee of Fifteen, 153

Committee on Church and State, 125, 126–27. *See also* Central Conference of American Rabbis

Comstock, Anthony, 13, 84, 87, 88

Comstock Act, 84

Condemned (film), 162

Congo Bongo Act, 28

Congress on Africa, 38

Conley, James, 49, 50

Connolly, James, 222 (n. 49)

Coon, as term, 28

Coon songs, 23. *See also* Minstrel shows

Cooper, William Fenimore, 165

Cooper and Bailey, 6

Courtney, Susan, 210

Crafts, Wilbur F., 183–84, 270 (n. 70)

Cressy, Will, 26

Criminality, in Stage Jew, 25–26, 121–25, 150, 159–60

Cripps, Thomas, 144–45, 150

Crisis (periodical), 44, 131, 132, 133, 136

Crossin, William, 235 (n. 79)

Crowder, Reuben. *See* Hogan, Ernest

Curley (film), 213

Daniel, Pete, 94

Daredevil Detective, The (film), 159

Daudet, Alphonse, 86

Daughters of the Confederacy, 89

"Daughters of the Poor" (Turner), 122

Davitt, Michael, 42

Dearborn Independent, 172, 199–200, 200–201, 273 (nn. 160, 163)

Deborah (film), 159

Decatur, AL, 93

DeMille, Cecil B., 191, 207, 208

Democracy: censorship and, 12, 13, 16, 88, 110, 113, 174, 184, 185–86, 211; culture and, 88; film and, 148, 173; free speech and, 12, 113, 212, 216, 223 (n. 56); hate speech and, 9; Irish and, 75; moral authority and, 13, 88; Progressive Era and, 11

Democratic Party, 7, 46, 47, 96, 119, 135, 154, 169

Department for the Promotion of Purity in Literature and Art, 128. *See also* National Council of Jewish Women

Department for the Suppression of Impure Literature, 128. *See also* Woman's Christian Temperance Union

De Priest, Oscar, 163

DeSilver, Albert, 200

Deslys, Gaby, 104–5

Des Moines, Iowa, 90, 100, 153, 243 (n. 45)

Desperate Chance, A (film), 162

Devoy, John, 41, 80, 198, 233–34 (n. 52)

Dictionary of Races or Peoples, The, 30, 33

Dillingham, William Paul, 30

Dillingham Commission, 30, 34

Dillon, Luke, 65

Diner, Hasia, 75

Dixon, Thomas, 83, 89, 96, 98–99, 110

Dockstader, Lew, 23

Donnelly, Patrick J., 66

"Don'ts and Be Carefuls," 193, 194, 203, 208–10

Douglass, Frederick, 37, 45

Draft Riots, 33, 46

Dreamland Burlesquers, 63–64, 235 (n. 71), 240 (n. 176)

Dreyfus Affair, 42

Drinking, 25, 71–72, 160

Drozda v. State, 201

Dubin, Al, 225 (n. 34)

Du Bois, W. E. B., 42, 43, 44, 131, 132, 134, 140, 196, 197–98

Dyer, Leonidas, 255 (n. 121)

Easter Rising, 80

Edison, Thomas, 171

Edison Trust, 149–50

Edmondson, Robert, 201, 276 (n. 49)

Eltinge, Julian, 73, 76

Emmet, Robert, 42

Emmett, Dan, 22–23

Epstein, Henry, 212

Erens, Patricia, 261 (n. 23)

Erlanger, A. L., 125

Ernst, Morris, 212–13, 216–17

Espionage Act, 39, 198

Ingham, Harvey, 153
Inside the White Slave Traffic (film), 178
Interdenominational Committee for the
    Suppression of Sunday Vaudeville, 172
International Federation of Catholic
    Alumnae (IFCA), 194, 205, 209
International Order of B'nai B'rith, 43, 50,
    127, 152, 207–8, 228 (n. 126)
In the Clutches of Gangsters (film), 264
    (n. 85)
In the Czar's Name (film), 161
Intolerance (film), 180–81
Ireland's Easter (play), 80
Irish: African Americans and, 3, 42, 45–
    47; anti-Semitism, 41; assimilation of,
    35–36, 40–41, 75, 233 (n. 50); Catholi-
    cism and, 194–95, 203–6; democracy
    and, 75; Democratic Party and, 46, 47;
    divisions within, 35–36; Draft Riots
    and, 33, 46; gender tensions with, 36;
    Germans and, 59–60, 221 (n. 29); het-
    erogeneity of, 8; Hogan and, 30; hos-
    tility toward Jews by, 46–47; identity
    of, 34–35, 194–95; immigration, 34–35,
    75, 240 (n. 164); Knights of Columbus
    and, 195; in melee, 24; migration of,
    34–35; in minstrel shows, 21, 22–23;
    Protestants and, 34–35, 62, 72, 75, 106;
    as race, 4, 30, 33; in racial comedies, 33;
    racism of, 41, 45–47; respectability of,
    67, 107; social class and, 35–36, 47, 65,
    66, 74; status of, 35; violence by, 62–63;
    as white, 4, 22, 33, 42, 229 (n. 143);
    women, 36, 70–71, 75, 240 (n. 164);
    World War I and, 198–99; Wyndham
    Act and, 68–69. *See also* Stage Irish
Irish American (newspaper), 232 (n. 22)
Irish and Proud of It (play), 80–81
"Irish Cause," 199
Irish Hearts (film), 203, 204, 205, 206
Irish nationalism, 40–43, 227 (n. 107);
    and Ancient Order of Hibernians, 54;
    of Ford, 233 (n. 52); free speech and,
    198–99; and *McFadden's Row of Flats*,
    59–60; and *Playboy of the Western
    World*, 100–101; and Russell Brothers,
    59–60; social class and, 236 (n. 96);

violence and, 66–67; in World War I,
    80–81, 198–99; Yale riots and, 105–6
Irish Parliamentary Party, 67
Irish Race Convention, 80
Irish Republican Brotherhood, 80, 227
    (n. 107)
"Irish Servant Girls, The" (vaudeville),
    51, 58–59, 61, 69–71, 72–73, 74–75,
    77–78
Irishwomen and the Home Language
    (Butler), 79
Irish World (periodical), 3, 60, 67, 69, 71,
    76, 78, 198, 220 (n. 21), 234 (n. 66)
Irwin, May, 23
Italians, 7

Jackson, Robert, 163, 166–67
Jazz Singer, The (film), 23, 203
Jeffries, Jim, 135
Jenkins, Henry, 97
Jew(s): African American experience vs.
    that of, 117; African Americans and,
    3, 47–50, 91–92, 120, 137–38, 162–63;
    assimilation of, 150, 229 (n. 153); *Birth
    of a Nation* and, 140, 220 (n. 24); in
    blackface, 23; Catholics and, 204, 206;
    as censors, 160–61, 167; in Chicago,
    151–52; and Chicago World's Fair, 43;
    as "Christ-killers," 92, 180, 207; *The
    Clansman* and, 91–92; *Dearborn Inde-
    pendent* and, 172, 199–201; divisions
    within community of, 36–37; Eastern
    European, 36, 43, 111, 122, 127; exclu-
    sion of, 116–18; German, 36–37; *God of
    Vengeance* and, 110–14; heterogeneity
    of, 8; in Hollywood, 150–51; and hotel
    discrimination, 117–18, 119; identity
    of, 33–34; immigration of, 36–37;
    Irish hostility toward, 46–47; *King of
    Kings* and, 203, 206–8; Levy Bill and,
    119–20; lynching of, 49–50; mail-order
    business and, 252 (n. 67); in minstrel
    shows, 21, 23; nationalism among, 42;
    organizations of, 43–44; pogroms
    against, 36, 49, 118, 127, 153; Protestants
    and, 91; as race, 4, 30, 33, 137–38, 226
    (n. 50); and racial comedy, 33; reform,